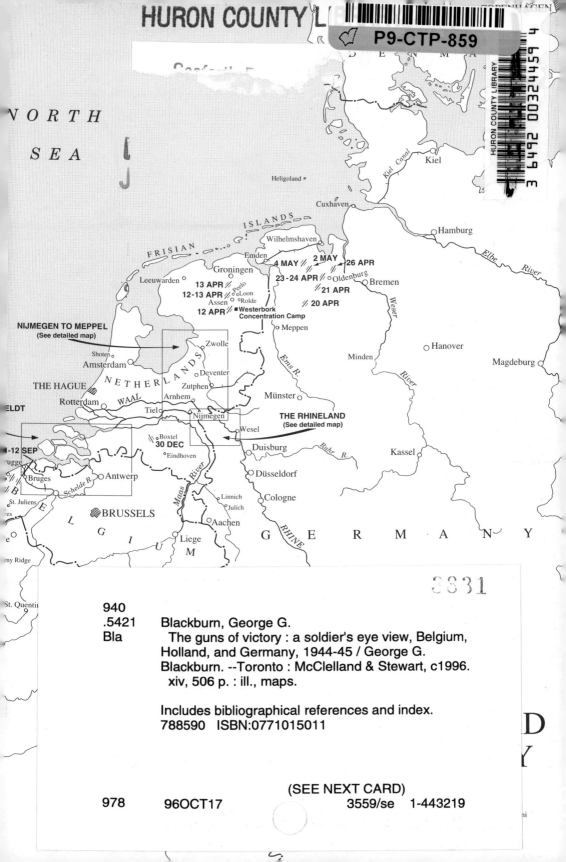

940
.5421
Bla

Blackburn, George G.
    The guns of victory : a soldier's eye view, Belgium,
Holland, and Germany, 1944-45 / George G.
Blackburn. --Toronto : McClelland & Stewart, c1996.
    xiv, 506 p. : ill., maps.

Includes bibliographical references and index.
788590   ISBN:0771015011

(SEE NEXT CARD)

978   96OCT17   3559/se   1-443219

Praise for George Blackburn's The Guns of Normandy, *1996 winner of the Ottawa Citizen Book of the Year Award and the Edna Staebler Award for Creative Non-Fiction, and a finalist for the 1996 Trillium Award:*

"This book may well contain the greatest Canadian memoirs of World War II."
— from the Trillium Award jury citation

"A very moving and poignant . . . account. . . . George Blackburn's book is a salute to the human spirit and its ability to rise to the challenges that confront it."
— *Vanguard*

"Entrancing. . . . One of the best books to come out of the Second World War."
— *Calgary Herald*

"George Blackburn . . . brings us as close as we will ever come to the tension, savagery, and turmoil of the fighting in Normandy half a century ago. The immediacy of Blackburn's narrative, his empathy with the fighting men, and his professional insight put *The Guns of Normandy* in a class of its own as a military memoir."
— *Quill & Quire*

"The most realistic and breathtaking account of what front-line action was like in World War II . . . not just by a Canadian soldier who was there, but by any combatant, Allied or Axis"
— *Moncton Times Transcript*

"A war book not to be missed."
— *Ottawa Citizen*

"[Blackburn] provides details so graphic that even the most unmilitary reader can appreciate artillery warfare. *The Guns of Normandy* is no glorious adventure story. Once into the front lines, war is hell. . . . Tension overlays every minute of every hour of every day for weeks on end."
— *Books in Canada*

"A remarkable book. . . . [It] promises to be definitive about wartime soldiering."
— *Toronto Sun*

"The finest personal account of the campaign in Northwest Europe written by a Canadian. . . . His description of what it was like to live through those desperate days . . . should be read by everyone who thinks that military history is about strategy and the views of generals."
— *Canadian Military History*

"Easily the best book yet produced on . . . the Canadian army's bloody campaign in Normandy. In terms of describing the nightmare of a massive mechanized war from the ground-level view of somebody who was in the thick of it, it is unique."
— *London Free Press*

THE GUNS OF VICTORY

The Guns of Victory

A Soldier's Eye View,
Belgium, Holland, and Germany, 1944-45

GEORGE G. BLACKBURN

Canadian Cataloguing in Publication Data

Blackburn, George G.
    The guns of victory: a soldier's eye view, Belgium, Holland,
and Germany, 1944-45

Includes bibliographical references and index.
ISBN 0-7710-1501-1

1. Blackburn, George, G. 2. World War, 1939-1945 – Personal narratives,
Canadian. 3. World War, 1939-1945 – Artillery operations, Canadian.
4. World War, 1939-1945 – Campaigns – Europe. 5. Canada. Canadian
Army – History – World War 1939-1945. I. Title.

D768.15.B55 1996   940.54'21   C96-931720-4

Maps by William Constable
Typesetting by M&S, Toronto

The publishers acknowledge the support of the Canada Council and the
Ontario Arts Council for their publishing program.

Printed and bound in Canada

McClelland & Stewart Inc.
The Canadian Publishers
481 University Avenue
Toronto, Ontario
M5G 2E9

1 2 3 4 5   00 99 98 97 96

To all the loved ones of all who didn't make it back – especially those who know their fathers only through fading photographs

CONTENTS

PART FOUR – MARCH 11–MAY 15
CROSSING THE RHINE TO SEVER HOLLAND FROM GERMANY

MAPS

INTRODUCTION

---- ✳ ----

In the final eleven months of the six-year struggle to gain unconditional surrender from Hitler's Nazis, Canadians made a contribution out of all proportion to their numbers, on land and sea and in the air, but particularly on land, starting on D-Day (June 6, 1944) when 3rd Canadian Division and tanks of the 2nd Armoured Brigade penetrated farther inland than either of the two British divisions or three American divisions in the assault.[*]

In three subsequent major operations – each of them crucial to an Allied victory in Western Europe – 1st Canadian Army played a pivotal or leading role. First, there was the formation and the sealing off of the Falaise pocket, dooming to destruction the German armies in Normandy. Then in October there was the clearing of the Scheldt estuary and the opening of the port of Antwerp, the only port big enough to supply all Allied armies with the mountains of essential supplies required for the final showdown battles with an enemy defending his homeland. Finally, in early spring, 1945, there was the last great battle on the Western Front – a

---

[*] Tanks of 6th Canadian Armoured Regiment reached the Bayeux–Caen road three kilometres ahead of their assaulting column, but turned back to the main Canadian line, ten kilometres inland. By evening 75,000 British and Canadians were ashore, compared to 57,500 Americans.

massive assault through the Siegfried Line to clear the lower
Rhineland and allow: crossings of the great river to be made by
irresistible forces; Holland to be severed from Germany; and Allied
spearheads to plunge with lethal force into the heart of the Reich.

In *The Guns of Normandy* an earnest attempt was made to allow
readers to live day-by-day, hour-by-hour (and occasionally minute-
by-minute) through the titanic struggle for Normandy in the summer
of 1944, which peaked in intensity in late July for the Canadians
along Verrières Ridge, when record-breaking shell consumption by
field guns reached "insane levels," laying down "curtains of fire" to
plug gaps in the line torn by the 1st Panzer (Leibstandarte Adolf
Hitler) SS Division with swarms of Panther and Tiger tanks.

The Guns of Victory, prepared with similar intent, carries on the
story through the last eight months of the war on the Western
Front. Some of the fighting was conducted in the drifting snows of
the worst winter in fifty years in Holland, but mostly in appalling
conditions of mud and flood-water that have been compared, by
veterans of both great wars, to the legendary miseries of the mud
and water of Passchendaele – both in the fall of 1944 along the
Scheldt and in the spring of 1945 along the Rhine, causing the men
of 3rd Canadian Division, who fought through the worst-flooded
landscape in the Rhineland, to assume the title "Water Rats."

As in *The Guns of Normandy*, the view of the war is usually from
the gunpits or forward observation posts of 4th Field Regiment (one
of three field artillery regiments supporting 2nd Infantry Division)
with particular responsibility for bringing down "Mike targets" (fire
from all its twenty-four guns) in support of the three battalions of
4th Infantry Brigade. But being constantly linked by radio and accurately oriented, by precise land-survey, with all the other Canadian
and British field guns in the theatre of operations, 4th Field guns
regularly participated in impromptu shoots on "Uncle targets"
(involving all seventy-two guns of the division); and, occasionally,
on "Victor targets" (involving all 216 field guns of 2nd Canadian
Corps) called down by a FOO (forward observation officer) to crush
counter-attacks threatening to roll up the whole front.

Though intended to be the story of the guns, this is as much the story of the infantry and the tanks, for without some picture of what the troops at the cutting edge faced in gaining objectives and maintaining tenuous holds on shell-tortured ridges, burned out farms, and smashed villages, the periodic demands on the guns for outrageous concentrations of shells would make no more sense than those endless scenes in war films of guns puffing mindlessly away at dear-knows-what, creating the impression that gunnery is simply a matter of pointing the guns in the direction of the enemy, tipping their muzzles up enough to ensure the shells won't land on their own troops, and periodically (at the whim of some senior officer somewhere) lobbing some rounds into enemy territory.

Without some appreciation of the objective of the troops and the severity of the resistance confronting the weary, hollow-eyed, mud-encrusted infantrymen, no one could possibly understand the constant calls for fire by FOOs at the mouth of South Beveland Peninsula and in the Breskens pocket in the autumn of 1944; let alone comprehend what impelled the gunners, in the struggle for the Rhineland the next spring, to carry on without complaint to the point of total exhaustion – day after day – manhandling their guns through the mud into each new position (when their towing quads bogged down and had to winch themselves back out to the road); shovelling tons of shells into guns glowing red; and endlessly slogging back and forth through the mud, carrying 115-pound cases of shells and 62-pound boxes of cartridges to their ravenous tubes from trucks stopped an indecent distance away, on roads barely distinguishable from the surrounding rutted and shell-gouged landscape of glistening mud and water.

The Guns of Normandy ended with Hitler's armies shredded in the Falaise pocket – the shattered remnants of his elite SS divisions largely devoid of tanks, guns, and transport after escaping across the bridgeless Seine by improvised rafts not capable of supporting heavy equipment – disorganized and mostly leaderless, scurrying to keep ahead of the Allied spearheads driving for the Fatherland, as behind them the sounds of wild cheering rose up from crowds delirious at the sight of Allied recce cars, tanks, and guns rolling into Paris, Rouen, Dieppe, Brussels, and Antwerp.

That the war was won and would soon be over seemed very clear – not so much from anything reported by official military sources, but from the excitement that sometimes crept into the delivery of the BBC news picked up on little 38-sets. The normally studiously impersonal newscasters seemed to be gloating as they read their bulletins – even showing a touch of nationalistic bias, by way of a sneering tone, as they revealed that Herr Goebbels, Hitler's Minister of Propaganda, was appealing to the population to engage in "a people's war in defence of the sacred soil of the Reich ... to fight in every street and every lane to save the Fatherland from the final humiliation of invasion by Allied armies."

The hopelessness of Goebbels' appeal seemed to be underlined by two other BBC bulletins: as many as ten thousand Germans a day were being taken prisoner, and the Reich was mobilizing fourteen-year-old school children in regions adjacent to their borders.

The Guns of Victory is the third volume of a trilogy about World War II from the perspective of one regiment of 25-pounders – the second volume being *The Guns of Normandy*, published in 1995.

The first volume, with the working title *Where On Earth Are the Guns?* (as much in deference to the fact the Regiment waited two years for its guns, as to the number of times they were lost during training in that maze of unsigned roads that was wartime Britain) will be published only if enough interest is aroused in readers curious to know how war came to a generation of young Canadians one sunny September weekend in 1939; and how a grab-bag of volunteers from all walks of life – many of them mavericks and misfits from a depression-ravaged land, more inclined to creating situations suitable to comic opera than to the conduct of His Majesty's business – gradually assumed the character of a proud regiment, which in 1942 was declared "the best field regiment in Britain," at a fire-and-movement competition on Salisbury Plain.

PART ONE: SEPTEMBER 6–NOVEMBER 8

Clearing the Channel Ports and the Battle for the Scheldt

I

BACK TO WAR IN
FLOODED COASTAL LOWLANDS

✳

"REVEILLE 0230, BREAKFAST 0300, MOVE OFF AT 0415."

These predawn orders sound more like instructions for a training scheme in England than a return to the stern business of war, after four euphoric days at Dieppe with the guns out of action for the first time in almost two months. Still, as 4th Field Regiment pulls out in the early-morning gloom, onto a road heading northeast to a 2nd Canadian Division concentration area near Montreuil, fifty miles away, there is a disturbing sense of returning to reality, and you have to work hard to suppress the ugly thought you may still buy it before Germany packs it in.

Your ultimate destination is a mystery. All you know is that Canadian Army is to clear the coastal areas of France and Belgium, and in the process to achieve two objectives of tremendous consequence: the elimination of the V-1 launching sites, bringing to an end the flying-bomb attacks on Britain, and the capture of ports required for landing the mountains of supplies still being trucked up from the Normandy beaches.

While 2nd Division was relaxing at Dieppe, British XXX Corps' tanks and recce cars were racing north through Amiens, Arras, and Douai – plunging deep into Belgium to occupy Brussels on September 2 and Antwerp on September 4, with even more dash, in terms of speed and distance, than the Yanks achieved on their highly acclaimed drive for Paris after their break-out from the Normandy bridgehead. The American spearheads, confronted by no organized resistance of consequence, in three days almost reached Le Mans on August 6, a truly exciting advance that captured the imagination of all the war correspondents after the long weeks of bloody containment – particularly when the general commanding this dashing force packed a pearl-handled pistol on his hip in traditional cowboy style.

However, General Patton's seventy-five-mile thrust in three days pales in comparison with Lt.-Gen. Brian Horrocks's XXX Corps' thrust north through France into Belgium after crossing the Seine – 230 miles in six days, the Guards Armour covering the final seventy miles from Douai to Brussels in a single day. In fact, so swift was the initial British hundred-mile run to the Somme that General Eberbach, Commander of Fifth Panzer Army, was captured in his pyjamas at Amiens.*

During today's long move – according to the diary assiduously kept by Bombardier Ken Hossack, your senior GPO Ack† since arrival on the continent on July 7 – there are only two events worth mentioning: the Regiment passing over the Somme river without anyone remarking on it; and your Number Four gun breaking its axle. Since broken axles on guns are unheard of, it is something of a miracle when Gun Artificer "Hank" Wilkins locates a replacement so promptly the gun is able to join the troop in time for another all-night move to Hazebrouck, twenty miles south of Dunkirk – to the disgust of Sgt. "Lefty" Phillips and his

---

* By comparison it took the swaggering Patton thirteen days (from August 6 to August 19), including three days clearing Chartres, to get from Le Mans to the Seine at Mantes, a distance of only about 140 miles.
† GPO stands for "gun position officer"; and Ack for "A," a carryover from the old British phonetic alphabet, stands for "assistant."

crew, who'd settled in a nearby café for an indefinite period of relaxation.

The night is inky black with driving rain, and there is only one map per troop. So when Troop Commander Len Harvey's universal carrier misses a turn and ends up in a water-filled ditch – submerging him and the map – GA, your armoured scout car, takes over the lead, and you make your way, according to Hossack, "By guess and by God." On safe arrival, though, his diary gives you full credit: "GPO guesses well."

Another all-night move (this time by moonlight) to Gistel, in Belgium, with you reading a map from a four-day-old London newspaper when the convoy leaves GA behind nosed over on its side beside a muddy stream.

Finally, on September 9, the guns deploy for action near Ostend, while the Rileys (Royal Hamilton Light Infantry) occupy the port seized yesterday by 18th Armoured Car Regiment (12th Manitoba Dragoons) feeling out the countryside in advance of 4th Division. Next day, with the Essex Scottish moving left towards Nieuwpoort, and the Royal Regiment of Canada moving right, along the coast towards Zeebrugge, the Regiment has to split up. Second Battery moves northeast behind the Royals, while the other two batteries (14th and 26th) go southwest to mark concrete coastal gun emplacements with red smoke for the rocket-firing Typhoon dive-bombers, affectionately known as "Tiffies."

Tootling about as a FOO (forward observation officer) at this time can be frustrating, as you discover when sent up to the Royals near Blankenberge. The daily allotment of shells is a mere twenty-five rounds per gun, and when these are used up, that's it. So later, when you are on reconnaissance along the west bank of the Bruges–Zeebrugge canal with Major Hank Caldwell, looking for a possible crossing point, and you spot Germans sunbathing on the far bank, you are unable to treat them to a single shell, which leaves Caldwell pawing the air.

Meanwhile, ammunition restrictions notwithstanding, the guns have to move often to stay within range, and Lieut. Bob Grout, your troop leader (as the assistant GPO is known), conducts the troop on a couple of dicey moves through flooded lowlands, where long stretches of roads are inundated. It's easy to drive off the road and submerge, as the Battery Command Post scout car did, soaking clothing, equipment, and stocks of cigarettes.

On September 11, 2nd and 14th batteries deploy just west of Bruges, a city of some fifty thousand with a large German garrison, including, according to local Resistance blokes, several thousand convalescent German soldiers wounded in Normandy. The Royals and the Royal Hamilton Light Infantry, after moving into the suburb of St. André to relieve units of 4th Division (the Royals taking over from the Lake Superior Regiment) that have had the city under mild siege for four days, are ordered "to make a show of strength," while 4th Division does a flanking move five kilometres southeast of the city from a bridgehead they have secured over the canal at Moerbrugge.

At noon on September 12, the guns move up into the outskirts of Bruges, Regimental Headquarters setting up shop in a notable building where King Leopold of Belgium capitulated to the Germans on May 28, 1940.

Soon reports of a city gone wild with joy reach the guns via "lost" truck drivers. Gunner Andy Turner, the Major's Don R (despatch rider), claims he was the first Canadian to enter Bruges – at least the first in that section of the city into which he blundered, to be overwhelmed by a mob of laughing, cheering people treating him to food and drink.

Later you hear Royals Capt. Tom Wilcox and his driver are being recognized as liberators of Bruges. Sent into the city on reconnaissance by his new CO, Lt.-Col. R. M. Lendrum, to discover the truth about reports that the enemy had flown, Wilcox was on his way back, after exchanging shots with some retreating Germans, when he was stopped by masses of cheering people pouring into the streets. Lendrum, hearing church bells ringing and cheering in the city, ordered the battalion to move in.*

The Rileys must have moved at about the same time, and no one will ever persuade Major Joe Pigott that *his* company was not the first to enter Bruges and be swallowed up in the surging mass of joyful humanity, which grabbed his soldiers, one after another, and hauled them off to parties, until he and his sergeant-major found they were leading no one.

However, officers and men of 4th Canadian Armoured Division will always claim they were the real liberators of Bruges, for it was they who first laid siege and who eventually negotiated, through a priest acting as the mayor's emissary, abandonment of the city by the Germans.

Most appropriately, when Brig. Robert Moncel, CO of 4th Armoured Brigade, enters the city – closely followed by Maj.-Gen. Harry Foster, OC of 4th Armoured Division – they are conducted by cheering crowds to the city hall to be made honorary citizens of Bruges.

Still, danger continues to lurk just north of the city, where FOO Len Harvey and his veteran carrier driver, Gunner George Ryckman, are wounded, seriously enough to be evacuated, by a booby trap attached to a German corpse.

By evening the sounds of revelry are everywhere, and men, women, and children crowd onto the gun position as though it's a freak show at a fair, paying their way with bottles of cognac, champagne, beer, and milk, and handfuls of eggs, apples, tomatoes, and onions.

At first it all seems harmless and amusing. But as the tippling goes on and the carnival atmosphere grows more and more pervasive, it becomes threatening and worrisome. You are not at all sorry when

---

* Wilcox was invited back on the first anniversary of Bruges' liberation to receive an engraved bronze medallion from the *Bürgermeister*.

the Germans intervene to the extent of attracting the attention of a
FOO somewhere on the north side of the city, resulting in a target
coming down and the gunners taking post. Just what these naïve
people crowding round the guns expected when they saw them
being loaded only they could say, but with the first deafening
smashes of muzzle blast, exaggerated by the surrounding buildings,
they turn into a panic-stricken mob, scattering in all directions as
though the devil himself is after them, dragging squealing children
by the hand and snatching up tiny tots who cannot keep up with
their headlong dash for homes and cellars.

At any rate, the guns are no longer treated as a sideshow, and
while the effects of gifts in bottles linger well into the night, no dis-
ciplinary problems are brought to your attention. And if some
gunners take advantage of the libertine spirits now abroad both
here and up at Middelkerke next day, when the Regiment returns
to the coast before the move back into France to lay siege to
Dunkirk, they do it with discretion.

Only one name makes it into Hossack's diary: "Bombardier Earl
Killeen celebrates his return to us by almost missing the early-
morning move."

2

BESIEGING DUNKIRK

——————————————— ✳ ———————————————

AT 4:00 A.M. ON SEPTEMBER 13, 4TH FIELD MOVES OFF ON its return to France, carrying all 4th Brigade infantry not conveyed by their own limited transport, many of them riding outside the vehicles – some even perched precariously on guns and ammunition limbers. Hossack's diary records this as "a first," and reports with obvious satisfaction that "the infantrymen speak well of our support, and we take turns buying drinks at a café that opens early as the convoy halts."

Within sight of Bergues, a hilltop German-held town six kilometres south of Dunkirk, the Royals are dropped off to make their way on foot to the village of Warhem, while the guns deploy.

A couple of days ago, at the same time the normally staid BBC was reporting, with undisguised pleasure, the end of five years of nightly blackouts in Britain, they announced an end to further training of the Home Guard, which had been frantically organized in 1940 in the grim days of Dunkirk, when Hitler's legions were expected to follow up their swift victory on the continent with a cross-Channel invasion. Now, with some relish, you recognize that your guns, laid on a zero line pointing at the Germans in Dunkirk, are deployed in the very fields from whence the Germans besieged the British rearguard. The British 25-pounders had gallantly held on until they had to be blown up to keep them from falling into enemy hands – while behind them on the beaches, thousands cowered among the sand dunes, exposed to shells, bombs, and strafing hour after hour, awaiting their turn to wade out to the little rescue boats shuttling back and forth from England.

Still, the cold reality is that you are again in action against determined forces: as many as ten thousand in Dunkirk, and a three-hundred-man garrison of grenadiers led by SS officers (according to the French Maquis) holding Bergues' medieval-walled heights, looking awfully formidable on that solitary hill humped up on the pancake-flat landscape. The full realization that you are again truly at war strikes with uncomfortable force as you are informing Troop Sgt.-Major Tommy Mann that your recommendation for his long-service leave to Canada has been accepted and that in a few days he'll be leaving for home. The sight of tears welling up in his eyes at the prospect of seeing his wife and son after more than four years does you in.

Like everyone else, you have been expecting to hear that an Allied armoured column has thrust deep into Germany and the war is over. The rapid moves following 4th Brigade hither and yon the past few days reinforced the idea the German war machine is disintegrating and the end is near. But as you joke with Mann that you'll not be far behind – may in fact pass him at the transit depot in Aldershot – you are plagued with the thought you may buy it from a sniper bullet or a mine, even as the Reich collapses. It is not a healthy thought, and when you learn you have been promoted captain, and as Able Troop Commander must now take up fooing full-time, you do your best to suppress it.

Late in the afternoon you are sent up to take over a Baker Troop carrier crew left leaderless and stranded beside an isolated barn out in the barren flatland that is no-man's-land. They are about a mile west of Warhem, and about the same distance east of the enemy-infested Bergues, glowering down on you from the left flank.

That there are snipers within range, your predecessor, Capt. John Bagley, a newcomer to 4th Field and the fooing business, discovered when he tried sneaking forward among the drainage ditches towards a canal some seven hundred yards in front, on an inexplicable mission of his own devising that left his veteran crewmen mystified and remarkably unsympathetic to the fact he absorbed a bullet in his nether end. When you express concern, they startle you with the vehemence and the extremely colourful language (even for gunners) they use to convince you he has only a minor wound and will crawl back after dark to the battalion aid post in Warhem.

You don't pursue the matter, for at this point you realize you have inherited a crew in various stages of inebriation, the most advanced being Gunner W. J. Jordan, generally known as "Biff," a likeable character, settled in at the radio set among a clutter of empty beer bottles in the left-rear compartment of the carrier. Red-faced and beaming, he provides a lasting impression of a signaller so well-trained in his discipline he could function perfectly well even when loaded to the gills. You might not have even noticed his condition had he not felt the need to explain, each time you came near him, "I'm entirely a victim of circumstances, sir."

According to another member of the crew, Signaller "Wally" Driemel, the "circumstances" were simply that for some considerable time this morning they'd been left to their own devices near a brewery. Naturally they'd filled the carrier with cases of the stuff (and a couple of bottles of Advocat) before coming over here, and when it seemed they had been abandoned for an indefinite period, they'd gotten their snoots into the brew again. Admittedly, old Biff is a little the worse for wear, but he is a good man, and they've all been through a lot together. He hopes you'll make allowances. And you are preparing to do just that (aware you haven't many options) when the third member of the crew, a very young signaller, staggers on the scene with faulty step and glazed eyes, determined to impress you with his superior wisdom and maturity, even if it means asserting his opinions in a loud and belligerent voice.

Establishing his name is Knox, you send him packing to the barn's hayloft to sleep it off, determined to pursue the matter with some severity when he sobers up. And you probably would have but for Driemel, who undertakes to plead the case for leniency: Bill is really a good lad, and he's been through a lot. He usually isn't like that at all – just had more to drink than he's used to. And are you aware he is only a kid – barely sixteen – having lied his way into the army when he was only fourteen?

Coming from almost any other gunner, such intercession would be intolerable, but back in England you had come to think highly of Driemel's judgement upon learning he shared your taste in music, at least to the extent of being an enthusiastic fan of a song you composed for your wife, after that swinging piano-player Signaller Ralph "Coop" Cooper and his regimental dance-band added it to their repertoire for Saturday night dances. Driemel's pleas have their effect, and as you cool down you try to imagine the extent of the lie a kid of sixteen has to live – emotionally and every other way – just to survive among his peers and not be spotted and sent home for being three years under the legal age for active service. You end up packing all of them off to bed in the barn and take over the radio-watch yourself for the next four hours.

At last light, two companies of Royals (Major Hank Caldwell's and Major Bob Suckling's) pass through on their way up to the canal in front, which they will cross using a rubber raft towed back and forth with ropes. Before dawn they must establish a firm base on the northern bank, in the eastern end of the only narrow strip of land still above water.

From your first view of this watery landscape, you have despaired of troops managing a successful assault on Dunkirk. That one road to Dunkirk – a skinny seven-kilometres-long causeway stretching through the water to infinity from that spit of land forming the far bank of the canal, under observation every foot of the way – must surely become a road to suicide.

Suckling and Caldwell are more than a little disappointed when they learn you won't be crossing with them. And, for a moment, you feel so uncomfortable you almost change your mind. But you know that here is a real test of the credo of your old friend Don Wilson, passed on to you by Stu Laurie back in Normandy. Wilson, your 1942 troop commander and a D-Day 3rd Division battery commander, visiting 4th Field briefly in July, had criticized the high casualty rate among FOOs. He'd derided the practice of artillery carriers crawling along with the infantry at walking pace, instead of moving at high speed by leaps and bounds to places of cover, as the infantry gained or passed such cover. He'd stressed the point that FOOs should take every precaution not to get pinned down with the infantry in the attack, declaring: "You're no damned good to them with your face down in the dirt beside theirs."

And as you explain this to Caldwell and Suckling, you seriously expect that enemy fire will shortly be erupting about them at the canal. Instead, before crossing, Caldwell's company accepts the surrender of five Germans who swim over the canal to him; and both companies of Royals cross without any opposition.

This, you reason later, could only have been due to the attention of the enemy being diverted from the canal and the Royals' crossings by the very heavy concentrations fired by 4th Field on Bergues and the furtive activities of the RHLI over on the left as they prepared the ground for an attack on the walled town at 4:30 A.M. The Riley plan called for their scout platoon to cut a gap through a wire barrier, with the Pioneers lifting mines as necessary, after which a platoon of Royal Canadian Engineers would blow a hole through the twenty-foot-high town wall to allow two companies to enter. However, the Riley attack was aborted even before it got going, for reasons later explained by your friend "Stevie" Stevenson, of 14th Battery, who went forward as a FOO with the assaulting force:

As the company I was supporting had to approach the wall over a wide flat area, I was on foot with a radio set on my back. The sappers were there with scaling ladders; but the wily Hun was prepared for us. He'd located drums of oil around the perimeter of the wall, and as we came up he applied a lighted torch until all were ablaze. Immediately our approach was light as day, and their enfiladed fire raked the front. Casualties were heavy, and only by crawling on one's gut did most of us manage to withdraw.

3

RELISHING REVENGE
AS GUNS SMASH ATTACK

✳

WHILE THE NAMES OF THOSE WHO SERVE AS SECOND-IN-command of infantry battalions may never appear among the postwar lists of commanding officers, some are chalking up more time in command of their battalions than many who will be so honoured in unit histories. Such a one is Major Ralph Young of the Royals, who recently acted as CO of the battalion for almost a month, from the day Lt.-Col. Jack Anderson was wounded until Lt.-Col. R. M. Lendrum arrived five days ago from the Canadian Scottish Regiment to take over.

Exuding a steely determination, which you sense could border on the ruthless if such were required to see the unit through a sticky go, he always manages to wear a big smile even in the most wretched circumstances. It is incomprehensible, unless you take his smile to be a kind of sardonic comment, a smile of contempt by one taking a cosmic view of the ongoing human condition. But whatever is behind that smile, you usually find it reassuring – except when he arrives unexpectedly at a company you are supporting, for his sudden appearance can mean a crisis is brewing or an attack is being planned.

So shortly after dawn today, September 15, your anxiety level rises sharply when, with uncanny clairvoyance, Young appears beside you in your hayloft overlooking the canal and the road leading up to Dunkirk just as a swarm of Germans mount a blazing counter-attack against two companies of Royals beyond the canal. He had spotted them streaming out of a house at the left end of the spit of land as he drove up to your barn in his Jeep, and scrambled up the ladder to your loft to alert you before the last of them spilled from the house into view.

Through holes you punched yesterday through the tiles in the barn roof, you can see them running crouched over, now and then dropping down, only to rise almost immediately with Schmeissers blazing in the direction of the Royals dug-in among some trees at the right end of the "island." With the canal house as a reference point, it is easy to give the guns a precise map reference, and you go right into "fire for effect" without ranging: "Scale 10" (ten rounds per gun), using one battery of eight guns only, for there isn't room between the attackers and the Royals to safely use all twenty-four. The target area you choose is slightly ahead of the advancing Germans, anticipating they'll arrive just in time to walk under your deluge of eighty shells. And so it happens.

Steadying your glasses on a rafter pole to counter the rocking sponginess of the hay under your feet, you focus on the hunched-over, running, blue-grey forms from whom streams of glittering white tracers periodically spurt into the trees ahead of them. You see their faces clearly as your shells sizzle overhead, and then violent black-and-orange puffs flash and spout among them. Only for a moment can you follow them – some go down immediately, others try to run, then crumple over and go down – then smoke from the torrent of explosions blots out everything. Satisfied with the way your shells are falling, you order "Scale 20 – Repeat" (twenty rounds per gun at the same line and range).

As your shells rip and tear that narrow strip of land where you saw them go to ground, you feel you are finally taking revenge. After all the times you and your comrades have cringed, paralyzed with fear, under *their* shelling, *their* mortaring, *their* strafing, and *their* bombing – without ever once being able to get them in your sights – you finally have them. And you find yourself mumbling: "That's for always-smiling Jack Cameron (who every night wrote his wife, whom he married only two days before being sent over-seas) . . . and that's for quiet Jack Thompson (who left his wife preg-nant on his last leave) . . . and that's for my Grace's gentle uncle George Marsh, the Birmingham air-raid warden (who died on duty) . . . and that's for Dawson and Knapp and Parker and Thorpe and Ament . . ."

The Royals' historian will record: "Three times the enemy massed for counter-attacks on A Company's position, but each time they were dispersed by accurate artillery and mortar fire, and the direct fire of a 40-mm Bofors ack-ack gun." But you will recall only ordering and reordering, "Scale 20 — Repeat" until the sur-vivors rise up with hands stretched high over their heads and walk into the Royals' position – thirty-six only, including two officers, of the 186 who marched down here from Dunkirk last night, accord-ing to the haggard prisoners.

For once you are able to give command posts and the men on the guns a graphic description of the results of their shooting. However, before they have time to take satisfaction from their morning's work, at about 11:00 A.M. they are on the receiving end of unusually heavy and accurate shelling from German guns around Dunkirk – something everybody had been expecting since 4th Field moved forward yesterday into full view of what the gunners call "Burg-on-the-hill."

Sgt. Bruce Hunt's diary will report: "Command posts, troops and kitchen – each in turn receives a well-directed, vicious effort." But while tires and gas tanks are punctured and kit of all sorts is blown to oblivion, 2nd and 26th batteries miraculously suffer no casual-ties. Less fortunate is 14th Battery; they suffer six casualties. As the guns are being limbered up to try to escape the shelling by moving back to the former gun position, Gunner John S. Sherwood is killed. And Sergeant Nicholas Ostapyck and gunners Edward J. Cuff, F. H. A. Nicholson, Michael McLeod, and John Rutherford are wounded.

And 14th Battery FOO "Stevie" Stevenson tells you later of another rough go for him with the RHLI. Shelled out of a church tower – his carrier damaged, his radio knocked out, and his signaller badly wounded – he's desperate as he wades back through a water-filled ditch to the Rileys' company headquarters.

They are in the process of withdrawing over the fields, but I can't join them because I don't want to leave my wounded signaller behind. I get through to Battalion on their radio and ask Jack Drewry, my battery commander, for smoke to cover the route I'll take.

Back at the church we load the wounded signaller into the carrier and lay on our route with the driver, who'll be driving blind through smoke. When it arrives, we move off with our heads down. All the way back, the sides of the carrier are pitted with small-arms fire, but we make it to Battalion HQ. Everybody seems rather surprised to see us.

The effectiveness of the German counter-battery fire creates an urgent demand for precise information on the location of the offending guns, and you are sent to spend the night flash-spotting the guns of Dunkirk from a towering church steeple in Hondschoote, right of Warhem.

As you settle down on an open stone balcony, far above the world, you wonder why in 1940 the British allowed this tower to survive overlooking their entire rearguard forces holding off the Germans. Never, in your wildest conjectures, while reading to your training troop in Petawawa from "Return Via Dunkirk," by a gunner officer using the pseudonym "Gunbuster" – the story of a British field regiment supporting the gallant rearguard – did you imagine that one day you'd be here at Dunkirk with the roles reversed. From up here you can readily identify that part of the "naked plain," some eight kilometres away near Rosendael on the eastern outskirts of Dunkirk, where those immortal 25-pounders were deployed in their final stand that last night before being blown up by their battery commanders at virtually the eleventh hour, while behind them burning Dunkirk "glowed red like a cinder."

Then, as now, much of the countryside was covered with water, flooded by the French opening sluice gates to discommode the Germans who had to cross that same canal glistening down there before you that the Royals crossed last night. And farther on, a mile from Dunkirk, though you can't identify it, is another canal into which the British gunners dumped all their shells "considered surplus" to their last-hour needs – an incredible move. Why they didn't fire them off at the enemy before spiking their guns is something that has always bothered you; and you wonder if those shells are still lying there on the bottom of that canal.

How remarkably different this whole business of seeking out targets and dropping shells on them has become since those days. The equipment you carry to do all required of a FOO – field-glasses, compass, Chinagraph pencil and map (frequently removed from its protective talc-covered case and stuffed in the front of your blouse) – would have seemed incredibly primitive to "Gunbuster" when the shooting war began for him, somewhere west of Brussels in May 1940. As that earnest gunner officer settled down in his tower to carry out the prescribed procedures of 1914–18 vintage – first to draw a panorama pencil sketch of the zone, then to carry out "silent registration" of potential targets – he had with him a survey instrument known as a No. 7 Artillery Director, a range finder, and an artillery board holding gridded paper and an "arm" and an "arc" to measure ranges and switches to targets. How he and his poor ack ever made it up a tower, lugging all that stuff, you can't imagine.

As it is, even without all that baggage, the number of steps and ladder rungs you have to climb to reach this eyrie leaves you breathless and heaving. And for your hungover, repentant crew, it is a penitential climb of intimidating proportions each time they have to ascend from ground level: first with cables and phone, and then down and up, down and up, to relieve the pangs of hunger, thirst, and other bodily functions, which seem to be functioning more than usual this evening. There has been no "hair of the dog" for them today, of that you have made certain, and as the night tips over into the early hours of September 16, and the telephone goes dead, they pay the price for their excessive indulgence yesterday, as, sweating and panting, they take turns climbing up and down the darkened interior of this great tower trying to get the thing to work.

The recalcitrant instrument went dead just when you collected a clean bearing on a gun firing from Dunkirk – a really big flash you suspect was from the muzzle of the coastal gun they have turned around and are using to harass major Allied supply roads many miles inland. Radio silence having been imposed tonight for some reason, it is essential to get the damned telephone to work.

Finally assuming there's a break in the line snaking back to Regiment, you wait for the Signal Section to fix it. But when the first misty predawn light appears and the line is still dead, you decide to pack everybody into the carrier and go back along the road to locate the break. Your weary men are soon patiently taking turns stumbling along the ditch, running the signal wire through their hands, when they meet the signal truck coming up, its crew industriously winding in the cable on a big spool!

Incredulous, you listen to Signal-Sgt. Ryder informing you that the Regiment pulled out an hour ago for Belgium, on their way to Antwerp. Hadn't anyone told you?

Surely he's joking, especially that ridiculous Antwerp bit.

He assures you the guns left at 0430 for a staging area ten miles east of here.

When finally you catch up with the Regiment at Hoogstade, you learn that 4th Brigade is being rushed to Antwerp to prevent the Germans returning to destroy the port facilities. It seems the nervous garrison had been more concerned with being cut off from *das Vaterland* by the tanks of British 11th Armoured Division than with blowing up the port facilities, and they have been left virtually intact in the control of the Belgian Resistance after the city was overrun by the British tanks and the garrison commander captured by the accompanying infantry. Now, realizing their error, the Germans are trying to return.

And Dunkirk? It will be screened off and left to rot.*

At 0915 on September 16, the Regiment, again carrying the infantry packed in and on the quads, trucks, and gun limbers, pulls out for Antwerp, following a route through the heart of "Flanders Fields." All morning you see road signs associated with legendary battles of the First War. Ten miles into the journey, there's the road leading to Poperinghe. Then comes Ypres with its Menin Gate, a great stone arch carrying the names of sixty thousand British and British Commonwealth soldiers of the First War for whom there were no known graves, and where each evening at sundown three members of the Ypres Fire Brigade assemble to raise their bugles and blow the Last Post in grateful memory of their sacrifice.

Six kilometres northeast of Ypres, and six west of Passchendaele, you pass the towering thirty-five-foot granite pillar supporting the famous "brooding soldier" – a giant bust of a soldier bowed over his folded hands which rest on the butt of his rifle standing muzzle-down at "arms reversed" – marking the entrance to a cemetery near St. Julien of two thousand graves of Canadians who fell during the Second Battle of Ypres in 1915.

The great helmeted head, bowed forever in reverent sorrow, is so striking and its message so powerful that for a while you are over-come with murderous hatred for a people who wildly cheered their leader as step by step he led them into vile aggressions that would plunge the world into another round of slaughter, within a mere twenty-one years of the end of the one commemorated here.

However, as emotional exhaustion adds its weight to the stupefying

---

* The Allied High Command sensibly decided it was not worth the price it would cost to pursue the attack across that flooded landscape. Dunkirk was left contained by a screen of armoured cars of the Czech Brigade for the rest of the war.

effects of some thirty hours with only catnaps, you slump down in the rocking carrier and drift off in a sleep so deep you don't wake until its tracks are clattering along a cobblestone street lined with substantial buildings whose façades of rich and intricate design suggest an ancient city of some consequence. Your driver, Gunner Bill Walkden, reveals you are passing through Ghent, seemingly unharmed by whatever the 7th Armoured Division (Desert Rats) had to do to capture it a couple of days ago.

Hazy memories of Browning's poem " 'How They Brought the Good News from Ghent to Aix' " are stirred: "I sprang to the stirrup, and Joris, and he;/ I galloped, Dirck galloped, we galloped all three. . . ." And though no "cocks crow" at Lokeren, and at Boom no "great yellow star" appears, you follow the very route Browning's imaginary horsemen galloped towards Aix until you reach Boom and 4th Field turns north to Antwerp. But unlike the over-stressed horses that began dropping dead as their awesome gallop reached a climax, not a single quad or other 4th Field vehicle breaks down on this long and strenuous drive.

The way the Regiment's vehicles are standing up on these long hauls through northern France and Belgium is a measure of their excellent maintenance by conscientious drivers and the support of dedicated battery motor-mechanics, who daily labour beyond the call of duty.

The reliability of the big trucks, travelling back and forth from supply dumps, bringing up tons of shells, petrol, and rations, is taken for granted by all except the "motor-mechs." Seldom have vehicles failed to keep their place in convoy on these all-night runs, and when on rare occasion vehicles have broken down, motor-mechs usually have them moving again in short order.

Major repairs are supposed to be by LAD (Light Aid Detachment), a section of REME (Royal Electrical and Mechanical Engineers) detached and travelling with the Regiment. If LAD can't handle the job, it is sent back to REME Base Work Shops set up in buildings suitable for machine shops and sophisticated repairs. But many major repairs are made at the side of the road, or in open fields, by 4th Field mechanics. Officially, batteries are limited in the stores they can carry with them, but battery motor-mechs never miss an opportunity to add to their stocks of spare parts, pirating fuel pumps, carburettors, water pumps, and the like from disabled vehicles along the way.

Whether the nature of the trade attracts a certain type of man, or whether it's because they are daily involved in pursuits of a constructive nature, while all about them others are sharpening their skills for destruction, motor-mechs invariably appear as men of greater maturity with strong leadership qualities. Without exception they are accorded high respect by all ranks. Some, like 2nd Battery Bombardier G. J. Vosdingh, are looked upon as supermen. Affectionately known as "Sledge," for sledgehammer, he is believed capable of fixing anything with "a bit of wire and a pair of pliers." And over the years you have heard this, or something similar, said of at least one mechanic in every battery.

Recently this legendary ingenuity was taxed to the limit when "Sledge" and 2nd Battery's Sgt. Keith McConnell replaced a clutch in the middle of the night in a truck bringing up a load of petrol to the Regiment. Obviously this was a job for a well-lit, well-equipped workshop, which in normal circumstances would have been turned over to LAD or towed back to REME.

However, in McConnell's judgement there wasn't time. Without that load of petrol, the Regiment could be immobilized, a very serious matter for the rapidly advancing infantry who have come to count on the continuous support of the guns of 4th Field, night and day, in fair weather and foul. Fortunately, they were carrying in Battery Stores a spare clutch for a 30-hundredweight truck, which they had the foresight to scrounge somewhere back in Normandy. Working under a tarpaulin draped over the vehicle to prevent light from their lantern attracting a marauding German bomber to this load of petrol, they removed the defective clutch and replaced it well before dawn, and were able to catch up with the Regiment before any gas tanks ran dry.

Motor-mechanics will never be awarded medals for keeping vehicles in operation, for the same reason signallers are not decorated for keeping wireless sets operating. Their work is now so taken for granted it is unlikely that any mention of them will ever appear in the Regimental war diary, let alone in despatches from war correspondents, who, quite naturally, overlook the dull, winding columns of trucks coming up behind, in favour of the flashing guns and the roaring tanks and armoured cars in the spearheads thrusting into enemy country.

Still, anyone choosing to reflect on the matter will agree that dependable transport, like constant communications, is crucial for the guns to be there whenever the infantry and tanks need them to support attacks and subdue counter-attacks. And the extent to which this is not always true of the German artillery may account for the ultimate success of our infantry against Hitler's élite divisions.

4

THE SOUND OF
REVELRY BY NIGHT

AFTER TEN HOURS, THE CONVOY ARRIVES IN ANTWERP JUST
as the sun is going down on a beautiful evening, the guns rolling
down the Grand Boulevard between dense, cheering crowds and
beneath a succession of giant elongated Belgian flags, hanging
down from cables stretched across the street, their red, orange, and
black stripes wavering gently like flames in the sunset as the quads
brush under them on their way across town to the docks in the
north end.

This great reception is totally unexpected. After all, twelve days
have passed since four British tanks nosed their way tentatively
into Antwerp, making it Allied territory. But tonight, with the
Germans in the northeastern suburb of Merxem, threatening to
reoccupy the city and perhaps carry out reprisals, people have
turned out to express their gratitude to the first large contingent of
Allied troops that has come this way with a comforting number of
guns. Men, women, and children, many on their fathers' shoulders,
line both curbs of the great boulevard's right roadway, cheering
the passing parade.

Now and then someone darts from the curb to pass up fruit,
cigars, wine, or beer to a gun sergeant leaning down from the roof-
hatch of a passing quad or to a soldier reaching out from his perch
on a gun or limber. A big bunch of grapes and a handful of fine
cigars land *plop* in your lap just as your carrier is passing what you'll

later learn is the opera house, a noble structure at an intersection with a main business artery that leads right, to the Rex movie theatre, sidewalk cafés, the railway station, and the Century Hotel.

The convoy pauses a moment later to drop off the infantry, and your carrier peels away to follow the marching Royals down narrow back streets to an area of factories and warehouses along the Albert Canal, which separates Antwerp from the Germans in Merxem. The guns proceed north to deploy on and about the docks, with muzzles pointing across the empty ships' basins towards Merxem. The luck of the draw places 2nd Battery in pre-prepared gun positions with excellent German-built dugouts just north of the docks at Noordkasteel. The cooks set up shop in splendour in an aquatic clubhouse complete with swimming pool.

As the guns are put on line, the infantry take up positions along the canal and at other strategic points, such as the installations known as "sluice gates," which, you are told, the Germans must seize if they are seriously to disable the harbour. Until now, these all-important gates controlling water levels at the port, eighty kilometres up the Scheldt river from the North Sea, have been held somewhat precariously through the gallant fighting and astute manoeuvring of Belgian Resistance fighters, now known as the White Brigade because of the white butchers' coats they assumed as their uniform on moving their operations "above ground."

You spend the entire first night finding your way from the Royals Tac HQ, in a school a few blocks from the canal, to 4th Brigade HQ, in a mansion on the other side of town, to pick up maps; and it's mid-morning before you finally settle in your OP, the attic of an empty multi-storey factory building down on the canal.

Almost encircling the gloomy vastness under the rafters on the top floor, is a substantial rubber conveyor-belt nearly five feet wide, resting, unmoving, on a bed of rollers on a waist-high steel frame. Placed a few feet from the windows, it provides a convenient springy-but-firm extended platform from which to view the zone through small dormer windows high up in the steeply slanting mansard roof. However, as an OP, to be occupied over a long period, it is seriously flawed. The slanting part of the roof is only the thickness of asphalt shingles laid over one-inch boards, offering little or no protection against anything but a spent bullet. Shells and mortar bombs could rip through it like paper. For the first time, you decide you must take advantage of a privilege extended by custom to artillery forward observers by the infantry, and ask them to provide you with "protection," which can be interpreted in many ways – in this case a "pillbox" built of sandbags on the conveyor-belt.

Company Commander Suckling is somewhat taken aback when you make your request as you are bedding down that night on one of the cots sitting on duck-boards in the partially flooded basement where he's established his headquarters. But sympathetic to your position, he arranges for a squad to haul the necessary number of sandbags up the several flights of stairs and stack them in a semi-circle on the belt, leaving a viewing-slot in front and roofing it over with more sandbags. When the nest is "floored" with chesterfield cushions, you're absolutely delighted, even though it immediately draws undisguised scorn from an observer crew for the Toronto Scottish's 4.2-inch mortars, the officer and his signaller lounging like oriental potentates in deeply upholstered chairs on the con-veyor-belt in front of neighbouring windows.

Unquestionably the war is serious business for the infantrymen along the canal and the gunners among the docks, but the drawing power of a city untouched by war – full of cafés, restaurants, hotels, and pretty women – is irresistible, and the powers-that-be know it. So the second night, five-hour leaves uptown are started for a portion of the gunners at a time.

When Sgt.-Maj. Tommy Mann, who leaves tomorrow for Canada, picks you up at the OP to drive you uptown, he brings along Sgt. "Lefty" Phillips, the man who'll succeed him as troop sergeant-major. After locating what seems to be the heart of the city and parking the Jeep by removing the rotor from the distribu-tor, there's still the puzzle of how to proceed. Uncertain where to go in the blackout, you stop and listen. The sounds of music and laughter lead you through a blackout curtain and upstairs to a beautifully appointed restaurant and dance floor jammed with people in evening dress. All over the room, smiling people beckon you and your companions to join them at their tables, and waiters follow you with chairs and a tray of drinks. But as you squeeze in between an immaculately dressed man and woman, you become conscious of your bulky sidearm, your dirty hands, and your stained and rumpled battledress.

Although they pooh-pooh your concerns, you get a waiter to lead you to a washroom. It turns out to be one that serves both women and men at the same time, and for the first time, you have the peculiar experience of being attended in such a place by a woman. She hands you a tiny sliver of soap and a towel; and when, after washing, you go into a cubicle and get comfortably seated, reflecting how much better this is than a Compo box with its top panel punched in, she knocks at the door and hands you in two sheets of toilet paper.

When you rejoin your companions, you find they've decided they can't stand such affluence and want to try somewhere else. Every other place is jammed, for it appears Antwerp has decided spontaneously to celebrate this day as their Liberation Day, something they had delayed doing until the few British tanks and infantry and their gallant resistance fighters were reinforced by the Canadian battalions and the 4th Field guns.

For a while it looks like a dry night, but suddenly you find a quiet side street full of small luxurious bars with nobody in them. It isn't until you have had a drink in four or five different establishments, and become bored with the utter stillness of the perfumed luxury of each of them in turn, that one of your companions asks the lady proprietor why they have so few customers. The Madam explains the facts of life as she knows them on this street, and offers him one of her "girls," a woman old enough to be his mother.

You go back to following the sound of revelry in the blackout, and are led to a small restaurant in a converted house. Inside, a pianist at an upright piano with a vase of roses on it accompanies an attractive lady singing "Roses of Picardy." Looking around the room, it dawns on you that these people, listening so intently with a far-away look in their eyes, are old enough to have gathered around a piano and sung this song at the height of its popularity in 1916. Having driven all the previous day along poplar-lined roads that "Colinette with the sea-blue eyes" would have recognized, you feel extraordinarily close to these people and their thoughts, and suddenly you realize the 1914–18 war, which always seemed so long ago, was really only yesterday.

Days later, when you visit the guns, you will find your GPO Bob Grout and new Troop Leader Lieut. Bernie Ackerman imbued with similar thoughts, having been led into the subject by Gunner John Elder's father. Brig. Herbert Elder, Deputy-Director Canadian Army Medical Services, and senior medical officer in this theatre of operations, had paid a surprise visit to the guns to see his son, who, until then, had kept the matter of his father's high rank hidden from his comrades. The Brigadier, a courtly gentleman six-foot-three-and-a-half-inches tall, had served as a bugler at his father's field hospital in Flanders in 1914 when he was only sixteen.

Bombardier Hossack's diary, however, presents a less sentimental view of Antwerp:

Collaborators are being rounded up daily, and the women who "informed" on the resistance forces, or were otherwise unpatriotic, are publicly shamed. Made to stand all day in a main-street window giving the Nazi salute, they are removed to the street at 5:00 P.M., where a barber clips them bald. A woman shorn of her locks loses much of her beauty. There follows the public march, or rather the chase, to the cages of the nearby zoo, with all civilian bystanders vying for a chance to slap or spit on the unfortunate ones. A particularly angry mob has torn the clothes from one young lady and she covers the route to the zoo in record time.

The cost of high-living is telling on the boys. Our extra smokes, soap, and chocolate disappear for francs, but we're still poor. In the end everything from Jeeps to dirty underwear claims its price. Enemy shells seldom land near us, but his mortars are active against other units. One shell does land on our cookhouse just ten minutes after we (including cooks) had dispersed.

For sixteen days, 4th Brigade and its supporting guns (along with the rest of 2nd Division from September 19) remain here, preventing the Germans from spoiling what the High Command considers a plum, while all priority of supply on the Western Front is given over to Montgomery's "Market-Garden" operation, which is meant to leap over the Rhine, utilizing huge British and American paratroop and glider forces to secure the vast Grave bridge over the Maas (Meuse) river, the Nijmegen bridge over the southern branch of the Rhine, and the Arnhem bridge over the Neder Rhine, while XXX Corps drives a corridor north towards them along the ground.

Most things still come all the way up from the Normandy beaches, and ammunition, while sufficient for emergencies and some harassing fire, is strictly rationed, which means you restrict your firing to targets you can clearly identify among the streets you overlook in Merxem. An exception to this is the great bulging roof of the ice-hockey arena, into which you drop a shell now and then to discourage its use by the enemy for storage or billetting.*

Your most intriguing target involves a dead-end street leading away from the canal directly opposite you. Each noon German soldiers trickle out in ones and twos from between two houses down

---

* Weeks later, on a balmy early winter day, as Belgian workmen strove to repair holes in the great arena's roof and stem the inward flow of warm air, 4th Field's regimental hockey team (managed by the FOO who'd punched all those holes) participated in a game (the only one they got to play on the continent) in fog so dense that, from behind the players' bench, only centre-ice faceoffs could be seen before the action disappeared into the white void; and only the sudden cessation of clicking and clacking of sticks and a return to visibility at centre ice of players and referee for another faceoff revealed the fact that a goal had been scored.

near the canal on the left side of the street and take off in a mad gallop to the far end, where they cross over and disappear. At first they'd strolled casually, one even walking a bicycle, obviously believing they were unobserved. But now, knowing the street is "registered," they run for their lives when they enter "Green Street," the name you've given it because of the carpet of grass growing up between the cobblestones through the absence of all vehicular traffic. Why they don't use a hidden route to their cook-house for their noon meal is beyond comprehension, but day after day without fail they maintain their routine, and each day your guns are loaded and waiting to ambush them. This greatly amuses Bob Suckling and neighbouring company commanders Caldwell and Stothers when he invites them over to inspect the "pillbox" his men built for you, and they time their visit to coincide with your noon-day show.

However, for the men on the guns who can't see the interesting effects of the fall of their shot, it's a matter of vast irritation that every noon, just as the cooks have doled out their hot meal, your order comes down to take post. And after loading and laying their guns on the target, they wait interminably for the order to fire, while their grub grows cold and greasy in their mess tins, and leathery membranes form in their mugs on the surface of their "Compo tea" – that unforgettable concoction obtained by boiling tea leaves, powdered milk, and sugar together.

When enemy mortars become active for short intervals from somewhere in the grounds of a castle-like structure among the trees over the canal, counter-measures are arranged for rocket-firing Typhoons, with your guns marking the suspected target area with red smoke. Then the night of September 20, the Essex Scottish, on the left, are attacked in such strength, one company is forced off its position; and the Germans are driven off only after 2,400 rounds are expended by the Regiment in a flurry of firing.* However, such

---

*   L/Sgt. Joseph Harold Lewis (Troop Signals NCO of 26th Battery) was

activity is unusual here. Apart from the loony Jerries in Green Street each noon, you seldom spot anything to hammer, and the hours from dawn to dusk pass very slowly – particularly in the cramped positions you must assume to fit into your sandbag nest, for while it is a masterpiece of strength and security, it is not spacious. Still, you sustain the belief that one of these days the Germans will have to conclude the observer for the guns harassing them each noon is up in a window high in this building directly opposite Green Street, and when they do, your caution will be vindicated.

At noon today it happens. As always you are curled up in your "cocoon," as your mildly insulting Tor Scots neighbours refer to it as they recline in their easy chairs to your left. As usual you've laid the guns on Green Street to await the stubbornly methodical Germans who, despite the fact you have shelled them every day for a week, will appear as usual to run their awful gauntlet. You wait impatiently, for you are scheduled to go uptown for a few hours this afternoon. But right on time the first appear, galloping up the street. You yell "Fire!" into the phone and immediately the guns start thumping behind. In seconds, sinister whispers pass overhead – a split-second silence – and then roaring vicious flashes, black smoke, and dust fill the street.

As you wait for the dust to settle, there is a nasty fluttering sound overhead and a mortar bomb crashes through the roof – then another and another and another in rapid succession, blacking out everything with choking attic dust. In the dark stillness that follows, there is the sound of groaning and then cries of "Stretcher!" from the mortar crew. Yelling to them that you are going for help, you feel your way over to the stairs, and skitter down to locate stretcher-bearers.

---

subsequently awarded a Military Medal for re-establishing communications between OP and guns by land line, "following a route that was under shellfire continually, and, at a critical stage, under direct fire from enemy automatic weapons." (Quoted from citation.)

This accomplished, you make your way out through the back alley, crouching over to keep out of sight. After a block or two you are able to straighten up, and wait for a free ride uptown on one of the little yellow streetcars that dare come down this far. When one arrives, it stops just long enough for a brisk and friendly motorman to swing the trolley arm around and change his control-crank from front to back, and it rattles and scrapes back the way it came, taking you to scenes of civilian life going on totally oblivious to the rumble of guns in the distance.

The streets are full of shoppers, including women with toddlers and baby carriages. Sidewalk cafés are crowded with civilians and soldiers watching the girls go by. The spacious lounge of the Century Hotel is filled with immaculately groomed people conversing over the gentle strains of a vintage salon orchestra, and dawdling over their glasses of Advocaat served by discreet waiters in dinner jackets. While up the block, the ice-cream parlour is doing a land-office business soothing throats that haven't tasted anything cold for months – let alone ice-cream – some customers starting at the top of a menu on the wall and successively ordering every sundae listed.

When your five-hour leave is up, you catch a streetcar back to the canal where you take up the business of war again. Tonight you fire diversionary shelling, to draw their attention away from friend Lieut. "Hefty" Ross, the now-legendary Royals' scout officer, who, in anticipation of the attack that everyone knows must soon be made over there, swims the canal and crawls around on his belly in the cinders of a dark Merxem parking lot, locating German positions by following the smell of cigarette smoke and the faint, desultory conversation between sentries meeting at the boundaries of their allotted rounds. Around 3:00 A.M., he returns via Suckling's company. Soaking wet and shuddering, black-faced with shoe polish, and with a balaclava pulled over his head, he pores over a map with Bob, identifying the enemy positions he's pinpointed.

5

CLEARING THE CHANNEL PORTS

❄

FATE MUST SURELY HAVE BEEN MINDFUL OF THE TERRIBLE sacrifices made by 2nd Division on the beaches of Dieppe in 1942 to have arranged events in such a way as to spare its units from fighting for a Channel port.

Remarkably, the only two Channel ports of consequence taken without a struggle were those assigned to 2nd Division for clearing: Dieppe and Ostend, which, according to Intelligence, were the only ports Hitler didn't place on his list to be held at all costs. Then on the eve of what surely would have been another blood-letting in the flooded land in front of Dunkirk, 2nd Division was suddenly withdrawn and rushed to Antwerp to occupy static positions in relative comfort, periodically enduring breathtaking brushes with civilian luxury on pass uptown.

Meanwhile, other divisions of First Canadian Army, including attached British divisions, have been forced to fight for every metre of ground in the vicinity of every one of their designated ports.

The first, Le Havre, earmarked for American use, required a heavy assault by two British divisions, the 49th West Riding and 51st Highland, supported by massive fire-power from land, sea, and air – most particularly the air from which 4,000 tons of bombs were dropped during the siege and 5,500 more during the attack itself, which began September 10. From the sea the 15-inch guns of HMS *Erebus* and *Warspite* shelled the coastal gun emplacements. And

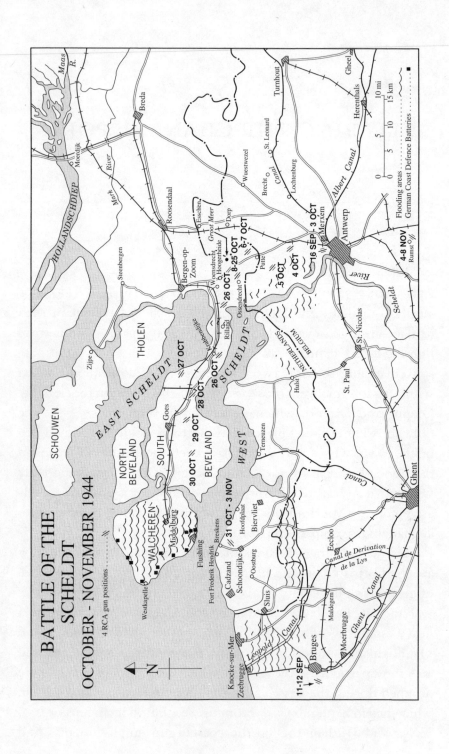

BATTLE OF THE
SCHELDT
OCTOBER - NOVEMBER 1944

4 RCA gun positions ....

N

SCHOUWEN

Maas R.

HOLLANDSCHDIEP

Moerdijk

Breda

Mark River

Steenbergen

Zijpe

THOLEN

EAST SCHELDT

NORTH
BEVELAND

Goes

SOUTH

27 OCT

28 OCT

26 OCT

29 OCT

30 OCT

Kreekrakdijk

Rilland

BEVELAND

Middelburg

WALCHEREN

31 OCT - 3 NOV

Westkapelle

Flushing

Fort Frederik Hendrik

Breskens

Cadzand

Schoondijke

Oostburg

Hoofdplaat

Biervliet

WEST

SCHELDT

Terneuzen

Hulst

NETHERLANDS
BELGIUM

St. Paul

St. Nicolas

Scheldt River

Roosendaal

Bergen-op-Zoom

Wouwsche Plantage

Esschen

Groot Meer

Dorp

Wensdrecht

Hoogerheide

8-25 OCT

26 OCT

Ossendrecht

5 OCT

4 OCT

Potte

6-7 OCT

16 SEP - 3 OCT

Merxem

Antwerp

4-8 NOV

Rumst

Wuestwezel

Brecht

Canal

Lochtenburg

St. Leonard

Turnhout

Herenthals

Gheel

Albert Canal

Ghent

Eecloo

Canal de Derivation
de la Lys

Canal

Canal

Ghent Canal

Maldegem

Moerbrugge

Bruges

Sluis

Zeebrugge

Knocke-sur-Mer

11-12 SEP

Leopold Canal

10 mi
15 km

0   5   10
0   5   10

Flooding areas ....
German Coast Defence Batteries ....

from the land, in addition to the fire from two divisional field artilleries, and a torrent of 100-pound shells from ninety-six medium guns, were the awesome *crumps* of 200-pound shells from sixteen 7.2-inch heavies blasting away at the strongpoints.

Hardly surprising that the siege ended after only forty-eight hours with the surrender of 9,500 survivors, and that the demolition of the docks was so complete, it would take more than a month to restore the port installations to usefulness.

Boulogne is in no better shape when captured. The assault by 3rd Division on its garrison of 10,000 and its ninety guns of various calibres up to great coastal guns, all well-protected by thick concrete emplacements, had to wait until Le Havre fell and the guns of 51st Highland Division and 9th British AGRA (Army Group Royal Artillery) could be moved north to join 2nd Cdn AGRA and double up the land-based fire-power.

In the meantime, German positions, marked by red smoke by the field guns, were subjected to twenty-nine attacks by medium bombers and swarms of rocketing Typhoons.

On September 16, opening day of the assault, the Typhoons carried out twenty additional strikes, but these were dwarfed by the 8,541 bombs (3,310 tons) dropped by 752 Lancaster and Halifax heavy bombers and 40 Mosquitoes on five target areas. And while the bombs were still falling, 328 guns opened up on a series of timed concentrations on strongpoints.

Brig. Stanley Todd, CRA of 3rd Division (ex-CO of 4th Field), had under his control five field regiments, five medium regiments, three heavy regiments, and one heavy ack-ack regiment. And considering the long hauls for ammunition, the scale accumulated was astounding: 38,400 rounds for ninety-six 25-pounders, 14,000 20-pound shells for forty-eight heavy ack-ack guns, 12,000 100-pound shells for eighty mediums, and 800 200-pound shells for eight 7.2-inch guns.

In addition to all this, to keep the big coastal guns of Boulogne preoccupied during the assault, Brig. H. O. N. Brownfield, the BRA (Brigadier Royal Artillery), the highest ranking gunner officer of

First Canadian Army, arranged for supporting cross-Channel fire from two 14-inch Dover guns, coyly known as "Winnie" and "Pooh," and two 15-inch monsters of 540th Coast Regiment at Wanston on St. Margaret's Bay, directed on targets by an Air OP officer, the CO of 660 Squadron, flying a little Auster aircraft above the Channel, augmented by observations by ground observers brought over from Dover.

The Wanston guns scored a direct hit on a 16-inch enemy gun at Sangatte before their 1,920-pound shells began to land in the sea – their worn barrels (the fourth replacements in three years) no longer capable of producing the muzzle velocity necessary to send their huge missiles to the continent. However, "Winnie" and "Pooh" fired again on the 19th and 20th, damaging three of the four 28-cm (11-inch) guns in the German coastal battery in the Cap Gris Nez area.

After six days of fighting for a seemingly endless number of strongpoints, the last of the Boulogne fortifications fell and 9,517 survivors of the 10,000-man garrison surrendered on September 22.

Canadian losses numbered 634 killed, wounded, and missing.

For the next two days long convoys of guns, Canadian and British, moved north for the attack on Calais, which opened on September 25 with another massive bombardment from sky and land. Five days before, 633 planes of Bomber Command had dropped 3,000 tons of bombs on Calais defences, reputedly with good results. But on the morning of the assault a thundering armada of 900 heavy bombers came over from England to plaster strong-points. Unfortunately, bad weather prevented many from completing their sorties, and much of the 1,300 tons of bombs dropped were off-target, leaving intact many pillboxes and gun emplacements.

Half an hour after the aerial bombing began, the positions of twenty-one known enemy batteries were bombarded for forty minutes by three heavy regiments, eight medium regiments, and two heavy ack-ack regiments – 224 guns in all. Then thirty minutes before H-Hour these same medium and heavy guns joined 144

25-pounders of six field regiments in several earth-shuddering concentrations on the objectives of the assaulting troops.

On the left of Calais, 8th Brigade, with only the guns of 13th Field providing close support, captured the garrison at Cap Blanc Nez, and next morning, September 26, the battery of giant 406-mm (16-inch) guns in the nearby hills surrendered.

During the day, close to seven hundred RAF planes dropped 3,600 tons of bombs on Calais and Cap Gris Nez. Still the big guns on this headland escaped damage and would not surrender.

Fortunately, not all strongpoints were defended with such tenacity. For instance, old Fort Nieulay – five miles in from the sea and dominating the plain before Calais – could have been a wretched business. Upgraded by the addition of machine-gun pits along the top of embanked walls, and 88-mm guns in corner emplacements, the ancient fort presented a formidable obstacle in the path of 7th Brigade, in particular the Royal Winnipeg Rifles, following a road east towards Calais, passing by the principal gate into the fort. However, when their Carrier Platoon, commanded by Sgt. Joe Roshick, went forward to recce the outskirts of Calais, and one of the three flame-throwers suddenly did a smart left turn and let fly a roiling ball of flame up against the wooden front door of the fort, setting it on fire, a white flag appeared.

Capt. Cliff Chadderton, whose "Charley" Company was following close behind and was first to enter the fort, met an astonishing scene:

The Commandant, a very fat officer, stood at the centre of the open courtyard holding a white flag. Clearly prepared for a ceremonious surrender, he stood beside a table covered with a white cloth on which were arranged glasses and a bottle of champagne. As he and several other officers were being disarmed, he was told to bring all his troops into this central square, including those on the parapet manning the 88-mm guns who were glaring down quizzically as though not sure what they should do. To the relief of the handful of Winnipegs in the fort, outnumbered at least ten to one, when the Commandant waved at them to come down, they came. All in all the garrison numbered about 200.

When, with the Commandant in tow, we entered the command post of the fort, a telephone was ringing. We ordered him to answer it, but he refused. So we picked up the phone and said, "We have your fort." A surprised voice answered in German and we turned for help to a Winnipeg soldier who could speak German. In the ensuing conversation the officer in Calais, obviously of superior rank, insisted we put the Commandant on. When the agitated man took the phone and confirmed the situation, he was given a severe dressing-down and promised a court martial.

Now the parapets, which seemed to rise forty or fifty feet above the square on all sides, were seized by Winnipegs running up the zigzagging stone steps to a succession of galleries that looked for all the world like those in that unforgettable fort in the old film *Beau Geste*. This accomplished we signalled the Canadian Scottish on our left and the Regina Rifles on our right that Fort Nieulay was no longer a threat to their advance.*

Next morning, September 27, 342 Lancasters cascaded 1,700 more tons of heavy explosive on the inner defences of the port. Then leading up to and during an attack by 9th Brigade with some tanks in support, against the Cap Gris Nez batteries (fifteen miles southwest along the coast from Calais), the huge guns were subjected to an eighty-minute non-stop bombardment by 14th Field, four regiments of mediums, a regiment of heavies, and a regiment of heavy ack-ack. The awesome bombardment produced results: all three batteries, which periodically had been turned inland on targets, were silenced, though not until they were overrun – one gun crew getting off a final round even as the infantrymen arrived on their gun platform.†

---

* Author interview
† Derived from G. W. L. Nicholson's *Gunners of Canada, Vol. II,*

On September 28, the commandant of Calais garrison was granted a forty-eight-hour truce by the Commander of 3rd Division (Maj.-Gen. Dan Spry) to allow for the evacuation of 20,000 civilians. This seemed to be in preparation for a final bitter showdown, but when the attack was resumed at noon on the 30th, German resistance was noticeably thin.

At 7:00 P.M. the German commandant surrendered the city, for which the bleary-eyed, unshaven, staggering-tired infantrymen of 3rd Division were profoundly grateful. They had suffered almost three hundred casualties subduing the outpost forts and gunsites, bringing their losses in dead, wounded, and missing in the taking of Boulogne and Calais to nearly one thousand.*

McClelland and Stewart, 1972, which also provided the statistics on shelling and bombing of objectives described in this chapter.

* From D-Day in Normandy, June 6, to October 1 when the clearing of the Scheldt began, 2nd and 3rd Canadian divisions suffered more casualties than any other divisions in 21st Army Group:

FORMATION	CASUALTIES	FORMATION	CASUALTIES
1. 3rd Cdn Div	9,263	9. 59 Inf Div	4,911
2. 2nd Cdn Div	8,211	10. 51 Inf Div	4,799
3. 43 Inf Div	7,605	11. 11 Armd Div	3,825
4. 15 Inf Div	7,601	12. Guards Armd Div	3,385
5. 3 Brit Div	7,342	13. 4 Cdn Armd Div	3,135
6. 50 Inf Div	6,701	14. 7 Armd Div	2,801
7. 49 Inf Div	5,894	15. Polish Armd Div	1,861
8. 53 Inf Div	4,984		

6

ONLY THE PORT OF
ANTWERP IS BIG ENOUGH

※

ON OCTOBER 2, 4TH BRIGADE AND 4TH FIELD REGIMENT
are required to abandon "Shangri-La" and with the rest of 2nd
Division finally undertake a full role in opening a port – the greatest of them all – capable of handling 40,000 tons a day, when both
shores of the Scheldt Estuary are cleared of Germans and ships are
able to sail in from the sea.

By now it is clear the war is not about to come to a swift end.
The ebullient view of only a few days ago – that Montgomery's
drive, September 17–25, to the Rhine, outflanking the Siegfried
Line at Nijmegen in Holland, was the start of a drive to Berlin –
shrivelled when General Brian Horrocks's XXX Corps failed to
reach the British 1st Airborne Division, which was holding the last
crucial bridge over the northern branch of the Rhine at Arnhem.

If this failure proved anything, it was that for the final drive into
Germany all Allied armies would have to be properly supplied,
with all necessary petrol and ammunition, not by shifting priorities
among formations, but by building up forward dumps and shortening supply lines. Currently the largest port in operation is Dieppe,
capable of handling only 7,000 tons a day. Obviously Antwerp, with
its unrivalled capacity to land all that is necessary for all Allied
armies on the Western Front, will have to be made usable. The job
is given to First Canadian Army. And, with General Harry Crerar
ill in hospital, Lt.-Gen. Guy Simonds is totally in charge.

With the fall of Calais, 3rd Division turns north to deal with the German 64th Division, confined by 4th and Polish Armoured divisions in what is known as the Breskens pocket — a sodden, dike-laced corner of Holland peculiarly placed southwest of the Scheldt, bounded on the west by the North Sea, on the south by the Leopold Canal, and on the east by Braakman Inlet jutting down from the Scheldt, twenty-eight miles west of Antwerp.

The 3rd Division will clear the south bank of the Scheldt to the sea, crushing the determined forces that were left behind to hold the Breskens shore when German Fifteenth Army (the Pas de Calais force) evacuated eastwards — by way of Antwerp until the British arrived, and since then across the Scheldt to Walcheren Island. The 2nd Division will clear the north shore as constituted by South Beveland Peninsula snaking west to Walcheren. Only when both banks of the broad estuary are clear of Germans, can the big coastal guns, denying Allied shipping the mouth of the river, be dealt with by sea-borne landings of British units under command of First Canadian Army.

Once again, as in the closing of the Falaise pocket, Canadians are to play the pivotal role in an operation crucial to the ultimate success of all Allied forces in Western Europe, and so recognized by Supreme Allied Commander Eisenhower in a signal to Field Marshal Montgomery on October 9: "Unless we have Antwerp producing by the middle of November, entire operations will come to a standstill. I emphasize, that of all our operations on the entire front from Switzerland to the Channel, I consider Antwerp of first importance."

Before 2nd Division, its right flank secured by 4th Armoured and Polish Armoured divisions pushing towards Bergen-op-Zoom and Breda, can begin clearing South Beveland, it first must take Merxem and push north 23 kilometres (14.4 miles) and secure the villages strung across the mouth of the peninsula.

Preparatory to joining in the divisional drive north (once 4th Brigade has cleared Merxem), 5th and 6th brigades, deployed on the right along the Albert Canal east of the city, must get over this obstacle and wheel west to gain still another barrier, the Antwerp–Turnhout Canal curling northeast from the Albert Canal near Merxem.

On the night of September 27, seven kilometres east of the docks, a Calgary Highlanders' patrol, crawling across a partially wrecked footbridge – for much of the way hanging by their hands over the dark water as they swing from one rusty remnant to another – manage to subdue all opposition long enough for the battalion to cross and establish a bridgehead firm enough to resist two strong counter-attacks, and to allow a bridge to be built. (The leader of this courageous patrol, Sgt. G. R. Crockett, was subsequently awarded the Distinguished Conduct Medal.)

Gaining a foothold on the far bank of the Turnhout Canal is more difficult. An assault by the Fusiliers Mont-Royal and the South Saskatchewan Regiment twelve kilometres northeast of Antwerp (September 24) is roughly treated by a strong force of infantry and tanks. The FMRs, after suffering 130 casualties, 27 of them among the Belgian White Brigade serving with them, pull back over the canal. The SSRs soon follow.

On September 28 another attack is tried further east. With the SSRs mounting a diversionary attack across the canal, Le Régiment de Maisonneuve gains a bridgehead, from whence the Black Watch takes St. Lenaarts and another town, Brecht, two or three kilometres further west. During the fighting many Germans are killed and 200 taken prisoner, but the Black Watch over the period of just three days lose 119 wounded and killed. The troops confronting the Canadians have received the following from General von Zangen, Commander of Fifteenth Army: "The German people are watching us. In this hour the fortifications along the Scheldt occupy a role which is decisive for the future of our people. Each additional day that you deny to the enemy the port of Antwerp, and all its resources, will be vital."

7

CANAL WATERS REFLECT
A FLAME–LIT SKY

✳

FOR SOME TIME, PERHAPS FROM THAT FIRST HOUR SIXTEEN days ago, when you occupied that OP in the attic of that abandoned furniture factory and peered across the canal for the first time into Merxem, you knew that one day you would have to accompany an infantry attack to clear it of the enemy. Still, as the moment approaches, you are filled with dread.

All day October 2, two companies of the Royals have been over there among the burning buildings and fearsome noises of battle. Shortly after midnight last night, Major "Paddy" Ryall's C Company crossed in assault boats, with two companies of the Belgian White Brigade.* Then just before first light today, Bob Suckling's D Company, accompanied by 4th Field FOO Lieut. Bill Dunning and a signaller, crossed over, penetrating deeper into Merxem.

A couple of hours ago (2130 hours) you got a signal to report to Royals' battalion headquarters in Antwerp with Major Hank

---

* The brigade was commanded by a former sea captain, Eugene "Harry" Colson, leader of 600 of the 3,500-strong Antwerp underground army – recruited by a regular Belgian army officer, Lieut. Urbain Remier – that early in September took control of the sluice gates, crucial to the maintenance of water level in Antwerp harbour, and prevented the retreating Germans from destroying them.

Caldwell when his company was ordered back from the detached vigil they had been sharing with fifty members of the White Brigade, guarding several miles of the Antwerp–Turnhout Canal that runs up from the Albert Canal past the village of Schoten northeast of the city.

As you approach the dark and deserted Sports Platz stadium where Caldwell's company has been ordered to assemble for the crossing, the guns in the docklands, northwest of the city, are pouring shells into Merxem, where several fires are burning fiercely, their ugly glow in the smoky sky reflecting disturbingly in the waters of the canal, turning it blood-red.

Nor is the news reassuring when you and Caldwell arrive back at Battalion Headquarters, in the principal's office of a school in Antwerp, for briefing by Col. Lendrum and your battery commander, Major Don Cornett. Interrogation by Intelligence Officers of the first prisoners taken – 25 Belgian SS and 44 Germans from the 1018th Grenadier Regiment, diverted from its intended role on the Russian front, for the purpose of regaining control of the Antwerp docks – suggests you are up against aggressive troops.

Passage over the Albert Canal by Ryall's company and the White Brigade contingent this morning was heavily contested, and casualties among the Belgians were severe. You'll be crossing where they did, passing through Ryall's company now consolidated among streets adjacent to the canal. However, beyond there progress may be "sticky," for Suckling's company, deeper in Merxem, is now cut off and in danger of being overwhelmed. At dusk the Germans infiltrated between the two companies, and are now attacking Suckling's position from the rear.

All day communications have been poor – wireless transmission by portable 18-sets inhibited by the densely built areas on both sides of the canal. Now the lack of sit reps is taking its toll of the normally calm and self-assured Lendrum sitting behind the principal's desk opposite Cornett. The decisive, firm manner you have come to expect is noticeably absent. His comments on what Caldwell may encounter over there are clearly speculative, and the long pauses between comments, during which he rearranges pads and pencils and desk accessories, are disconcerting. Like Cornett, hunched over his map, he is obviously more concerned with the immediate plight of D Company.

Suddenly the civilian phone on the desk starts ringing. Lendrum reaches over and picks it up, a reflex action only, for the civilian phone system has not been working. To his astonishment, Suckling is on the line explaining that two White Brigade men – phone technicians – have just connected the phone in the Tramways Office in Merxem to a line they have maintained with Antwerp comrades throughout the siege. As the conversation continues, Suckling's voice sinks lower and lower, and you and the other onlookers surrounding the desk are alerted to this fact when Lendrum asks: "Bob, why are you whispering?"

His answer, inaudible to the eavesdroppers, sends Lendrum into gales of laughter. Looking up and covering the phone mouthpiece, he reports: "Bob says, 'The frigging Germans are just outside the door!'"

A moment later Lendrum hands the phone to Cornett, explaining the Germans have been advancing down the street with a light gun, periodically shelling selected buildings, and are being held at bay by one platoon showering grenades down on them from an upstairs window of a house. But if they are to hold on, they must have some arty support. Suckling is turning over the phone to a White Brigade operator on the ground floor of the building who will transmit fire orders shouted down to him by FOO Bill Dunning observing from an upper storey. Even as he grabs the phone, Cornett is calling to his signaller: "Mike target! Mike target! Mike target!" And it seems the signaller hardly finishes transmitting the map reference and "Scale 5 . . . Fire" before the guns are thumping, sending 120 shells crashing where needed. A couple of "repeats" and the counter-attack is snuffed out.

You have no inkling that from this hour resistance in Merxem will begin to crumble, and as you walk back with Hank to his company, waiting in the gloomy infield of the big stadium, you can't shake the image of a company cut off and fighting for its life. So when a platoon commander, who has been down at the canal checking on the assault boats deposited there earlier, returns to report to Caldwell that all but two have been sunk by mortar fire, and that the two survivors are half full of water, you really start to "get the wind up."

On your way to your carrier to fill your pockets with hardtack and bully beef, and to advise Gnr. Bob Stevenson, who'll be going over with you carrying the 18-set radio, to do the same since there's no telling how long it will be before you'll see the carrier again, an unfamiliar voice calls out your name and hands you a letter. Curious, since mail normally only comes up with the rations, and no rations came up tonight, you seek out an empty dressing room under the grandstand where you can show a light. The little blue airmail envelope is from your father who seldom writes to you. As usual he has little to say, his excuse being "your mother will have given you all the news." But few as they are, his casual offhand comments have a remarkably soothing effect. You find yourself recalling one dark fall evening when you were a little squirt. He'd asked you to go to the barn, locate a lantern hanging (unlit of course) on a nail in the dark cow stable, and bring it back. Seeing you hesitate, he'd smiled and said, "You're not afraid of the dark, are you?" And though you were terrified of the sinister creaking sounds in the dark barn, and the strange crunching and snuffling noises animals make when eating, you simply had to go and fetch that lantern to prove you were not. Afterwards you glowed with joy at his pride in you. Now holding the little airmail in your hand, you can almost hear his voice again asking, "You're not afraid of the dark, are you?"

Suddenly you realize that all the painful anxiety and tension afflicting you only a moment ago have disappeared, and when you and Stevenson go down to the boats with Hank, you paddle across a canal that is as silent as a country night, the only sound the swirl and gurgle of paddles dipping and pulling at the water. Even the fires, which earlier seemed to be consuming Merxem, have calmed down; and shells no longer explode anywhere in the town.

On the roadway along the canal bank near where you land is a veritable mountain of parkas and sheepskin coats, obviously abandoned by the German brigade, which was diverted to Belgium (currently enjoying balmy fall weather) after being equipped for the Russian winter. As you go forward with Caldwell to find Ryall, you leave Stevenson, resting with the Royals on the pile of parkas, using his 18-set to alert his buddies back in the Sports Platz so that when 4th Field passes this way, they pick up some of the coats.

Ryall's company headquarters turns out to be in a tiny, cramped cellar of a nearby house, and you are left alone down there sitting on a trunk while the two company commanders go off to decide where Caldwell should locate his company. The cellar is dimly lit by a candle on a table in the corner, and in the shadowy light you could swear that just there on the floor ahead of you a pile of sheepskin coats, similar to those you just passed on the dock, is moving gently up and down as though breathing. For a moment you think you're going batty, but when you bend over and lift one of the fluffy skins, the tousled head of a beautiful teenage girl appears, and as you continue to hold up the coat, staring in disbelief, two stunning, if sleepy, eyes open wide on yours, and a husky voice says, "Eh-low."

Yawning and rubbing her eyes, she gets up, and sitting down on the trunk beside you asks if she may have a cigarette. Then for the next half hour you are enthralled with the proximity of this lovely young creature and everything she has to say.

No, she is not a refugee; she and that other girl, still asleep under that other pile of sheepskin on the floor, came over as "nurses" with the White Brigade soldiers accompanying the Royals. Of course they aren't really nurses, you understand. Actually, she is a student who has been working as a volunteer at the headquarters of the White Brigade in Antwerp. When she learned they needed people to go along on the attack to help with the wounded – like stretcher-bearers, you know – she and her friend, having had first-aid courses at school, volunteered. Oh, it was awful! The White Brigade men had no training or experience for fighting like this. Major Ryall said they should have spread out, but they were all bunched up on the canal bank, and when the mortar bombs started coming down on them, it was terrible . . . so many wounded . . .

Their supply of bandages, a mere handful, and a bottle of iodine, so pitifully inadequate in the face of so many terrible wounds . . . It was so horrible that she and her friend wanted to cry. If she lives to be a hundred, she will never be able to forget.

Abruptly, as though to get her mind off the events of this day, she starts discussing her favourite American hit tunes, which she has been able to keep up with using the radio her family had hidden away to listen to the BBC news.

Now that the war is almost over, she can start thinking of things like going to a ball. This has been her dream for a long time – that one day she would get a long, backless evening gown and go to a beautiful ball. That was the way she had come to visualize what it would be like when freedom finally came, for, of course, she was too young to remember much about what it was like before the war.

You could have gone on listening to her all night, but Paddy Ryall returns and tells you Hank and his company have started off up a side street. And so you are wrenched back to the reality of the war in the sinister darkness outside.

Though at one point a German patrol clumps noisily across an intersection just up ahead, causing the company to freeze in the shadows of a building abutting the sidewalk, the company doesn't fire a shot this night. After walking silently for a time towards the eastern outskirts of the suburb, Hank distributes his platoons, establishing company headquarters in an empty house to which he gains entrance by sending a man up over the back kitchen to break in an upstairs window.

Next morning, October 3, you are wounded, but not by the enemy, who appear to have pulled out overnight.

In preparation for a move north from Merxem, you and Hank had gone up to the end of the street to gain a view of the land beyond, on the way traversing endless backyards, which, though this is Tuesday, are filled with fluttering lines of laundry – the war having interfered with the Merxem ladies' traditional washday yesterday. It's on your way back, having decided to chance the open streets, that you and Hank meet a Royals' patrol – a sergeant and a private with a Sten gun slung over his shoulder. Fortunately the gun, cradled in his right arm facing you, is pointed down at the pavement, for suddenly – *bang!* – it goes off and you feel a thump on the calf of your left leg. Instantly a torrent of expletives from Hank draws attention to the fact his knees have taken the brunt of the concrete bits dislodged by the bullet ricocheting off the sidewalk. Cursing, he rolls up his pant-legs and starts picking cinder-like bits out of his kneecaps.

"That's the third time it's done that this morning," says the soldier in wonderment as he pulls back the cocking-lever of the Sten, now pointing directly at your stomach, and doesn't turn the knob into its safety notch.

Pushing the muzzle away from you, you tell him, "For God's sake, man, put it on safety!"

In obvious bewilderment, he asks, "What's that?"

Hank, hearing this, bobs up from attending to his smarting knees, demanding, "Where the hell did you get your weapons training, soldier?"

"I never had any weapons training, sir," says he apologetically, "I was a cook with Army Service until I was sent up to the Royals."

Now as you rub the numbness from your leg, you realize it's wet. And when you pull up your pant-leg, you see two little holes where the bullet passed in and out of the calf, barely beneath the skin – the absolutely perfect flesh wound that everybody hopes to get! But it is too perfect. By the time you get the opportunity to visit the Royals' MO (Dr. Ken Mickleborough, a fellow ex-Glebe Collegiate type) the bleeding has stopped. Daubing it with antiseptic, he applies a kind of oversized, homemade Band-Aid, and wishes you better luck next time as you return to duty. So much for old collegiate connections!

However, on balance it is a good day. Passing through Schoten at noon you learn from a White Brigade man over a bottle of Belgian beer, partaken in the street, that your shells on the church tower yesterday wiped out an enemy artillery observation crew in residence there.

Your new friend is much impressed when you manage to get through to him by way of atrocious French and pointing at the tower and then at yourself that it was you who shelled it. And he proceeds to attract a crowd when, in stentorian tones, he announces to passersby that it was you who destroyed the Boche in the tower. Flattered by the smiles and the admiration shining in eyes on all sides, you share with them the interesting fact that the gun you'd used had actually faced you from the other side of Antwerp – showing them on the map the unusual positioning of the target between you and your gun, supporting your explanation with pantomime to show how your shells snarled directly at your face before landing. However, you choose not to describe the blind ranging you conducted on that damned tower, when each ranging round aroused in you an uncontrollable urge to flatten out on the floor below the window sill of the upstairs bedroom you were using for an OP.

Somehow you feel it might leave the wrong impression of the calibre of their liberators, if you tried to explain to this excited, chattering crowd the meaning of "cellarosis" (timidity unbecoming a soldier developed from spending too much time in cellars or other relatively safe havens). And of course it is impossible to describe in any language the incredible difference between the casual sound of a 25-pound shell sizzling overhead on its way out into no-man's-land, and one coming in to burst in front of you.

8

SUDDENLY TRAFFIC
IS NOTICEABLY SPARSE

❋

NEXT MORNING, OCTOBER 4, THE DRIVE NORTH BY 2ND Division towards the mouth of South Beveland begins in earnest – not with a massive attack preceded by heavy artillery preparations, but with silent infantrymen trudging single-file up the verges of narrow roads crowded with rumbling armoured cars, growling half-tracks, clinking carriers, and purring Jeeps. Some of the Jeeps with tall aerials wavering above them carry red-tabbed, frowning brigadiers exuding urgency and seemingly bent on giving the impression they are riding close herd on this business of clearing the Scheldt – suddenly top priority with First Canadian Army, 21st Army Group, and General Eisenhower's Supreme Headquarters.

By mid-morning, however, shelling of crossroads by lone German guns and periodic bursts of MG 42-fire from wooded flanks have given notice that troops passing this way must pay a toll, and soon traffic becomes noticeably sparse. In fact, as you approach a blown culvert over a narrow stream, following the Royals' leading company, and a German field gun starts dropping shells randomly to harass anyone trying to reconnoitre another way over this obstacle, your carrier is the only vehicle within sight or sound.

As you shrink well down below the rim of its steel walls, you have your driver, Gunner William Walkden, turn off the engine. Suddenly it's so quiet you can hear the water burbling along the swollen ditches and, more importantly, the *thunk* of the gun as it fires from somewhere in the bush beyond the field on the right. You count the seconds it takes the shell to arrive: six. It's a small-calibre field gun, and judging by its drawn-out whine, of low velocity. Using the muzzle velocity (MV) for Charge II of a 25-pounder and applying your rule of thumb of three seconds per 1,000 yards, the gun is only 2,000 yards away.*

But to get a compass bearing on the sound of the gun you'd have to get out and away from this steel box, exposing yourself to all the shell fragments whipping around out there. As you contemplate the prospect with distaste, and are about to conclude "not bloody likely, old boy," you see out of the corner of your eye, passing no more than twelve inches away, the head and shoulders of Col. Mac Young! Though he knows perfectly well he's passing your carrier, he doesn't even glance your way as he walks on. You, of course, pile out and follow him.

As you catch up, he asks, "Any theory as to where it may be?"

You tell him that judging by the time-of-flight of its missiles, it's only about 2,000 yards away, but you don't yet have a bearing.

He stops and holds out his hand: "Let me have your compass."

At that moment you hear the gun *thunk* over on the right, and this time the tone of its whine clearly indicates it's coming directly this way. The Colonel seems to realize this too, and as he receives the compass he leaps for the water-filled ditch. Instantly you follow. Too late, you realize he doesn't mean to jump into the ditch, but over it. You land floundering in icy-cold water up to your hips. Struggling to regain your feet, you look up just in time to see him unconcernedly kneeling, squinting into the compass, outlined against a flashing geyser of black mud and smoke spouting up with an awesome roar no more than fifty yards in front of his unflinching face.

He makes no comment as he stands up, leaps back over the ditch to the roadway, and leads you, dripping, back to your carrier. There,

---

* Charge I (MV 640 fps): 5 seconds for 1,065 yards; Charge II (970 fps): 3 seconds for 970 yards; Charge III (1,450 fps): 2 seconds for 966 yards.

after only a moment's study of your map, he puts his finger on a clearing in the bush and in his calm drawl says, "Try plastering around there."

With that he turns away and starts back down the road as casually as he'd come, ignoring the next round that comes whistling over the carrier to land just beyond the road. Feeling you have been bracketed, you rush to get some rounds down where he suggested – a Mike target of Scale 3. After it kicks up quite a fuss over there, you wait a while to see if the gun opens up again, before ordering a repeat. But no more shells are needed. Either it was hit, or the reign of terror from near-misses persuaded it to move somewhere else. At any rate, the result is totally satisfactory and the advance continues.

Opposition is uneven for all brigades at the outset. But on the next day, October 5, the Essex Scottish come up against the stiffest opposition since Merxem, when they are hit by a counter-attack in a long, skinny town called Putte straddling the Belgium–Holland border, and strung out a remarkable distance along the main road that runs through it from Antwerp to Bergen-op-Zoom. The leading platoons are driven back, leaving Fox Troop Commander Ted Adams stranded in a church tower.

Subjecting the town to heavy mortar and shell-fire, the Germans manage to close within 150 yards of Adams's OP, but the excellent overview of the town afforded by his tower allows him to catch many of them in the open street with all twenty-four guns of 4th Field concentrated on a Mike target. The effect is devastating, and the Essex not only are able to retake the ground they lost, but are able to seize possession of the whole town, thus establishing a bridgehead over a canal cutting the main road north. (The gunners will later learn the importance of their contribution when Capt. A. E. Adams is awarded a Military Cross and his ack, Bombardier Ernie Hodgkinson, is awarded a Military Medal.)

At the same time as the drama in Putte is being played out, over on the left, around the Belgian village of Berendrecht, about four kilometres west of the track the Royals are following north, there is a rattle of heavy machine guns, punctuated now and then by sharp cracks of high velocity guns. Later you'll learn that this flurry of firing is mainly by the weapons of a troop of 8th Recce Regiment armoured cars, pushing into the heart of Berendrecht with such intimidating agressiveness that a hundred Germans, grateful they survived the furious onslaught, surrender to the troop commander, Lieut. Colin Ridgway.*

Meanwhile, a couple of kilometres west of Putte, after crossing the canal by another bridge, the Royals push on about two miles in open country with Zandvhiet visible on their left, before taking up a defensive position for the night.

Here an enemy plane drops propaganda leaflets containing a clumsy attempt to arouse suspicions among the "Boys of the 2nd Canadian Division" that they are being sacrificed as at Dieppe "to fight and bleed for England" in the upcoming "God damn slaughter." That the German High Command would, in spite of diminishing resources that now must be strained to the limit, give priority to preparing and printing large quantities of a special message for the Canadians, and assign a precious plane and crew to dropping it over this spearhead of 4th Brigade approaching the mouth of South Beveland, means you are in for special attention of a more intimate nature very soon.†

----

* Lieut. Ridgway was subsequently awarded the Military Cross.

† This same night, October 5, Col.-Gen. Kurt Student, Commander of German First Parachute Army, ordered Lt.-Col. F. A. von der Heydte to break off holding up the Polish Armour, near Alphen, and move in haste his 6th Paratroop Regiment southwest to confront a Canadian force reported on its way to Ossendrecht with the obvious intention of capturing the mouth of South Beveland and cutting off all access to Walcheren garrison. Student's 30,000-strong First Parachute Army had been brought into being on Hitler's orders September 3, by recruitment from odd sources including convalescent Luftwaffe airmen and redundant Luftwaffe ground crew, but it was larded with well-trained and highly motivated survivors of paratroop regiments and the remnants of SS units that escaped the Falaise pocket. Von der Heydte's 4,000-strong 6th Paratroop Regiment, the élite of the élite, who'd been given top priority for equipment, began its counterattack against the Royal Regiment the next afternoon, October 6.

9

A NOT-SO-COMIC

OPERA

❋

BY FIVE O'CLOCK IN THE MORNING OF OCTOBER 6, THE
Royals are on the move again, with you walking at the rear of the
leading company with its commander, your eyes searching for
indentations of sinister portent in the road or track over which
must pass the tracks of your carrier clinking along behind you in
bull-low. During the past two days casualties have been light, the
battalion suffering only one officer and four Other Ranks killed,
and one officer and seven ORs wounded, mostly from mines.

The drill is now well-established and will continue as long as
enemy opposition remains light. Companies take turns passing
through each other to take the next objective, which is normally a
concession road crossing the line of advance at right angles. A FOO
is expected to take off with each leading company as it passes
through, and proceed with it to the next objective, where you
again take up with the next company passing through. Normally
there would be two FOOs, with the battalion taking turns going
forward with leapfrogging companies, but Baker Troop is currently without a troop commander, acting troop commander Bill
Dunning having been posted to 2nd Division Headquarters as a
liaison officer.

By late afternoon, D company, the leading company, reaches an
east–west lateral road – Middel Straat, Hageland – on high land
overlooking open fields towards Hoogerheide village, which lies
just beyond the immediate objective, Ossendrecht, mostly hidden

down on the left, beyond where this lateral road turns north past a row of houses.

While there is still no sign of Germans, your imagination begins to work as you study some substantial buildings in the middle distance; brickworks, according to the map. In the deadly still fields and roads, they look sinister and forbidding, as lifeless buildings in no-man's-land always do. You find yourself exercising a degree of caution you haven't been concerned with all day when you instruct Walkden to drive the carrier farther west along Middel Straat and park it out of sight behind a farmhouse at the corner, where the road turns north down the hill past that row of houses. And when you peer around the corner of the first house, and you see a church steeple poking up malevolently out of Ossendrecht in the valley, you immediately seek out a six-pounder gun crew, commanded by Corporal Jack Williams, to put some rounds through its belfry.

In the meantime a second company of Royals, to whom you normally would attach yourself for the next move forward, arrives at Middel Straat, believing they have arrived at their objective. They claim D company did not identify an earlier farm track back yonder as their objective, and came on a concession too far. As maps are being studied and claims discussed, a third company arrives and pauses in confusion. Before things are properly sorted out, the fourth company arrives. By now things are sufficiently complicated that advice must be sought from Battalion Tac Headquarters following somewhere behind.

There is a great deal of milling about. Altogether too many men have assembled along a short section of road in an overlapping mess.

Suddenly a Jerry gun begins shelling beyond that row of houses – a high velocity gun that is out of sight but very close, for there is almost no lapse of time between the *wham* of its firing and the roar of its missile landing against those houses. Fortunately it is concentrating on something other than this clutter of troops here, but those stunning, reverberating roars, enveloping the whole area, cause great consternation among men with no trenches in which to shelter.

Then a clutch of 8th Recce armoured cars, of the towering, heavily armed Daimler variety (coaxially-mounted two-pounder cannon and Besa machine gun), which had just come up and were last seen moving cautiously down the road past the row of houses, roar back up the hill. As they skid around the corner and disappear along Middel Straat, causing some soldiers to scramble out of their way and others to exchange sober glances, you hear a voice call: "Tank!"

And you are not immune to the drawing power of those retreating recce cars. Common sense tells you, as it must all who witnessed their unseemly haste, that those courageous types, whose job it is to take tremendous risks as they scout uncleared hostile territory, would not be retiring so fast if they hadn't seen something coming this way that they with all their fire-power couldn't handle. For a few minutes the situation threatens to dissolve into utter panic, as the roar of the retreating Daimlers and the crashing shells drown out the shouting of four company commanders and several platoon commanders, competing for attention as they disentangle their companies and move them back along the road to form some kind of defensive position.

Since it is not at all clear which companies are to stay put and which are to move, and with everybody suddenly consumed by the urge to travel, it appears you may be left stranded if you don't watch out. Not relishing having your carrier trapped forward of all this, with a German tank crawling up the hill, you run to where it is parked in a confined, brick-paved entryway behind the house at the corner, and get your crew packing up everything for a hasty withdrawal. But just as you finish coiling up the last few feet of remote-control cable and are helping your ack, Gnr. William Hiltz, to heave the heavy spool into the carrier, making ready to follow the recce cars and infantry, Bob Suckling suddenly appears around the corner of the house yelling over the crash of the German gun:

"Come with me! I've located it. It's a self-propelled gun – not a tank. Come – I'll show you!"

Yelling at Stevenson, who is manning the radio in the carrier, to order the guns to "take post," you take Hiltz and Walkden with you, telling them to space themselves out as human relay-stations so they can get your fire orders back to Stevenson.

The German shells continue one at a time, horribly close, but still mystifyingly out of sight, as you and Suckling take turns pounding on locked front doors of the row of houses on the left side of the street, where an upstairs back window could provide observation of the field sloping down to Ossendrecht where Suckling says the gun is.

When at last a door opens, he unceremoniously brushes aside the bewildered woman standing there, and leads you thumping up the stairs two at a time to a back bedroom window.

"There!" he yells, pointing down a broad, grassy slope towards a tree-lined ditch or creek, "Right there!"

And there indeed it is, your attention drawn by the spurt of smoke that jets from its muzzle as it fires, its vicious *wham* coupling with the instantaneous smash of its shell on the back of a house just a few doors down to the right, creating intimidating reverberations.

Crash!

Panic threatens to blind you as you glance from map to gun and back again, trying to establish a map reference. It seems to be sitting on a culvert over a tree-enshrouded ditch or creek. You *must* be right – you may only get one chance! But speed is paramount! You scribble down a six-figure coordinate and dash across the hall into a bedroom at the front of the house. Throwing open a casement window, you yell the figures to Hiltz standing down in the street, coupling them with "Mike target – Mike target – Mike target! Scale 5 – Fire!"

As you listen to him call your orders up the road to Walkden at the corner, who will relay them to Stevenson in the carrier behind the house, who in turn will send them to the guns, the crash of shells from the SP measures its relentless march up the line of houses, coming ever closer, each unnerving roar causing everything to shake and rattle. Though you've never seen Jerry use such tactics before, and it's hard to think clearly, it appears the gun is systematically working over each house in turn, starting at the bottom of the street. And when he gets to the top, they'll attack.

As you rejoin Suckling in the back bedroom where he continues to maintain a vigil from well back in the shadows, you do your best to suppress your dread of the guns not getting enough shells up here in time to stop that gun before it puts a round in through this window.

The explosions are very close now. And when you throw up your field-glasses to study the SP, to your horror you seem to be looking right down its muzzle. How on earth can Suckling stand here so calmly watching that gun gradually ratcheting this way? Any minute now it will rip a shell in this window, and yet he remains standing here!

Crash!

Fully aware, even in your fuzzy-headed anxiety, that the success or failure of the German attack hinges on whether you are able to silence that demoralizing gun, you know you should remain here where you can observe the fall of your shells and make corrections until it is knocked out or driven off. But as the acrid fumes of those terrible explosions drift in through the open window, the only course that makes any sense to you is to run down the stairs and find a door to the cellar, if there is one, before it's too late. The problem is, you can't leave Suckling up here alone.

As you turn to face him, you wonder how you should put it. With all your heart and soul you want to say right out: "For God's sake, Bob, let's go downstairs to the back of the house where at least we'll have a chance. To stay up here is plain suicide." But something in the eyes of this resolute man as he looks at you makes you clam up. He seems confident you will silence the German gun. There is even a slight smile of amusement on his face as he waits to see you do it. My God, doesn't he realize how bad the odds have grown, and what is about to happen? But then in a calm voice he poses a question that makes it clear he's well aware that time is of the essence:

"How long should it normally take them to get something up here?"

You tell him, two . . . three minutes . . . four at most . . . depending . . .

Crash!

You retreat to the front bedroom overlooking the street, where you'll be able to hear Hiltz when he relays the message from the guns, "Shot Mike One" – the signaller's message that the shells are on their way. You start pacing back and forth and try to imagine current activities at the guns.

Crash!

By now the Tannoy loudspeakers in the gun pits are spewing out line, range, and angle of sight; gun-layers are twiddling their dials, whirling fine-tuning gears, and levelling their bubbles; shells are being rammed in the chamber, cartridge cases inserted behind them, breech-blocks closed with their distinctive metallic clunks . . .

CRASH!

A particularly awesome concussion, followed by the sound of glass and debris cascading down out back, ends your imaginings. That's it. They've started on the house next door. You're next. God – what are they doing back there at the guns? Why aren't they getting something up here? Are they all asleep? But then you hear Walkden calling, and immediately there is Hiltz's welcome shout: "Shot Mike One!"

Even before you get settled in the back room with your glasses to your eyes, the first shells are sizzling overhead. Instantly, furious orange and black eruptions engulf the creek area and the SP in the gap in the trees, building and building into a continuous roaring inferno.

Just before you lose sight of the SP in the smoke and dirt, you think you see a round strike it, but you can't be sure, for many are striking trees around it.

Suckling is now tapping you on the back and shouting excitedly in your ear, "Look! Look! Don't you see them? There's your target! Can you move some of your shells down there?"

Since you are concentrating on a maelstrom that's blotting out everything in your vision, you have no idea what he's talking about.

Pulling your arm and your glasses down from your eyes, he says, "You don't need your glasses. Look – right down there in the field, lying on their bellies!"

For a moment you still don't see any Germans, for you are looking for distant figures. But then you look where he's jabbing his finger, down at the ground, at a point barely visible beyond the window sill which can only be seen by moving dangerously close to the window; and, there they are – a great many of them incredibly close – more than halfway up the slope – no more than a couple of hundred yards away!

Quickly you estimate the distance from the creek and the SP, and running back to the street bedroom window, yell down, "Southeast three hundred – Repeat!"

As you rejoin Suckling, you wonder how in the world all those Germans could have crawled that close without him spotting them. He explains that just seconds before your shelling began, a platoon of Germans appeared and started to move up the slope towards the houses in an open-V formation. The whine of your incoming shells had driven them to earth. Now he starts laughing and pointing: "Look at those silly buggers."

And while you fail to see the humour in the situation, you have to admit it's a unique sight. If you didn't know it's impossible to follow a 25-pounder shell in flight, you'd swear they were watching the shells sail over their heads and land behind them; all are looking skyward or back towards the creek.

In the brief lull, while the guns are applying new lines and ranges in response to your correction, a single German soldier stands up and runs back down the slope towards the trees – then another and another and another. Then groups of two or three jump up and tear off down the hill to disappear in the bushes. So by the time the new batch of shells start blotting out the field and the running figures in geysers of dirt and smoke, a lot of the prone figures have disappeared from the slope.

And when the shells cease coming and the smoke clears, only a few grey forms can be seen lying crumpled and unmoving in the grass. But in your profound relief and happiness at the way things have turned out, you are totally unconcerned that most of them managed to escape. It's enough that the guns turned them back and sent them running. And you glow with pride in the gunners of 4th Field when the veteran infantry officer at your side labels their performance "a really good show."

Scanning the bushes along the creek-bed with your glasses, half expecting the SP to have disappeared, you are delighted to find it sitting silent, obviously immobilized or it would have pulled back. But to make certain you send Hiltz off to find Royals Corporal Jack Williams and his anti-tank crew and ask them to bring up their six-pounder gun to puncture its vitals with some armour-piercing shot.

Never before have you knowingly disabled a tank or a self-propelled gun, let alone one about to blow apart your OP, and it is with feelings of satisfaction bordering on ecstasy that you focus your glasses and feast your eyes on the silent monster and its awesome gun jammed askew at a peculiar angle that most certainly would have blown you and Bob Suckling to eternity had your shells not arrived when they did. But then you remember that the principal role in frustrating the German attack was played by this calm, modest man – that Suckling alone was responsible for preventing them from taking this line of houses, which they clearly intended to do once the SP had finished its shelling of them.

Later that night, holed-up at D Company HQ in a house down the hill, Suckling makes it all sound like a comic opera as he regales Major Tim Beatty with the story of the aborted attack. According to him it was all terribly amusing, with the Jerries scuttling away one after another, abandoning their officer until he too, finding himself alone, jumped up and ran. This outrageously understated version is triggered when you try to make sure Beatty, who has just returned to take over D Company after recovering from a wound suffered at Louvigny in July, is fully aware of Bob's cool-headed action, and will view it as worthy of official recognition, perhaps a gong.

However, the very earnestness of your appeal backfires. Suckling's modesty, as much a part of him as his courage, compels him to turn your story into a joke, thus downplaying his role. Obviously if there was no serious attack, there was no serious role for him to play — completely ignoring the fact it had been a very close thing.* Even a minute or two more delay in the arrival of your shells and the Germans would have made it into these houses unopposed, and the Royals, instead of taking Ossendrecht against light opposition, would still be back there in the fields somewhere, having to mount another attack against an alert and reinforced enemy ready to contest every house and barn.

The extent of the enemy's disorganization in Ossendrecht, since their counter-attacking force was sent packing, is revealed by a leading platoon of Royals penetrating deep into the village after dark. After overrunning a German headquarters, they wait quietly in the dark and capture enemy patrols as they report in. A total of thirty prisoners are taken that night, and next morning another fifty while clearing the village.

But it could have been quite another story. Just how ferociously the Germans are prepared to fight to retain possession of these little villages strung out across the mouth of South Beveland and the bleak polders in the neck of the isthmus, quickly becomes evident when the Calgary Highlanders, the Maisonneuves, and the Black Watch combine to try to drive through Hoogerheide, only three kilometres north of here, on their way past Woensdrecht to Korteven.

---

* Suckling's jolly version ended up in *Battle Royal*, the history of the Royal Regiment. However, corroboration of the facts, as described herein, is found in the Artillery Operations Log — RCA 2nd Cdn Div for 6/7 Oct 44, Serial 2249: "Time 1755, from 4 Fd. OP 41 reports at 1730 SP gun at 633158 knocked out. Casualties seen, enemy dispersed. SP gun finished by high velocity friends. No fire coming from this sector now. Sub units moving to objective." — National Archives of Canada RG 24 Vol. 14325.

10

TWO BRAVE MEN DIE
DEFENDING THE GUNS

——————————— ✳ ———————————

THE GUN POSITION, NO MATTER WHERE IT IS OR HOW BRIEFLY occupied, is home to all who serve in an artillery regiment, regardless of rank. In the speech and language of the gunner lies evidence of this. He is forever talking about "going up to the guns" or "going back to the guns," "moving with the guns," or "leaving the guns" to go somewhere. Always, the guns are his point of reference.

For carrier crews spending most of their time with the infantry, the gun position may exist only as a map reference that is forever changing. But in this transitory world, it's important to know it's there – that you have a place with which you can identify, in much the way people identify with a village or a town in Civvy Street. When on rare occasions you make it back to the guns, it truly feels like you are returning to your home town. Everything looks as familiar as Main Street. All the faces are friendly and you could put a name to most of them if you had to. Many call out greetings and inquire, "How you doin' – okay?" And when you tell them, Okay, and ask how things are with *them*, they tell you it could be a lot worse. And have you time for a cuppa – they've just whipped up a fresh brew?

You get the feeling you are visiting a very special place – one of the most welcoming places you will ever visit in your whole life – even though you are conscious that tomorrow, or before today is out, this field will be abandoned, never to be seen again by you or any of these fellows. How strange that something that has no permanence by way of form or location should become fixed in your mind as something of substance, something reliable to be counted on in this shaky, impermanent world, an island of stability and order in a churning ocean of disorder, an ultimate refuge to which you can withdraw if everything else disintegrates: home.

And just as you would on Civvy Street, you try to get back home whenever there's a death in the family. And there were two at the gun position late yesterday when Able Troop, fulfilling the tradition of gunners "to fight their guns to the muzzles" if need be, drove off an enemy fighting-patrol that attacked the guns as they were deploying in scrubby bush and sand-dune country, two kilometres south of Ossendrecht. The universally popular George "Lefty" Phillips, your Troop Sergeant-Major, died while directing one of the guns onto the Germans. And the earnest and brave Fred Edwards, the troop's ack-ack Bren gunner, who, with Bombardier Scott, brought in those first German prisoners back at Fleury-sur-Orne in Normandy, died with his Bren gun blazing from the hip.

The news reached you during the night of October 6 in Ossendrecht, and at dawn you have permission to go back for a brief visit with your troop, which you expect has been badly shaken by the experience.

You hitch a ride back and are let off at RHQ, just west of the main road from Putte, where you can get directions to 2nd Battery.

Regimental Sgt.-Maj. A. J. Addie meets you with tears in his eyes for the loss of his pal "Lefty," inquiring bitterly: "Why the hell is it that it's always the good guys who get killed?"

You try not to let the implications of his question bother you as you walk over to 2nd Battery, about a quarter of a mile east of there, up a bush track leading through some scrubby pine woods to an open area of sand dunes with patches of low bushes. As you come within sight of the position, the guns are firing due north over the sandy track you are following. Then suddenly, to your astonishment, all the guns in the battery swing around 180 degrees and start firing at a target directly south towards Putte! And by the time you make it to Able Troop Command Post, at the far end of the positions, the guns have completed the target to their rear and have swung back again onto their zero line pointing north.

You find your GPO Bob Grout and his troop leader, Lieut. Bernie Ackerman, swept up in wonderment at these extraordinary demands on the guns, but glowing with relief that they were able to handle such an unprecedented target. The arm and arc on the artillery board, set up to plot targets in the zone in front of the guns, were totally useless of course, and they were forced to improvise, working out the range and switch from zero line from the map.

The target? Obviously 5th or 6th Brigade coming up on the right hit a pocket of Germans just as the guns here did yesterday. Lurking in the bush some four hundred yards right and forward of the gun position, the Germans had not bothered anyone on the regimental advance party, and only began to spatter Able Troop guns with small-arms fire as they were being put on line by Ackerman.

At first no one was too concerned. All had heard similar sounds before without anything serious developing. But soon the fire became so intense, all were forced to take cover behind vehicles or guns.

Grout first became aware of the enemy small-arms fire when he mounted the lip of a saucerlike sand-dune in which GA had parked and where his crew were setting up the troop command post. He'd climbed up there to watch the guns being put on line by Ackerman, who had joined Bombardier Hossack at the director out in front of the guns:

At first I thought the loud buzzing I heard was the sound of a swarm of angry bees. I remembered seeing several beehives only thirty or forty yards away when I was choosing this spot for my command post, and I turned in that direction expecting to have to order some curious gunners away from the hives. Instead I saw a stream of tracers passing waist-high. Immediately hitting the dirt, I crawled down the protected side of the dune and dashed to the command post, where, with the help of the others, I tried to pin down where the fire was coming from. The consensus was it was coming from the ridge about four hundred yards out in front.

Edwards, our ack-ack gunner, was keen on going out to locate the source and taking it on with his Bren. Sgt.-Maj. Phillips volunteered to go with him. He was instructed to pinpoint the enemy and assess their strength, but not engage.

I put in a request to RHQ for permission to engage with open sights [gun laid directly on target using the anti-tank telescopic sight] as soon as a target was identified. Then Phillips returned, covered with blood, reporting he and Edwards had spotted the machine-gun and had been fired on – and that before he could stop him, Edwards had sprung up and charged the MG's position, and had been cut down almost immediately. He had crawled to him and tried to help him, but shell-dressings were insufficient to handle the series of wounds across Edwards's lower abdomen, and so he'd come back for help.

We decided our armoured scout car should go out to pick him up. But it took time to unload the command post equipment, essential if the guns were to be prepared to fire in support of the infantry, always our number-one priority. Edwards was dead when it got out to him.

Meanwhile, Ackerman and Hossack, in their exposed position out in front of the guns at the director, had managed to pass the zero line to only one gun before the bullets, buzzing around them, drove them back to the guns. There Ackerman was able to put the other three guns on line using the "dial-sight method," meaning that guns were brought parallel by one gun passing reverse bearings from its dial-sight to the dial-sights of the others. By this time, Grout had received permission to engage the machine-guns, and was about to go over and direct a gun onto them, when Phillips suggested he should go, since he knew exactly where the fire was coming from. Ackerman recalled the final moments of the sad story:

I decided to take over Sgt. Graham's gun and act as gun sergeant, with Graham acting as gun-layer, and his bombardier loading the gun. I called for a target at 600 yards using Charge II. It was then Sgt.-Maj. Phillips came running over to me to point out the exact location of the enemy fire. We fired three shells. He stood at my right shoulder, and pointed to my left: "Sir, look! Over there!" I started to swing the trail of the gun to fire the way he directed, when they opened up on us. Two shots penetrated the shield of our gun like it was cardboard and one bullet hit him in the temple, above his left eye. We all dropped flat, and I had the unpleasant task of pushing Lefty's brains back into his head and using my field dressing to bandage it. I escaped with only a nick in the end of my nose – either from a splinter from the shield or the same bullet that hit Lefty. Gunner John Rawlings was wounded in the shoulder.*

Later you learn there were other casualties that day: Sgt. Walter Brown and Gunners Roy Seabrook and Harold Wiens. Wiens, however, was wounded not by enemy action, but by a phosphorous grenade he had taken away from a Dutchman walking through the wagon lines. On his way to burying it, it went off in his hand, splattering burning, clinging phosphorus onto various parts of his body, producing frightful wounds.†

---

* Sgt.-Major George R. Phillips was posthumously awarded the Belgian Croix de Guerre avec Palme, and a Commander-in-Chief Certificate.
† So frightful were his burns that one year and ten days would pass before he would be discharged from his last hospital. Arriving at his first hospital in Brussels, stripped of his clothes, his bandages and his stretcher kept soaking wet to prevent his body from smoking, they scraped off the phosphorus, shot him with penicillin and painkiller, and shipped him on to a civilian hospital in Basingstoke, England. After skin grafting on his neck and arm, he was shipped to a hospital in Canada.

II

EPIC STRUGGLE
FOR HOOGERHEIDE

✳

BY OCTOBER 8, HOOGERHEIDE, THE FIRST OBJECTIVE OF the Calgary Highlanders and the Maisonneuves, is barely secure, after three days and nights of close, bitter fighting, during which individual houses change hands several times. The German para-troopers show a bold tenacity matched only by the SS back in Normandy. In fact, the Black Watch, who were to push on past Woensdrecht to Korteven, are forced to add their strength to the defence of Hoogerheide just to maintain the Brigade's hold there, as the paratroopers, supported by heavy mortar- and shell-fire of a strength not encountered since last July around Verrières Ridge, not only prevent the Calgarians and Maisonneuves from securing the startline for the Black Watch, but push them back and threaten to drive them out of Hoogerheide as well.

The Black Watch, attempting to gain an intermediate objective only 300 yards beyond their unsecured startline, suffer eighty-one casualties including three officers and nine soldiers killed. However, that evening the paratroopers, infiltrating Hoogerheide in large numbers, pay severely for their boldness when they attack D Company just as the battalion Scout Platoon, alert and ready, joins it.

The battalion war diarist will record with evident satisfaction: "They held their fire until the enemy was fifty or sixty yards away and then opened up with everything they had, killing more than fifty." Still the enemy persists: ". . . the attack develops throughout the sector. Very heavy fighting ensues and it is more than two hours before the enemy decides he has had enough. We lose no ground and account for many Germans."

Similar notes in the Calgary Highlanders' war diary of October 9 will further underline the stubborn aggressiveness of the paratroopers:

0400 hours: Able Company reports "Hun infiltration"...

0421: Dog Company busily engaged in breaking up Jerry infiltrating party ... To discourage the bold Hun, arty [5th Field] dropped a few rounds ... an extremely effective shoot!

0515: Able Company's situation not clear ... fighting still going on in some of the houses around the company area, but in general there is a perceptible decline in the ferocity of the Hun attack ...

0602: ... Able Company again in the throes of another counter-attack.

0640:... infiltration definitely beaten off and prisoners taken ... Fighting still continuing in Charley Company area ... Tracked vehicles heard again in Able Company direction ... arty called in to do a little dusting off ... 10 more prisoners taken ...

1615: Able Company again being counter-attacked ... coming in from all three sides. Able and Dog under heavy mortars and terrific shelling.

1655: Word comes Able withdrawing ... Dog Company was able to put up a determined stand and hold out against strong pressure. Tank and arty assistance required ...

1705: Able Company is still trying to rally for a stand and will try to hold on until assistance comes. The battle increases in intensity ... communications with Able Company cease ... when contact is made the Company commander and another officer are casualties and a lieutenant is in charge.

0248: Acting Able Company Commander returning to his company (from reporting in at Battalion Tac Headquarters) finds his original position occupied by the enemy. Travelling about between Dog and Charley companies he locates survivors of his own company. Gets the arty [5th Field] to shell about 40 Huns (spotted during his travels) approaching from the west across a field. The shells fall directly on target with devastating effect . . . the enemy can be heard screaming. Apparently the German officers and NCOs kept driving the survivors forward.

The Black Watch war diarist is clearly impressed with the vigour of the enemy:

Identification of bodies and of live prisoners taken (24) show the troops we are meeting are definitely the cream of the crop. They . . . range in age from 20 to 26, and are fine physical specimens, keen, with excellent morale.

At 1600 they opened an artillery bombardment that lasted two hours. Then came in on a counter-attack. Once again the attack was general on the sector, but more heavily on Calgary High-landers. For a while things were very sticky, but once again this attack was repulsed without loss of any ground. There has been close cooperation between the artillery [5th Field] and our forward companies, and our guns have been firing continually on targets . . .

The grim determination of the hard-nosed paratroop battalions, grouped under the intimidating name "Battle Group Chill," rushed here to hold open the mouth of South Beveland at any cost, is reminiscent of the fanatical resistance of the SS units along Verrières Ridge in Normandy last summer. However, as in Normandy, their stubborn reluctance to withdraw, inspired by fanatical loyalty to their Führer, is costing them dearly in numbers killed, wounded, and captured. And in the end, as in Normandy, the dogged, unforgiving pressure by ordinary Canadian foot-sloggers "in baggy pants covered with mud, their boots and socks always wet" (to quote a local Dutch woman) – carrying an unemo-tional, unspoken, but unquenchable desire to destroy anything in a field-grey uniform and "get this goddamn war over and done with" – prevails at Hoogerheide.

Battalion commanders may mutter under their breath that the Army is now "scraping the bottom of the barrel" to fill up the ranks of the infantry (even posting gunners to rifle companies instead of back to their own artillery units when they recover from wounds). And they may curse the politically-minded staff officers who send up reinforcements so seriously deficient in training they don't even know their personal weapons, as witness the still tender bullet-hole in the calf of your left leg. But let no one ever fault their courage. Though many of them, if not most, are experiencing full battle conditions for the first time, and fear, as on any battlefield, is the dominant emotion, they are showing bags of courage. No one writing of these days will ever do justice to the courage of those who refuse to be driven from Hoogerheide, or those who will go forward to take Woensdrecht, or those who must push out into the misty, forbidding polders in the neck of South Beveland to wrest long, dismal stretches of muddy dikes from stubborn defenders and drive off counter-attack after counter-attack by screaming para-troopers.*

---

* A German report of these days makes much of "the stubborn resis-tance of the Canadian troops" in repulsing the "vigorous attacks" of their "battle-seasoned" paratroopers to try to regain Hoogerheide: "In the two following days [October 9 and 10] attack and counter-attack alternated. Three times the vanguard unit, Combat Group von der Heydte [formed from two battalions of 6th Paratroop Regiment] succeeded in thrusting [from the north] through the southern edge of Hoogerheide. Every time, the position gained had to be given up again for lack of force against the enemy counter-attack." – British Imperial War Museum MS/B798.

12

OUT IN THE

MIST–ENSHROUDED POLDERS

✳

AT THE SAME TIME 5TH BRIGADE UNITS ARE FIGHTING FOR
Hoogerheide, the Royals move west into South Beveland.

All of the peninsula, stretching west some twenty-six miles to
Walcheren Island, is land reclaimed from the sea by the Dutch, who
for five hundred years have progressively diked off the sea into large
rectangular areas, pumping them dry and producing fertile fields –
perfectly flat and enclosed by dikes twelve feet or more high. These
fields are known as "polders." Here and there, tucked away in a
corner of a polder, partially hidden from its neighbour by looming
dikes, is a little farmhouse with its barn.

Major Beatty's D Company moves out on "a reconnaissance in
force" from Ossendrecht along a dike road between two flooded
polders, to polders not flooded on the way to a "sluice basin pumphouse" at the narrowest part of the isthmus, four and a half kilometres west of Woensdrecht.

Walking with Beatty, behind the long line of infantrymen
snaking through the mist, is 4th Field FOO Capt. Leslie "Hutch"
Hutcheon, while his carrier, with his crew (Gunners Wally
Driemel, Mel Squissato, and John Copeland) grinds along behind.
Following them are two sections of 3-inch mortars, two anti-tank
guns, a troop of 8th Recce armoured cars, a Toronto Scottish
platoon of machine-guns, a detachment of Engineers, and a
number of Dutch maquis.

Some polders, like the one D Company is approaching, are three kilometres long and half a kilometre wide. Here, the advantages are all with the defenders. Attackers can obtain no concealment from an enemy dug-in along the dikes; and vehicles, forced to travel on top of the dikes, provide easy targets for anti-tank guns located at intersections. Thus, without the heavy mists – to which the soggy polders are susceptible on cold days – the Royals could never make it out there, let alone overcome by surprise (as they do) a German outpost, and push on almost to the pumphouse and important sluice gates, using a series of platoon attacks with guns preceding each attack with a healthy "stonk."*

At dusk when Hank Caldwell's A Company moves out to rein-force Beatty's, they hold between them an area two miles wide, and while not close to cutting off the isthmus, they present a menace to the main road from Walcheren, passing north of Woensdrecht, to Bergen-op-Zoom.

Next day, October 9, the Germans engage in really dirty pool. After Hutch lays down some fire on "a threatening counter-attack," some fifty Germans indicate they wish to surrender. But when a platoon is sent out to escort them in, they open fire with machine-guns, and the Royals just manage to get back with the aid of smoke laid down by their own 3-inch mortars.

Today, October 10, you and your crew take part in an attempt by the Royals to move north from where the two companies are entrenched in the polders, to close off the isthmus by fire if not by occupation. In early afternoon, Tom Whitley's B Company and Paddy Ryall's C Company move out from Ossendrecht.

Fortunately, again today, there is a heavy ground mist screening you from the German artillery observers in Woensdrecht, barely visible on its ledge. Even so you feel naked as you walk along the dike, which is like a causeway, conscious that for eight hundred

---

* In a "stonk," guns are laid in such a way as to ensure their shells land in a line along the compass bearing of a linear target.

yards, the only available shelter from shelling and mortaring is the icy ten-foot-deep water lapping the verges of the road.

At first Whitley's company is in the lead, and it is with him you walk with your carrier grinding beside you. As always there is about him that intimidating aura of determination to see things through regardless, of which you first became conscious back in that terrible orchard at Eterville in Normandy. And it is just as reassuring now as it was then, when, exhausted from constant bombardment, and looking like a scarecrow, he snarled his defiance. How different he looks today, so beautifully turned out: his tie perfectly knotted, his web-belt with holster in place, and his boots clean enough to be going out on a battalion parade square, rather than on their way into battle in the muddy polders.

Some distance beyond the flooded polders, there is a rendezvous at a farm that is to become Battalion Tac HQ. There you leave your carrier to go forward with Signaller Stevenson, who is back-packing an 18-set radio, walking north with Ryall's company in extended line towards the pointed end of this narrow polder hidden in the deep mist a thousand yards ahead. Their ultimate objective is a farmhouse in the next polder, just beyond where the left-hand dike converges on the dike angling up diagonally on the right.

As you walk in the swirling mists through the short wet grass of a mowing meadow, with only the sound of many feet rustling and squishing, and the deep breathing of men on each side of you, there is a sense of unreality.

To achieve maximum surprise there will be no arty preparation or covering fire until you've walked the length of the polder. But then there will be concentrated fire for ten minutes by the 25-pounders, with the mediums joining in for the last five minutes, as you shelter on this side of that next dike somewhere up ahead in the fog.

The fire-plan is precisely timed, so everyone is urged to walk briskly to make sure all are there at the dike, ready to rush over the top and hit the farm as soon as the firing ends. What will happen if they are on the dike waiting for you when you appear out of the fog is too unpleasant to contemplate. But clearly it is on everyone's mind, for when the dike looms up out of the mist, and no Schmeissers *bur-rup bur-rup*, the body language of deep relief of all within view is un-mistakable, as shoulders unhunch, necks lengthen, backs straighten, and firm, confident strides replace the irregular, stumbling footfalls induced by fear and foreboding.

Seconds after you and Stevenson – breathing heavily – flop down with the infantrymen against the wet, grassy slope of the dike, there is a distant booming of guns from behind Ossendrecht. Shortly the air sizzles overhead and a crashing storm of shells exploding just beyond the dike rises to a hellish din that shakes the ground. You time the firing so as to help the infantrymen to be ready to go over the top as soon as the last shell arrives. But when the firing ends, before you can say anything, a bull-moose voice close by yells: "Okay, let's go!"

As you look that way, a thick-set sergeant scrambles up the dike, and immediately men on all sides are scrambling up and over with him. Small-arms fire starts snapping and crackling, and you and Stevenson move to the top of the dike where you can observe what's going on. The shooting is over so quickly you wonder if the farm was really occupied. But then you see bodies lying on the ground in the barnyard.

You have Stevenson send a message back on his 18-set that the carrier can come up now, for you want the more reliable 19-set radio in the carrier available to bring down fire when the inevitable counter-attack comes in. As you move down and across the farm-yard towards the house to check out its possibilities as an OP, you pass among the German casualties.

· They lie sprawled here and there between the barn and the house. Your shells had caught them in the open as they were trying to get at you and the Royals crouching behind the crest of the dike waiting for the fire-plan to lift. Most of them lie as they fell, but some are squirming and dying in agony, ignored by the Royals' stretcher-bearers who are fully occupied attending their own wounded. You are overcome with inexpressible horror. Until now you have never had occasion to pause on the ground immediately afterwards, and walk among men dead and dying from the high explosives and flying steel you had called down on them. Over the past four months you'd fired tons of shells on suspected enemy positions, but if you saw any movement at all, it was as though you were watching a movie playing in your field-glasses of shells bursting among little distant figures running for cover.

There had been that time in front of Dunkirk when you'd caught eighty of them in the open attacking a company of the Royals trapped between a canal and flooded land. Many had fallen and disappeared in the flashing, black puffs of your shells, and you'd watched with satisfaction, mumbling your grim litany: "That's for big, smiling Jack Cameron . . . and that's for quiet Jack Thompson . . . and that's for Dawson and Knapp and Thorpe and Ament and . . ." through a long list of dead comrades.

But now, staring down at the young German whose boots have just stopped twitching, you feel confused as you fight a flood of compassion that threatens to overwhelm you. You tell yourself that had he got the chance to use the Schmeisser lying beside him, you might now be lying dead here instead of him. But logic doesn't work, and you know you'll never be quite the same again. Time and again in the months ahead you will shell them with hate in your heart, but never again with the simple, straightforward satisfaction and enthusiasm of that young Forward Observation Officer in front of Dunkirk.

As you gain control of your emotions, you notice the dead man's jack-boots are almost new, and you wish you had a pair like them so you could pull them off at night and dry your feet; and when a counter-attack came in, you could pull them on without having to lace them up.

As though reading your mind a rough voice behind you says: "Nice boots, eh? Why don't you take them?" Receiving no reply, and undoubtedly sensing your queasiness, the Sergeant reaches down, yanks off the boots, and hands them to you.

You mumble, "Uh . . . thanks." And gingerly holding them by

your fingertips, you dump them into your carrier that has just arrived, grateful to be rid of them, for the warmth of the dead man's feet still breathes up from within the leather.

(A couple of days later, when they are cold, you will cut them down into Wellingtons and wear them with great comfort.)

On checking out the second storey of the little brick house, with most of its roof missing, you decide you can observe the zone from the dike in front just as well and with a lot less risk.

Ryall, worried about his right flank, which produced a strong counter-attack against Tim Beatty's company yesterday, directs his right-hand platoon to spread out to the right along the dike carrying the road to Woensdrecht, to a point about two hundred yards beyond a junction with another dike running north towards a prominent road-and-rail junction, a reputed strongpoint, with (according to the Dutch Underground) deep, bricked-in trench-works. As it turns out, there are some Germans along the dike over on the right, manning a 75-mm anti-tank gun, which the Royals capture with remarkable ease after a brief skirmish.

Your only contribution is to drop neutralizing shell-fire around some farm buildings on the right flank, but it brings you to the attention of a sniper who almost ends your war, when you cross over the north-south dike skirting the right side of your little house, and walk with Paddy a short way out in the polder to try to make out what's going on. You have your field-glasses to your eyes, when there's a shocking smack in your left ear as painful as the slap of an open hand. From experience working the rifle butts, where bullets flying at paper targets just inches over your head make that smacking sound, you know its significance. Paddy's ear must have caught a similar smack, for he drops as quickly as you. Without comment, you both scramble back over the dike into the barnyard.

The Royals have their slits only half-finished when the German counter-attack comes in. But the dike offers excellent protection against small-arms fire, while providing almost rifle-range conditions, with an incomparable field of fire, for the riflemen and machine-gunners confronting the shadowy, grey-green, helmeted figures in flapping, mottled smocks materializing in the mists.

They come in a stumbling run across the muddy field, flopping down among the sugar beets, firing bursts of flickering tracers and then rising to run forward again.

As you call back over the remote control for a Mike target to land in front of their line of advance, Lee Enfields are cracking, Stens are sputtering, and Brens are hammering away methodically all along the dike. And by the time your shells start sending up geysers of mud and smoke in the field just beyond the dike, putting an end to the attack, many of the paratroopers already have ceased to rise and run forward.

Then in the brief lull before their mortars and airbursts begin, a veteran sergeant – festooned with two captured Mauser rifles, one hanging down from each shoulder on its sling – starts marching back and forth along the crest of the dike in full view of the enemy, haranguing his men who crouch down behind the dike, sheltering from the menacing buzzing sounds that follow him as he passes back and forth.

Your first thought is the poor guy has cracked up. But when he comes close to where you are lying against the leeward side of the dike, you detect the smell of rum on the evening breeze. It's obvious he's had a bit too much spine-stiffener on the way up here today. Yet as you listen, it becomes clear this is not just an alcohol-induced display of bravado. He has a serious message to get over to his boys, and he's running a big risk to make his point. He most certainly has their attention, as he tells them he didn't hear enough fire from their weapons when they were attacked just now (a common complaint of company commanders): "The more you fire at them, the less they'll fire at you. Here now! Keep your heads up! There aren't any Heinies within miles. If there were, would they let me walk around up here?"

At that moment he's tramping just above where you are lying back against the dike, and you notice there's now a nasty, intimate *snick-snick* to the bullets. And when a smirking rifleman, on his knees working on his trench below the crest nearby, catches your eye and winks knowingly, you decide it's time the sergeant came down before he's shot down, an eventuality that will benefit no one's morale.

It will probably take the persuasive authority of the company commander, Paddy Ryall, or his second-in-command, Len Gage. But before you go looking for them, you call and beckon him to come over where you might talk to him quietly. To your astonishment and relief he not only comes over, but slides down the side of the dike beside you, inquiring: "Yeh, Foo?"

Clearly it is a day of honour for the Royals. By 5:00 P.M. Whitley's company is on the near side of the embankment carrying the railway through the isthmus less than three hundred yards from the sea lapping its north shore, in position to dominate by fire all roads to and from Walcheren Island, denying their use, at least in daylight, and ultimately contributing something of consequence to the island's downfall. In taking their objectives the assaulting companies had destroyed many of the enemy and taken 104 prisoners at the relatively low cost of three dead and twenty wounded. And in all this, the guns played a significant role.

Buoyed by success, the Royals decide Hank Caldwell's A Company should go forth next day, October 11, to clean out that strongpoint 1,000 yards north of Ryall's company and about the same distance east of Whitley's where his railway embankment meets a dike.

Overnight the balmy fall weather, the one decent feature of life here, disappears. By morning the chill of approaching winter is descending from dark grey skies in the form of an icy drizzle that later turns to rain. Thus bomb-carrying Spits and Tiffies, which could have helped, are unavailable. Still, a heavy fire-plan is laid on by Col. Mac Young at Brigade, involving field and medium guns, along with Tor Scots' 4.2-inch mortars and the Royals' 3-inch mortars plastering the objective, while heavy ack-ack fills the air above it with airbursts.

The attack goes in about 3:30 P.M. over the dike directly in front of your OP. You have them in view all the way. Jerry lets them get almost to the railway embankment before he opens up. By then they are much too close to the enemy for you to safely shell the source of their torment. When Hank comes back to use Paddy's communication with Battalion HQ to request permission to withdraw, he is badly shaken. His leading platoon has been severely mauled, and the rest are pinned down under heavy mortar and machine-gun fire short of the crossroads. To aid them in getting back, you pop smoke shells along the railway up to the crossroads. Already misty, the polder is soon blanketed in dense, white fog from your fuming canisters. But you can't use H.E. Some wounded Royals may be lying close to the objective and unable to crawl away.

While they gained no territory and suffered thirty-three known casualties, Hank's men must have fought with intimidating aggressiveness, for they managed to bring back forty prisoners!

That night the Germans launch a strong counter-attack involving flame-throwers on both Paddy's company and Tom Whitley's over on the left. You are asleep in your bedroll on the floor of the little storage room attached to the kitchen at the rear of the house, the only room that can be blacked out, other than the tiny cellar beneath the kitchen in which company headquarters is set up.

Paddy wakes you and tells you the heaviest firing (judging by the amount of tracer bullets) is originating from the polder just over the dike in front, and from over on the right where they captured the German gun this afternoon. Still half in your bedroll, leaning on one arm and holding a dim lamp-electric over your map-board on the floor beside you, you are able to give Stevenson, manning the radio only a couple of feet away, a Mike target to send back to the guns. Having registered several spots in the polder just beyond that dike before dark, it's a simple matter to choose one near the source of trouble and identify it for the guns by its code name. After plastering it with a heavy scale of fire a few minutes, you move the shelling: "West 200 . . . Repeat!" Then: "East 400 . . . Repeat!" Back and forth you move the fire.

In each successive lull, as the guns are being "switched," the snap and chatter of small arms along the dikes is noticeably reduced, until it dies away completely. When it does, a weary Paddy Ryall, coming in the back door and passing through your storeroom into the kitchen on his way to his headquarters in the cellar, calls out, "Good shooting, old boy! Thank your gunners for us, will you?"

High praise from an infantry officer, for which they will be most grateful. Thank goodness he saw nothing incongruous in a FOO shooting from the map while still ensconced in his bedroll.

It takes a while to go back to sleep; you keep expecting the Krauts to try again. And while you wait for sleep to return, you amuse yourself watching the shadows cast on the wall behind the table by the signaller's candle as he tries to read the *Reader's Digest* your wife sent you in a recent parcel. Outside, a basin of Moaning Minnies end their howling flight with tremendous crashes, and suddenly you are conscious of the vulnerability of that wall to a shell or mortar – an outside wall of light construction facing Woensdrecht.* Not good. Not good at all. In the morning you must get the crew to erect an inner wall of sandbags. In addition to greatly improving the sheltering quality of the room, it will give them something constructive to do and perhaps get their minds off the rather awful vistas of death that surround them on all sides here. Morale is still quite good considering, but . . .

---

* Nebelwerfers (or Moaning Minnies to the troops) were rocket mortars, with six to ten barrels, of varying calibres and ranges.

CALIBRE	PROJECTILE	RANGE IN YARDS
150 mm	75 pounds	7,300
210 mm	248 pounds	8,600
300 mm	277 pounds	5,000

13

A FARM HAS BECOME
A PLACE OF DEATH

BODIES OF MEN AND BEASTS LIE EVERYWHERE UNBURIED. The initial shelling, preceding the move in here, killed the horses and cows. Even the chickens lie dead in the yard.

One old driving-horse, which somehow survived the awful torrent of shells and was still standing in the yard halfway between the house and the barn when you arrived, became the special concern of the boys on your crew for a while. Though he stood rooted to the spot as though paralyzed by shock, his hide perforated with shell fragments, there was no sign of serious bleeding, so they were encouraged to hope he might survive if sheltered from further wounding from the Jerry airbursts and mortar bombs, which began to arrive with increasing frequency. But when they tried to lead him to the barn, they couldn't budge him. Gradually, his head hung lower and lower, and when for more than three days he didn't move an inch from where he stood, and began to weave on his feet, they decided he should be put out of his misery. A bullet through the head from one of the captured Mauser rifles, stacked in the corner of your room off the kitchen, and he crumpled down only a few yards from the unburied Germans.

In the barn, three big work-horses died, convulsing in great agony from shell splinters while tethered side by side in their stall. They lie in a repulsive confusion of legs, heads, and bodies, so completely and so consistently covered with red brick-dust – from the roof tiles pulverized by the shells, which had slowly settled on them over a period of days – that the effect is of a sculpture moulded of red clay designed to illustrate the madness of war. Bulging eyeballs, tongues hanging from agonized mouths, great hoofs and fetlocks that died pawing the air, lacerations and blood-matted manes and tails – all equally and evenly coated with red dust of one tone and one texture – on first sight arouse within you a new sense of horror, unlike anything you have experienced before on gazing upon the face of death.

And in the fields are dead cows and God knows how many dead men. Two German stretcher-bearers with red crosses on their smocks appear out there this morning, wandering around in the mist in front of the junction of roads and railway, stopping every so often and bending down – obviously checking bodies to make sure none are still alive. For half an hour they are left to go about their business unmolested – but then the Royals begin to get suspicious.

When their zig-zagging brings them close enough to the dike to pinpoint the Royals' trenches if that is their intention, a sergeant stands up and waves them in with a Bren. After a slight hesitation, they obey. But when they are paraded in front of a stern Major Ryall in the kitchen they vigorously protest, in highly accented English, being taken prisoner – boldly demanding their rights under the clause in the Geneva Convention covering the safe conduct of non-combatant stretcher-bearers. Paddy shouts them down, telling them they should count themselves lucky they were taken prisoner and not shot, as they shot one of his stretcher-bearers only a couple of days ago in broad daylight.

During a long lull in the German mortaring (probably due to their not knowing where their meandering stretcher-bearers are), the farmer, Sief Pijnen, who'd taken refuge at a neighbouring farm, comes up with a horse and cart to rescue any animals still alive.

All he can find are a few little pigs in a sheltered pen near the back door. As they are hastily loaded and driven off, you believe you are watching the last living creatures (other than soldiers) depart this place of death. However, this belief is shattered late in the day when an ungodly screech – unlike any sound ever uttered by anything of this world – draws your eyes to the attic crawl-space above the kitchen. Up there, barely visible in the gloom, stands a wild-eyed little dog.

How it's been able to resist coming forth to beg food before now is incomprehensible, until you try to reach for it to bring it down for some of the M & V stew giving off the odour that enticed it from its hiding place. As your hands touch its shivering body, the screech it emits is so horrific you topple backward off your precarious perch on an upturned Compo box. Clearly the poor mutt has been driven insane by the shells that blew off chunks of roof and ceiling from the bedroom in which it was seeking refuge from the terrifying explosions.

Reassembling your courage, you mount the box. This time, prepared for its awesome bellow, you grab the quivering bundle of stiffness and drop it to the floor, where it scuttles under the table. There it lurks, screeching at every pretext, even when food is pushed towards it, until the next day when you drive it out the back door, your nerves unable to cope with its insane shrieks each time your feet pass close by.*

During the afternoon you receive a signal from Col. Mac Young at Brigade to mark with red smoke that strongpoint on the next dike where it joins the railway embankment – now becoming infamous under the complete misnomer "Five Ways Crossroads" – and subsequently to observe and report the effectiveness of the 500-pound bombs the Spitfires will try to drop on it.

While it's easy enough to produce red smoke shells on target, judging the effectiveness of bombs is something else, even when observed from a superior vantage point among the ragged rafters of

---

* On visiting the farm twenty-five years later the author felt foolish at the depth of his relief on learning from Sief's brother Louis (who shared the farm, but was trapped north of Woensdrecht during the battle) that "Fanny," the little "hounde," recovered and lived to a ripe old age.

the upper storey of your house, creaking and rattling from the cold wind of almost-gale force that has been blowing all day. One after another, a few seconds apart, five Spits sweep in over the polders from the east, arousing a fury of black flak from around Woens-drecht. You follow each of them in turn with your glasses as they close in on the crossroads. Clearly you see each black bomb plunge earthward in a wobbly arc to a tremendous flashing gush of smoke and mud, feel the earth-quaking jar even before you hear the roar of the explosion that seems almost under the tail of the plane as it scurries away from the concussion wave.

It all looks mighty impressive, but what they accomplished is impossible to tell. And all you can report with certainty is that all five Spits delivered their bombs in the target area and got away from the flak unharmed. Later, when the CO unexpectedly drops in on you (for no reason that you can discern other than to make it clear he fully understands how sticky it is up here) he tells you the bombing of the crossroads is in preparation for a full battalion attack by the Black Watch through here tomorrow.

However, as it turns out, the first attack in the morning is against the Royals holding the Black Watch startline, of which their historian will one day write: "Action on the 13th opened at four o'clock in the morning with an enemy counter-attack, which began against B Company (Whitley's) and continued on down the battalion line. This was repulsed within twenty minutes with the aid of strong artillery support."

(No mention, of course, of the artillery FOO, aroused once more by his company commander, again shooting from the map while still in his bedroll propped up on one elbow.)

14

WHAT PRICE ANTWERP?

---　✳　---

SOMETIMES YOU FORGET THAT THE REAL PURPOSE OF ALL this costly fighting to choke off the neck of the isthmus of South Beveland and drive the Germans from the length and breadth of the peninsula, is to open up the back door to Walcheren Island and silence the big guns there, so Antwerp's port can be used. And when the sense of purpose disappears, the whole wretched business takes on the bleak and hopeless aspects of a blood-letting. If you can have these lapses, what must it be like for the weary riflemen of the Royals clinging to their miserable, rainsodden dikes out there; and for the men of the Black Watch, who, at 0615 this morning, tried to make it across that misty sugar-beet field behind artillery and 4.2-inch mortar concentrations, but got no more than 250 yards before being pinned down and driven back by a hurricane of airbursting shells, mortars, and machine-gun fire?

Now, just before last light, as they wait to be sent out there again to try to clear out that meeting of road and rail-line running along the top of the next dike less than a kilometre away, what are they thinking? Can they have anything else on their minds but survival?

They've been told, of course, that, since the battalion was driven back at 0830 this morning, a dozen Spitfires have dropped bombs and strafed a brickworks north of Woensdrecht, from whence offending mortars have been originating; and that twice, once at 2:30 P.M. and again at 3:00 P.M., "Angus," the code name for that fortified crossroads, was treated to attacks by rocket-firing Typhoons, led there by your red smoke shells. They'll have ten tanks in support, including heavy flame-throwers, and while they cannot move forward with them, they'll be firing from the flank. Also, belt-fed Vickers machine-guns, firing from the top of the dike over the heads of the advancing soldiers, will attempt to neutralize enemy fire from distant dikes, while 17-pounder anti-tank guns will fire over open sights at possible enemy OPs in Woensdrecht on its high ground only 1,500 yards away. And of course the artillery "preparation" and prearranged concentrations of field, medium, and heavy ack-ack will be heavier than this morning.

Still, you look with pity at the men sheltering behind the dike waiting for zero hour, saying little, having a last cigarette. Just above them, along the brow of the dike, vaguely silhouetted against the darkening sky, sit the Vickers, their silent muzzles pointing out over the flat, forbidding polder, completely devoid of cover of any kind.

Casualties are bound to be high, though you can hardly antici-pate that by midnight all their company commanders will be killed or wounded, and ten men – all that can be mustered by one surviv-ing officer in that churning cauldron – will be requesting permis-sion to withdraw.*

As Spitfires hum in and drop more bombs, the guns over behind Ossendrecht open up and pour shells into the polder beyond your dike in a deafening roar. The Vickers are now chattering, and Jerry starts to respond, ploughing the dike with mortars. One flashes right beside a Vickers' crew, and the gunner falls over backward down the dike. Immediately another leaps up behind the gun, and it continues firing with barely a pause. You glance at young Gunner Hiltz, who has crept out beside you on the dike, and he wags his head in the odd way that men do when they marvel at the courage of other men.

---

* On this "Black Friday" the Black Watch lose 183 officers and men, 56 of them dead, bringing their total losses to 264 since they began fighting at Hoogerheide to close off South Beveland five days ago.

Most of the Black Watch are either cut down as they go over the dike, or are down and crawling before they get very far. Fewer than a dozen manage to get across the muddy beet-field anywhere close to those crossroads on the enemy-held dike. At least that's what one surviving officer (Major Bill Ewing) who comes back to the house about 11 o'clock seeking permission to withdraw, tells his CO on the phone connecting Paddy's cellar to a farm in the rear shared by tactical headquarters of both the Royals and the Black Watch: "We're at the railway dike, but still at least four hundred yards from the objective, and all we're able to muster is ten men."

By now the number of wounded coming back is so heavy, the walking-wounded have to be directed to the barn to await their turn on one of the ambulance Jeeps provided by many regiments, arriving and departing in a steady stream – one at least driven by a Dutch civilian lad from a neighbouring farm. An MO (you assume he's Black Watch) has set up in the gloomy kitchen in discouragingly poor light, which must be kept subdued since that room, unlike yours, cannot be blacked out. There, using the kitchen table as an operating table, he provides emergency treatment for some. But the majority of stretcher cases are patched with shell dressings and shot with morphine in your little storeroom by the stretcher-bearers who bring them in, and then are put aboard stretcher-carrying Jeeps bound for hospital as they become available.

For hours the Black Watch stretcher-bearers have been going out into the darkness of no-man's-land before Five Ways Crossroads, the only light the flashes of mortar bombs, carrying in the most severely wounded and propping them up around the walls of this room you've sandbagged and made as liveable as possible.

As they cut out arms and legs of battledresses and pack on shell dressings, you marvel at their cheerful demeanour. One of them in particular, a robust lad, pours forth a steady stream of reassuring nonsense at the stunned men with white faces, many of whom will never live to see the inside of the hospitals back in Antwerp, where the stretcher-bearing Jeeps are now taking them.

"Will I make it?" asks a boy with a row of holes across his chest.

"Of course you will – you lucky devil! You'll be home in Canada for Christmas!" And he lights a cigarette and shoves it between the boy's pale lips, before he goes on to the next man.

You're fascinated with the idea the Black Watch would have been issued with special blood-red underwear, until finally the truth dawns on you. Feeling yourself growing dizzy, you go out into the night and sit down in the darkness of the little outside toilet, putting your head down between your legs until the dizziness goes away. Back inside, you notice your crew look pale and drawn, and to break the spell of horror, you get them brewing up tea and handing it around to those who can drink it.

Now one of the stretcher-bearers – a mere boy – his humanity stretched beyond the limit, breaks down and starts to cry, repeating over and over between sobs: "Did you see those guys out there? It was plain murder. They never had a chance." For a while no one says anything. Then the robust, cheerful stretcher-bearer, still going about the business of bandaging a man's belly, yells at him ferociously: "Why don't you go home and suck your mother's teat? Talk about women – talk about anything else, but shut your goddam mouth!" A murmur of approval goes up around the room, and you know they're justified, for some will never see the dawn. But still you feel sorry for the poor, sensitive boy, who now slinks out into the darkness where his sobbing will be unobserved.

Insensitivity now dominates life. If it didn't, everyone surely would go mad. But when Ralph Young, second-in-command of the Royals, making a visit relates "a shocking incident" he witnessed shortly after dawn at 5th Brigade HQ (now sharing a farmhouse with Royals' Tac HQ), you agree there are unacceptable levels of insensitivity. "Hefty" Ross, intrepid leader of the Royals' Scout Platoon, was tongue-lashed unmercifully by the Brigadier of 5th Brigade for picking up, and bringing back in his Jeep for medical attention, two seriously battle-exhausted Black Watch lads he met staggering away from the front with unseeing eyes.

15

A TOWER SILHOUETTED
AGAINST THE SKY

✳

ON THE AFTERNOON OF THEIR SEVENTH DAY IN THE POLDERS, the Royals are relieved by the Calgary Highlanders and undertake a long route march of some thirteen kilometres, from the extreme left of the line in South Beveland to the bush area east of Ossendrecht near a lake called Groote Meer, where the topography is so strikingly different from the treeless, mud-and-water polder-lands in the isthmus as to seem of another country. A land of sand dunes and pine woods, all above sea level, it even has a hill of respectable height, thirty-one metres (more than one hundred feet) according to the map. And on its crest stands a fire-ranger's tower.

It's a long trek for the heavily laden, weary troops plodding back through Ossendrecht and east to the main highway from Putte to the mouth of a bush road that leads in to the lake; and, on the way there, there are several delays from enemy shelling. Then just after dark – word having been received that the South Saskatchewan Regiment, now attached to 4th Brigade, whose right flank the Royals are moving to strengthen against increasingly violent counter-attacks by infantry and tanks, is again under severe attack – the tired men are broken off for a hot meal in the grounds of a secluded, substantial building left of the highway. And while this is being served, an Orders Group is held in a brightly lit, sterile room the like of which you'd forgotten existed. Company commanders are briefed on their holding role and assigned areas in which to deploy around and about the northwestern end of the lake, about one and a half kilometres from here. You make sure Cornett attaches you to the company that will be closest to that hill with the wooden watch-tower. This turns out to be Hank Caldwell's A Company.

A great storm of shell-fire is now roaring over in the area where you are headed, but no one seems greatly concerned. As the companies form up in single file, by platoons, to continue their shuffling way up the highway to turn right into the bush road towards Groote Meer, you marvel at the degree to which everyone has become blasé about German counter-attacks that seem to hit selected spots in each sector at least once or twice a day or night. In a matter-of-fact way Cornett reports that all the shelling up ahead is by 6th Field on map reference 662184, directly northwest of Groote Meer. The fact that that is right next to where the Royals are headed, and that those shells are designed to help extricate a sub-unit of the South Saskatchewan Regiment that has been overrun, seems to concern no one, least of all your Battery Commander.

He tells you that last night Bill Carr, 26th Battery Commander, currently attached to the SSRs, reported firing on targets over in this same zone to gain relief for another company of SSRs "cut off," and that about 4:00 A.M. he'd reported the "sub-unit of friends in great difficulty." However, by mid-afternoon today the tide had turned, and Carr was reporting the SSRs had taken thirty prisoners and that "forty more were on their way back."

While the Major admits conditions up there currently appear a bit sticky, the situation will stabilize in due course – a conclusion, you believe, more readily arrived at by one who will be remaining here at Battalion Headquarters, than by one heading off at 9:00 P.M. in the pitch-black with Hank's company nosing up the narrow, bush-lined road for Groote Meer, just as an Uncle target is being shot by the 72 guns of 2nd Division on "four tanks and 100 infantry . . . at map reference 658181," only 800 yards from the lake.

Taking up positions in the dark in unknown territory must

always be fraught with nerve-wracking difficulties, but confusion can assume terrifying proportions when the occupation is attempted during an enemy counter-attack. For what seems like hours, bewildered and anxious, the column is stalled in the inky-black confinement of the narrow, bush road, while Schmeissers *bur-rup bur-rup* close by and high explosive is liberally dumped up ahead where the companies are to deploy.

However, fulfilling Cornett's optimism, things eventually get sorted out, and though shells from the direction of the enemy keep roaring and flashing in the woods nearby, the Royals continue to move forward.

Miraculously, all companies make it to their positions without bumping into hostile troops, though it takes them until well past midnight to dig in because of periodic sessions of some very heavy enemy shelling.

On the map, Groote Meer shows as a good-sized lake about one and a half kilometres long and about half that wide if measured across its western end, where is situated the only building for miles around. Hank heads for this. It turns out to be a sizeable lakeside residence with some out-buildings, and there he establishes his company headquarters in the basement, making full use of what appears to be a formidable water barrier out front in placing his platoons on the flanks.

Damage within the house on the side facing the lake suggests it has been the object of machine-gunning and mortaring. All the glass is missing from the windows and French doors.

With no room in the basement for you and crew a ground-floor room off the living room is made as safe as possible by blocking off a window in a side wall with an upturned mattress held in place by a bureau pushed against it, and by installing a blanket over the door as a blackout curtain to prevent light from spilling out into the living room every time someone goes in or out at night. Hardly a bomb shelter, but the wide lake out front provides a sense of security you haven't felt for a long while as you bed down for a couple of hours.

But when dawn comes and you go out into the shadowy living room to peer through the ragged windows over the lake, you can hardly believe your eyes. You rush down into the cellar and bring up Hank to have a look. He is aghast. The lake, on which he had based the defensive disposition of all his platoons, does not exist. From shore to shore, it is completely dry – its exposed clay bottom veined with wide cracks. An enemy patrol could have walked over here last night and entered this open lakefront door unmolested.*

However, the fire-ranger's tower on the crest of the hill, which starts to rise only a short distance from the circular drive at the rear of the house, is real enough. On your first trip up there you are pleasantly surprised to find one of Hank's platoons dug-in among the pine trees at the base of the wooden structure. This you didn't expect since the tower is so distant from company headquarters – at least half a mile by way of a torturous trail winding up through the bush. It seems you are not alone in looking upon this height of land as an asset that must not fall into enemy hands.

When you crawl up the ladderlike, open stairway to the top, you find it really is a very high structure, rising well above the mature pine trees of the forest in which it stands. Any higher and you might not have the stomach to climb it. And you anticipate that as time goes by, there will be periods of irrepressible anxiety springing from the thought that if you can see so far, this tower silhouetted against the sky must be visible to every German 88-mm on the whole front.

But for a while you are almost drunk with the view and the power it gives you as an arty FOO. Accustomed to looking out from

---

* When in 1973 the author visited the restored lakeside house, Groote Meer was still dry – a sorry, tangled mess of weeds. Local residents had concluded that earth-quaking tremors from bombs or a heavy artillery bombardment opened an underground fissure, allowing the lake to drain out into the low lands beyond Ossendrecht. Since the war the question of how the lake might be rehabilitated was raised again and again in political forums without results.

a hole at ground level, or through a narrow hole poked among the tiles of a roof of a house or barn, this is a dream OP. The only problem is communications, and this is solved the first day by the signallers running a line from your room in the house, where the 19-set radio from your carrier is manned twenty-four hours a day, to a field telephone installed up in the tower. And for the next six days you spend most of the daylight hours, and a great many hours of darkness, crouched behind the low, wooden barrier-wall around the platform at the top of the tower, peering out at the zone.

The yellow telephone line, snaking up an incline of varying steepness to the pine-covered rolling plateau where the tower stands, follows a trail of sorts through the underbrush – very rough and laced with fallen trees and other obstacles, including a dead German soldier lying face-up right across the path, which could trip the unwary. The trail is well enough defined to be followed easily in daylight. But at night it's necessary to run the signal line through your hand and exercise care if you're not to trip and go crashing headlong into the underbrush that always seems to be dripping wet from mist or rain.

The combined height of the hill and tower provides a view from the top of the platform for many miles in all directions, but, because of the continual misty weather, very little detail is identifiable beyond a couple of miles. In a way, this is just as well, for ammunition expenditure, except on DF (defensive fire) tasks, has been restricted to sixty rounds per gun in each twenty-four-hour period.

Apart from shelling one made-to-order target of enemy soldiers attempting to dig-in in broad daylight, and dropping some red smoke shells around a distant church tower to mark it for demolition by 500-pound bombs dropped by Spitfires at its base (after you'd spotted what looked like a long wireless antenna sticking out of the louvres of its belfry), your observed fire has consisted mainly of spattering a few shells from one troop of four guns on suspicious-looking scars of new earth that could be enemy trench-works.

To conserve shells while extending the harassing aspect of such shelling you use "troop fire," whereby each of the four guns of your troop fire in turn at prescribed intervals. Thus "three rounds troop fire at ten-second intervals" means the enemy will be harassed for almost two minutes instead of less than half a minute at the regular "gunfire" rate.

Three days after arriving here, you are called upon to provide a small fire-plan involving smoke mixed with H.E. in support of an attack by a strong fighting patrol sent out by D Company, with a troop of tanks, to clean out positions directly in front of them, from which the enemy has been making life difficult for the Royals by way of machine-gunning, shelling, and mortaring – the severity of which reached an intolerable level yesterday, October 16, with the Battalion reporting one bomb or shell arriving in company areas every twenty seconds.

From your tower you have a grandstand view of the attack as it moves out through fairly open country with the odd sandy bank showing among patches of gorse and clumps of scraggly pine so reminiscent of Petawawa. Right at the outset a Sherman runs over a mine and humps up in a cloud of dust and smoke. Though it doesn't catch fire, it is immobilized, and its crew, expecting it to brew up, pile out, and the other tanks, fearing the same fate, leave the infantry to go on alone.

About the time your bombardment is to end, you notice the odd shell is failing to clear the tops of some tall, widely spaced trees through which the troops are passing, bursting with a wicked flash and violent black puff right over their heads. While none appears to have been hurt by the shower of steel and branches, you later learn those airbursts were devastating to the nervous systems of some men who only recently returned from hospital after recovering from that RAF bombing back at Hautmesnil last August. Two at least are again being evacuated as casualties of battle exhaustion. Otherwise the attack proceeds so smoothly that by mid-morning all objectives are attained and you are left with the impression you have been watching a training manoeuvre.

Clearly not all the Germans fighting around here are taking

seriously Hitler's edict (revealed by prisoners) to fight to the death. You might reasonably suppose that the less aggressive are members of the "White Bread Brigade," men with stomach ulcers or other digestive-tract problems, requiring a special diet, who reputedly were posted to garrison this zone when it was still isolated and quiet.*

Knowing Signal-Sgt. Ryder is due to come up from the guns this morning with a box of Compo rations, and hoping he'll have some mail this time, maybe even a parcel of goodies from home, you go down the hill to the house for lunch.

Ryder's visits, which occur every three days when conditions allow, have become real highlights of the limited existence you pursue up here. Always a cheerful fellow, ready to share the latest bit of scuttlebutt and news about what's been going on back at the guns, he is like a breath of fresh air, and he never fails to leave you and your crew feeling better for hours after his visit.

Ever since he accidentally put a bullet hole in the wall just above your head as you lay resting on your bedroll on the floor of the little room off the kitchen at Paddy Ryall's headquarters at that farm out in the polders – missing your skull by no more than a couple of inches with a shot from a supposedly empty rifle he'd selected for examination from a pile of captured Mausers stacked in the corner – he has taken an outsized proprietary interest in your well-being. And in recent days, before coming up, he noticeably is taking the trouble to go beyond the Battery (to RHQ you suspect) to equip himself with information he thinks may be of interest to you.

---

* More of the "White Bread Brigade" might have surrendered had it not been for fear of their officers. Years after, Sief Pijnen, of the battered farm out in the polders, told you of spurning (out of fear of treachery) an offer of a Luger pistol from the German soldier in whose trench he was sheltering from your shells, prior to the Royals' attack. The German private urged him to take it and shoot his officer in the next trench so he and his buddies could surrender.

Thus you learn that Capt. Sammy Grange has become the Adjutant replacing Capt. "Tim" Welch, the Adjutant since way back at Horsham in England, who has taken a job back at Division.

You also learn that a Capt. Jack Cooper, an older brother of Major Don Cooper, who commanded 26th Battery when you were with it back in 1942–43, and who for a while was second-in-command of the Regiment late in 1943, has joined 4th Field and been posted as a troop commander to his brother's old battery.

16

WOENSDRECHT

———————————— ✳ ————————————

AFTER THE EXPERIENCE OF THE ROYALS AND THE BLACK
Watch out in the polders under fire from guns and mortars controlled by observers in Woensdrecht, it is clear the village must be
taken, and the RHLI are chosen to do the job.

Woensdrecht is only a short walk northwest of Hoogerheide, but
conscious of what it cost 5th Brigade battalions to take and hold
this smashed and forlorn place – in a battle that swayed back and
forth over a few houses for three bloody days and nights – every
Riley moving up to the startline, accompanied by tanks of the Fort
Garry Horse, knows it could be the longest walk of his life.

When they set out in the black early hours of October 16, following a creeping barrage, they do their best to follow the spirit, if
not the letter, of the advice given them "to lean into it and get there
before Jerry has a chance to recover and get his head up." Shivering
and sweating at the same time – half-intimidated and half-stimu-
lated by the raging linear inferno of blinding flashes and hot concussions, seemingly erupting just before their faces – they plunge
through the sour fumes and stumble over steaming gashes left by
the violence that just passed, desperate to keep up, but at the same
time dreading the moment when they will confront the enemy.

The enemy, however, anticipating the barrage, has pulled back,
and the leading companies are allowed to move through Woensdrecht and out onto the low ridge beyond. Then about 10:00 A.M.,

A Company, still settling in on their exposed slope, is hit with such force by paratroopers, tanks, and self-propelled guns, they are routed in disarray, and within minutes paratroopers and tanks are dominating the northern part of the village – one tank stopping just outside the house 4th Field FOO "Stevie" Stevenson has chosen as an OP.

Clearly, the battalion is in a desperate way – its only hope for recovering and stabilizing the front resting on the shoulders of Major Joe Pigott's reserve company and what help they can draw from the demoralized remnants of A Company, turned around to face the enemy by Pigott and Lt.-Col.Whitaker brandishing pistols.* But first the enemy about Stevenson's OP and Pigott's company must be dealt with; and with the approval of that intrepid Riley officer, Stevenson pulls down on the position an Uncle target – all seventy-two guns of the division.

That this does all it's meant to is confirmed in a situation report to Div Headquarters RCA at 6:35 P.M.: "Now much quieter. Believe U 203 held position for RHLI. First [Uncle target] brought down deliberately on our forward troops. They were pleased. Killed many Jerries." And the gunners receive a message of gratitude from the Rileys' CO (that will one day find expression in the history of the gunners of Canada): "The fire caught the enemy in the open, whereas our men were deep in slit trenches having been warned. Our troops cheered; the slaughter was terrific."

But, when, in their turn, the Rileys counter-attack and regain their positions with the help of a company of Essex Scottish and more tanks, they are hit again and again with fierce counter-attacks by paratroopers and tanks, each attack preceded by fearful doses of shelling and mortaring, including endless heart-stopping airbursts of 88-mm shells arriving unheralded, and streams of blood-curdling banshee-wailing flights of Moaning Minnies,

---

* *Tug of War* by Lt.-Col. Denis W. and Shelagh Whitaker, Beaufort Books, New York and Toronto, 1984, p. 194.

looping in and crashing with monstrous reverberating booms among the ravaged buildings.

After Stevenson's house is struck by four shells or mortars, it collapses about him, forcing him to set up elsewhere. Casualties mount – ninety-one in the first few hours,* and the Rileys maintain their tenuous hold on the smashed and fire-gutted houses and barns only with the help of rocket-firing Typhoons attacking the German armour, and by the shattering concentrations of shells called down at crucial moments by Stevenson and another 4RCA FOO, Capt. Douglas McDonald, getting his first taste of battle, having just joined the Regiment from Canada.

Back at the guns, the action is reminiscent of Normandy: first, the thundering roar of the orderly fire-plan by the guns of 2nd Division and three medium regiments (7th Canadian, and 84th and 121st British) lighting up the black dome of cloudy predawn sky with ragged flashes; then the strange calm, when all the guns go silent, extending until daylight, when the expected report comes that the infantry have gained their objectives. Then comes the inevitable enemy counter-attack. At 7:35 A.M., over all earphones in the Regiment comes the urgent call: DF (SOS) 1029 – Scale 2 – enemy infantry concentrating for attack."

Then from a FOO: "Mike target – Mike target – Mike target . . . Enemy attacking in force with tanks." And for the rest of the day, the guns thump away, consuming 5,000 shells in response to calls for fire – the demand rising and falling with the intensity of the attacks.

Late in the day the Flying OP, in his little Auster plane, scudding back and forth behind the guns, low to the ground so as to not present a target for the Jerry 88s – only rising up a couple of hundred feet to observe the fall of his shot – helps direct 4th Field guns on "enemy guns now firing" and "enemy infantry."

After dark, the infantry's position about Woensdrecht remaining precarious, on urgent appeals from 14th Battery Commander

---

* RHLI casualties over five days totalled 167, including 21 dead.

Major Jack Drewry at RHLI Tac Headquarters permission is obtained by Col. Young from Brigadier H. Keefler, CRA, at 2nd Division Headquarters, to fire DF (defensive fire) tasks normally allowable only by brigadiers or up.*

At 11:16 "attempted enemy infiltration" is hammered by DF 112; and half an hour later DF 1019 and DF 1012 are shot for similar purposes. And in the next twelve hours four more DF tasks are fired, the last at 10:45 A.M. "to frustrate enemy forming up to attack."

When eventually there is a lull in demand for defensive fire by 4th Field, a thank-you message from the CO of the RHLI is passed on to the gunners. Without reservation Col. Whitaker gives the guns full credit for preventing a disaster.

The guns of 4th Field, helping to stabilize the front, are some five kilometres south of Woensdrecht, deployed in a muddy field just east of Ossendrecht, near the east–west road known as Middel Straat, Hageland, having moved here eight days ago on October 8.

All day long it is grey, cold, and miserable, with occasional showers, but the gunners, sweating from their exertions, have little time to notice. During lulls in the firing, as they take time to collect and pile up the latest crop of spent cartridges – some 200 per gun to add to the 675 per gun already in piles – they carefully stack the empty green shell and cartridge boxes in such a way as to suggest they have shelters in mind, and for very good reason. Though battery and troop command posts are set up in nearby buildings, the

---

* This is to prevent nervous front-line officers giving away the defensive fire-plan in response to enemy feints. Defensive fire targets (areas designated as vulnerable to enemy attack so that lines and ranges may be worked out by battery command posts in advance, allowing the guns to respond instantly without ranging in the event of a serious enemy attack) call for three minutes "intense" (five rounds per gun per minute for three minutes) for field guns (25-pounders); three minutes "rapid fire" (one and a half rounds per minute) for the mediums; and three minutes "rapid" (one round a minute) for the heavies when available.

men on the guns have been without any shelter since moving here, and the cold wind, with the smell of approaching winter in it, has begun to gust strongly.

Over the next four days, as the guns are called upon to break up a string of counter-attacks by some two thousand paratroopers clearly determined to regain all the ground they've lost, regardless of cost, 4th Field guns fire 13,104 more rounds, emptying 3,276 shell boxes and 1,638 cartridge boxes – thus providing each gun crew with 204 additional "building blocks."*

During the final twenty-nine hours of the paratroopers' attacks, ending at about 4:15 P.M. on October 20, 2nd Division Headquarters RCA will log no fewer than 32 Mike targets fired by 4th Field. And at one point this afternoon, Mike targets from FOOs are "queued up three deep waiting their turn," according to Sgt. Hunt's diary that carries a good description of life at the guns during the seventeen days they are here getting off 37,000 rounds:

Flood waters encroach on the area, and the wind sweeps across in terms of a gale, as meteor telegrams show. The gunners have few tarps under which to shelter from the rain. In the morning, those off duty rise warily from underneath their inadequate ground sheets, so as to not disturb the rivulets of water gathered in the creases. The signallers have their exchange in a pigsty inhabited at the same time by those for whom it was constructed. Here they sleep, eat, and work in great good humour. Battery Headquarters is more fortunate, with a dry barn, good straw, and a sufficiency of onions to make even bully beef palatable.

The mobile bath we patronized a few days ago was hit by a

---

* In Woensdrecht municipality, shells and mortars destroyed 427 homes – 72 by fire and 355 so ravaged by high explosive as to be not worth repairing. Another 235 were damaged but repairable. (Official figures of Woensdrecht Town Council)

flying bomb, resulting in 9 dead and 27 wounded, including two
from the Regiment – L/Sgt. Howard Hill and Gunner Joseph
Mikituk.

The YMCA (Curt Embleton and helper) set up their moving
pictures in the barn. We hear that Jerry is planning a counter-
attack in this area on a large scale. Orders are to dig in. Slit
trenches fill with water and don't invite occupation. More rain
and consequent discomfort for the gunners who have no shelter
nor place for drying clothes.

Among the battle casualties are veteran carrier crew members
Gunners P. J. "Pooch" Pelletier and Gordon Henry. Bombardier
Ivan Cook is wounded while laying a signal line to an OP during
the first day of the RHLI attack. And that same day, October 16,
Gunner George Garrity dies of wounds. Two days later, Gunner
James MacFarlane also succumbs to wounds.

The security blanket laid over the sister front southwest of the
Scheldt ensures you will forever carry a confused and foggy picture
of the bitter struggles under appalling conditions of mud and water
in the Breskens pocket, though the rumours of the moment, and
the tales told weeks later over beer-soaked tables in Belgian cafes,
will one day be authenticated in published works.

The initial assault on October 6 had been across the Leopold
Canal by 7th Brigade (Canadian Scottish, Regina Rifles, and the
Royal Winnipeg Rifles), following a barrage of searing flames from
an extended line of twenty-seven Wasps (flame-throwing Bren carriers with big fuel tanks to sustain the roiling blasts).

The crossing had been successful, but it took seven days to gain a
thousand yards. Meanwhile 9th Brigade (The Highland Light
Infantry, the Stormont, Dundas and Glengarry Highlanders, and The
North Nova Scotia Highlanders), to relieve the pressure on 7th Brigade, crossed the Braakman inlet in Buffaloes (amphibious tracked
vehicles able to carry thirty infantrymen) and gained a lodgement
behind the enemy, menacing the strongpoint of Oostburg.

17

THANKSGIVING DINNER
ON GROOTE MEER

✳

A FORWARD OBSERVATION OFFICER'S CREW IS NOW NORMALLY made up of a carrier driver, a signaller, and an ack, who may not be trained in both signals and OP work sufficiently to qualify in the technical sense as an "observation post assistant," since the supply of trained OP acks available for OP work has tended to dry up as the grand tour of the continent continues.

When the Regiment first entered battle, carrier crews were so completely trained that in a pinch anyone could substitute for anyone else with reasonable proficiency. However, from the earliest days of Normandy, demand has tended to put a strain on supply, since all who serve on carrier crews, other than the officers, must be volunteers.

Common sense demands this, for the casualty rate among FOOs and their crews is inclined to be high, not only because FOOs are always attached to the leading rifle companies, which suffer most of the infantry casualties, but because their tracked vehicle is very conspicuous in the attack; and unlike the foot-soldiers with whom it is travelling, it cannot go to ground and remain invisible in drainage ditches or among bushes and rocks – even lying doggo in unharvested grain – until the situation is sorted out. And if an 88 or a mortar fails to get it, it can always blow itself up on a mine, being, more often than not, the first Allied vehicle to traverse roads and fields in the attack or on the line of march.

Thus it would not be fair to fill vacancies in carrier crews with anything but volunteers. While as yet there is no shortage of men ready to serve on OP crews, you suspect that as time goes by it could become a problem. Already it is noticeable that vacancies are being filled more and more by newcomers to the Regiment – those least likely to know the score – leading you to suspect that they are being conned into taking on this "exciting work . . . up where the action is . . . where there's lots of loot and Luger pistols to be had," by troop sergeant-majors desperate to fill out replacement crews.

However, there are some who still look upon attachment to an OP crew as they did during training in England: a privilege reserved for the élite. So when you split up a brother act – sending the younger one (Walkden, B.) back to the guns so two boys from the same family won't be wiped out by a single 88-mm shell or an errant mortar bomb landing in the carrier – the older brother (Walkden, Wm.), your driver, could not have been more disgusted.

Now the morale of a carrier crew is a fragile thing, and his resentment, taking the form of silence – simply not communicating with you or anyone else – has begun to irritate everybody, with the result that all are beginning to act in an irritating fashion towards each other. If he wasn't such a good carrier driver, you'd send him back to the guns too. Of course, he'll get over his resentment in time, but meanwhile something has to be done to raise the morale of the others. Even before this problem arose, spirits had been wilting, as day after day, surrounded by dead and dying men and animals at that smashed farm out in the gloomy polders in the neck of the isthmus, they'd had nothing to look forward to but more of the same.

Then during the move over here to Groote Meer (October 14) their spirits had sunk to a new low when Capt. Len Gage, Major Ryall's second-in-command, was killed by a shell shortly after you left him along the line of march. You had just been walking with him, and unquestionably would have died with him, had not your carrier, bringing up the rear of the company, stalled and refused to start again without a tow from a tank, forcing you to leave the Royals and drive back to the gun position in a nearby field to get a fresh starter-battery. It was on the way back up, racing along the same road to catch up to the Royals, that they'd spotted Len lying dead beside the road, not a hundred yards beyond where you had said goodbye to him.

Though they had had little direct contact with Len during the five days they spent out at the bleak farm in the polders, they had become very conscious of the tall, quiet man holed up behind a table in the tiny cellar, looking up with sad eyes at visitors over a wavering candle and a water-glass never less than half full of rum. At first they'd been inclined to write him off with joking disdain, until you brought them up short – pointing out you met him first at a hellish place called Eterville near Caen, where some men came apart at the seams with nerves permanently shattered . . . that his platoon led the way into Louvigny where 112 fell in the first attack by the Royals in Normandy . . . and God knows what all else he'd lived through since then.

From then on he had ceased to be a curiosity, and their attitude changed first to one of respect, and then to real affection when one day the unsmiling, reserved man split his last precious package of cigarettes with them on learning their canned ration of Goldflakes (to have lasted them for three days) had come out of a Compo box covered with green mould.

His death hit them hard and the collective morale of the whole crew is suffering. Something is needed to take their minds off the lousy war, at least for a few hours. But what? If only you could send them off overnight to some place where they could remove their dirty clothes, have a bath, and sleep in a real bed. Even a civilized meal would help, a change from the eternal Compo – the everlasting sameness of homogeneous M & V stew and glutinous steak-and-kidney pudding. Suddenly it strikes you that this could be the answer: a special meal – one of those hens wandering out there behind the house – a real feast – a Thanksgiving dinner – it must be close to Thanksgiving Day in Canada; as you recall, it was always around this time in October.

The proposal is warmly received, at least by Stevenson and Hiltz.

They too are ignorant as to the date Canadians celebrate Thanks-giving, but recommend that this very day, October 21, be arbitrarily declared Thanksgiving Day so as to get one of those hens into the pot before the infantry get them all. Immediately they volunteer to contribute tasty homemade items for dessert from recent parcels – including some brownies and macaroons. All you can find in your private hoard in your ammunition box are some rather soggy salted peanuts and some greying chocolate-coated after-dinner mints.

Obviously it won't be the greatest Thanksgiving dinner menu of all time, but to the delight and surprise of all, Walkden begins to show an interest, pointing out you can't have a chicken potpie without vegetables, and he spotted vegetables unharvested out behind the shed – some carrots and onions for sure, and maybe some potatoes too. And so, during the day, while you are up at the OP in the tower, they put together a great chicken stew. You swear you can smell it even while you are still on the trail going down at last light, long before you arrive in the circular drive before the house, where you are surprised to find Stevenson and Hiltz waiting in the gathering gloom.

They explain that during the afternoon the same delicious aroma from their bubbling stew, wafting down into the cellar to A Com-pany headquarters, had drawn Major Caldwell and his second-in-command, Capt. Ross Newman, upstairs to investigate. The subsequent drooling and groaning of those cunning gentlemen, as they leaned over the steaming pot, had been so pitiful, they had momentarily succumbed to Christian charity and invited them to return and share it when it was ready. They earnestly hope this is all right with you, for the aforementioned officers are even now back upstairs, waiting in the little room off the living room you have been using as living quarters.

When you hesitate, Stevenson, reading your mind, assures you there is more than enough for everybody, Walkden having rather overdone the quantity of vegetables he'd tossed in the pot with the dismembered hen, which had turned out to be a monster.

Naturally you approve; after all, they'd done all the work. And it turns out to be a truly memorable Thanksgiving dinner, even though those conscienceless foot-sloggers will forever after spread a scurrilous rumour that gunners can live in an atmosphere devoid of oxygen. (Some days later you'll actually overhear Major Caldwell asking one Major Ryall if he is aware that gunners prefer to breathe carbon dioxide, saturated blue with cigarette smoke and thickened with steamy cabbage and onion fumes, in an oxygen-free room sealed off by a mattress over the window and a blanket over a closed hallway door.)

However, they do contribute a nearly full bottle of Johnnie Walker and some real Canadian fruitcake for the table; and if you overlook their periodic melodramatic gasping and coughing spasms, they contribute much to the general conviviality of the evening. After dinner, Hank, an accomplished jazz piano player with a wicked right hand, accompanies you through a series of duets covering much of the music of the Thirties on the piano out in the dark living room near the glassless French windows, sending wild, syncopated cadenzas across the waterless lake, until complaints begin to come in by runners from nearby platoon commanders worried that "your goddam racket" is drawing unnecessary attention to this area.

Deflated, but not defeated, you push the piano into your lighted room, making it even more crowded than during dinner, and enhancing the title it already has been awarded by your uncharitable guests: "The Black Hole of Groote Meer."

The party might well have gone on the whole night, but for a signal from Sunray (the commanding officer) ordering you back up to your tower, to spend the night flash-spotting German guns and mortars presently doing a job on Woensdrecht.

Hiltz seems unnaturally anxious to accompany you, and while there is no more reason for him to go up with you tonight than on previous nights when you went up alone, you don't turn him down, for you really feel the need of company tonight.

18

THE STORY OF A STARRY NIGHT

❋

IT TAKES FIFTEEN MINUTES OR SO TO MAKE IT UP TO THE tower, running the telephone line through your hand as a guide – a spooky trip in the dark, becoming particularly tense about halfway up where you must use some form of animal radar to avoid stepping on the bloated body of the dead German lying directly across the path. Up near the top there is always the chance a nervous infantryman will let fly at you if you wander off the route you are expected to take through the trenches of the platoon position near the tower – a real possibility since you must navigate the last one hundred yards across the spongy floor of a rather open pine forest, without the guidance of the signal wire, it having taken off on a shortcut of its own through a thick tangle of undergrowth.

Slightly fuzzy from all the good spirits you shared tonight, it's comforting to hear Hiltz behind you, whistling softly his favourite tune – the theme from Tchaikovsky's Sixth Symphony – which, according to him, has been popularized back home under the charming title "This Is the Story of a Starry Night." His whistling suggests he had something more in mind than simply keeping you company when he volunteered to come with you. You've noticed his whistling is involuntary; whenever he's engrossed in repairing equipment or mulling over something, he whistles. And always it's that same appealing little melody.

Of course there's no conversation on the way up as you both

concentrate on not tripping and falling into the damp bushes, for while it's a frosty, clear, starlit night in the open, it is very dark in the forest. (Astonishingly once again, in the same mysterious way you have on previous nights, you both avoid stepping on the dead German.) But when finally you climb up the tall tower and settle down to your watch, under a sky filled with stars, Hiltz launches into his subject.

He wants your advice: he's fallen in love with a girl in Antwerp. You will recall he has spoken of her before – the one living with her parents in a penthouse on a tall building on the main street . . . the people with the grand piano he wanted you to meet. Well, that's still his wish. When you both next get leave, will you go with him to meet her and her parents, so you can assess the situation and help him decide what to do? He is so intensely earnest, you assure him you will, even as you wonder what on earth you're getting into.

And from then until the endless vault of star-drenched sky begins to decay with the first light of dawn, he talks of her.

In a hundred ways he describes all the things about her that make her so utterly charming, and how hospitable her nice parents have been, while posing innumerable rhetorical questions clearly indicating how worried he is about the ultimate effect on their relationship of all the apparent wealth and affluence surrounding her. How could he ever hope to support her in the manner to which she is accustomed? Is she not just mesmerized by the romantic circumstances of liberation and his appearance as a gallant liberator from across the seas?

The more he talks, the more impressed you are. While you liked his fresh, open countenance, and his relaxed, good-natured style from the first day he came up to the troop as an ack back at Fleury-sur-Orne in Normandy, you realize you are only getting to know him as he talks away the night. And what impresses most is the depth of his love for the girl, which is causing him to worry more about the risks to her happiness than to his own.

By dawn he's talked out, and you send him down to the house to get breakfast started. Stand-to passes without any problems from

Jerry, but just as you are preparing to climb down, "Hutch" Hutcheon comes thumping up the tower ladders, with the welcome news that he and his crew are relieving you so that you and your crew can go back for a couple of days' rest.

While you are putting him on the ground (pointing out prominent points in the wide panorama of enemy territory and relating them to the map), he undertakes a line of inquiry that makes it plain that he questions the advisability of using this tower as an OP. Why, the bloody thing sticks up like a sore thumb above the bush!

You frankly admit you have never been entirely comfortable up here in the daytime, but so far Jerry has restricted his shelling to the other Company positions around and about and has left the tower strictly alone.

But why on earth has he left it standing?

You can only suggest that the Germans can't believe any sensible person would risk occupying such an obvious OP.

How long do you usually stay up here at a stretch?

You feel a little silly as you explain that in daylight you remain only until you get the creepy feeling that somewhere out there the muzzle of an 88 is swinging around and lining up the tower in its sights. Then you scramble down to the ground as fast as you can.

To Hutch, a natural-born pragmatist, this must sound insane. As you prepare to take your leave, he remarks that since he had no breakfast, he might as well go down and have an early lunch before settling in up here for the afternoon.

Strolling down through the bush, comparing notes on your recent experiences in the polders – in complete agreement that fighting a war below sea level is totally without virtue – you're vaguely conscious of some loud banging up behind you, in the woods you just left. But since shells and mortar bombs are constantly dropping throughout the area, you don't consider it at all significant. However, reaching the foot of the hill, you find Hank Caldwell standing uncharacteristically at the door of the house waiting, and as you draw near, you notice he's staring at you strangely and wagging his head in disbelief.

"Wow – am I glad to see you guys! How the devil did you manage to get down from your tower without anybody seeing you?"

You and Hutch can only exchange quizzical looks.

"You don't know what happened, then?"

Receiving only stares of bewilderment, he proceeds to enlighten you: "I just got a call from my platoon up there – the Krauts shelled the hell out of your tower – cut it to pieces, apparently – left it a shambles! Surely you must have heard it going on when you were on your way down? I thought for sure you'd bought it when they said no one had seen you come down from the tower. I was just on my way to inform your crew when I spotted you walking out of the bush!"

"Jesus," Hutch is murmuring to himself, "if I hadn't decided to come down with you for lunch!"

You look his way, but you are not seeing him. You are remembering all those hours in that tower during the past five days, during which you'd suppressed your imagination, putting out of mind the image of the very thing that has just occurred. You begin to feel dizzy.

Hank notices and says heartily:

"I think a shot of rum all around would be in order just about now – a stirrup cup for the lucky buggers going out for a rest."

For a moment you'd forgotten. You're only too happy to supply the rum. When you go to the carrier to fetch a water-bottle full of it, you see the boys have everything packed and ready to move. And when you go in the house to collect them, you find them in a buoyant mood. Obviously yesterday's Thanksgiving dinner worked wonders. And after a hefty slug of the dark, over-proof issue liquor, all are in splendid spirits as you pull out to go first to the guns near Ossendrecht for rations and mail, and then another three miles to Putte, the first town along the road to Antwerp, straddling the Dutch–Belgium border.

Hiltz is vastly disappointed when you stop in Putte. It seems that from the moment he heard you all were going back for a rest, he nurtured the belief you would be going all the way back to Antwerp. To him the chance was heaven-sent. Regretfully, you have to point out that you have not been given leave, but a short rest behind the lines, subject to instant cancellation without warning. Even coming back as far as Putte might be thought by some to be stretching things.

Putte gives the impression of being a one-street town, albeit a very long one – lined on both sides with stores, cafés, churches, municipal buildings, etc., the southern half Belgian, the northern half Dutch. The first night you hole up on the Dutch side of the border in the municipal office building, which cannot be locked because of shell damage. However, Monday morning a Dutch-man arrives while breakfast is being heated over your Primus stove on what may be his desk, and he makes it quite clear he doesn't care for this invasion of his bureaucratic domain, even by his country's liberators.

That afternoon and evening old friend Len Harvey, just back from hospital after recovering from an encounter with a booby-trapped German body back at Bruges September 12, joins you in a search for new digs. Influenced by his normal cavalier improvidence in such matters, this quickly turns into a search for cognac when he finds the cafés are offering nothing but sweet, insipid beer.

The logical place to locate cognac would seem to be in a liquor store on the main street in the Belgium sector, but the pleasant couple operating the little store explain they have no stock left for sale – that all the bottles on display are fakes. However, if you would care to join them in their living quarters at the rear of the store, they'd be glad to share some of their own personal supply with you. Their living room is exceedingly modest, but this being the first time you've been socially welcomed into any home anywhere on the continent, the sense of returning to civilization is even stronger than it was in the luxury of the Century Hotel in Antwerp.

When it comes time to bed down somewhere, rain is descending in torrents outside. On learning you have no accommodation, they offer a small but completely empty attic room over the kitchen, just big enough to accommodate five prostrate bodies and their kit, including your precious cartridge case containing the contents of the parcel from home you picked up at the gun position yesterday. This linoleum-floored oasis is reached by a steep set of board-ladder stairs, leading up to a trap door.

The trap door has to be left open for ventilation, and as you bed down right next to it, advice is exchanged on why one shouldn't go sleepwalking in the night. The room is lit by one light bulb hanging directly over the trap door, and when this is turned off, the room is as black as the inside of an ink bottle.

At dawn, you're awakened by *slap-slap, scrub-scrub* sounds coming from the kitchen down below; and when you open your eyes, you find yourself looking directly into the eyes of a tiny little girl who has climbed up the stairs to a level just high enough to allow her to peek over the edge at the strange Canadian soldiers snoring in the gloom. Suddenly you identify the sound coming from below as someone mopping the kitchen floor – and immediately you are overwhelmed with a terrible sense of remorse, as you remember what you did last night.

Sometime during the night, your kidneys had produced a desperate urge requiring immediate attention. Very hazy from the generous shots of cognac you'd taken on board earlier, you realize that even with a light, it would be difficult for you to manage that stairwell, and without a light impossible. Standing, teetering dangerously close to the yawning chasm, you stretch out an arm and try to catch hold of the light bulb you know is suspended there. But in vain you paw the inky darkness, while you struggle to keep your balance and resist gross incontinency.

Finally you lose the battle and do the only thing that seems logical to your feeble wits at the time. Now, in the cold, dim light of dawn, as you listen to the sounds of that poor woman down there mopping the floor, and stare into her little girl's big, round eyes that seem to be accusing you, you are paying the price!

You can't confess your crime and apologize. But you can make restitution in secret: you open your ammo case and start lifting out cans of salmon, Spam, corn niblets, candy, chocolate bars, and tobacco, and handing them to the little tyke. She takes them without uttering a peep, but her eyes grow bigger as her arms grow fuller.

At last her little arms can hold no more, and she starts her descent, going down backwards, one step at a time (the only safe way on such steep stairs), excitedly calling out to her mother, at each step, the Belgian equivalent of "Mummy, Mummy, look what I've got!" And the sensation caused by her arrival at the foot of the stairs with her loot does your heart good, and goes a long way towards assuaging your conscience.

Your open-handed gesture pretty well empties your ammo box of all the precious stuff you got in your last parcel, but satisfied you've made restitution without embarrassing yourself, you descend incognito with the others to a breakfast of delicious home-fried potatoes.

But you reckoned without the child. As soon as she spots you, she points you out to her mother, and while you don't understand her words you know very well what she's saying. And the smile the mother beams at you is not so much a smile of gratitude, as a smile of amusement, the smile of a charitable woman who knows perfectly well what prompted one man among these soldiers to be so generous this morning.

As you're leaving and saying goodbye to the family, you see Hiltz remove his beret, complete with brass gun-badge, and give it to the pretty little ten-year-old. Strictly against the rules, but you say nothing, for you remember how much he misses his kid brother back in Halifax.

On the way back up the line, you drop in at A Echelon in the bush south of Hoogerheide for a fresh box of Compo rations.

Just as you and your gang are pulling out to go up to rejoin the infantry as they turn west into South Beveland in the big 2nd Division push going in this morning (October 24), you are waved down by Harvey who has been ordered to take over your carrier and crew. You are to report to the Colonel at Brigade Headquarters. Someone will take you up.

You feel a rush of resentment and more than a little jealousy as you dig your bedroll and kit out of what has been "your" carrier for so long, and pile it into the back of the waiting Jeep. But as you pull away you manage to smile and wave at them, for they must be feeling a little uneasy too. And for a moment they stop stowing away Harvey's kit and smile and wave at you.

When you arrive at Brigade, the news is waiting. They've run over a mine – Hiltz and Stevenson are dead.

19

AN ARTY REP CONTROLS
AWESOME FIRE-POWER

❋

YOU KNOW YOU WILL ALWAYS MOURN THEM; YOU KNOW you will forever carry in your mind a picture of them smiling and waving goodbye a few minutes ago; that their faces will always be among those who "shall not grow old as we who are left grow old." You know that for the rest of your life every time you play that plaintive Tchaikovsky theme, or hear it played, you'll hear Hiltz whistling "This Is the Story of a Starry Night"...

But at this moment your sensibilities are totally unreliable, short-circuited by the all-enveloping grossness of war, and your mourning is shallow and transient as you head for the barn to report in to the Brigadier with mounting apprehension as to what may be expected of you up here at this level of command.

On the way here you hadn't worried, believing you were merely joining the Colonel to assist him in some minor way or other, perhaps providing liaison with the battery commanders at battalion headquarters some distance ahead. However, when his batman was breaking the news to you about your crew (even before you climbed out of the Jeep in the barnyard), he also informed you the Colonel had already left for the headquarters of one of the battalions in the attack, and that you are to cover off for him here at Brigade.

Inside the barn you stop to look around, dumbfounded by the scene that confronts you – totally strange to eyes accustomed to the primitive set-up at battalion tactical headquarters confined almost always to poorly lit basements, cow stables, abandoned German dug-outs, and even open trenches. This brightly lit scene of officers on folding benches, sitting at folding tables on which papers and maps are spread out, with remote-control units and field telephones at their elbows – while behind them others plot coloured dots and arrows on large map-boards standing on easels, electrically lit by little shaded bulbs hanging over them – provides an immediate impression of a well-ordered office.

The only incongruous feature is an oversized caravan-truck that has been backed in on the barn floor and rests just inside the big closed doors. You are received perfunctorily at the back door of this mobile command post by the Brigade Major (handsome, aloof Jim Knox) who assumes you know what you are here for, and merely points out Col. Young's spot at a central folding-table a few feet to the rear of the stubby little steps leading to the back door of the caravan.

Opposite you at the table lounge two British officers, a captain and a major. The captain, a tall, handsome, outgoing type, stands up and offers his hand as he explains they too are "arty reps" – the major representing a medium regiment, and he a regiment of heavy ack-ack guns (3.7-inch) now being used in a ground role.* Each in his own way assures you that on demand they can, as the Captain puts it, "add considerably to the general din when the need arises," and not to hesitate to call on their support.

The major is a reserved, reticent chap, and the amiable captain, a career officer with the regular British Army (1st Brigade Royal Marines you later learn) is obviously happy to have someone to talk

---

* Attached directly to 4th Field Regiment at this time were the heavy ack-ack guns of 1st Brigade Royal Marines and the 118th Heavy Ack-Ack Regiment. Attached to 2nd Division Headquarters were the British 115th Heavy Ack-Ack and two medium regiments, the 84th and the 121st.

to. With vast amusement he speaks of a Scottish Division (52nd Lowland) about to enter battle for the first time in the war – establishing a bridgehead on South Beveland ahead of our troops – fighting below sea level though all its training has been for mountain warfare involving packhorses and special 3.7-inch guns that can be disassembled for easier transport.

Thoughtfully he makes you aware of the fact you also have at your disposal a squadron of Spitfire fighter-bombers and a squadron of Typhoons, which, he explains, you can "whistle up using that signaller sitting over there at that radio set."

Suddenly you realize they are taking for granted that you are assuming the role of coordinator in the planning and use of all this fire-power, since you are substituting for the colonel of a field regiment (normally the senior gunner officer at Brigade) – which means that if the need arises, they will expect you to act as the senior artillery advisor to the Brigadier, rank notwithstanding! Even the thought of playing such a role is subduing. All you can do, if by chance you are called upon to allot all that fire-power to an attack, is try to recall the scale and timing on behalf of other attacks of similar size in which your guns have participated.

But you earnestly hope the Colonel will get back before the need arises. How typical of the man to want to be forward with his battery commanders. He knows things are sticky up there, and maybe he can be of help, bringing into play more of the heavy stuff at his disposal, if he gets a better feel for the battle at a battalion headquarters.

Just as he had appeared out of nowhere beside your carrier under bombardment that first day when the push north from Antwerp was being held up, or the morning he arrived without warning at your OP in the polders at dawn after listening for much of the night to you calling for Mike targets on screaming paratroopers attacking the Royals with flame-throwers, you visualize him now suddenly appearing at the side of one of his battery commanders. Don Cornett would be your guess. He is now short a FOO with Harvey out of action, and Lendrum will be anxious. Of this morning,

October 24, British war correspondent R. W. Thompson will one day write in his book *The 85 Days*:

Frankly one would have thought these Canadians would have had enough; too much ... death had become personal, a daily and nightly lottery in which each man of the forward battalions held a ticket. .... After Woensdrecht the Canadians had become welded together, kindred, a tight community. The truth is they wanted to feel alone – alone with the sustained and terrible experience which they began to clasp to themselves as something personal, and upon which no one had a right to intrude. I marvelled then, and I marvel now, at the spirit of the Canadian 4th Infantry Brigade of 2nd Division as they turned to force their way through the narrow neck of the isthmus. Some craters on the main road were gigantic – huge cavities defeating the bulldozers. One was seventy feet across, measured by an engineer.*

Thin trees had been felled to add to the obstacles. Schumines, Teller mines, mines with names known only to engineers, mines in scores were sown carefully over all that way. Absurd to attempt to account in detail the water-logged progress. In individual minds it lives merely as discomfort, a blurred memory of men's feet blown off in a grey, futuristic landscape, something of Dali's. Waves of 20-mm fire held men tight against dike banks and made others thankful even of the water. Airbursts from 88s worked in with the hideous barrage of mortars with a sound like green seas on iron decks, a drenching sound, horribly threatening.

---

* An electrically wired buried torpedo (according to the Dutch) that blew up the Able Troop carrier, killing Hiltz and Stevenson. The awesome charge blew everything, including the engine, out of the steel box of the carrier that landed beyond the next dike. Miraculously, Capt. Harvey and Walkden, saved by a bulkhead, escaped with minor cuts and bruises.

20

ROUGH TREATMENT
FOR A TOUGH BROAD

✳

WHATEVER ROLE THE COLONEL HAS IN MIND FOR YOU WHEN he gets back – liaison with Div or whatever – it would seem imperative that you gain some kind of overall picture of what's going on. You study the big "I" map, and ask questions of your gunner confederates. They are, you find, surprisingly well-informed, and if somewhat fuzzy as to what precisely is occurring at the moment, they at least can construct a very detailed picture of what is supposed to be happening, both on the Brigade front and elsewhere – something entirely new to your experience. Of course, on reflection the extent of their knowledge is understandable, this being one of the principal nerve centres for the conduct of the battle, and they having little else to do but follow what's going on.

You learn the final clearing of the area immediately north of Woensdrecht was completed yesterday, October 23, by the Calgary Highlanders and the Queen's Own Cameron Highlanders of Canada, supported by a great fire-plan, including two barrages. Resistance undoubtedly was weakened by the drive by 4th Armoured Division that began two days ago as a right hook from the southeast eight miles north of Woensdrecht to the next sizeable town with the intriguing name of Bergen-op-Zoom. Here in South Beveland the plan calls for the Royal Regiment to open the attack into the isthmus, overcome the forward line of defence, reconnoitre in force the one major road and a minor road south of the narrowest part of the isthmus, and seize this area as a base for further exploitation. The Royals started out shortly after midnight to ensure their startline is secure in a partially inundated salt marsh, bounded on the left by a dike and on the right by the main dike road. Both flanking dikes are separated from the marsh by ten-foot-wide drainage ditches. The enemy are dug-in the full length of both these east–west dikes, and where they meet a lateral dike that is the objective of the Royals, the Germans have built strongholds of bricked-in trench-works and concrete emplacements for anti-tank guns and machine-gun nests covering both the dikes leading up to the junctions and the surrounding marsh.

Covered approaches being non-existent, and any manoeuvring impossible because of deep drainage ditches criss-crossing the marsh, the attack is made by two companies of Royals moving up the two dikes behind a creeping barrage, with the northern flank covered by timed concentrations, and the heavy mortars of the Tor Scots bombarding the objective to shut down fire from there.

The guns had opened up at 4:00 A.M. and the soldiers following close behind had to almost feel their way forward in the flashing, roaring, confusing darkness, as they bumped into successive German posts along the dike and subdued them in what the Royals' historian would describe as "bitter hand-to-hand fighting."

By now (7:00 A.M.) all companies are on their objectives. There is a report that the Germans are shelling themselves, until it becomes known that the shells are being laid on them by the mediums and the heavies of 9th British AGRA firing from across the Scheldt.

Still, Germans do die from their own fire. Capt. Bob Suckling of D Company will not soon forget the grim business of witnessing the death of fifteen German prisoners collected from posts overrun by D Company moving along a dike. Told to lie down behind the twelve-foot-high embankment until they could be evacuated, they were all killed by one of the first salvoes of German mortars landing right on them.

The original plan called for exploitation of the Royals' success by two mixed columns of armour from 10th Armoured Regiment and the 8th Recce Regiment, with the Essex Scottish riding with them in Kangaroos as back in Normandy the night of the break-through at Verrières Ridge.

However, Brig. F. N. Cabeldu, on being informed by the Royals that the secondary road along the southern part of the isthmus was impassable due to cratering, mines, and mud, decided the second phase of the attack should be launched along the railway embankment nearer the northern rim of the isthmus.

And so the Essex Scottish and their armoured escort are ordered forward at 10:00 A.M.

The columns are to debouch through gaps bulldozed in the first dike and rumble up onto the main highway up the isthmus.

Privately you question the ability of tanks and armoured cars to operate anywhere out there. Many polders are flooded deeply and the others, criss-crossed by swollen drainage ditches, are too soggy to sustain heavy vehicles. Thus restricted to moving along roads on the tops of dikes, silhouetted against the sky, tanks and recce cars must be picked off like sitting ducks. And it comes as no surprise when the Essex Scottish attack bogs down shortly after take-off.

Before noon a signal comes in from Major Carr at Essex Scottish Tac Headquarters, somewhere near the leading edge of their attack on "Mary," the code name for a line running through a junction of dikes in the isthmus: "Fetch Sunray to the blower."

Properly interpreted by the signaller on the set, this means: "Bring the Commanding Officer to the radio and turn over the earphones and mike to him." So when you go on the air, Carr is taken aback. For a moment he hesitates, but only a moment, for the imperative demands of the battle in which the Essex are involved allow him no time to fritter away in merely satisfying curiosity. From the growling tension in his voice, it is obvious the Essex have suffered a bloody nose in their attack on the junction of dikes with that sweet and gentle code name "Mary." And this is underlined by the facetious style he uses in reporting: "Our Mary is turning out to be a very tough broad."

He needs a fire-plan – a heavy concentration of short duration directly on Mary in support of a renewed attack by the Essex. He asks for a stonk along the dike by the guns for at least ten minutes before H-hour, thickened up by whatever heavier stuff is available at the time, including help from "our fine-feathered friends." He assures you that for the bombing the Essex will be pulled back four hundred yards.

Somehow you manage to carry on in a manner you hope will appear to him and the others watching you as confident and self-possessed, while feeling entirely otherwise. As you assure him "Roger Wilco, Out" (message understood – will carry out orders – ceasing transmission), and turn from the radio, you are momentarily afflicted with a brain-numbing case of nerves. Never, in your wildest dreams, did you imagine being thrust into a situation like this. Realizing the eyes of your colleagues are on you, you fight down a rising sense of inadequacy and carry on as though you know exactly what you are doing. A battalion attack is being mounted, the success of which will depend largely on the effectiveness of your fire-plan. Many of the Essex will die if your plan is inadequate.

Though conscious of the current need to conserve ammunition which has to be trucked so far, you decide to use everything available to you. You will send in the Spits with 500-pound bombs for the intersection of the dikes thirty minutes before H-hour (which is 1330), and Typhoons at H minus-15 to rocket-bomb whatever they can see by way of trench-works or guns along the dikes on the flanks. The medium guns will lay a stonk along the dike at the objective, firing at their normal rate from H minus-10 to H-hour; the heavy ack-ack will airburst over the target area for the same period; and 4th Field will fire a stonk on the objective, using the intense rate of fire from H minus-5 to H plus-5; at which time they will move their fire to a point four hundred yards farther west along the same dike from H plus-10 to H plus-15.

When you are ready, you call your artillery colleagues together for an "O" group. They listen intently to your every word and scribble notes. Watches are synchronized. Then they go quickly about translating your orders into their own lingo and transmitting them back to their guns. Meanwhile you lay on the aircraft support and give 4th Field guns their part in the show. Finally you go on the air to tell Carr the fire-plan is ready to go and that he can expect the air support to begin at a time you transmit in code.

And that, seemingly, is all there is to it. Your job is done. Now others are responsible for seeing that the many tons of high explosive you ordered are moved and shifted and dumped on the enemy in and around the objective at the times you have ordered. How astonishingly easy it all is when you don't have to do any of the dirty, heavy work, or the critically accurate technical computations to get the job done, while responding to endless other problems connected with "man-management."

And still you feel pleased with yourself, as though you actually have done something worthwhile. Is this the way generals and high-ranking staff officers feel? Is this what men find fascinating in the conduct of war? You find yourself recalling an article in a London paper by American columnist Dorothy Thompson last winter, describing similar notions as she watched wooden blocks, representing squadrons of planes, being moved about like pawns on a giant chessboard at tactical headquarters of RAF Fighter Command during an air raid on Britain.

The fire-plan goes ahead without a hitch and Carr is able to report "Attack successful – Mary taken." But later, when you have the chance to get a first-hand account of the effectiveness of your fire-plan, you will learn that the attack was not as neat and tidy as Carr's terse report of the moment suggested. According to Ted Adams, the FOO with the leading company in the attack, it was "a very sticky go." And to illustrate, he tells the story of an infantry subaltern who collapsed in a dead faint when he learned he would have to lead his platoon through a gap in a dike covered by a German machine-gun, clearly perceiving he had been condemned to die: "When he came to, he alerted his platoon and they took off. He was the first man around the end of the dike. As he anticipated he was met by a burst of Spandau fire. He died instantly with a bullet in his forehead."

Concentrated neutralizing fire by the guns always helps, and in cases like "Mary" is essential, but if any objective is ever to be taken, the enemy must ultimately be subdued by the P.B.I. (the poor bloody infantry) who always pay the worst "butcher bills."

You learn that real progress has been made over on the 3rd Division front across the Scheldt. Breskens fell a couple of days ago (October 22) to the Stormont, Dundas and Glengarry Highlanders breaking out of the right flank of 9th Brigade's bridgehead across the Braakman inlet. After many days and nights of stiff fighting with German troops anxious to prove their loyalty to their Fuhrer's orders to fight to the death and save their families from retaliation back in Germany — first, just to stay ashore, when in one day they fought off (with the aid of 4th Division guns) six furious counter-attacks, and then during the taking and holding of the town of Hoofdplaat beyond the range of the guns — "the Glens" were able to take the highly fortified town of Breskens with comparable ease. Conducting a daring attack along a seawall, using buoyant kapok equipment to get over a twelve-foot-deep and twenty-foot-wide anti-tank ditch filled with water (something the enemy didn't think possible) they took the garrison by surprise and 150 surrendered.*

---

* The CO of the Glens, Lt.-Col. Roger Rowley, was subsequently awarded a bar to his DSO for his "brilliance," "courage," and "speed" in mounting the attack.

21

WORDS WILL NEVER DO
THE INFANTRY JUSTICE

❋

NEVER DRY, ALWAYS COVERED WITH MUD, NEVER STANDING completely upright, always hunched over well below the crest of the dike he is following, never able to relax in the dread of mortar and machine-gun fire that can arrive with little or no warning as he moves crablike along its sloping side, forcing him to throw himself against the steep incline, pressing his body into the spongy wet turf as tightly as he can until they stop, or until they stop him – perhaps forever . . .

That is how the FOOs and their signallers, weighed down by heavy 18-sets on their backs, will remember the infantry with whom they move day after day across the flat, sodden country, attacking still another junction of dikes to gain domination of another polder, as indistinguishable from the last polder as it is from the next – another and another and another – polders and dikes seemingly without end.

Words will never do justice to the courage of the infantryman – eternally cold, eternally wet, eternally bone-weary – who at any instant may be blown apart by a mortar or cut down by machine-gun fire even as he waits at the rear of the battalion stretched out along the dike – waits to take his turn in what he knows will be a lottery of death when his section takes over the lead for the platoon crawling up along the dike or wading through a flooded polder churned by mortar bombs and rippled with machine-gun bullets.

While tanks and armoured cars can briefly lace strongpoints with intimidating fire from afar, they are next to useless in taking ground in polder country. And while artillery FOOs can bring down prompt and accurate concentrations of shells on suspected mortar positions and on a section of dike from which tracers are originating, cooling down enemy fire and occasionally snuffing it out, the ground must be taken by flesh-and-blood men with haggard faces and mud-encrusted hands, doing their best to keep their weapons clean and functioning while they themselves grow filthier and more exhausted with each passing hour. And it is only by extraordinary and continuing acts of courage by ordinary soldiers of the rifle companies and their leaders – the subalterns, the sergeants, and the corporals – that any forward movement is possible.

At the outset, passing through the slender neck of the isthmus barely fifteen hundred yards wide, only one battalion at a time can be utilized, and it must leap-frog its companies, and companies leap-frog their platoons, edging their way up a single road.

And even beyond the neck, where South Beveland widens to four or more kilometres for the next ten miles to a major water barrier, a wide ship canal, only two battalions can be used at a time, following two dike routes roughly pointing up the axis of advance.

At the outset you despair that the peninsula can be taken in less than a month, and then only at terrible cost. From the beginning of the fighting out here among the polders almost three weeks ago, it seemed transparently obvious that in this flat land, ribbed with high dikes, the defenders holding the dikes with unobstructed fields of fire have almost insurmountable advantage over the attackers.

However, what quickly becomes evident, that was not evident during those first battles for the most heavily defended strongpoints in all the polders west of Woensdrecht, are the serious drawbacks to defensive positions located on well-defined, narrow dikes, particularly at well-defined junctions of two dikes. Every artillery rep, from the FOOs with forward companies, back through the majors at battalion headquarters to the colonels at brigades and the Brigadier CRA at Division, knows exactly where the enemy will be dug-in and where the neutralizing fire should be concentrated before any attack, in contrast to trying to pin down enemy positions in other terrain confused by hills, woodlands, gullies, orchards, tree-enshrouded farms and villages, where the Germans can be remarkably cunning at disguising their positions and holding their fire until it can be most effective in halting an attack.

Here, apart from the odd farmhouse, defenders must dig in on the dikes, for holes dug down in polders simply fill with water. Of course dike junctions – providing fields of fire up the roads in all directions and across the polders – inevitably are infested with machine-guns, and frequently anti-tank and ack-ack guns, making them prime targets for fire-plans designed to shoot the infantry onto their objective. And on top of this, contesting only dike positions seriously inhibits the flexibility of the German defensive tactics. Ordinarily their drill is to pull back from the opening artillery concentrations, allowing the attackers to get on their objective before counter-attacking to drive the intruders back in disorder. However, this initial pulling-back won't work when the only cover to which they can retire is the next dike several hundred yards to their rear.

The result is six hundred prisoners are taken by 4th Brigade in its three-day assault up the peninsula, before they turn over responsibility to 6th Brigade for finding a way over the Beveland canal twenty kilometres west of Woensdrecht and halfway to the causeway to Walcheren Island.

The next day, October 26, the guns of 4th Field finally move from their Ossendrecht positions out into South Beveland peninsula, and move again within hours to keep within range of the front which, according to 4th Field's war diary, appears to crack wide open.

Bombardier Hossack's personal log sets down his impressions of the miserable battlefields of Hoogerheide, Woensdrecht, and the polders – most particularly the infamous junction of dikes and railroad for which so many died in vain on Black Friday the 13th – as the guns roll out into South Beveland isthmus to deploy in the very polder where the Black Watch soldiers were cut down in front of your old OP at Pijnen farm:

Nearly all buildings show signs of the ravages of war as we advance to open fields near Woensdrecht. This is our first position on South Beveland peninsula and the battle against rain, mud, water, and the Germans is only beginning. There is no point digging trenches here – no sooner started than water rises in them.

A few hours here and we move on without firing a shot. We've lost interest in days and dates as we advance in bad weather over soggy terrain. . . . Numerous dead Jerries are sprawled over roadways and dikes – mute evidence of fierce fighting. All the fields are pock-marked with water-filled shell holes, and the litter of a battlefield is everywhere – mess tins, rifles, machine-guns, tin hats, greatcoats, boots, rations, etc., etc., spilled all over the place in disorder. Railway tracks running atop a dike are broken and curled up in the air [from the bombs dropped by the Spitfires on the red smoke canisters with which your guns marked that target]. Well-sighted enemy SP and anti-tank guns have knocked out all too many of our Recce cars, tanks, and carriers.

Rilland on our left is the target for many enemy shells. We do considerable firing ourselves.

Dutch youth sell crates of apples for ten Belgian francs or a few cigarettes – very good apples too. The rain continues steadily, and those of us who are not housed in the one large barn are soon drenched.

Hunt's diary will note that mines have become a greater hazard than usual and expresses gratitude for the thoughtfulness of Dutch civilians marking German mines embedded in the roads of a dark town:

At night, when all good folk are abed save those whom providence has condemned to duty, minimum recce parties are called

for 2300 hours. A considerable cavalcade, with the CRA [Briga-
dier R. H. Keefler] leading, sets off into the darkness. We pass
through a deserted town whose noble burgers had marked mine
emplacements with chairs and other pieces of furniture. That
this was a worthwhile precaution we realize later when an RHQ
vehicle strikes a mine (unmarked) and is wrecked with casualties.

Of this same night (October 26), the regimental war diary notes:
"Many vehicle casualties. RHQ [on arrival at new position] finds the
advance party has five German prisoners locked in the cellar."

At 4th Brigade HQ there is real relief that 6th Brigade is now
passing through (the FMRs on the left, heading for Hansweert, and
the Queen's Own Cameron Highlanders of Canada moving
through Yerkse), closing on the wide Beveland ship-canal cutting
across the peninsula. To head off a repeat of the bloody struggle that
ensued for so many days at the mouth of South Beveland, Army
Commander Simonds has arranged for the Germans holding the
canal to be outflanked by the British 52nd Lowland Division,
coming across the Scheldt estuary and landing beyond the canal in
waves of amphibious vehicles. This is another first for Simonds,
though the amphibious tracked vehicles (Buffaloes), amphibious
wheeled vehicles (DUWKs), and amphibious tanks (DDs) are all the
product of the fertile mind of British genius General Sir Percy
Hobart, who equipped 79th Division with its "funnies." Your
British friends tell you that many of the platoon commanders of
52nd Division are Canadians.*

---

* Known as "Canloan Officers," 673 (mostly lieutenants) volunteered in
1944-45 to serve with British units, who were short of trained subalterns.
All British divisions, and most battalions, had Canadian subalterns serving
in them throughout the campaign. Seventy-six per cent of them were
wounded or killed.

22

THE FIRST AMPHIBIOUS
ARMADA IN HISTORY

✳

THE TEN-KILOMETRE SHIP CANAL, RUNNING NORTH AND south across the start of the main bulging body of South Beveland, joining the Ooster Scheldt with the Wester Scheldt, is twenty-one feet deep and sixty-four yards from bank to bank at its narrowest point. With banks rising five feet above the water, and twenty-foot-wide drainage ditches flanking it, it constitutes a formidable obstacle to assaulting forces.

The map shows locks with roads at each end of the canal. A road and railway pass over it a mile and a half from its south end. At the north end the main road from Yerseke to Goes passes over a bridge a mile and a half from the canal mouth. Of course all crossing points are covered by enemy guns and all bridges are blown as soon as the first Canadians approach the canal. Troops must resort to assault boats.

To aid the Canadian crossing, by outflanking and menacing the German rear, at 4:45 A.M. October 26, about the time the Canadians are making their canal move, two brigades of the British 52nd (Lowland) Division (156th and 157th in two waves) carry out a seaborne operation the like of which has never been seen before.

Using an unprecedented number of amphibious tracked and wheeled vehicles – Buffaloes, Alligators, and Weasels – they cross the Scheldt Estuary from Terneuzen to points ten kilometres beyond the canal, with all their equipment, including a small bulldozer to pull vehicles through weeds and the silt and mud up to two feet deep over the sand at marshy landing places. More than 175 amphibious craft of limited seaworthiness manage to wallow through nine miles of choppy black water and deliver the first wave – the 6th Cameronians and the Royal Scots Fusiliers – reasonably intact on objectives, guided only by tracers from ack-ack guns sailing overhead through the blackness towards the jagged flashes on the distant shore, where thunderous shells, weighing 200, 240, and 360 pounds, end their moaning flight across the estuary from the heavy and superheavy guns of 9th AGRA, deployed in the Breskens pocket for the ultimate assault on Walcheren Island.

Only four DD (Duplex Drive) Tanks (British-converted Shermans made buoyant by a huge collapsible bucket of canvas affixed to and enclosing its body, turret, and gun), propelled through the water by two screws, which swivel to provide steering, manage to make it ashore. But firm lodgements are secured by infantrymen clawing their way through the water, weeds, and mud onto the solid land beyond the marshes along the southeast corner of Beveland's bulging body. Despite mines and bombardment of landing areas by guns and mortars, which grows more severe as Jerry reacts to what is happening on his right rear, the bridgeheads build up rapidly and are joined and expanded by following waves of men and supplies.*

Despite this, the Germans defending the canal against the Canadian assaults, unaware of the extent of the landings far to their right rear, continue to defend the crossings with vigour, and when patrols of 6th Brigade try to use the lock gates to gain the far bank, they are driven back by intense fire. However, by midnight October 26–27, the South Saskatchewan Regiment has established

---

* Night and day for three days the Buffaloes (each capable of carrying thirty men), Weasels, and the rest of the strange flotilla churned back and forth, bringing more than seven hundred loads of men and supplies to the beaches.

a bridgehead, near the remnants of the road bridge blown by the Germans, sufficiently firm that in the afternoon of October 28 the Engineers are able to put a bridge in place to allow the vehicles of 4th Brigade HQ to pass over.

As soon as the SSRs are firmly established, 4th Brigade, led by the Rileys, return to action, paddling across in assault boats and pushing west against light opposition towards Gravenpolder five miles away. It is now obvious that things have been made easier by the Scots expanding their bridgehead beyond Oudelande. When the Royals cross that afternoon to take over the westward thrust, they meet little opposition until Gravenpolder. There Jerry decides to make a stand, and Major Tim Beatty's D Company, not strong enough to drive them out, watches from a nearby farm as the unfortunate village is subjected to an awesome bombardment by those 9th AGRA guns from over the Scheldt.

The Royals take twenty-two prisoners on the 28th, along with four 75-mm howitzers, a number of heavy mortars, fourteen horses, and seventeen wagons loaded with ammunition. Most of this loot is captured by Beatty's D Company when they ambush two enemy reinforcement columns. After the first ambush, Beatty sends the horses and prisoners back to Battalion, but the second time he is told "Just send the men back – keep the horses and wagons." At this they turn the horses loose, and tip the wagons over and spill the ammunition into the water beside the road.

A 3rd Division liaison officer arriving at 4th Brigade makes it clear the fighting in the Breskens pocket is at least as bad, with water and mud forcing attacks along the dikes to be undertaken by single, "leap-frogging" companies. Before he left, a Chaudière company was wiped out on the way to Oostburg, and another was saved only by a company commander getting 13th Field FOO Capt. Jimmy Else (formerly of 4th Field) to plaster the enemy over-running his newly taken concrete trenchworks, the startline for the Queen's Own Rifles to take the town.*

---

* The company commander, Major Michel Gauvin, was awarded a DSO.

23

DRESS STANDARDS LAX, BUT REALLY, OLD BOY!

✳

FROM THE CANAL ONWARDS, FOR FOUR KILOMETRES, GRID lines are marked as objectives for leap-frogging battalions and assigned the names of literary giants, starting with Shakespeare at the canal and going on to Dryden, Browning, Chaucer, and Kipling. Somewhere just beyond Kipling in the direction of Gravenpolder contact is made with British 52nd Division. Capt. Tom Wilcox of the Royals' Carrier Platoon, on standing patrol on the left flank, comes across a Scottish lieutenant-colonel carrying a shepherd's crook in place of a swagger stick, so perfectly turned out in all respects that the bedraggled, mud-spattered Canadian will remember him forever as "the finest soldier I have ever seen in my life." Wilcox is so impressed and voluble on the subject, his description – involving a comparison with his own shoddy appearance that would fit most any Canadian officer in a forward position these days – will one day find its way into the official history of the Royals:

> He had a small pack neatly adjusted on his back. (I had absolutely no idea where mine was and couldn't care less.) His gas-cape was neatly rolled above the pack. (I'd last seen mine about Eterville, last July.) He had his pistol in a neatly blancoed web holster. (I had mine in my hip pocket.) He had a neatly kept map case. (I had mine in my breast pocket.) His boots were nicely polished. (I was wearing turned-down rubber boots.) . . . He asked if I

could direct him to Battalion Headquarters. I did better than that. I escorted him there. I was taking no chances of losing such a beautiful specimen of a soldier to the German Army.*

While standards of dress take a low priority with Canadians along the Scheldt, there are limits, and you realize you have gone a bit beyond the generous limits allowed around 4th Brigade Headquarters when you begin to notice the startled looks on faces as you pass by in your German parka — not mottled with the normal green, grey, and black camouflage, but striped with orange, yellow, and black configurations resembling an ostentatious tiger.

Selected as a curiosity by your carrier crew when they grabbed several from the great mountain of grey, green, and black parkas as they passed through Merxem several days ago, it was the only one left unclaimed in the carrier when suddenly it turned cold and you felt the need of warmer clothing.

You are normally unconcerned about your appearance, but your weird parka, obviously designed for a sniper lurking amidst the colourful foliage of fall, induces a self-consciousness which is unendurable, and you resolve to get rid of it as soon as you can get your hands on a replacement. Fortunately, before you get around to tossing the damned thing in an ashcan, you make the acquaintance of an American flyer and, amazingly, the jacket provides the key to the acquisition of a garment that allows you to dress in style. This comes about when 4th Brigade Headquarters' trucks are pulling into a barnyard, and a young fellow, dressed in ill-fitting farmer's garb, calls out to you: "Hi, Bud, got a deck of cigarettes to spare?"

On questioning by the Brigade Intelligence Officer, he reveals his glider-towing plane was shot down six weeks earlier on its way back from up near the Rhine (Groesbeek) where they had towed gliders and dropped parachutists to secure the bridges at Grave,

---

* Major D. J. Goodspeed, *Battle Royal* (Toronto: Royal Regiment of Canada Association, 1962), p. 509.

Nijmegen, and Arnhem. To prove his story, he digs up from the garden behind the farmhouse a box containing his papers and his flyer's uniform, including a fur-collared, olive-green, nylon flying jacket, lined with silky brush wool, which is glistening new, having been issued to him just before he took off on his last flight.

Desperately hiding all signs of envy, you obliquely plant the idea of a possible trade for the priceless garment you are wearing, "an authentic German sniper's parka from the Russian front."

To your astonishment, he responds with enthusiasm. He reveals he is entitled to a complete new kit and a month's leave back in the States for managing to escape from enemy-held territory after being shot down, and would be delighted to return home with such an unusual war souvenir. In a twinkling you change from being unquestionably the weirdest dressed, if not the worst dressed, officer in Canadian Army, to one of the best.

And of profoundly greater importance, it is the most comfortable cold-weather garment you have ever donned in your life. So light in weight you wouldn't know you had anything on, when its zephyr-smooth zipper is run up from its snug, knitted-wool bellyband to its soft furry neck, the wondrous garment is so roomy, warm, and comfortable (the designer even thought to place eyelets in the armpits for ventilation) you believe you could, if necessary, sleep in it without further cover.

The depth of ignorance in which fighting troops are kept as to what is going on on their flanks strikes you with particular force when provided with news on Operation "Suitcase," which, until now, had not been mentioned at 4th Brigade, although the security of 2nd Division's rear is totally dependent on it. It involves 4th Division's driving north to take Bergen-op-Zoom (October 27), and the Polish Armoured Division advancing to Breda (October 28) before pushing on, with the 49th British Division on their right and the American 104th Division (now under Simonds's command) on their extreme right, to clear the lowlands to the mouth of the Maas river at Moerdijk.

24

LIKE THIRTEEN FOOTBALL
FIELDS LAID END TO END

❊

FOR A DAY AND A HALF, VILLAGES OF CENTRAL SOUTH BEVE-
land, with names like Nisse, Heinkenszand, and Veldzicht, fall one
after the other, the enemy offering only relatively light resistance
when they do choose to make a stand at a crossroads or a village
against 4th or 5th Brigade, pushing on towards the mouth of the
great causeway stretching almost three-quarters of a mile across the
sea to Walcheren Island.

Moving on parallel but separate axes, each brigade of 2nd
Division is driven by the need to be first to the causeway and thus
to escape having to take part in the assault across that pitiless plateau
of embanked rock and earth, which rises more than twenty feet
above the high-water mark, some 1,300 yards long and 45 yards
wide, like thirteen football fields laid end to end.

Now there is about Brig. Cabeldu and his Brigade Major a disquieting aura of anxiety and concern when they deign to consult
you as to the whereabouts of Col. MacGregor Young, who seems
to have disappeared (by design you suspect) among the battalions
churning their way forward. Before the Brigadier returns to his
caravan, he asks you to let your Colonel know he wishes to see him
as soon as possible. The Brigade Major explains the Brigadier is
uneasy at being out of touch with Col. Young at this time. It seems
the Acting Division Commander (Brig. R. H. Keefler) has made it
clear that the brigade that seizes the fortified positions at the near

end of the causeway will not have to participate in the assault across it, and Brig. Cabeldu is determined 4th Brigade will be the reserve brigade this time.

Although by now all the sodden, mud-encrusted troops of 2nd Division are nearing exhaustion from almost continuous forward movement with little sleep, under constant strain of knowing sudden death or frightful dismemberment is always just a step away from the next basin of mortars dumped along the road, or the next burst of Schmeisser fire from that farmhouse up ahead, 4th Brigade units plod on, and by the afternoon of October 30, the Royals are less than three kilometres from the causeway.

Here, however, real resistance is encountered, and when 8th Recce armoured cars and an Essex Scottish patrol cautiously feel their way forward, they are driven back by heavy fire from field guns and machine-guns set up in pillboxes, weapon pits, and emplacements, arranged in a semi-circle behind rolls of barbed wire, trip wires, and a minefield.

Thus the Royals are committed to a full battalion attack supported by a heavy fire-plan involving the guns of 4th and 5th Field, and all available mediums and heavy ack-ack, as well as the 4.2-inch mortars and medium machine-guns of the Toronto Scottish Regiment.

While the target area of the objective itself is relatively small, the timed artillery concentrations are designed to not only neutralize known forward enemy positions and prevent them from being reinforced by way of the causeway, but discourage, as far as possible, fire from their reserve positions on Walcheren Island, which, according to Dutch Resistance people, are concrete shelters and emplacements recently sunk along that far shore to which an estimated two thousand Germans have retired.

The fire-plan is designed in complete detail by the Colonel, still up with the infantry at Royals' tac headquarters. All that is required of you is to acquaint yourself and your two British arty reps with the plan; see that Brig. Cabeldu gets one of the two copies delivered to you by Don R; and get off the other by Don R to the

Brigadier CRA at Div Headquarters where the whole business can be coordinated, including alerting Army Service Corps to ensure ammunition needs are met at all gun positions well before H-hour, set for 2:00 A.M. October 31.

Lendrum's plan is for A Company, now commanded by Capt. Jack Stothers, to push north along the sea dike, while Major Tim Beatty's B Company pushes west along the dikes of the north shore towards the entrenched positions. The remaining two companies are to keep the enemy preoccupied meeting their pressure from the front.

One day Stothers will tell you it worked only because he was able to persuade Lendrum to allow him to attack along the muddy shoreline beyond the sea-dike, in behind the enemy trench-works, pillboxes, and gun emplacements, for, while they still had to contend with barbed wire, mines, and booby traps, they had the advantage of surprise when they hit the Germans from the rear. One strongpoint required the action of a flame-thrower, but before 3:00 A.M. Stothers's A Company, reinforced by platoons from C Company, reached the mouth of the causeway, and by dawn, with B and D companies closed in from the east, the Royals dominate it.*

Your only problem throughout the night has been your inability to respond to a demand from Brig. Cabeldu, passed on frequently and with increasing impatience by his Brigade Major, to produce your commanding officer. Throughout the length of South Beveland the Brigadier seemed perfectly content not to have his senior artillery adviser at his side, but from the moment his fire-plan for the Royals' attack arrived, the whereabouts of his trusted "Mac" seems to have become a matter of prime importance, and he is threatening to lose patience, if you can judge by the deepening frown of the Brigade Major each time he comes out the back

---

* Major John Stothers, Lieut. Morris Berry, and Lieut. A. C. Gillespie were awarded Military Crosses for "conspicuous gallantry and leadership."

door of the command vehicle to inquire if you have had any luck, and all you can tell him is what you've told him before: that Major Cornett says the Colonel is on his way back and should have been here long ago.

With each passing minute, you start worrying more. Something must have happened to this good and courageous man who need never have gone forward of this headquarters, but did so because he was concerned with the unusual need of gun support for the battalions of the brigade attempting to get to the causeway first so as not to have to attack across the damned thing. And if nothing serious has happened to him, then won't he be in trouble for not being around when the Brigade Commander needed him? When finally the Colonel's batman appears and whispers in your ear that Col. Young is back, the relief is great. But it is only temporary, and you become even more concerned when he whispers: "But he's flaked out on his cot in the HUP . . . a bit the worse for wear . . . had one over the eight, I think, sir. He already had his boots off and was flopping down on his cot when he got your message that the Brigadier wanted to see him. He just laughed, and curled up in a blanket and started to snore."

As you go rushing out to the HUP parked in the gloom of the barnyard, temporarily blind and stumbling from having just left the relatively bright light in the barn, you wonder how much force a captain can use in persuading his Colonel to wake up, get on his boots, and make his way to the Brigadier's command vehicle? Inside the HUP, you can see nothing until the batman produces a lamp-electric. In its dull glow you shake the Colonel. Surprisingly he comes awake without too much shaking, but on hearing your plea to get up and accompany you to the Brigadier, he tells you in a slow drawl: "Go away . . . tell the Brigadier, the war is over . . . the Royals have the mouth of the causeway . . . Tell him to go to bed . . . there's nothing more for him to do." And this he repeats, without losing his temper, each time you plead with him just to come with you.

Finally, more in exasperation at your stubbornness than compliance, he allows you to pull him to a sitting position on the side of the cot and push his feet into his boots. As you are lacing them up you ask why it took him so long to get back to Brigade. He tells you he got lost. Then, chuckling, he explains that after suffering the greatest fright of his life, he stopped in at the Rileys for a smash or two with Jack Drewry to settle his nerves. It seems that when he realized he was lost on a dark road in no-man's-land, and was turning around, he managed to get the bumper of his Jeep hooked into some fence-wire at the side of the road, and when he reversed the vehicle, up in front of him rose a German, first the unmistakable helmet, then the whole man, no more than six feet from his face. Dead of course. But in the brief moment it took to recognize this, it was an awesome experience.

On the way to the barn on your arm, he doesn't stagger, but when you leave him on his own to mount the few steps to the door of the caravan, he stumbles and plunges dramatically through the door. Your British friends purse their lips and wag their heads significantly as you return to the table. But soon a storm of laughter shakes the whole caravan. You suspect "Mac" has just reached the part of his story where the German cadaver rose up in front of his Jeep. Almost immediately the caravan door opens, and Brigadier and Colonel descend arm in arm, followed closely by a smiling Brigade Major. And all are laughing at something the Colonel is saying, as they disappear out the back door, clearly on their way to raising some toasts to the Brigade's success.

The war, which a moment ago seemed to be of such desperate importance, goes into a state of suspension, at least here at 4th Brigade. Telephones, which were ringing and buzzing urgently, go silent. Radios, though continuing to hiss and blabber, produce no messages for the sigs to rush to the caravan door. When a clerk goes about switching off the lights on the map-boards to save batteries, the friendlier of the two British officers suggests you and he might also relax a bit. He has a crock in his kit out in the cow stable, and if you can get that pesky acetylene lamp of yours working to provide light, there are a couple of feed barrels for chairs and a table of sorts at one end . . .

So when at 4:00 A.M., October 31, 4th and 6th Field are ordered to pull out of action and drive back through Antwerp to what had been the Breskens pocket, to join the mass of guns assembling to support two seaborne attacks on Walcheren Island scheduled for 0445 next day, November 1, the Colonel and you proceed "independently" after the Colonel manages a few hours' sleep.

This day, with a bridgehead over a north–south canal at Retrachment, on the western Dutch–Belgian border (gained by the Stormont, Dundas and Glengarry Highlanders and the Highland Light Infantry), the last and largest town in the Breskens pocket, Knocke-Heist, is threatened by the North Novas advancing during the night, taking outposts and prisoners. At 4:00 P.M., November 1, Major-Gen. Knut Eberding, commander of 64th Division, and his staff of one hundred, emerge from deep concrete bunkers with their hands up, ignoring the spirit and letter of his own order at the start of the campaign to fight to the death,* and now only concerned with the security of the cases of kit he will be taking with him onto captivity.†

---

* Eberding had warned that premature surrender would be considered desertion, and "in cases where the names of deserters are ascertained these will be made known to the civilian population at home and their next of kin will be looked upon as enemies of the German people."(Quoted in Wilmot, *Struggle for Europe* [London: Collins, 1952], p. 546.)

† "He [Eberding] told his servant Frank to pack his bags for a long captivity, and not to forget his chess-set and books. So Frank piled in the staff officer's trousers, the polished high boots, the suit of civvies, the fur-lined gloves, the extra stock of general's insignia, hats various, the underwear, and above all the General's chess library – some fifteen printed works and manuscript notebooks." (Intelligence Summary #52 HQ 3rd Inf. Division Appendix B, Public Archives)

25

HELL IS A CAUSEWAY
SWEPT BY ENEMY FIRE

❋

THE ROYALS' ATTACK TO CLEAR THE MOUTH OF THE CAUSE-
way proceeded with such despatch that by dawn all companies were
on their objectives and the enemy troops in the vicinity were so
demoralized that they surrendered in droves. Two officers and 153
men came in with their hands up, abandoning three 75-mm guns,
two anti-tank guns, many machine-guns, and quantities of essential quarter-master stores.

However, with the coming of daylight, though the enemy makes
no attempt to recover their position, their guns and mortars on the
far shore undertake to make life miserable for the Royals, bombarding them all day as they wait for the Black Watch to come up and
take over after last light, preparatory to attacking across the long
land-bridge.

Until now that bleak neck of rock and earth, stretching flat and
featureless, except for rows of poplars bordering the railway and
roadway it was built to carry across the water to Walcheren, has
been known simply as "the causeway." Now with its mouth and
western approaches under intense bombardment from enemy shells
and mortars, it becomes that "goddamned causeway" or something
equally suggestive of its accursed nature.

Under fire from noon until dark from machine-guns, an anti-
tank gun ricocheting shots down the centre of the roadway, and
field guns and mortars of various calibres dropping H.E. along the

length of the causeway, most of the Black Watch are only halfway across, and a mere handful have made it to within twenty-five yards of the far end, when around 7:30 P.M. they are ordered to withdraw. Evacuation of the wounded is naturally slow, particularly those from the far end of the causeway, and many are still out there at 11:40 P.M. when an artillery concentration is brought down.

Before midnight the Calgary Highlanders are ordered to take a crack at getting across the causeway, but when their leading company loses most of its first platoon just getting halfway to the objective, they are withdrawn.

At dawn November 1, they are ordered to try again, and this time they manage to get across and overrun the roadblock at the far end, taking fifteen prisoners. By 9:33 A.M. they have established a shallow bridgehead, but enemy pressure mounts during the day, and before night falls strong enemy counter-attacks supported by intense mortaring and shelling drive them back onto the causeway, back to a giant crater about halfway along its length.

Next morning, November 2, at 4:00 A.M., with the support of a stormy barrage laid down by three field regiments, and the thunder of three medium regiments conducting counter-battery fire, the Maisonneuves are sent on the same mission. Their D Company, at least those who manage to survive the torrent of enemy fire they are exposed to all the way along the causeway, reach the Walcheren end and seize a bridgehead some four hundred yards wide, from which they expect to be relieved at 5:00 A.M. by the Glasgow Highlanders of British 52nd (Lowland) Division whose responsibility it will be to debouch from the bridgehead into Walcheren.

For nine hours the Maisonneuves courageously maintain their holding, saved on occasion by the guns of 5th Field and the timely intervention of rocketing Typhoons diving on marauding tanks, while reinforcing companies try to reach them. During the morning one platoon of the Glasgow Highlanders crosses the causeway and joins the remnants of D Company in the bridgehead, and the rest of the British battalion gradually makes its way up the causeway, replacing the Maisonneuves. But conditions on the fire-swept

Prisoners streaming out of Boulogne over the rubble of an overpass that had been blown up and dropped to impede Allied vehicles. (Donald I. Grant, National Archives of Canada, PA-137309)

Boulogne gun captured and silenced by 3rd Division. Sitting on the great barrel is Pte. F. J. Coakley of the North Shore Regiment, September 21, 1944. (Donald I. Grant, National Archives of Canada, PA-167981)

Hawker Typhoons ("Tiffies") of 121 (RAF) Squadron, armed with eight rockets, each with the blasting-power of a medium shell (four under each wing on their launching rails, below two 20-mm cannon), readying for take-off from Antwerp, September 22, 1944, to strike targets marked by red smoke shells fired by FOOs. (National Archives of Canada, PA-115087)

"Flying mattresses" of rocket bombs were launched from each of these projectors when all 32 barrels, or "rails" as they were known, were fully loaded. The 1st Canadian Rocket Battery had twelve projectors in use in the Rhineland. Twelve more were added for the Rhine crossing. (National Archives of Canada, PA-192038)

Spent cartridges at Ossendrecht gun position are stacked by Gnr. E. G. Westover, their carrying boxes having been put to use as sand-filled building blocks for shelters for gun crews. (G. Kenneth Bell, National Archives of Canada, PA-143928)

Sitting outside their hovel (built in the manner described above) two 4th Field men take advantage of a sunny day and a lull in the action before the big push (on October 24, 1944): Bdr. J. H. Wilson to write a letter, and Bdr. G. M. Hart to sew a button on his battledress sleeve. (G. Kenneth Bell, National Archives of Canada, PA-143931)

Louis and Seif Pijnen's farm before the war, when Canadian shellfire and later German mortar-fire turned it into a smashed and forlorn place of death. Restored after the war, and Louis Pijnen's family home for some forty years, it was finally obliterated to make way for a superhighway. (Photo courtesy of the Pijnen family)

The people of Hoogerheide and Woensdrecht gaze in awe at Major Bill Ewing, the only Black Watch company commander to come through the attacks on "Black Friday," October 13, 1944, without serious wounds and able to attend the funeral service on October 24 for fifty-six of his comrades. (G. Kenneth Bell, National Archives of Canada, PA-136755)

Dutch children placing flowers on each grave that day set the pattern for memorial services in military cemeteries in Holland to the present. (G. Kenneth Bell, National Archives of Canada, PA-176844)

Where's the gun? Artillery quad (gun tractor) and ammunition limber, to which there is normally attached a 25-pounder, off the road on the way up South Beveland to the canal, October 28, 1944. (G. Kenneth Bell, National Archives of Canada, PA-131257)

Bdr. Morty Hughes plots his artillery board at Baker Troop (2nd Battery) command post near Ossendrecht, reading off the line and range for his GPO to give the guns for another Mike Target on a map reference radioed back by a FOO desperate to break up still another counterattack, October 1944. (G. Kenneth Bell, National Archives of Canada, PA-137648)

The Groesbeek Zuid mill provided an overview of enemy territory unequalled in the Nijmegen salient. Normally the cupola is rotated to face the vanes into the wind, but throughout the winter of 1944-45, the skeleton vanes hung lifeless, away from the enemy, so that observers at the fan window in the rear of the cupola (not visible in the photo) could see for miles into Germany. (Author's photo)

Properly dressed for the occasion, the Queen's Own Rifles move out on patrol from the Nijmegen salient, January 22, 1945. (B. J. Gloster, National Archives of Canada, PA-114073)

Amphibious vehicles (2.5-ton DUKWs, built like flat-nosed boats with wheels) pass along the tree-lined route of the submerged Kranenburg-to-Cleve road, bringing up food and ammunition to the front and taking back the wounded, February 14, 1945. (B. J. Gloster, National Archives of Canada, PA-132422)

causeway are such that their battalion historian will record that it was like being "led into hell . . . to move a foot in daylight was nearly impossible; to advance at night was an adventurous success.*

At 2:45 in the afternoon the survivors of D Company, now numbering no more than twenty, and the one platoon of the Glasgow Highlanders that first came up and made it to the bridge-head, withdraw under a smokescreen laid down by 5th Field guns, directed by their FOO, Lieut. D. G. Innes, who, though wounded, remained with the Maisies throughout.†

There will be no more attacks along the causeway. That night 52nd Division, led by 6th Battalion of Cameronians, cross the Slooe Channel two kilometres south of the causeway, walking in single file along a narrow ford through treacherous mud and sand that two intrepid British sappers had reconnoitred and marked with white tape the previous night.

While the heroic effort by 5th Brigade – unsurpassed in the matter of courage anywhere along the Scheldt – will be deemed a failure, no one should ever refer to it as such in front of a Maisonneuve. Lieut. Guy deMerlis, who, with Lieut. Charles Forbes, the other surviving platoon commander of D Company, played leading roles in the affairs of the beleaguered company, will tell you: "We did exactly what we were asked; we crossed the damned causeway and established a bridgehead from which the British were to attack into Walcheren Island. They chose not to."‡

While all this was going on at the causeway, 8th Reconnaissance Regiment (14th Canadian Hussars) engages in a saltwater sea-crossing of its own to North Beveland, an island eleven kilometres long and five wide lying just one hundred metres off the northern shore of South Beveland, along which a squadron of recce cars under

---

* George Blake, *Mountain and Flood: The History of the 52nd (Lowland) Division* (Glasgow: Jackson, Son & Co., 1950).

† Lieut. D. G. Innes was subsequently awarded the Military Cross.

‡ Author interview.

Major Dick Porteous has been pushing for some days, protecting the right flank of 4th Brigade.

On learning from the Dutch Resistance that North Beveland was being used as a transfer point for enemy movement to and from Walcheren Island, Porteous, with the full support of his commanding officer, Lt.-Col. Mowbray Alway, commandeered a long barge and some fishing boats at a ferry station and crossed to North Beveland on the night of November 1, taking with them, besides their own vehicles, a company of heavy mortars (4.2-inch) and medium machine-guns (Vickers) of the Tor Scots, as well as about twenty-five armed members of the Dutch Resistance.

Their first success was the capture of a German hospital ship. Then, though the commandant of the German garrison in Kamperland, the principal town on the island, first scorned an 8th Recce ultimatum to capitulate – promising to fight to the death – 250 of his men and two officers promptly surrendered when the Tor Scots lobbed a few 4.2-inch mortar bombs at them, and a squadron of Typhoons swooped over them as though to attack them on their way to targets on Walcheren.

The final bag of prisoners taken in clearing the island totalled 367, and the invasion force did not suffer a single casualty.[*]

---

[*] Details of North Beveland invasion by 8th Recce from Denis and Shelagh Whitaker, *Tug of War* (Toronto: Beaufort Books, 1984).

26

MASS OF GUNS IN
A SEA OF MUD

✳

AFTER AN ELEVEN-HOUR DRIVE VIA PUTTE, MERXEM, Antwerp, the Ghent tunnel, and then northwest along the south shore of the Scheldt Estuary through villages, completely smashed and desolate, 4th Field arrives at the village of Schoondijcke in what had been the Breskens pocket, to deploy amidst a vast array of field guns, mediums, heavies, and superheavies, at about 3:00 P.M., October 31.

After weeks among the flooded fields, mud, mists, and rain of South Beveland, you should be used to the bleak vistas of polder country in these bitter wet days of fall, but the sight of the grim, grey sea of mud into which the guns are ordered to deploy next to the shattered village is appalling. This must surely be the ultimate in miserable living conditions, which no human being should ever be asked to endure.

However, as you slosh about on your way to locating shelter for the night in a partially intact building near RHQ in the remnants of the village, despairing for those poor devils at the guns who face the descending night without shelter, you hear not one single word of complaint. On the contrary, as you pass by your old Able Troop, there are attempts at humour and good-natured joshing: "Great weather for ducks, eh, sir? Tell me, have you looked between your toes lately?" And when he receives no reply, "To see if any webbing has sprouted yet?"

The gun sergeants, ready as always to strike an upbeat note, assure you they'll "make out all right." They've been told that to gain surprise for the seaborne commando attacks on Walcheren Island gun sites there will be no firing until H-hour just before dawn, which means the boys can take turns getting some rest in nearby buildings.

Fortunately, all battery and troop command posts find space they can black out among the derelict buildings. Able Troop's command post is in an abandoned tobacco kiln made remarkably cosy by the heat from a little Primus stove. As the night progresses, the temperature falls, and when ammunition thermometers at the troop positions are read for the purpose of working out the "corrections of the moment" to apply to the gun forms, adjusting ranges and switches to accommodate the latest meteorological conditions just before the big shoot begins, the mean temperature is a chilly 50 degrees Fahrenheit.

To gain maximum range for weapons of various calibres, Corps CRA Brig. Bruce Matthews has had to jam gun positions together in closer proximity than you've ever seen them deployed before.

Field gunners seldom pass a 7.2-inch gun position, and until now superheavies have entered your consciousness only as distant deep-throated booms. Here, at last light, the 7.2s and the 155-mm "Long Toms," along with their superbrethren of 8-inch and 240-mm calibres, are visible silhouettes on the horizon at the rear. There are, you are told, 314 guns assembled here. In addition to those heavies and superheavies (3rd Cdn and 9th AGRAs) capable of reaching the big guns at Westkapelle and delivering a weight of shell to do them damage, there are 240 25-pounders, 112 5.5-inch mediums, and 48 3.7-inch anti-aircraft guns to engage the area of Flushing, only three miles from this shore and about six miles from the field and medium guns. Also, for the first time ever on the Western Front, from the Allied side, a battery of rocket launchers, manned by Canadians, will fire three salvoes of 96 rockets per salvo onto ack-ack positions north of Flushing.

All these weapons crowded together do not escape the notice of the big guns on Walcheren. However, all the shells that moan over from the Island in late afternoon and evening land well out in front of 4th Field.

The extensive fire-plan for the early-morning shoot, received by Regimental Headquarters this evening, is considered "a work of art." This will be a very big show, second only, you are told, to Normandy in complexity, for the snout of Walcheren facing into the North Sea is more strongly defended than were any of the Normandy beaches.

A disaster equalling Dieppe might have occurred without Lt.-Gen. Guy Simonds's insistence on Bomber Command opening up four great gaps in the saucerlike outer rim of the Island (a dike thirty-two feet high and in places one hundred feet wide at its base), thereby letting in the sea and rip tides and forcing friend and foe to take refuge on scanty high ground or in upper storeys of buildings, reducing German mobility and cutting his supply lines. As it is, casualties are bound to be high for those in small naval craft moving just offshore and attracting enemy fire while commando boats surge through the gaps in the dikes to attack the guns from the rear.

It is raining at 4:30 A.M. when, with a thundering wave of sound and concussion, enveloping everything and everybody on the crowded gun positions and blowing tiles from the roofs of buildings still blessed with roofs in the village, the great shoot begins – 4th Field adding "just a small voice in the roar of cannons around us," to quote the war diary. For two and a half hours the guns continue to pump fire on designated targets, including the hostile guns that could be brought to bear on the commando forces and the assaulting brigade (155th) of 52nd Division constituting "Infatuate I," who'll be taking Flushing.

Four hours after "Infatuate I" goes in, the assault in the gap in the dike south of Westkapelle is to be carried out by the 4th Special Services Brigade with very heavy naval support. H-hour for this is

9:45 A.M. and another timed program for the mediums and the heavies begins seventy minutes before then – continuing in bursts of firing for varying periods up to 10:45 A.M. on the casemated guns west of Flushing and about Westkapelle.

The second seaborne attack of the day, "Infatuate II," involving a large flotilla from Ostend directed at Westkapelle on the nose of Walcheren Island, is engaged by the enemy shore batteries around 8:00 A.M. Later you will learn that while some German guns are knocked out by the naval ships escorting the flotilla, most of them are taken out by the commandos who get ashore while small naval ships purposely attract the attention of the gunners.

All elements of the assaulting forces from the sea are British, except for medical services, which are provided by the Royal Canadian Medical Corps going in with the commandos.*

---

* One day you will read a vivid account of what those gallant doctors and their helpers faced when they sailed in through the Westkapelle gap, in a book by the leader of Number 8 Canadian Field Surgical Unit, D.r Major John Hillsman, an American surgeon who gave up his citizenship to join the Canadian forces before the United States was drawn into the war by the Japanese attack on Pearl Harbor in December 1941. Hillsman landed on a shoulder of the Westkapelle gap before most of the assaulting commandos. Burbling ashore in a wallowing Buffalo from a landing craft laced with fire, he and his gallant band immediately became involved in collecting and treating casualties among burning vehicles and enemy fire. By the end of the day they'd treated 150 casualties. At noon next day, three Buffaloes, loaded with seven tons of ammunition, were hit by hostile shells and began to burn and explode, causing many casualties to both Brits and German prisoners. Hillsman and Captain Lou Ptak, of his transfusion unit, had to crawl around on their bellies with the exploding ammunition shooting at them from one side and the Germans from the other. "For the next half hour," Hillsman writes, "we lay on our faces in the sand, dressing wounds, stopping hemorrhages, and splinting fractures." That night a gale blew and he operated in a tent six feet by nine, so crowded (by five men) he had to crawl under the operating table when he

News is sketchy, but seemingly the assaulting forces are gaining one position after another of those still above water in the flooded basin. Early on November 2, the guns fire on the Flushing area. Otherwise they are quiet all day.

Again, early next morning, heavy fire is called for about Flushing. And in the afternoon some Victor (Corps) targets are engaged, even as a regimental recce party is sent sixteen kilometres south of Antwerp to a place called Rumst to find "billets" for a rest out of action once all the guns of Walcheren are silenced.

Today (November 4), as usual, the guns open up early on a strongpoint near Flushing, but this turns out to be the last shelling needed. During the morning all resistance on Walcheren appears to end, and the order "prepare to move" comes down at noon. At 3:00 P.M. 4th Field, with no regrets, pulls out of the churned mud and water, heading for the village of Rumst, chosen, you are told, because Antwerp has been under bombardment by V-1s and V-2s since early last month. However, just before the Regiment arrives, the chosen billet is flattened by a V-1, and new digs must be found in schools, cafés, and factories.*

Officers are billeted in private homes, and you draw a sweet-smelling house, redolent with odours of the fruit maturing on vines and trees flourishing in a glass-roofed conservatory opening on the dining room of your hosts, two charming middle-aged ladies.

"wanted to change sides." In two days he and his team performed fifty-two operations, using instruments sterilized in basins of fluid sitting on the floor, and on occasion operating by the light of an acetylene lamp when the generator packed it in. See John Hillsman M.D., *Eleven Men and a Scalpel* (Winnipeg: Columbia Press, 1948), p. 101.

* From October 7, 1944, until March 30, 1945, 3,709 V-weapons (2,448 flying bombs and 1,261 giant rockets) exploded in the Antwerp area. At least 1,214 landed in the city itself, killing 3,000 (including 131 dock workers) and wounding 15,000.

27

SEDATED IN MALINES –
REVIVED IN ANTWERP

—————————— ✳ ——————————

FOR FOUR DAYS THE REGIMENT PAYS ATTENTION TO ITS OWN
needs with no outside obligations, apart from a Corps Commander's briefing for officers and warrant officers in a theatre in
Malines.

Observed from your place far up in the balcony, deeply embedded in blessed anonymity, the solitary figure striding forth unan-
nounced from the darkness of the vast empty stage has your
sympathy. Dwarfed by the towering proscenium arch as he plants
himself at the centre of the wide stage apron to face this audience
of hardened veterans of two of the bitterest campaigns in the long
story of war, he is not in an enviable position, you think.

However, Lt.-Gen. Guy Simonds is no ordinary mortal, and he
proceeds with such self-confidence in every word, gesture, and
posture, you find yourself marvelling at the bold arrogance of great
generals that allows them to conduct themselves with such assur-
ance in circumstances such as this – obviously the same arrogance
that sustains them in making awesome decisions that send thousands to death and disablement, the unavoidable consequence of
every major operation.

However, the content of his address, mainly a dry, pragmatic
appreciation of accomplishments in Normandy, at the Channel
ports, and along the Scheldt, coupled with an uninspiring view of
a future that holds out months of tedious, uncomfortable times

before the enemy is finally defeated, is less than impressive, particularly when, by implication, he suggests officers and NCOs are currently showing levels of leadership and discipline that must be improved remarkably if a lowering in morale throughout the Army is not to occur this winter in static positions up in the Nijmegen salient.

Having come to admire Simonds greatly from afar for his remarkable originality and imagination in devising unique operational plans never before attempted, and for utilizing equipment in novel ways to keep casualty rates as low as possible, his talk, that seems to go on for ever, is a great disappointment. Not only do you not learn anything of real consequence, but he succeeds in creating an atmosphere you thought safely buried in old diaries of training days, as he affects that cold, glowering, threatening style used universally in England by patronizing senior officers as they delivered pep talks on morale-building and the need for junior officers "to take over" – larded with endless platitudes that have become meaningless over here.

The result is a stupefied audience that files out of the theatre in silence, resisting comment until they are safely ensconced with trusted peers in neighbouring watering-holes. The consensus of your peers is that the Regiment, like every other outfit in Canadian Army, is tired and filthy, but all it needs is time for personal maintenance, equipment maintenance, rest, and recreation – with special emphasis on the latter – and it will immediately regain its resilience.

Divisional commanders appear to agree with this consensus, for twenty-four-hour leaves to Antwerp are immediately introduced, and every day for four memorable days, a quota of officers and Other Ranks, enough to fill three or four 60-hundredweight trucks, proceed into the city, replacing an equal number who have spent the previous night in this beautiful city – so alive, so pleasant, so civilized – revisiting familiar haunts and looking up civilian acquaintances made while the guns were in position in the dock area back in September.

Devoid of all official duties (the Colonel having no need for an assistant while 4th Brigade is out of action) you move into the Century Hotel to live in splendid luxury, represented especially by an incredibly soft bed with white sheets and pillows, a gleaming white bathtub with endless hot water at the twist of a tap, and something you had almost forgotten existed, a smooth, clean floor beneath your bare feet when you get out of bed and pad to the bathroom, and a warm toilet seat, properly formed to receive a human posterior comfortably.

As long as there are others from the Regiment on overnight leave in town, you know you can't be left behind by a sudden move of the Regiment called back into action without warning. But each noon your position feels mildly illicit and slightly precarious as you say goodbye to fellow officers dutifully returning to Rumst, leaving you alone in a relatively deserted hotel.

There are, of course, late each afternoon, a couple of anxious hours' waiting to see if new truckloads come in. But the very uncertainty – that this may be your last day in this marvellous place – revives a full appreciation of your privileged status, when, with dusk falling in the wet and windy streets outside and the warmth of the soothingly lit lobby of the Century assuming its most welcoming aspect, you at last spot a friendly face from the Regiment among the arriving guests, and know you will spend another enjoyable night in the new glittering cabaret they've established for officers in the ballroom of the Excelsior Hotel adjoining the Century Hotel.

Then, over and beyond partaking of the amenities of this luxury hotel and amiable city, there is always the chance you may meet up with a friend you haven't seen for years, for Antwerp is a strong magnet these days for anyone getting time off. Your current run of luck produces a wonderful reunion with old Pembroke friend Ramsay Garrow, now a captain with the Sherbrooke Fusiliers, who without warning drops down on a chair beside you at your table in the Excelsior Cabaret.

For hours, completely oblivious to the swirling dancers, the swinging big band, and the ebb and flow of the laughing gabble of voices trying to make themselves heard all around you, you shout and laugh, exchanging precious news of family and friends back home and showing each other your latest batch of snapshots of loved ones, in your case particularly those of your little girl now almost two years old.

Only this morning, while wandering up the main boulevard, eating ice cream cones purchased at the famous ice cream parlour, does the conversation get around to the war. But when it does, the grey morning turns even greyer and all the exuberance – the like of which you haven't felt in years – immediately disappears as he provides you with some truly horrifying insights into the life of tank-men. He has managed to survive all the way from the D-Day beaches with the Sherbrooke Fusiliers, but in the process has formed quite a low opinion of most Allied tanks – so low you find it astonishing that tankmen can go on accepting their inferior equipment with such equanimity.

In fact there's an upbeat quality to his description of ways the Sherbrookes have tried to make up for the inferior armour and armament of their "Ronsons," as Shermans are known for their proclivity for "brewing up" when punctured. Sqdn Commander Major "Woppy" Radley-Walters, DSO, MC, who has had three tanks and three armoured cars shot out from under him (not to mention nine other tanks holed but left serviceable), claims that if the armour-piercing shot from the 75-mm gun of a regular Sherman (incapable of penetrating the frontal armour of a German Panther) is ricocheted down off the bottom of the bulging mantelet of the Panther, the slug will drive through the thin surface armour. And to ensure incoming enemy slugs meet an uneven surface and are diverted ever so slightly from their normal, lethal course, the ingenious "Woppy" has started a trend of welding hunks of track from derelicts around the Shermans' bodies and turrets.*

---

* When an Ordnance pooh-bah decreed this "junk" must be removed, since the extra weight could reduce a tank's running life by five hundred miles, Radley-Walter's blunt answer was that without that "junk" those tanks might not make it even to the next hill.

28

OUR HEARTS LAID BARE
BY LYRIC WRITERS

"WISH ME LUCK AS YOU WAVE ME GOODBYE..."

"I'll walk alone..."

"I'll be seeing you – in all the old familiar places..."

"We'll meet again – don't know where, don't know when – but I know we'll meet again some sunny day..."

"I haven't said thanks for that lovely weekend – those two days of heaven you helped me to spend – the thrill of your kiss as you stepped off the train – the smile in your eyes like the sun after rain ... Then you had to go – the time was so short – we both had so much to say – your kit to be packed, the train to be caught – sorry I cried but I just felt that way. But now you have gone, Dear, this letter I pen, my heart travels with you, till we meet again. Keep smiling my Darling and someday we'll spend, a lifetime of peace as that lovely weekend."

Words like those in the lyrics of current songs, expressing so poignantly the thoughts and feelings of lovers wrenched apart today by the war, perhaps permanently, may appear to future generations of youth as embarrassingly sentimental, or just plain dreary, as lyrics of many of the First War songs appeared to you when you were growing up.

However, it should be clearly understood and recorded, while our memories of this war are with us, still living-fresh, that no collection of official documents now being filed away by the great political leaders and military commanders for their memoirs, no scrapbook of newspaper and magazine clippings, nothing now being placed in print and on film that historians one day will claim for posterity to be the true story of the War, will ever capture the spirit and soul of these days in the way popular song lyrics are doing.

Could any statesman's diary or news report ever come close to matching the childish bravado embraced by the British public during the "phoney war" – when nobody on the western front fired a shot either way – expressed in the lyrics: "We're gonna hang out our washing on the Siegfried Line . . ." and "Run Rabbit Run."

And when the seemingly invincible German hordes overran Western Europe, forcing the British soldiers to abandon all their weapons and equipment in France and make it home as best they could, and when the need to fight despair was paramount, it was a song lyric that captured the spirit of the times and the feelings of the British and their friends all over the world: "There'll always be an England, and England shall be free, as long as England means to you, what England means to me."

For years now, most Englishmen would be too embarrassed to sing words like that. But let the world remember, there was a time after the fall of France – when the droning and stuttering noises of the battle for domination of the sky over Britain filled the air – when those words were sung loud and clear, not only by the British, but by people across the seas.

For you the picture is still fresh of several hundred men at a service club luncheon in the Château Laurier in Ottawa standing and singing those words with tears in their eyes, just after applauding the speaker of the day, British poet Sir Alfred Noyes (of "The Highwayman" fame) for calling author H. G. Wells "a liar" in alleging the soldiers at Dunkirk had been abandoned by their officers.

As inspiring as Churchill's stirring declarations of defiance were in 1940, when he hurled them at the Germans in the face of over-powering odds ("We shall fight on the beaches . . .") the spirit abroad among the common people during that awful period of suspense, awaiting the expected invasion from the continent, was more accurately captured by the lyrics of a gentle little song expressing the longing for a return to normalcy, for the days when the children were at home: "There'll be blue birds over, the white cliffs of Dover – tomorrow just you wait and see . . . The shepherd will tend his sheep, the valley will bloom again, and Jimmy will go to sleep in his own little room again . . ."

Will these words someday be labelled sentimental twaddle? Perhaps, but let those who choose in the distant future to research this era take note that in the early 1940s, when thousands of children were being sent away from the danger of the Blitz to live apart from their parents, people found those words profoundly moving, expressing the very essence of the civilized values they believed worth fighting for.

Song lyrics have captured a wide spectrum of the strangeness of life for the new recruit: the great contrast between pampered life in Civvy Street and the coarse conditions of the training barracks ("This is the army, Mr. Jones, no private room or telephones . . ."); the tedium and drudgery of life for common soldiers buried in helpless anonymity in some drab depot or reinforcement unit ("You'll get used to it – you gotta get used to it . . ."); and the pervasive need of all those new to hard service discipline to put down those in authority who are making life miserable for all the lowly odds and sods of this world ("Don't forget to wake me in the morning and bring me in a nice, hot cup of tea – Kiss me good-night Sergeant Major – Sergeant Major be a mother to me").

But no song exposes the secret yearnings of the soldier on his way up to the front as well as the German song about Lilli Marlene, said to have been "captured" by 8th Army Desert Rats in North Africa.

Nightly it is the piece most requested of the Belgian swing band playing at the dances in the Excelsior ballroom cabaret. These remarkable affairs, that only came into being this week when Antwerp was suddenly flooded with men and officers on twenty-four-hour leaves from exhausted Canadian Army divisions released from the mud along the Scheldt, and that will cease abruptly in a couple of days when First Canadian Army moves north to the Nijmegen salient, are providing those lucky enough to share in them memories that will last a lifetime.

Tonight, as always, every seat at every table is taken. Most wear holstered pistols and some have knives slung on web-belts around the shirred waists of their battledresses, still wrinkled and baggy from crouching in the rain in water-logged holes on the Scheldt – survivors of struggles in which hundreds of their buddies were struck down.*

There are dark circles under their eyes and their faces are weatherbeaten and lined with fatigue, and for some time after they arrive, they seem like old men unable to smile. They stare around the bright, noisy, merry room and at the lovely-gowned girls out on the dance floor in utter disbelief. Then after a couple of cognacs they spot some friend they haven't seen since OCTU or a boyhood chum they haven't met since school days, and join in the general hubbub, adding to the noise level rising to a din that threatens to drown out the orchestra playing the song hits of the Thirties: "Marie, You're Laughing At Me," "Sunrise Serenade," "Deep in a Dream of You," "Star Dust"...

Then, for at least the sixth time tonight, the Belgian musicians on the bandstand succumb to calls from the room and start whistling "Lilli Marlene," stomping their feet rhythmically as though marching – softly at first, then more loudly, and still more loudly as the room grows quiet and attentive. Now the musicians pick up their instruments and play as though a military band is passing by, their feet marching heavily. Gradually they drop the volume, until there is only the faintest sound of men marching away whistling "Lilli Marlene." Finally that too disappears, and for a long moment there is silence.

---

* First Canadian Army losses on the Scheldt totalled 12,873 killed, wounded, and missing. Of this total, 6,367 were Canadians.

PART TWO: NOVEMBER 9–
FEBRUARY 15

The Nijmegen Salient

29

SETTLING IN THE

NIJMEGEN SALIENT

✳

THE REGIMENT ARRIVES IN THE NIJMEGEN SALIENT NEAR Groesbeek just before noon November 9 after a 110-mile overnight drive from Antwerp. It has travelled over roads laced by rain and hail and severely congested by other Canadian units moving up to take over from a mixture of American paratroopers and British artillery who have been holding this zone since September 21, when XXX British Corps, driving north from the Meuse–Escaut canal in Belgium, reached here in its ill-fated attempt to reach 1st British Airborne Division still holding Arnhem bridge over the Neder Rhine.

At a roadside briefing of officers, deep in a pine woods where the Regiment bivouacs waiting for the British 112th Field Regiment to vacate their gun positions next day, Col. Young makes it clear the troops must be encouraged to build substantial dug-outs – not only to withstand the rigours of winter, but to gain maximum protection from expected heavy counter-battery activity by the enemy. Senior officers of the American 82nd Airborne Division, briefing senior officers of 2nd Division this morning, gave the impression that this is a very sticky sector, absorbing an unholy amount of Jerry shells and mortars along the front line running through Groesbeek and among the gun positions spotted in clearings in the bushland behind the village. And since the unflappable Colonel is known to

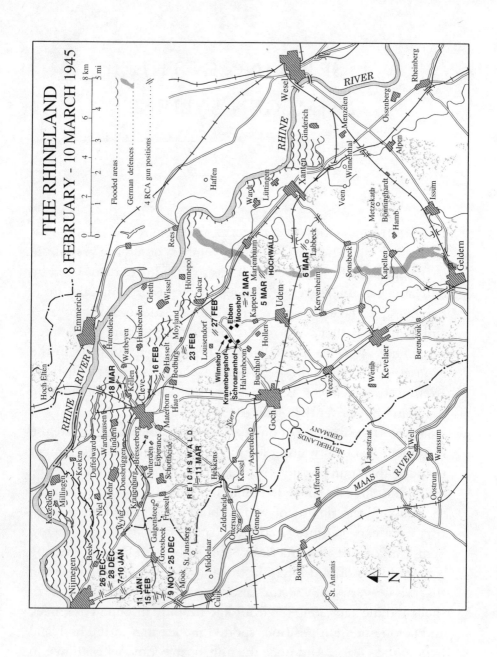

THE RHINELAND
— 8 FEBRUARY - 10 MARCH 1945

Flooded areas ....
German defences ....
4 RCA gun positions ....

km
mi

be totally disinclined to dramatize conditions, this information is taken seriously by all ranks.

From the first days in action it has never been necessary to issue orders to the troops to dig in. Early experience with horrendous enemy bombardments of gun positions in front of Carpiquet sorted out that matter for all time. However, until now, the troops have never had the opportunity to do a real job on dug-outs and command posts. Now, with bags of time available, there develops a sense of competition to see who can build the most comfortable underground living-quarters, usually constructed by pairs of men or small syndicates – some even felling trees and building log cabins in holes to be covered with earth. Most, however, build shacks below grade, using, in place of plywood, doors from the ruined houses of Groesbeek village, inside doors as well as outside doors, to shore up earthen walls and provide sheathing for roofs to receive their thick covering of soil.

At the outset, they utilize shelters left by the British, while working hard and long with a sense of urgency, improving dug-outs and excavating new ones, bracing themselves for the expected bombardments.

However, either Jerry has suddenly decided to lay off shelling this sector, or those American paratroopers, never having been sub-jected to the weight of shelling endured by 4th Field in Normandy or along the Scheldt, are not equipped to judge what constitutes heavy shelling, for these gun positions behind Groesbeek turn out to be among the quietest ever occupied by the Regiment in action. Apart from some widely spaced shelling on the flanks, and the odd airburst over the gun positions, Jerry restricts his attention to the infantry. And even up front, though OP logs regularly record a bit of shelling by 75-mm or 105-mm guns, he seldom shows any real inclination to expend large numbers of shells or mortar bombs.

Periodically a basin of Moaning Minnies descends on Groesbeek, and now and then the desolate and deserted village is subjected to a leisurely bombardment by one gun of fairly large calibre – ten or fifteen wailing shells arriving one at a time, with long intervals between, their ground-shuddering concussions and roars reverberating among the confined streets and derelict buildings, creating the impression of something very large and terribly lethal.

Your OP is a ridiculously exposed and atrociously vulnerable tall windmill standing forth on the brow of a height of land to the right of Groesbeek village, looking across an enemy-dominated valley of misty, low-lying farmland stretching to the German frontier three kilometres away, easily distinguishable by the fact the map shows the border running along the foot of the distant formidable ridge, covered with a dark and dense evergreen state forest called the Reichswald.

The main part of the tower is quite substantial, with thick, brick walls capable of stopping small-arms fire and shell fragments, with a base virtually impregnable to any ordinary field piece or anti-tank gun, surrounded as it is by a deep, earthen berm of fortresslike proportions between eight and ten feet high. Moreover, there is a truly splendid means of access to what might be described as the basement of the mill. Cut deeply through the berm, fortuitously away from the enemy and completely hidden from their view, the entry doors are wide enough to allow your carrier to drive inside and be hidden from air reconnaissance. However, to observe the zone, you must use the cupola at the very top, with its fan-window opening almost down to floor level of the moveable dome, and hunch down, back in the shadows, next to the huge wooden gears and the thick shaft supporting the great windvanes now hanging sail-less outside the rear of the mill, facing back in the direction of the guns.

In normal times the cupola would be turned by the miller's pushing on a great brace, running from the back of the cupola down to the base of the mill, so the vanes face into the prevailing wind, but now, while the valley in front remains no-man's-land, the cupola will stay as is with its fan-window facing the Reichswald.

The mill is, at the same time, the best and the worst of OPs: the best for providing the widest panoramic view of no-man's-land and enemy-held territory, and the worst for its ridiculous vulnerability.

Its fan-window must appear to the enemy as an evil, menacing eye, complete with looping eyebrow, an open invitation to a burst of machine-gun fire or a shell from an 88. The thin wooden boards that form the roof and walls of the cupola wouldn't inhibit the passage of a bullet, let alone high explosive. A single shell of respectable calibre would blow this flimsy loft away in a shower of matchwood.

Nevertheless, until now the Germans have chosen not to attack the cupola with any kind of fire. Why they continue to leave it alone, you can only speculate. There is lots of evidence that the mill's dominant position in the village was seriously contested in the early hours of the American paratroop and the glider landings. A German soldier lies dead on one of the lower floors, and though the heavy brick structure shows few scars of battle, the surrounding turf is cratered and torn by shells that barely missed it.

It is, of course, idiotic to use the mill as an OP, for any tower that provides wide observation must be suspect. If it were in German-held territory, you wouldn't rest until it was chopped to ribbons by your shells, anti-tank solid-shot, and Typhoon rockets. But even as you realize the risk involved in using it to observe the zone, you continue to climb up to the cupola each morning simply because the broad panorama it provides from the top is irresistible to a FOO. It surely is the outstanding OP in the Nijmegen salient, and may well be without peer on the whole Western Front.

The fact the Germans have left it alone until now encourages you to believe they may continue to do so. Still, you never completely suppress the memory of that fire-ranger's tower you occupied for several days unmolested on that hill in the bush back at Groote Meer near Woensdrecht, and the way it was smashed by Heinie shells just moments after you vacated it for the last time.

For the first few days, you occupy the mill around the clock, observing the zone from the cupola during daylight hours, retiring to a lower floor during the hours of darkness.

However, there being no way to black-out completely any part of the tower, it isn't possible to expose a light strong enough for reading, which makes the longest nights of the year seem longer still. Also, continuous exposure day and night to the chimney effect of the tall tower, which induces unpleasant, icy draughts to sweep up through the completely open stairwells from floor to floor has given everybody on your crew a head cold.

Thus, when the weather turns particularly nasty one afternoon, you agree that the crew should check out a farm they like the looks of down on the right a couple of hundred yards, on the west side of the road, labelled on the map Herwendaalsche Straat.

And though you are a bit uneasy about its unprotected location in a sort of no-man's-land between the Royals and their neighbours, with no evidence of men from either battalion nearby, as darkness falls and a gusting wind sends snowflakes swirling in through your fan-window, their enthusiastic reports of a pile of dry firewood in the kitchen and a full bin of coal at the back of the farmhouse make the idea of moving over there for the night irresistible.

However, the dream of spending your first evening in the cosy luxury of a dry kitchen, warmed by a glowing range, is ruined by the Germans early in the evening, when they open up with a variety of guns and mortars all along the front. While they are not disturbing your house, you get a signal to return to your OP in the mill to flash-spot hostile guns and mortars until dawn.

This means sitting alone in the cold and gloom in utter boredom, fighting sleep, watching the dark zone in front of you until you catch sight of a flash of a gun or mortar. Then with your prismatic compass, lit by a shielded lamp-electric, you read the bearing, and report it to the Regiment for passage on to Div, along with the precise time the flash was observed – being careful not to report flashes of our own shells or mortars sent over by other units. On receipt of two or more reports of flashes, recorded at the same point in time, Counter Battery at Div, knowing the map location of each OP reporting, can use the bearings to establish by triangulation a map reference for the enemy gun, on which counter-battery bombards can be arranged.

The accuracy of the map reference thus arrived at is of course totally dependent on the accuracy of the compass bearings supplied, and accurate readings are extremely difficult since the flashes are, more often than not, vague by virtue of coming from behind a crest, or diffused by fog and mist.

Usually the spotting FOO does not try to engage the flashing weapon, since it is next to impossible for him to establish the offending gun's position from a split-second, pinpoint flicker or a splash of light on the horizon. But during the first part of the night, the urgent need to cool down Jerry's heavy harassing fire on Groesbeek and vicinity, and in recognition of his habit of removing his Moaning Minnies and guns to other locations after firing a few rounds so as to frustrate flash-spotting efforts, you immediately engage any suspected area in the vicinity of the flashes with a few rounds' gunfire, in addition to reporting the bearings to Counter-Mortar.*

While the chances of hitting a hostile gun or mortar with this kind of random firing at flashes on the horizon are slight, the small expenditure of shells is, in your opinion, still very worthwhile as a morale-booster for the harassed men living out a wretched existence in filthy, cold, fearful conditions along the front here.

Many of those poor fellows are bound to be recent reinforcements, some of them experiencing their first tour of duty in the front line crouching on muddy straw or pine boughs strewn across the slightly congealed, half-frozen ooze on the bottom of their

---

* Where practical to instal and maintain the equipment, more-accurate readings on locations of hostile mortars and guns were obtained by the Sound Ranging Troops of 2nd Survey Regiment of 2nd Corps. Close-in mortars were monitered by microphones spaced out across the front, hooked up to jiggling four-pen recorders; and distant guns by six microphones placed in overturned pots in camouflaged holes in the ground, 1,500 metres apart across the front, hooked up to a recording device of running film-negative registering impulses from each microphone – from the "gun-firing wave," the "incoming-shell wave," and the "shell-bursting wave" – each showing up on the film as meaningful "blips" to the trained eyes of sound rangers.

partially covered slit trenches. To those men, cringing out there in the dark, praying their hole won't receive a direct hit – helpless, unable to fight back – the sound of some friendly guns thumping behind them, followed by the sizzle of shells passing overhead on their way to land with flashing roars on distant enemy territory, must surely be music to their ears.

On the 17th of November, 1st Canadian Calibration Troop arrives at the Regiment, and over three days all the guns are measured for wear and calibrated. All gun barrels absorb wear from each and every shell driven out their length with such tremendous force. As time goes by the stream of shells reams the bore larger and larger, until the gases, expelling the shells, start escaping past the copper drivingbands meant to provide a seal between shells and the rifling of the bore. This causes a lowering of the velocity of the shell and a drop-off in the distance it will travel at any given range setting.

Up to a certain point, the drop-off in muzzle velocity from wear can be compensated for by acute adjustments to the ranging sights by expert artificers, which in effect tip the gun muzzle slightly higher when each elevation is applied by the gun-layer. Though the FOOs have not discerned any fall-off in the range of 4th Field guns, it is only reasonable to assume that after the record-breaking firing they have engaged in, their barrels will prove to be badly worn when measurements are taken by the calibrators using photo-electric cell equipment.

However, the drop-off in muzzle velocity is astonishingly slight for 1940 tubes that, during the past four months, have fired an average of 10,128 rounds each, including occasions in Normandy when they glowed red-hot and, which, by all logic, should have caused severe wear. Typical of the calibration results were those for Sgt. McEwan's gun, as recorded in his gun log:

On November 17, 1944, the muzzle velocities of 25-pounder gun barrel L/24006, of "D" Sub of Easy Troop, 26 Battery, 4RCA, was measured at each of the four levels of propellant charges, and recorded against the original muzzle velocities in feet per second:

	Original MV	*17 Nov 1944*
Charge I	645 f.p.s.	635 f.p.s.
Charge II	987 "	971 "
Charge III	1463 "	1433 "
Super Charge	1742 "	1698 "

No one seems particularly impressed with the staying power of their superstars. Field gunners are inclined to take for granted the extraordinary flexibility of their weapons, which can be brought into action in less than a minute, ready to fulfil their role as howitzers or guns – capable of traversing 360 degrees on their own steel platforms – something no other field gun in the world can do. And so they also take for granted their remarkable durability, and on countless occasions have demanded of them more than should ever be expected of any gun, pounding away for outrageously long periods, at firing rates far in excess of the limits laid down by those who should know their capabilities. For the reliability of the 25-pounder to be fully appreciated, it must be compared to other formidable weapons earning honoured places in the history of this war – the 5.5-inch medium gun and the 40-mm Bofors ack-ack gun – whose barrels frequently must be replaced after intensive fire.*

---

* During August 1944 the replacement rate of 5.5-inch barrels in the Canadian Army was eight per day. Rated for 7,000 rounds of E.F.C. (equivalent full charge), 5.5-inch barrels generally accomplished only a third of that, ending life at 2,400 E.F.C. And Bofors barrels were inclined to bulge when furious firing rates were sustained, as during their use in a ground role during the opening of Operation "Veritable" in the Rhineland in February 1945. 38th battery reported eleven barrels bulged among twenty-four guns of two troops.

30

BIT OF AN OVERSIGHT,
EH WHAT?

✳

AFTER THE ENEMY WAS CLEARED FROM THE SCHELDT AND the big guns of Walcheren silenced, it took nearly one hundred British minesweepers three weeks to clear the eighty kilometres of winding estuary from Antwerp to the open North Sea, blowing up or neutralizing 267 German mines.

Those first ocean-going freighters, led by Canadian-built *Fort Cataraqui*, and manned by the Royal Navy, steaming up to Antwerp quays on November 28, near where 4th Field guns once stood, represent the culmination of a great operation by the Canadian Army – a victory of decisive importance to the prosecution of the war, and so recognized by both General Eisenhower and Field Marshal Montgomery.

The Supreme Allied Commander in Western Europe will say: "The end of Nazism was in clear view when the first ship moved unmolested up the Scheldt."

And the 21st Army Group commander will write: "The Canadians have proved themselves magnificent fighters, truly magnificent. Their job along the Channel Coast and clearing of the Scheldt was a great military achievement for which they deserve the fullest credit. It was a job that could have been done only by first-rate troops. Second-rate troops would have failed."

And surely no one is unmindful of the terrible cost in Canadian blood of this day of triumph – that in thirty-eight days of merciless struggle, in the most appalling conditions men could ever be asked to fight, 3rd Canadian Division suffered 2,672 casualties, and 2nd Division even more, 3,364 dead and wounded.

Thus it is entirely fitting that there be a ceremony to mark the port opening. And one is held, appropriately involving a salute by bands playing national anthems as the first ship of a nineteen-ship convoy is escorted into harbour by a boatload of dignitaries, including the *Bürgermeister* of Antwerp, Field Marshal Montgomery, and a number of naval and military chiefs of Belgium, Britain, and the United States. However, the Canadian anthem is *not* played. For reasons never explained, no Canadian – from Lt.-Gen. Simonds, who planned and led this huge and complex operation, down through all levels of Canadian officers and men who fought those awful battles – was invited to the ceremony.

And since Antwerp is out of bounds to all military personnel except those on official business, ever since a V-1 landed on the Rex movie theatre with awful results, few Canadians could have been in the city today.* Therefore, to be able, one day, to casually drop the fact you were in Antwerp on this historic occasion, being in possession of a pass for "official business," will surely sound impressive – particularly if you neglect to explain you weren't aware of any ceremony and your business was to purchase a supply of booze so that some officers, residing in the cold, misty Nijmegen salient, might get together for a drink in a remarkably large dug-out at 14th Battery gun position near Groesbeek.

This underground phenomenon, constituting the first, last, and only "officers' mess" ever established during action in Northwest Europe by any battery in the Regiment, completed the third week of November, is something of a triumph in design and decoration,

---

* On November 28 the ack-ack ringing Antwerp shot down 35 V-weapons, but one of the fifteen that got through landed with a roar at an intersection, killing eleven civilians just as the first ship was arriving at the docks.

being a room ten feet by fifteen feet with seven feet of headroom, entirely below grade, with an exotic decor that could best be described as a blend of Eastern Mediterranean and the South Seas.

The basic wall-covering is bamboo matting, plainly suggestive of palm trees and Dorothy Lamour. Draped over this are rich tapestries, and covering the earthen floor is a thick oriental rug. Finally, adding to the sense of glowing opulence is the subdued lighting supplied by wall lamps with sexy little brown shades, powered by current from 12-volt radio batteries fed through a 110-volt converter salvaged from a broken 19-set.

A velour curtain hangs across the doorway at the foot of the stairs to prevent the winter draughts, now swirling through the frozen bushland above, from leaking into the room. A Nederland version of the Quebec Heater, the venerable Canadian parlour stove, fed with coal filched from the tender of the nearby abandoned locomotive, keeps the place warm and cosy, and dries out the upholstered chairs, which, like the rug and tapestries, were "rescued" from sodden houses in Groesbeek. Distributed around the perimeter, between some rather splendid casual tables, the chairs are fairly dry – at least visitors no longer appear wraithed in steam when they arise from them and go above ground.

Never will you forget the first time you descended the slippery steps from the bleak, wintry landscape above, and passing through a stained and ragged piece of tarpaulin, hanging just outside the velour curtain at the doorway, burst into that beautifully appointed room. Just back from a two-week stretch in a dirty, cold OP your first thought was that the thing must surely be some kind of elaborate joke. And the 14th Battery batman, showing it to you – obviously harbouring mixed feelings about this masterpiece on which he'd been obliged to lavish so much ingenuity and labour – said it so well: "Ain't war hell, sir?"

Major Jack Drewry, the battery commander, whose enthusiasm alone brought it to fruition, naturally wants to show it off at a regimental officers' bash, to which he's invited the officers of the RHLI at whose tac headquarters he spends his time when they are in the line. Justification for the bash is contained in a pious title on the invitations: "Get-to-know-your-neighbour Cocktail Party" – meaning of course the "Rileys." However, the objective could apply equally well to 4th Field, for casualties and promotions during the last few months have produced a multitude of strange faces among the officers. It is because 14th Battery has so many new officers of limited experience that Drewry requested you be transferred to 14th "to thicken up their experience," at least until the spring offensive starts.

So the great party is scheduled for 5:00 P.M. tomorrow, November 29. But even as the invitations were being distributed yesterday, Drewry discovered the 14th Battery officers' booze cupboard (more precisely an ammo box in his possession designated to carry such goodies) was in a particularly barren state. While issue rum was considered quite a pukka base for a mess punch in England, and an extra gallon could have been scrounged for the purpose, rum, now being of daily issue, does not seem quite special enough. Someone must go to Antwerp on a buying expedition and Drewry, knowing you are about to be seconded to 14th Battery to take over D Troop, invites you to take on the job. Old friend Len Harvey decides to keep you company, being free of regimental duties as he awaits posting to a training course for pilots for a new Canadian Air OP Squadron being formed under Major Dave Ely, once your troop commander in Britain.

Thus you and Harvey are in Antwerp when the history-making opening of the harbour takes place. However, having no access to English papers or the BBC, you would have remained totally ignorant of the event except for a precocious little ten-year-old girl, enthroned on a high stool beside her mother behind the bar in a café in Rumst, when you are persuaded by Harvey to take the thirty-minute drive south of the city so he may revisit his favourite Flemish watering-hole and deliver some candy bars to the effervescent tyke, who captured his heart when the Regiment was billeted here just three weeks ago.

As you enter, she is filling the bar with her laughter in typical fashion. And what has set her off? Well, it seems the newspaper lying before her on the bar, showing pictures of the ceremony in Antwerp harbour, reports the first ship to dock was carrying salt. To her this is hilarious. In English, extraordinarily good for one who only began to pick it up three weeks ago, she declares:

"All that fighting you did to open up the port, and what do they bring us? Salt!!" (a gale of laughter) "With the sea full of saltwater, and saltwater flooding everywhere through the broken dikes, they bring us a ship loaded with salt!!"

She laughs so hard, she almost falls off her high stool. But suddenly she stops, and covers her mouth with her hand, as she spots the candy bars Len is holding out to her.

Back at the Century Hotel, you find the lobby absolutely empty of people – not one customer. Three weeks ago this long, high-ceilinged reception room was pulsing with life every afternoon and night. When you remark on this to the desk clerk booking you in, he sighs:

"Ah yes . . . no more . . . the joy has gone . . . the hotel is almost empty of guests . . . the v-bombs you see."

And the ballroom next door in the annex hotel – the Excelsior?

"The same . . . nothing. If you wish a drink, gentlemen, the bar in the basement is open."

You go down and look in. Except for the barman, it's deserted. Len decides to hit the sack. You hang on for a while with the object of taking advantage of the baby grand piano on the platform in the corner, which you recall is well-tuned, a rarity on the continent of Europe.

But before you move to it, two colonels with red-banded forage caps – one distinguished by a black patch over one eye, and the other by white hair – come in and sit down on the bar stools beside you. The white-haired colonel looks familiar, and when he introduces himself, the name Eric Harris rings a bell. You met him at Barnham Junction when he visited his old 26th Battery he'd brought to England in 1940.

He and his companion, Colonel Wardell, were over on Walcheren today examining gun sites hit by the rockets that were fired by weapons designed by Colonel Wardell. Perhaps you saw them in action in the Breskens area when your guns supported the attack on Walcheren? "No . . . well, you will . . . in all major operations in the future . . . you most certainly will!"*

Before you can ask for more details, he inquires, "Where is this swinging Antwerp we've heard so much about? We were told Antwerp was the swinging capital of Europe."

You explain they should have been here a month ago, before the v-1s and v-2s started arriving.

He then asks how 4th Field made out in Normandy. But as you begin telling him how rough it was, you realize he's not listening. He starts to tell Wardell about leaves he had here in Belgium in the last war, and you don't think he even notices as you excuse yourself to leave for bed, thoroughly depressed by having been patronized and then ignored by an old soldier trying to recapture his youth.

---

* While rocket artillery was designed and developed through the initiative of a British Guards officer, Lt.-Col. Michael Wardell, full credit must go to Lt.-Col. Eric Harris that Canadian gunners introduced it on the Western Front for the first time in World War II, on November 1, 1944. Wardell had been the champion of rockets as ground artillery from when he'd improvised the defence of his position in North Africa in 1942 and dispersed the enemy using an anti-aircraft rocket projector. He lost an eye in the engagement, but he became a staff officer, and got the chance to promote his ideas. Though he successfully demonstrated his rockets in trials at Larkhill in the winter of 1944, the British brass decided it was too late in the war to refine the weapon and develop a supply of rockets. Among the spectators was Harris, former 26th Battery commander, who had set up the Canadian School of Artillery at Seaford. To him Wardell's "collection of pipes" was too good to be relegated to the scrap heap. He recommended Canadian Army should develop a rocket-firing battery. To the credit of Gen. Harry Crerar and the BRA Brig. H. O. N. Brownfield, senior gunner officer at Canadian Army Headquarters, approval came quickly.

31

FILET MIGNON FOR BREAKFAST

❊

FROM DAWN UNTIL DUSK EACH DAY, AND SOMETIMES AT night when required to flash-spot active enemy guns and mortars, FOOs keep enemy-held territory through to the Reichswald under constant observation. The "O Pip," or "Oboe Peters" (as observation posts are now sometimes known, under the bastard phonetic alphabet produced by an amalgam of British and American versions) from which all this surveillance is conducted in the Nijmegen salient, are, topographically speaking, quite superior, providing broad and deep overviews of the zone.

However, the quality of accommodation for bones and muscles, which remain crouched, slouched, hunched, or otherwise cramped in awkward postures for hours on end, varies greatly from one OP to another. Sometimes you hunker down under the slanting rafter-poles of a frigid farmhouse attic or a barn loft, with the wind whistling through the cracks between the tiles, and scuttle about crablike when you change position, as much to keep yourself from fossilizing in some grotesque shape as to gain a different view of no-man's-land.

All observation from buildings tends to be restricted, for it must be conducted discreetly so as not to draw attention to a position that will be continually occupied by FOOs for weeks. So viewing of the zone always is from back in the shadows, away from openings such as the holes blown in the roof by unfriendly mortars, or purposely opened by your unwiring some of the tiles from the rafter-poles and letting them skitter off down to the ground.

One of the strangest OPs on this whole front is with an isolated company of Royals in some battered buildings forming an island several hundred yards out in a broad lake of flood water, created by the Maas river overflowing its banks in the general area of Middelaar.

One chilly, black night in early December, you are sent up to meet the rowboat coming back for rations for "Paddy" Ryall's company, then occupying that island. This entails a nerve-wracking drive in a 15-hundredweight, at a snail's pace up a narrow road only barely above the level of the flood waters lapping the road on both sides.

One moment the water is glistening black right next to the left front wheel, and the next instant it is menacing the right wheel, as the veteran driver, Gunner Ed Crosier, struggles to track an imaginary centre line in total blackout. Breathing hard, he explains it isn't just the possibility of running off into the water that bothers him; the verges have not been cleared of mines, and if he fails to recognize the rendezvous point, he'll deliver you to the Jerries, whom he's been told are not far beyond here.

About the time you become convinced he has long since passed the crucial point and that you may expect a burst of Spandau fire through the windshield at any moment, you spot some white tape draped on stakes at a widening of the road. With nerves thoroughly frazzled, you leave the truck, collect your bedroll and your signaller with his 18-set from the back, and climb into the canvas rowboat to sit atop a load of Compo rations. Straddling a kitbag full of mail and parcels, as you are rowed through the blackness, you face the future with some trepidation, expecting to be delivered to a partially submerged, waterlogged hovel.

But when Paddy receives you with such obvious pleasure at his island-building – a sort of mill warehouse – "handing you out" with courtly grace onto what in normal times would be a loading dock for wagons, and leads you upstairs to a dry candlelit storeroom with mellow wooden floors and partitions exuding comfortable odours of corn or bran, you start thanking your lucky stars and relishing the prospect of spending the next two weeks here.*

Alas, next night you are hauled back to become Dog Troop commander and occupy OP 46 with the RHLI two kilometres southwest of Groesbeek.

Along this sector the distance between opposing forces varies tremendously, from just the width of a village street in a crossroads hamlet, such as Knapheide, to a thousand yards in the open, soggy fields, though the gap between the lines narrows considerably at night when both sides send out patrols and listening posts among the derelict American gliders strewn about the valley.

Artillery OPs are sometimes so close to the enemy the FOO must move in after dark, and then quietly, if he doesn't want to attract a shattering burst of Schmeisser fire of hair-raising intimacy. Such a place is OP 46. And going up after dark without a guide, trying to follow an ill-defined track across muddy fields intersected by deep drainage ditches filled to the brim with ice-water, can be treacherous. This you learn on a black and rainy December night when one of these water hazards claims you, up to your hips, when, attempting to jump over it, you misjudge the distance between its slippery banks.

It happens just after you abandon the dry snugness of the cab of a 15-hundredweight truck, following a disconcerting conversation with the driver, again Gunner Crosier, when the track he's been following begins to peter out in suspicious fashion, suggesting it no longer is a road but a farmer's lane. From long experience with drivers, who always seem to know the best route to a neighbouring unit or the safest way to an awkwardly placed OP, you took for

---

* This island position was not without its drawbacks. One was the unavoidable delay in evacuating casualties. Frank, the younger brother of 2nd Battery Don R Gunner Andy Turner, serving with Ryall's company and wounded here, was dead on arrival at hospital because of such a delay.

granted that Crosier would know the way up to the Riley company to which you've been assigned. He, on the other hand, never having been up here before, carried on in the belief you knew precisely where you were going and would make sure he didn't stray off the track. If you hadn't become worried, when the muddy road grew less and less distinct, and questioned the wisdom of driving on, he would have driven out into no-man's-land never realizing the blind was leading the blind. As it is, you land at Major Joe Pigott's company headquarters, set up in a partially wrecked, tiny brick farmhouse, a sodden mess, covered with mud and cursing after dragging your lower extremities dripping out of the ditch.

In the morning you learn that as a place for observing no-man's-land this sad little farmhouse, sitting in an open field halfway down a forward slope, isn't in it with most of the other OPs along this front, but as a position in close and continuing contact with the enemy it surely would top any list. Now and then a Spandau sprays bullets at the north and east windows of the house to discourage their use for observation purposes; and when, in a fruitless search for a better OP, you spend an educational day with a forward platoon, you experience one of their regular exchanges of rifle-grenades with the Germans in the houses on the opposite side of the *straat* that runs through the hamlet.

Later this becomes one of the most interesting targets you are required to engage at any time on this front, when Pigott, after experiencing firsthand one of these bizarre grenade exchanges during a visit to his forward troops, decides those German grenadiers should receive a sharp reprimand. On returning to his headquarters in the little farmhouse, he insists you shell them, even though no more than seventy or eighty feet separate the enemy houses from those on the near side of the street.

You warn him that even by using Charge I, to ensure the highest possible trajectory for the shells looping onto the target, it is entirely possible that every one will strike the first row of houses going in – that is, those within which his troops will be sheltering.

He understands but is ready to take the chance. So with the

connivance of his troops, who are warned to take shelter as best they can, you drop a stonk along that street – a "stonk" being a target requiring all the guns to drop their shells in a line, for a specified distance, along a selected bearing running through a map reference. Dispensing with prior ranging so as to catch a maximum number of the enemy by surprise with the first salvo, all possible care is required at the guns to ensure extreme accuracy, including application of "corrections of the moment" for meteorological conditions, and the use of their Sands Graphs to adjust the range of each individual gun, to compensate for the way gun pits are intentionally staggered to present a less concentrated target for marauding planes.

While no one is able to say what proportion of the shells hit the intended target, since none of the forward troops can keep their heads up, and it is far too foggy for you to gauge their effectiveness with any accuracy, some undoubtedly land where they are supposed to, providing a terrifying experience for any Heinie caught on the upper floors of any of those houses. At any rate, for a time at least, they stop firing grenades across the road.

Every day, from dawn to dusk, misty rain and fog enshroud the whole front, often restricting visibility to less than two hundred yards, which encourages patrol activity in both directions and makes everybody a little jumpy. But apart from some light mortaring, and those random burp guns splattering the house now and then, there is no really serious enemy activity. As the days pass you become convinced that the greatest threat to your continued existence comes not from the enemy, but from a mechanical monster devised by an ingenious member of Pigott's headquarters gang: a stove – a roaring, house-shuddering stove, roughly based on the principle of a blow torch and occupying much of the free floor-space in the little kitchen.

The principle is childishly simple: A couple of inches of petrol, in the bottom of a jerrycan, is set to boil on a little gas-operated Primus stove. While the lid is tightly secured on the jerrycan, a nail hole has been drilled about two-thirds of the way up the side of the can. As the gasoline heats up, a white spume of fumes begins to shoot out the nail hole in a steady, horizontal stream for a distance of about four feet. And when a match is tossed into this spume, it flashes into bluish white roiling flames with a pulsing roar, resembling, to an uncanny degree, the sound of the German jets periodically scooting overhead trying for the Nijmegen Bridge.

To contain the flames and turn them into something useful, this flame-thrower is set up at the open end of a rectangular structure built of bricks from the rubble outside — about a foot and a half wide, four feet long, and about three feet high, open at the top, with a base of bricks laid on the kitchen floor. Utilizing the grills from the oven of the regular kitchen range, to span the open top and hold pots and pans, this energetic cooker is capable of bringing potatoes to the boil in two or three minutes.

Its invention is not just an exercise in ingenuity to pass the time. When company Sgt.-Maj. Stewart "Pinky" Moffatt and two other volunteers of commendable initiative lure a cow, grazing in the field across from the kitchen door, into a barn beyond the orchard, where it can be turned into meat for the table, the need arises for a large-capacity stove that won't give off tell-tale smoke when fired up in the daytime, as would the conventional kitchen range.

Though the battalion kitchen prepares two hot meals a day for delivery in insulated Hay Boxes to the forward companies — supper after dark, and breakfast before dawn — the basic grub is still Compo M & V and the like, the same boring stuff all have been eating for months. Once the idea of cutting into a real honest-to-goodness steak takes hold of the mind, it easily becomes an obsession, particularly since within this company headquarters group is a man who was a professional butcher in Civvy Street — one Danny Butler.

Thus, peering out into the drizzle from the door of the woodshed late one foggy afternoon, you fully understand the awful frustration of Moffatt and his fellow conspirators (one grasping the cow by the tail), when they fail to persuade the suspicious beast to saunter in orderly fashion to her doom in the barn. And when at last the Sergeant-Major, whose feet are only now and then touching the ground, lets go of her neck and falls head-over-heels down the muddy slope, cursing mightily (in preference to being carried by the bellowing animal into no-man's-land and on into Germany) you bleed for him, while at the same time struggling to suppress the idea there is anything funny about him calling out, just before he lets go, "Oh to hell with it, lads, let her go!" – unaware that he alone is trying to restrain the indignant animal, the other two having abandoned him to his fate at least a hundred yards back.

However, during the night additional cowboys are enlisted, and next morning there are great chunks of meat on the dining-room table, which, you are told by Private Butler, will provide the choicest of steaks, the rest of the carcass having been sent back to the battalion cooks.

When the group decides there should be filet mignon steaks for breakfast, and they light a little Primus stove and place its hissing, blue flame under a jerrycan quarter-filled with gasoline, you retreat out the back door, believing the odds are better in risking a sniper's bullet in the mist than remaining in that cluttered kitchen where they are boiling a substance with an explosive power equal to TNT. But after a few minutes, as you get used to the muffled roar, and the delicious smell of frying beef drifts out through the passageway into the woodshed, you assemble enough nerve to return inside.

In the crowded kitchen the resemblance of the Rube Goldberg stove to a jet engine is even more remarkable, as the roiling flames fill the brick cavity and overflow upwards, licking around the frying pan so that the cook must turn the steaks almost continually to keep them from burning. The gas is expelled at such pressure from the jerrycan that the flame doesn't start until it is eight or ten inches from the nail hole. And as you study it, you become aware that that remarkably durable can, designed to withstand the impact of a drop to earth from a low-flying aircraft, is bulging out on both sides from the extreme pressure. When you point this out to the designer of this set-up, he bends down quickly and turns down the Primus stove flame. Slowly the jerrycan subsides to a more normal shape. And from then on whenever the stove is operating you make it your business to stand by and protect the size and shape of the jerrycan, reducing the Primus stove flame when necessary.

At lunchtime, you, along with all the others in Company HQ, have your second steak of the day – a full sirloin. And for supper you have your third steak. And around about midnight, the fourth steak of the day is delivered to you as you lie in your bedroll on the floor at the foot of the stove. You don't ask for it, and don't particularly want it, when you awake to the sound of the stove roaring and the sight of flames darting out between the loosely laid bricks a few inches from your nose.

Sgt.-Maj. Moffatt, obviously feeling the need for a midnight snack after returning from delivering the rations, rum, and mail to the forward troops, is standing at the frying pan with spatula in hand. When he spots you pulling back from the licking flames, he leans down and hands you a knife and fork, and places a dinner plate with an enormous brown, steaming steak on it on the floor before you. And you, leaning on one elbow, proceed to eat it with relish.

Next day, you consume nothing but the odd cup of tea. You aren't ill. You simply do not feel the need for food.

32

'TWAS THE EVE OF
THE FEAST OF SAINT NICK

❋

BY NOW THE DUG-OUTS BACK AT THE GUN POSITIONS ARE extraordinarily comfortable. No one, taking a casual walk through the gorse patches and stubby pines close by the battery gun positions, would ever suspect the snug comfort of the dwellings lying beneath the columns of blue smoke issuing from stubby, ground-level chimneys, manufactured from 25-pounder brass cartridge cases or pieces of regular stovepipe, sticking up here and there through the frost-covered ground.

The men have ransacked shell-ravaged, deserted Groesbeek for every conceivable thing useable for building; especially doors, handy substitutes for plywood. By the last days of November, poor old Groesbeek was virtually doorless, inside and out.

To this you can testify, for right after you were posted to 14th Battery, 4th Brigade was pulled out of the line and you and Gnr. Alexander Whitehawk were forced to set up new housekeeping arrangements from scratch near your D Troop guns. As Johnnies-come-lately, you searched through the ghostly empty village for the better part of one afternoon without turning up one door still hanging on its hinges. Finally you'd been forced to knock apart a chicken coop and haul it back to your chosen allotment in the frosty bushland near the guns.

Without Whitehawk's awesome capacity to get things done –

springing as much from his placid optimism and quiet staying power as from his extraordinary energy and initiative – that discouraging pile of weathered old lumber full of rusty nails would have lain where it dropped until spring. However, to your amazement, a few hours after he'd politely suggested you occupy yourself somewhere else and leave him be, he'd converted that unprepossessing pile of splintered junk into the snuggest dug-out anyone could ever hope for; not big – not much more than six-feet square – but big enough to accommodate two built-in wooden bunks stacked one over the other, while leaving enough room for one man at a time to get up, dress, shave, wash, and sort out kit.

And all of this in warm comfort, for, while engineering this veritable miracle, his ingenuity brought into being, using an empty petrol tin and a piece of clay drain-pipe embedded upright in the earthen wall at the foot of the stairs, an incredibly efficient little stove capable of heating up the dug-out in minutes when fed but a few sticks of wood.

If you live to be a hundred, you'll never forget the sense of total luxury the first night you occupied it, lying cosy and warm on your top bunk listening to a "Mary of Arnhem" broadcast on the 38-set – putting up with periodic interruptions by that saccharine-voiced *Fräulein* inviting you to defect and spend Christmas on the other side of the Rhine – to hear Crosby croon "I'm Dreaming of a White Christmas" and a swatch of familiar ballads from the vintage years of pop music before the war. As you read and reread special letters from home and exchange reminiscences with the taciturn Whitehawk each time he arises from his lower bunk to brew up still another cuppa char, it all seemed too good to be true.

By now only those few free spirits, who scorn secondhand building materials and have harvested piles of logs to erect cabins underground, are still involved in construction. The outstanding example is Major Bill Carr, of 26th Battery, an energetic soul determined to create an underground log cabin of such staggering proportions it is fast earning the title "Carr's Folly."

Candles and petrol lanterns are principal sources of lighting, but many dug-outs are lit in the manner of Major Drewry's subterranean wonder using rechargeable 12-volt radio batteries hooked up to 110-volt converters "borrowed" from derelict 19-sets and fed into electric lamps scrounged in Groesbeek. And some 2nd Battery dug-outs along the railway cutting are hooked into the regular power line running close to their position, the electricity reputedly coming from a generating station which the Germans have agreed not to shell or bomb as long as the power is allowed to cross the Rhine for their use as well.

However, since plumbing and drains do not exist here, latrines manage to maintain the primitive aspects you've come to associate with them in spite of noble engineering efforts by troop and battery sergeant-majors – including Sgt.-Maj. Ed Blodgett – to enhance seating arrangements with boards and timbers and burlap screens. And as the weather has worsened and the snows have come, on mornings or nights when arctic winds billow and whip those protective burlap screens about like sails in a gale, it takes great courage, courage born of sheer desperation, to bare one's extremities and press them down on boards freshly cleared of snow. You so detest using these primitive obscenities that, when back at the guns, you plan your daily routine to include regular visits to the RHQ building to coincide with certain cycles of your metabolism with which you have become familiar, so as to take full advantage of a truly great luxury: a flush toilet with a warm seat!

However, all things considered, all at the guns seem quite happy with their living conditions, and so no one in Dog Troop is particularly enthusiastic when, on the afternoon of December 5, orders are received from RHQ to pull their guns out of action and tow them back a few miles to a village called Groot Linden for forty-eight hours' rest and maintenance. By contrast, you and your crew, called back from a frigid OP to share the experience with the troop, are quite enthusiastic – visualizing warm billets and maybe even real beds.

But by the time Sgt.-Maj. Hill has led you to the modest little house in the village where he's arranged for you to sleep, and you've dumped off your bedroll and personal "ammunition box" with its precious goodies you've been hoarding from Christmas parcels from home, your enthusiasm is beginning to fade. The space allotted you is a clammy, unheated, narrow, ground-floor room off the living room, devoid of all furnishings except a kitchen chair and a Singer sewing-machine.

From then on, though you force yourself to maintain a suitably cheerful front (trying not to overdo it and appear deranged in the eyes of the troop), you secretly sympathize with the point of view frequently expressed by the Other Ranks during a very boring evening. According to the schedule decreed by RHQ, the troop is supposed to enjoy relaxation and good-fellowship, aided by a keg of wishy-washy Belgian beer and a double ration of rum served in their own chipped and battered enamelled mugs on stained wooden trestle-tables in a dimly lit hall, while nibbling distractedly on Compo cheese and hardtack.

As time goes on the gunners express their dim view of all this loudly and distinctly (if obliquely) in a variety of colourful ways to each other – sometimes using revised song lyrics, one of the most popular being sung to the tune of "Auld Lang Syne" – "Sit down you bum, sit down you bum, sit down you bum, sit dow-w-n!" – whenever one of their peers assembles the nerve to stand up and tries to get their attention.

But when they want to make their point of view known to their Troop Commander, it is expressed in the form of a question, such as: Why the hell, sir, didn't they let us just pull the guns out of action and do our maintenance on them right there in our pits – and let us relax in our own dug-outs?

You, of course, must manufacture phoney reasons. You know that they know they are phoney. But this doesn't worry you, for most of them are veterans of many years' experience with the ways of the army, who know that officers always have to defend the orders of officers senior to them, even when (as on many occasions in England) orders appeared to all ranks to be plain, unadulterated crap. And you remind them that whatever they think of the arrangements, they were made with the best of intentions and the sole purpose of making life a little more pleasant.

Around 10:00 P.M. you excuse yourself and return to your billet, intending to write some letters. The house is black, except for the lamp in the kitchen, but the lady supplies you with a kerosene lamp and you use the sewing-machine as a desk. Very soon your hands are so cold you can't hold the pen. You decide to get warmed up before piling into your bedroll on the floor, and go out and rap on the kitchen door. When they invite you in, you sit at the end of the kitchen table, facing the big range glowing with heat, opposite the man of the house who is writing with pen and ink – slowly and meticulously drawing each letter of each word as though he is engraving. Resting just beyond his writing pad on the table is a homemade cardboard house obviously coloured with wax crayons.

Immediately it is clear what he is doing. Late in the afternoon, just as you were being shown to your billet by the Sergeant-Major, you had witnessed a fascinating tabloid: A tall man with long, white beard, dressed like a bishop in mitred hat and flowing robe of purple and gold, accompanied by a black-faced man in fancy maroon, oriental dress with a turban in matching colour, carrying a bishop's staff – surrounded by a swarm of very young children – made their way slowly down the village street. The Sergeant-Major, who'd been here since morning with the advance party, was able to explain. This, the fifth of December, is the Eve of the Feast of Saint Nicholas, the day that benevolent gentleman and his black servant traditionally bring gifts to the good children of Holland. This year, however, he was having to tell the children that with the war on, some gifts might not be possible.

Now, that must be what this father is doing – writing his children individual letters from St. Nicholas. You question him as best you can with the odd Dutch word, while pointing at the cardboard house and the writing pad. And while he replies only in Dutch, his meaning is clear when he adds some pantomime; the cardboard house is the one and only thing they have from St. Nicholas for their two little kids now asleep upstairs.

You jump to your feet and rush to your room, where your ammunition box with its goodies rests beside your bedroll on the floor.

A can of real Canadian red salmon, a bag of saltwater kisses, and a bag of gumdrops (from your mother's latest parcel), and two giant-sized milk chocolate bars and a full pound of salted peanuts (from your wife) make quite a respectable pile when you carry them in and dump them on the kitchen table before the astonished father.

The tearful, joyous reaction of the man and then his wife – who turns from stirring something on the stove, on hearing him cry out – is almost enough to make tears come to your eyes. You point to the things and say "St. Nicholas" and then point upstairs to where the kids are sleeping. Then you point to yourself and wag your head "no, no" – and repeat again "St. Nicholas" as you point at the candies and peanuts. When finally they understand that the kids must think the stuff came from St. Nick, they smile and nod vigorously, and wipe away their tears.

The lady insists on giving you a cup of tea, while the man, with great ceremony for your benefit, tears up the letters he had written to the children, and throws the bits into the stove, brushing his hands with obvious satisfaction. And after you've had your tea, they wring your hand, and escort you to your bedroll. And you go to sleep feeling absolutely wonderful.

33

NO MAIL FOR MORIN

---　✳　---

MAIL, SOME WRITTEN A MONTH AGO, COMES UP TO THE OP with the rum ration this morning, December 24. The real Christmas mail including parcels arrived days ago, so this was a grand surprise.

Reading letters from home is a reverent matter, one demanding as much privacy as conditions will allow, for it is the closest thing to sharing intimacy with your beloved you can have over here. You drink in each sentence, sometimes each word, savouring the meaning. Some letters are reread a dozen times, as you squeeze out every last drop of meaning where you sense more meaning was intended than mere words can convey, or that she has dared express on paper.

But even so you ration yourself – one reading now and another reading later tonight, or maybe two tonight, if you are in a dry place where you can show a light. You are starved for love, but still you must be careful not to suffer from overexposure to its afterglow. This peculiarly subtle, self-imposed dehumanization process, for which you were entirely unprepared when you first arrived overseas, involves the forced forgetting of your beloved wife, the repression of your most tender and loving memories of her so as to retain your sanity. Through long practice this has become an almost automatic process, so different from those first few weeks of separation – when memories of those last days and hours before you parted were still fresh and vivid, and "forgetting" required an act of will almost as painful as the searing heartache and desire from which you were trying to escape.

There's a widely held belief that the Army Postal Corps each year holds up delivery of mail on this side of the Atlantic during the first part of December, letting it accumulate so as to make sure that everybody gets at least one letter just before Christmas. This may be a myth, since letters from home tend to bunch up at any time because of the peculiarities of the system, and frequently you've received on the same day four or five letters from your wife mailed days apart from Canada.

However, if they don't play games with the mail at this time of the year, they should. Mail matters a great deal at any time, but at this season it matters very, very much; particularly to those who have been away from home for years. This will be the fifth Christmas overseas for most of the Regiment. And for Lieut. Jack Bigg of Baker Troop, who arrived in Britain with 1st Division before Christmas 1939 as a gunner with the RCHA, it will be his sixth Christmas away from his beloved wife, Gladys, and his little daughter, Phyllis.

It was nice that everybody on your crew got mail for Christmas, and, as you press her little blue air letter to your nose to smell her Evening in Paris perfume before opening it, you find yourself hoping everybody back at the guns did too. But as your mind is forming the wish, you also know there is at least one who will receive nothing from his family: Gunner Morin (Joseph Jean Conrad Paul Henri), a batman in 2nd Battery. A friendly, outgoing, cheerful man, always whistling happily – strong, robust, blessed with seemingly boundless vigour – he never appears tired or out of sorts. And most of all he is a man sincerely concerned about the welfare of others.

It was he and he alone, who, when the Regiment was brought together last winter to live in Nissen huts at Monks Common near Horsham, Sussex, became aware that a new man, Gunner White-hawk, was suffering racial harassment. While this apparently was no more than mild slurs on his Indian heritage couched in barrack-room humour, no worse than other slurs being tossed about daily at other racial groups and individuals (frequently by members of minority groups themselves), it was nonetheless hurtful. And in bringing it to your attention, Morin suggested his competent friend would appreciate being invited to become your batman – a move that proved mutually beneficial.

How damnably unfair that this admirable, warm-hearted man, of all men, should not be getting mail from home; and not just at Christmas, but at any time, all because he'd volunteered for service in the Canadian Forces against the wishes of his stepfather. He came from a small place in Quebec, and when he'd enlisted on November 1, 1939, it seems his stepfather had sworn never to forgive him for volunteering to fight the war for *les anglais*, and even had forbidden his mother and other members of the family to write to him or send him parcels.

Typically, he'd never complained to you or anyone. One day when you'd offered him a cigarette, he'd told you he'd quit smoking; and when you'd asked if he'd done so for health reasons, he'd volunteered the story. Unlike everybody else, he never received smokes from home, and since he couldn't afford to keep himself supplied with English cigarettes, he'd been forced to bum from his pals. This of course had been much too embarrassing, so he'd quit.

Back at the guns a few days ago, on a cold, grey day preparing to snow, he went out of his way to come over to the 14th Battery position to look you up just after coming back from hospital. You recognized his friendly, vibrant, tenor voice, calling your name across a wide expanse of frost-whitened gorse before you recognized him, for he was wearing dark glasses. His greeting, always warm, was especially so. At first you ascribed it to the fact you hadn't bumped into each other for some time, but his effusive manner as he wrung your hand made it clear that for him at least this was in the nature of a reunion. Not aware that he'd been wounded and had been away for some time, you were forced to do some fancy footwork to cover up your ignorance when you asked him why he was wearing dark sunglasses on such a dark day, and he told you that he'd been blind for some time in hospital in England.

"You knew, of course, Captain, I'd been wounded?"

"Oh yes . . . yes, of course!"

"It was back in Normandy in August – just after Falaise."

"Ah yes . . . How stupid of me to have forgotten!"

"But of course there were many wounded that day."

"Yes, a great many."

"Twenty-six, I'm told – and four of the boys died . . ."

Of course – the smell of marigolds! Friardel on the way to Orbec: the heavy shelling of the churchyard – those damp and pungent flowers as you pressed your face down into that flowerbed beside the little stone house. The wagon lines (where Morin would have been) were particularly hard hit.

"But did I hear you correctly, Morin, that you actually were blind for a while?"

"Oh yes, Captain, the doctors at the hospital in England said I'd never be able to see again. And when the nurse told me they were going to ship me back to Canada, she said they had applied for a seeing-eye dog for me. But one morning I think I see a little bit of light – and I call the nurse and tell her, 'I think I see a little bit of light.' She says that is most unlikely – that perhaps I am mistaken, and not to get my hopes up. But she goes and gets the doctor, and when he removes the bandages and shines a bright light into my eyes, I tell him, 'The light is so bright it hurts.' And he says he thinks I am right – that my eyesight is coming back. They move me into a dark room, and every day they let in a little more light. Finally I get that I can see everything, and then they give me these dark glasses to wear and move me out into the ward with everybody else. But when I ask them when can I go back to my regiment, they tell me, never. They say it is a miracle that my sight has come back at all, that my eyes are so delicate they must never again be exposed to bright light, and I will have to wear dark glasses during daylight for the rest of my life. And because the risk of losing my dark glasses, or having them broken in action, is so great, I am being sent home to Canada."

"But Morin," you protest, "you're still here?"

"Next day I get the nurse to bring me my clothes, and to allow me to get up and walk around a bit – in preparation, I say, for leaving for Canada. That night I climb out through the window of the hospital and start hitchhiking back to the Regiment."

"But why," you ask, "when you know you are running such a great risk? You were safely out of it – why didn't you go home? You could have gone back to Canada with honour – you'd done your share."

For a moment he looks at you in bewilderment that you, of all people, should have to ask: "But, Captain, all my friends are here in the Regiment."

Down in your little dug-out, sharing a piece of Christmas cake and a couple of drams of Scotch with him and his pal Whitehawk, listening to them compare notes and bring each other up to date, you come to realize the full significance of his declaration.

You know this modest, self-effacing man would explode into uproarious laughter if anyone were to suggest he is a hero for just being here, carrying on like thousands of others. But for you, he is and always will be one of the truly admirable, courageous men of this war.

Comparing your situation with his at the time of enlistment, you come off rather badly. Within your family and the society in which you were raised, it would have been very difficult, if not impossible, to remain a civilian. While no one ever said anything, the pressure to enlist had been there from the hour war broke out. But Morin knew as he volunteered to go and fight for his country that he not only faced the possibility of disablement or death, he risked being ostracized by his own family. And now, when he could have gone home, he hitchhiked back to the Regiment, wearing dark glasses!

34

THE TOXIC BREW THAT
SICKENS THE MIND

❄

ANTICIPATING THEY WOULD BE IN THE LINE FOR CHRISTMAS, all three infantry battalions of 4th Brigade held their Christmas dinners a few days early – the Royals four days ago, not as a battalion affair, since no accommodation of suitable size was available, but as company dinners.

Their special Christmas rations, which you assume the gunners will also enjoy when they attend dinners in two shifts, half at noon today and half at noon tomorrow, Christmas day, included canned turkey and cranberry sauce, fruitcake and Christmas pudding, oranges, apples, and an issue of canned beer.

This you know only because you happened to visit Bob Suckling for a mug of seasonal cheer just as his D Company was preparing to hold their dinner in a convent billets. It was only December 20, but as you stood with Bob, just inside their kitchen door out of the way of the nuns and soldier cooks, sipping your whisky from a delicate glass – now and then enshrouded in clouds of steam full of the most delicious odours of things you'd almost forgotten existed – it was suddenly, truly Christmas morning as you remembered the special atmosphere of such mornings in other times.

It may have been the way the nuns bustled about with supplies of civilized cutlery and plates, fine tablecloths and candles, reminding you of the bustling about of other ladies on other Christmas mornings, that gave substance to the illusion.

In every possible way they were trying their best to ensure the occasion would be memorable for the soldiers – something the Mother Superior guaranteed for you and Bob at least, when, in her hesitant English, she remarked, "How nice to hear the boys singing their songs of Christmas!" as she passed the cooks of D Company attending their burners in the snowy courtyard and singing lustily: "Roll me over in the clover – roll me over, lay me down, and do it again!"

Bob had pressed you to stay and share dinner with them, and you'd been sorely tempted, but knowing that the turkey was rationed at four ounces per man, it would have been criminal to accept. But the illusion that it was Christmas day persisted, and undoubtedly accounted for a rare bout of homesickness that night, which took the miserable form of feeling trapped, shut off from everyone you hold dear.

Normally you are not inclined to chafe under the confining rules of military dictatorship, though they are real enough, with most of your choices of movement, action, dress, words, and manners (even facial expressions) restrained by the whims, orders, and decrees of others, fully authorized by rules and regulations ascribed to the Monarch himself, and carrying the full force of law. These matters have been the very fabric of life as you have known it far too long to cause you any concern. After all, it was of your own free will, and for the very best of reasons, you voluntarily exchanged your wide-ranging civilian freedom for the peculiar imprisonment of a service uniform in wartime. From the first hour of enlistment you have been conscious that until your service ends, you are restricted to whatever part of the globe the army cares to post you, that your comings and goings must be accounted for every hour of the day and night, that you cannot travel any distance from your unit without an authorized pass, and that you must not expect to recross the Atlantic and see your home again until this war ends.

All of this has long since been accepted by you and everyone else over here, and arouses no unmanageable feelings of resentment throughout most of the year. However, at Christmas, the traditional

time for families to gather to share in the seasonal joy, the rigid con-
straints of the cold-hearted military, shutting you away from home
and loved ones in Canada even to the extent of prohibiting you the
use of the trans-Atlantic telephone for the duration, can suddenly
become a suffocating burden of cruel bondage.

Fortunately homesickness is an infrequent visitor, for it is
absolute torture when the insidious forces of sweet, poignant memories, and the desire to hug and be hugged in love once more in the
bosom of your family, combine – as they did four nights ago – to
form the toxic brew that sickens the mind, body, and soul; that
cannot be willed away, but must pass in slow agony through diminishing levels of melancholia, leaving you hung-over in an aching
void for hours or even days.

You and Whitehawk had settled down in your bunks for the
night in your cosy dug-out at the guns, rereading letters from home
and listening to Christmas carols broadcast by the sugar-voiced
"Mary of Arnhem" spilling from the big earphones of the little 38-
set hanging on a nail at the head of the bunks. Somewhere between
"Hark! The Herald-Angels Sing," "Joy to the World!" and "O Little
Town of Bethlehem," you succumbed to a flood of warm, glowing
memories, memories going back through her shining eyes on
Christmas Eve 1939, when you gave her your engagement ring
beside the blazing hearth at your family home.

Once unlocked, memories swirled out of the treasury of the
years in heart-smothering vividness – memories of old love-filled
houses, always overheated on Christmas Eve for the sake of little,
bare feet creeping down the dark stairs before dawn to see what
Santa had left at the tree.

As during other pre-Christmas bouts with homesickness, you've
done your best to suppress the effects of memories too vividly
recalled, by telling yourself how lucky you are compared to
Russians facing their fourth winter battling the Germans in the
cruel snows of the Eastern Front, or those poor guys captured at
Dieppe in 1942, including twenty-two from the Regiment, spending their third Christmas in a Heinie prison camp. And, dammit,

you are still alive and whole, in mind and body, which, in the face of the awful casualties in Normandy and along the Scheldt, is something you should be grateful for.*

Still, such efforts to divert your thoughts from Christmases past are only partially successful, for deep within you there smoulders a craving to live again those shining memories, even if it means being left with an aching heart and damp eyes. Nor does the prospect of spending Christmas in an OP help, and as you climb up inside the frigid windmill tower this morning, you simply can't resist feeling sorry for yourself. Thus, when, soon after settling down on the frost-laden cushions in the cupola, you get a message to report back to the Colonel at Brigade Headquarters, prepared to spend Christmas eve and Christmas day at their imposing Swiss-style chalet hidden deep in the bush west of Groesbeek, you respond with undisguised enthusiasm.

---

* By December 31, 1944, the Canadians in Northwest Europe had suffered 30,719 casualties. The severity of 2nd Division casualties from July 11 to December 31 – 11,875 in five and a half months – is brought into focus when placed against 3rd Division's 11,575 with a month more service, and the 10,586 suffered in eighteen months by 1st Division, involved in some of the harshest fighting of the war in Sicily and Italy. By war's end, though in action only ten months, 2nd Division's 15,493 casualties exceeded all other Canadian divisions. Of course the bulk of these were infantry casualties: 13,051 in ten months, compared to 3rd Division's 12,315 in eleven months, and 1st Division's 11,262 in nineteen months (allowing for a month's travel time from the Italian front to Holland in the spring of 1945). Armoured units suffered fewer casualties: 4th Armoured Division, 4,592; and 2nd Armoured Brigade, 1,077.

35

JERRY CAROLS, THEN
SHELLS TANNENBAUMS

※

THERE WILL BE SOME IN THE NIJMEGEN SALIENT WHO WILL remember Christmas 1944 as a day when a truce of sorts existed along their part of the line. During the morning, 4th Brigade Headquarters receives reports from the Royals that some forward positions hear Germans in nearby trenches singing carols. And over on 3rd Division front, Lieut. Donald Pierce, with a platoon of the North Nova Scotia Highlanders, on a dike half a mile from the misty Rhine, will record in his journal that will one day become a book:

> Not a sound anywhere, not a shot. I have a strong sense of being able to see silence. The river, which is clearly visible beyond the icy fields, bearing a few floating branches, and the snowflakes that are rather idly falling, are the only things with any motion. A few minutes ago I was sure I could hear the snowflakes dropping onto my battle jacket. A shout would carry for miles. I have never seen such stillness. I wonder if it's the same along the entire front? Up here both sides seem to have decided to call everything off, as though this day were beyond the war.*

---

* From *Journal of a War* (Toronto: Macmillan Co. of Canada, 1965).

However, others only a few miles away will remember this day as one of violence with little seasonal charity being shown by either side. Sgt. Hunt, in 26th Battery Command Post at the harassing-fire position among the snowy *tannenbaum*s, will report in his diary: "Air full of such exchanges as are in order between us and friend Hun. We appear to be giving more than getting, and the extent of our seasonal rejoicing is limited to the difference. Even so, Jerry lays down a heavy concentration on Easy Troop, which despite its density results in only one casualty."

Logging the same incident, Sgt. McEwan, of Easy Troop, implies a generous amount of good cheer of some potency has been passed around among 4th Field drivers Christmas morning: "Jerry threw over a few 88s, and Sgt. Morley Stokes was wounded in the leg. After a hectic ride back to the MO, during which the wounded man threatened to drive the vehicle himself, he was removed to the Casualty Clearing Station on his way to hospital."

Then back at the wagon lines, just before noon, Jerry sends over more 88s, seriously wounding Gunner Leon Batke and "drawing blood" from Gunner Ken Brock. Brock is just about to climb aboard his gun tractor to drive a load of fellow drivers over to RHQ for Christmas dinner when the first 88 arrives and he is struck by a fragment.

Being wounded is never a laughing matter, but Brock succeeds in breaking up those who come to his aid, when, as he is being carted off for medical treatment, growls: "The dirty bastards have done me out of my Christmas dinner!"

And when you hear the story, you know exactly how Brock feels, and you fully appreciate his sentiments, because those same "bastards," indirectly, but just as effectively, are in the process of cheating you out of what was to be a legendary feast at 4th Brigade, an event to which you have been looking forward with a degree of anticipation that only a man who has not seen a Christmas dinner since 1941 can develop.

When, the night before last, December 23, 4th Brigade moved back into the line, and you had to go up to occupy an OP, it looked

like you might miss Christmas dinner for the third year in a row —
thus setting some sort of record in view of the importance the
powers-that-be, both military and political, attach to the matter of
seeing "the boys" have at least one good meal a year.

The first Yuletide dinner you missed was back in 1942 at
Barnham Junction. Just as your 26th Battery was about to sit down
to a festive board in the village hall, you were sent off in a Jeep to
collect some British ack-ack blokes on isolated gun sites around
Tangmere and Ford airfields, and deliver them to a dinner at regimental headquarters. So well-camouflaged were their gun sites,
hidden behind high thorny hedges in far-off corners of fields, that
by the time you delivered them, and got back to your own meal at
Barnham, there wasn't even a spoonful of gravy left. So it had been
fried bully beef hash in the deserted kitchen of the officers' mess.

Christmas Day 1943 topped even that sad tale, when, designated
duty officer for the day, you were stuck alone and forgotten in the
deserted regimental office, waiting in vain for someone to bring
you dinner. Regimental Clerk Sgt. George Lloyd had been with
you, but you'd sent him off to have his dinner, from which he did
not return.

Bemused by the merrymaking sounds of a roaring party in the
sergeants' mess that could be heard now and then through the walls
of the Nissen hut, you'd gone on waiting for someone to relieve
you, or at least to bring you some food. However, not until mid-
afternoon did a good Samaritan, in the guise of longtime buddy
Lieut. W. G. "Sink" Sinclair, arrive with a deck of cards, a cribbage
board, two glasses, and a bottle of gin — but no food, of course.

So, when yesterday morning the CO called you back to take over
for him at Brigade so he might participate in a regimental carol and
communion service at midnight, and be present at the two Christmas
dinners scheduled for Rusthuis — half the unit on Christmas Eve and
half today — it seemed the gastronomic gods were at last about to
smile on you. Before taking leave of you, the CO made it clear you
were in for a real treat, explaining that Brig. Cabeldu decided a
month ago that Christmas dinner 1944 at 4th Brigade Headquarters

would be, for those lucky enough to partake of it, their most memorable meal since leaving home. He had even sent his Belgian liaison officer, who was an Antwerp wine-exporter in peacetime, to the south of France to select and bring back an exotic range of the finest vintage wines his educated palate could locate.

Thus the staggering impact of the news at noon today, just as you join others assembling for a predinner drink: the meal is off – not postponed, but *off*! It is unbelievable, until it is explained that 3rd Division has been ordered to take over this front, so that 2nd Division can become a mobile force to deal with an imminent airborne attack related to the Battle of the Bulge on the American front in the south. According to Dutch Underground sources, a German airborne division is poised to strike a blow in front of Von Rundstedt's spearheads, driving with astonishing speed through the Americans towards the Meuse (as the Maas is known in Belgium) – their ultimate objective Antwerp, cutting off the British and Canadian armies in Holland.

Though 3rd Division units will not move in until dark, it will take all afternoon to load the Brigade vehicles because of the tedious procedure laid down to prevent enemy air reconnaissance from discovering the chalet is an important headquarters. Only one vehicle at a time will be brought to the front steps for loading, and it must follow the track through the snow made by its predecessor.

While this preserves a single set of innocent-looking tracks in the snow, the pale winter sun is going down before all Brigade Headquarters vehicles are loaded and parked with motors shut off under the trees along the road in front of the chalet.

Now, as long, dark shadows form in the snow-filled woods, you receive a message from the Brigade Major, Jim Knox, to join him and Brig. Cabeldu in his command caravan up ahead, prepared to arrange diversionary fire, as it may be required during the turnover of battalions. As you head up past the line of vehicles towards the rear door of the big caravan, the first of the 3rd Division vehicles begin to arrive at the chalet.

From the raucous shouting back and forth among their drivers, as they crowd their vehicles helter-skelter into the area in front of the chalet creating a minor traffic jam, it's pretty obvious they haven't allowed their move over here to interfere with having their full share of Christmas cheer — in whatever form it may have been presented.

Big flakes of snow are beginning to drift down as you mount the steps to the door of the van. Inside an officer shifts over on one of the padded benches that line both sides, so you can sit down facing the Brigadier. There are no lights on in the van at the moment, for the blackout curtains on the windows are still open, but it's nice and warm, and very quiet and very civilized. Even the normal radio garbage that continually spews out of the earphones of the signallers, two of whom can be seen sitting behind a glass partition at the front end of the van, is very subdued.

No one is talking. Everybody seems fascinated with what is going on out there among the newcomers. And what they can observe leaves them speechless. With none of the ebullient 3rd Division crowd showing the slightest concern, the pristine single set of tracks leading to the door — so tediously preserved by 4th Brigade at the sacrifice of their gourmet dinner with wines of matchless vintage — has already disappeared under an intricate maze of tell-tale tracks from the clutter of vehicles filling the whole of the snow-covered circular space in front of the chalet.

The Brigadier stands up to look, but immediately, as though he can't stand to watch it, he waves his hands together to have the blackout curtains closed. This allows for a gas lantern to be lit and hung from the ceiling, and the van turns into quite a cosy little room. You wish a conversation would start, but the initiative is clearly up to the Brigadier, and he chooses to remain silent, staring down at the floor, concerned, you suppose, with what could happen to his battalions on their way out of the line.

As you study his face as he sits frowning down at his feet, you try to imagine the cumulative effect of the awful strain on the minds and souls of men of high command whose orders continually place the lives of hundreds at risk, and who, more than anyone else, must be eternally conscious of the awesome numbers of their brigade, or division, or corps, who didn't make it through to Christmas.

You become conscious of the muffled voice of a signaller on the other side of the glass panel talking into his mike, repeating weird code names as he writes down a message. Sliding open the glass, he hands the paper out to the Brigade Major. Decoded, it means two companies of the Royals are safely out of the line.

As more and more reports come through of an orderly turnover without incident, the atmosphere in the caravan noticeably relaxes. Behind the glass the signallers start to sing in harmony:

"Si-lent night – Ho-ly night – all is calm – all is bright . . ."

The Brigadier looks up frowning quizzically. Then, as though suddenly remembering what day it is, in a wondering voice he exclaims:

"My God, gentlemen, it's Christmas night."

No one says anything; everyone is too deeply immersed in his own thoughts. Even the Brigade Major, who always seems capable of coming up with a suitable comment of a reassuring nature when the Brigadier expresses himself, is now totally possessed by his own reveries.

Soon the changeover of brigades is reported complete and you are released to return to your own vehicle to get ready to move out.

As you walk back past pine trees laden with snow, now falling steadily and mercifully to cover the messy lacework of vehicle tracks around the front yard of the chalet, you recall with a pang snowy winter nights like this in Canada shared with your beloved, such as a memorable sleigh-ride to Teskey's dance hall at Hog's Back outside Ottawa. You can almost smell the hot chocolate and hear the joyful bantering over the booming jukebox. Colin Ross, the Royals' Scout Platoon officer, was on that sleigh ride. You must remember to ask him some time if he remembers.

Oh, God, how you envy Major Bill Carr, who was notified yesterday he is to return immediately to Canada for a staff job in Ottawa!

36

MORE FUN THAN

A BARREL OF OYSTERS

❋

THE DAY AFTER CHRISTMAS 4TH FIELD IS ORDERED TO SAY goodbye to the cosy dug-outs on which so much effort has been lavished, and move north three kilometres to new positions in the frozen land, where empty boxcars – draughty, frigid, and smelly – sitting in the drifting snow of a railway siding, are considered prime billets, coveted by all but the few who gain their barren possession. Two days later, with snow lying thick on the ground, the guns are deployed in battle positions two kilometres southeast of there.

And then on December 30, with the sun going down on what feels like the frostiest evening of the winter, the Regiment moves off in convoy to travel some fifty miles south to Boxtel, halfway between Eindhoven and 's-Hertogenbosch, where the German paratroopers are expected to drop in aid of their armoured spearheads driving through the Yanks towards Antwerp, which already have created on Allied maps an ominous bulge.

All night you follow a truck with white smoke pouring out of a stovepipe protruding out the back between the canvas flaps. Riding in your open steel bucket, your envy of the occupants of that truck, warmed by a coal-burning stove hidden within, rises with each passing hour. The trip, over ice-glazed roads, takes seven hours, and at one halt, when you try to climb out to relieve yourself and have a smoke, you find you are too stiff to make it over the side without help from your driver, Gunner "Palm" Knight. Only with the greatest difficulty are you able to undo the necessary buttons, and without his help you cannot secure a cigarette and light it. Though he too rides in the open front cockpit, separated from the hot engine box against which the signallers keep warm, his blood is kept moving by his driving exertions.

When at last the Regiment arrives at Boxtel and disembarks at a school, which is a medical college when in use, marvellously over-heated with steam coils, the like of which you haven't encountered since leaving Petawawa, it is as though you have arrived in heaven. Your body drinks in the heat, and when told you must sleep in your clothes (the Regiment being on four hours' notice and FOO crews on one-hour notice) you go to sleep with a complete sense of luxury.

As the first day of 1945 dawns frigid and misty, 4th Field, along with 4th Brigade and the rest of 2nd Division, is held out of action, but in a high state of readiness. Recce parties are out at dawn plotting the defence of Tilburg and a nearby airdrome. The rest have no duties.

While some brave souls take the opportunity to borrow skates from Dutch residents skating merrily on the frozen moat of a nearby castle, you and most others are quite content, after that marrow-freezing ride last night, to drowse away the day inside the warm school.

However, this delicious prospect is nipped in the bud by orders from above that troop route-marches are to be held "to enliven the spirit and bring tone to the muscles" of all below the rank of major. (Why majors and up don't require enlivening of the spirit and muscle toning is not explained.) Thus it happens that at 9:00 A.M. almost every worthwhile member of 4th Field is outdoors moving in various directions among the narrow streets of Boxtel to witness, at least in part, the swan song of the Luftwaffe.

The streets are glazed with a thick coating of ice, guaranteeing there is more slipping and sliding than marching. Remaining upright while making discernible forward progress demands not only acute mental alertness but more than a little acrobatic ability. Thus no one shows much interest in the succession of fighter planes scudding in from the east over the rooftops and disappearing in the early morning mists. All are too busy trying to maintain their footing on the glassy cobblestones of a confined street that echoes and re-echoes with the clattering and scraping of hobnailed boots finding it impossible to keep in step. Then one plane, circling leisurely over the village, attracts attention when it banks very low, just above the street.

For a split-second you find yourself looking right into the eyes of the pilot. Then, just as your unbelieving eyes spot the German cross on the side of the plane, somebody yells: "It's a Jerry!"

And you shout: "Take cover! Take cover!"

This is easier said than done. Even when, slipping and sliding, all manage to make it up over the curb, the only cover available is in the shallow doorways of the old stone buildings that line the street cheek by jowl, forming a solid wall tight against the narrow side-walk abutting the vehicular road. Mighty poor cover if Jerry returns and strafes the street. Fortunately he doesn't. And you are left wondering whether the swarm of planes you hear in the distance, periodically whining and stuttering, are German. And what are the implications?

In the afternoon you hear that the Allied tactical air forces based in Western Europe have been put out of action by German fighters simultaneously attacking all the mist-shrouded airfields in Holland, Belgium, and France this morning. Flying down on the deck, to avoid radar detection, they caught squadrons totally unprepared.

Weather conditions being so poor, few standing patrols were up over any of the airfields at the time; and hangovers from New Year's Eve partying had not enhanced the speed of response to the raids.

Those enemy fighter planes curling leisurely over Boxtel this morning were obviously getting their bearings before going into a slashing attack on the airdrome near Eindhoven. The attack lasted only twenty-two minutes but created chaos resulting in many deaths and in the destruction of dozens of Spits and Typhoons still sitting on the ground.*

Eindhoven, you recall, is the base of a Spitfire pilot posted for a couple of days over Christmas to 4th Brigade Headquarters to learn firsthand what war on the ground is like for the troops he is supporting. A most pleasant chap, he'd told you he cherished a dream of leading a crusade for seatbelts in automobiles in Canada after the war, convinced seatbelts in Spitfires saved his life twice when his planes pranged and were complete write-offs. While his idea sounds like a pipe dream, he was so very earnest in his desire to see car seatbelts brought into universal use, you hope he made it through those grim attacks this morning.

At the New Year's "at home" thrown by the officers of 4th Field in an improvised mess here at 4:00 P.M., with all the senior officers of 4th Brigade, including their Brig. Fred Cabeldu, in attendance, the devastating German fighter attack is a topic of lively discussion, second only to the sensational trays of oysters on the half-shell passing to and fro among the astonished guests.

All of this, of course, is entirely hearsay since you – along with several other officers of commendable initiative but no experience in and even less talent for opening oysters – are closeted in the scullery, chopping notches in oyster shells and prying open an endless number of the gnarled darlings from a seemingly bottomless

---

* Ten Luftwaffe fighter groups, consisting of nearly one thousand aircraft from more than thirty-eight German airdromes, some of them two hundred miles from their targets, converged on sixteen forward Allied airfields in Holland, Belgium, and France at precisely 0920 hours New Year's morning, 1945, and with cannon and rocket fire attempted to destroy parked aircraft and vital ground installations. Total Allied losses were 46 airmen killed and 241 aircraft put out of action, 130 of them totally destroyed. But in gaining this victory the Luftwaffe suffered irreparable losses: more than 300 planes and 253 of their most experienced pilots.

barrel in a losing struggle to maintain supply in some semblance of balance with demand.

Junior officers, who go forth to pass around the trays of the bivalve mollusks, report a smash hit, that this "at home" will go down in history as the most remarkable of all time. Which is all very nice if you can open the obstinate critters.

Secretly you curse the unique initiative of Lieut. Jack Bigg (Baker Troop Leader) and Capt. Ted Adams (Fox Troop), who, appalled at the prospect of corned beef sandwiches being served at a 4th Field reception, took off at dawn this morning to South Beveland to rake the oyster beds shown on the map. And then on their way back added further lustre to their glittering reputations as master scroungers, when they "borrowed" a barrel of rum that somehow tipped off a loading dock of a British supply depot into their passing Jeep.

Strange carryings-on for two ex-RCMP constables, you might say. But then anyone who knows their story is aware that Adams and Bigg, buddies ever since they conspired to get themselves kicked out of the RCMP in the fall of 1939 so they might join "C" Battery 1st Field RCHA in Winnipeg as gunners in time to sail for England before Christmas, are not men to stand on ceremony. Denied by their superiors the right to enlist in anything but the Provost Corps when Canada went to war, they simply revealed they were both married men, which in the eyes of the RCMP constituted an unforgivable misdemeanour before a constable completed at least five years with the force.*

---

* The RCMP did not forgive Captain John Bigg for marrying without permission. At war's end, on returning to the force, he was treated as a rookie, assigned to opening doors on Parliament Hill and posing in his scarlet tunic, breeches, riding boots, spurs, and all, for pictures with American tourists. Later, with some satisfaction, he returned to Parliament Hill, as the Member for Athabaska, to serve seventeen years with the Diefenbaker government and after.

But, damn their eyes, you wish today they'd scrounged some chickens or a suckling pig – something not requiring shelling. Just about the time you decide that before you go mad you must have a change of pace, and are preparing to go out among the guests to pass your own tray – a great, round affair you have just finished loading with a mass of glistening oysters on half-shells on a thick bed of ice garnished with seaweed – into the kitchen comes one of the newer subalterns, Lieut. J. L. McLean, begging you to allow him to take the tray and serve the Colonel and the 2 IC who are at that moment talking to Brig. Cabeldu.

While his weird reasoning that the moment is propitious for him to become a waiter – that serving oysters with élan to the Brigadier and the Colonel will somehow get him out of the doghouse in which he is presently residing – makes no sense whatsoever, his begging is so pitiful and your present mood so sour, it strikes you this pioneering experiment in "sucking-up" might provide some fresh insight into human relations.

From the half-open swinging door, you watch as he staggers towards the little group of distinguished officers in the centre of the room, carrying high over his head your carefully arranged great tray of oysters, seaweed, and ice. Just as he reaches them he seems to fumble the tray as he is lowering it to a presentable level, and dumps the entire mess on the head and down the front of the Brigadier.

Feeling a twinge of conscience, you make for the unfortunate subaltern as fast as you can. As you are passing the 2 IC, he snarls:

"Get him out of here, and place him under close arrest!"

When you come up behind him, he is engaged in picking seaweed off the chest of the Brigadier – pawing away with all the delicacy of a nearsighted bear. For a moment, as you take hold of his arms to turn him around, you really feel sorry for him, for it seems he's crying in boyish anguish, horrified at what he's done. But then you realize those strange moaning sounds he is making are unsuccessful attempts to suppress laughter! And as he turns to come away with you, he breaks into such a fit of laughing, it stops the last remnants of polite, covering conversation still being attempted.

"Oh, my gawd," says he in a hoarse, gurgling whisper that can be clearly heard in the farthest corner of the now attentive room, as you steer him to the hallway door, "Did you see the seaweed in his hair?"

In other days of other COs and CRAs, such conduct would have been enough to write finis to a potentially illustrious military career. But current senior officers must have a sense of humour. Not only does Lieut. McLean survive, he's posted as a liaison officer to Brig. Frank Lace's staff at Division.*

For five days the Regiment marks time with lectures and troop deployments, while the senior officers work on operation orders to cover every possible emergency deriving from enemy parachute landings. Then on January 6 a regimental parade is held to watch Brig. Lace present four brave men with Commander-in-Chief Certificates: Gunner Art Harder, Bombardier M. E. Jeffery, Lance-Bombardier J. W. Schneider, and Signals Corps Lance-Cpl. Priest, attached to RHQ.

Next day, the threat of an enemy parachute landing having faded, the Regiment returns to the Nijmegen salient, with everybody looking forward to getting back into their snug old dug-outs. But before this happens, the guns are deployed elsewhere in the snowy bush, and the gunners have to make the best of what they can find. Some get billets in houses, but most have to make do in nearby boxcars or in the poor-excuses-for-dug-outs left by 12th Field.

---

* Still, a unique penalty for overindulgence was devised by Brigadier Lace to rein in the ebullient McLean. At war's end 2nd Division Headquarters was in a beautifully preserved stone castle (Godens Schloss, near Oldenburg) complete with portcullis, drawbridge, and moat. When McLean had you up for dinner, he sorrowfully told you he'd been "put on the wagon" and warned that if he fell off, he'd have to mount the battlements in his best serge, complete with Sam Brown, and dive into the moat among the lilypads and frogs. Of course the inevitable happened, and he took the plunge in full view of the CRA and staff.

The day the Regiment moves back into the old positions behind Groesbeek, January 11, your D Troop is ordered northwest of Nijmegen over many miles of ice-glazed dike roads to deploy two and a half miles southeast of the villages of Leeuwen and Druten near the Rhine, to support the rescue by motorized assault boats of a number of walking-wounded from the far shore who have been in hiding over there since the parachute drop at Arnhem failed last September. The operation is called "Heaps" after Capt. Leo Heaps, a survivor of the parachute landing, who persuaded the High Command that many wounded parachutists, including a "high-ranking officer" (Brig. John Hackett), left behind during the fast evacuation, could be brought back if his plan were followed.

During the day you remain out of sight at the HQ of Major D. G. Mackenzie's D Squadron, 7th Recce Regiment, in what normally would be the principal's office of a regular school that has been converted to a convent school by nuns whose convent was burned over their heads when the Polish armour took this area many weeks ago. At night you go down to where the assault boats are hidden in a brickyard near the water's edge, to watch for the signal that the refugees have arrived at the far bank (the flare of a Very light looping briefly in the black sky), at which time you are to start your diversionary shelling a mile to the left of where the assault boats are to land. Night after night you wait with Heaps and his boatmen in the cold windy darkness, but no signal comes, and after eight days your troop is ordered to rejoin the unit.*

---

* How Hackett and others, aided by the Dutch, eventually made it back over the Rhine is told in Leo Heaps's *The Grey Goose of Arnhem*, Paper-Jacks, Markham, Ontario, 1977.

37

A HELMET LEFT HANGING

ON A SNOWY CROSS

———————————— ✳ ————————————

IN A LAND THAT IS FROZEN SOLID MOST OF DECEMBER
and January, and where a succession of blustery storms do their best
to fill in all uncovered trenches with drifting snow, some OPs are
just open holes dug into the forward slope of a hill and floored with
straw or pine boughs to cover the muddy sludge that continually
forms in the bottom from the body heat of their occupants. And
when you rejoin the Regiment and the Rileys return to the line for
two weeks, your OP is such a trench, almost lost among the deep
undisturbed white drifts billowing across the brow of a sparsely
wooded ridge rising 250 feet above the nearby Maas river's flood
plain.

With no Rileys within sight or sound, it is a remarkably lonely
spot, in distinct contrast to Battalion Headquarters down in the
valley behind you, where each morning, as you pass on your way to
the trail up the steep slope to your OP, a boisterous group, including
their CO, Lt.-Col. Denny Whitaker, and your Battery Commander,
Jack Drewry, make something of a Spartan ritual out of shaving and
washing in the snowbanks among the pines – bare to the waist and
steaming like walruses in the frosty, predawn grey light, some even
engaging in roaring snowball fights as you go by.

But once beyond the range of their cheerful bantering, you hear
no other human voice until you come back down this way again at
dusk.

Sometimes when you climb up through the deep snow, threading your way between the young pines, about the size of Christmas trees, and reach the crest of the hill, your trench has been so well camouflaged by snowdrifts you are able to identify it only by the Canadian steel helmet hanging by its web strap on a melancholy wooden cross poking up in the snow. The solitary grave lies right on the floor of the dog-leg entrance to a deep, well-constructed trench constituting the OP, and you spend hours trying to imagine how he was killed, starting with a jumping anti-personnel "S"-mine (Schützenmine), in wide use around here.*

Or perhaps it was a mortar bomb? Or maybe a Jerry crept up and heaved a grenade into the trench? But after days of considering the matter, you are inclined towards the likelihood it was a sniper – who right now could be lining up your head in his telescopic sights.

Because the weather is so cold and miserable, and you don't really need a signaller up here with the telephone line laid right up to the OP, you come up alone each morning. But with no one to talk to, it does make for a long day, even with the few hours of daylight. Almost nothing is ever seen moving in the valley below you, though it is reputed to be infested with German outposts.

On particularly cold days, when something piping hot at midday would go down well, you recall that miraculous self-heating can of oxtail soup they issued you on the ship coming to Normandy, and wonder whatever became of the supply. If ever issued, it has been creamed off by the rear echelons. Never once has your carrier crew, or any infantry unit with whom you've served, received one can, however much it would mean by way of nourishment for the body

---

* The much hated and feared "S" mine consisted of a canister of 350 ball-bearings packed with explosive, dug in the ground with only a stubby neck, ringed with little prongs, showing. Brushed by a boot, a broken prong triggered the canister to jump up about three feet above the ground, exploding the charge and ball bearings.

and comfort for the soul to men shivering in the sodden, flooded polders of the Scheldt last fall, and now huddled in open trenches among the drifting snowbanks of Groesbeek and Mook.

Sitting for hours without moving, snuggled down in your flying jacket, worn under your windproof Don R coat, the cold air makes you intolerably drowsy. Now and then you go to sleep, which disturbs you greatly, for you have been around long enough to realize fully how vulnerable you are up here even when you are awake and alert – completely isolated, alone, and devoid of all infantry protection. But no matter how you lecture yourself, chainsmoke and eat boiled sweets to stay awake, you frequently doze off.

Once it is quite dark when you wake up, and for a brief moment you have to fight down panic when you try to stand up and remove yourself in haste from what has become a cold, dark tomb and find it impossible to walk, let alone walk quickly. With all your instincts tuned to flight, your muscles and joints are too stiff with cold to function. Mentally coaching yourself, you thresh your arms back and forth across your chest as strenuously as possible, while stomping your feet with all the vigour you can muster. At first the efforts of your arms and legs are so feeble, it's as though you are still dreaming. But shortly you become mobile enough to stumble, trip, and slide down the dark snowy trail to light and warmth and human companionship – not to mention scalding hot tea laced with rum.

Apart from being mildly curious, no member of your crew shows any sign of having been worried about you not appearing at last light. They'd just gone ahead and eaten supper, and for this you are entirely grateful, for on the way down, you'd been unable to invent a credible substitute for the truth. But when the current ongoing argument, as to whether any malt whisky could ever match a fine blended Scotch, peters out, and before the next argument begins, it occurs to your driver, Gunner "Palm" Knight, to ask what held you up.

Preparing to shade the truth, you take a deep breath, but before you can begin, Gunner Eugene Bowers – who handles the duties of

OP ack and likes to pose as the "elder statesman" on the crew to the continuing irritation of Knight – offers to bet any reasonable sum with anyone that you merely had fallen asleep.

This is an irresistible challenge to Knight, who, when back at the guns, allegedly runs an illegal "crown and anchor" casino, though this is yet to be proven, for, his unique round shack is built entirely of Groesbeek doors standing upright, and with all the door-handles still in place and only one door actually operating, a surprise raid is almost impossible when the snow is tamped down equally all the way around the structure. Before you can intervene, Knight has taken an even-money bet of 200 Belgian francs that you didn't fall asleep.

When finally they turn their attention to you, you can't help bursting into a fit of uncontrollable laughter. Your esteemed driver scowls, curses, and pays Bowers.

Each night you and your crew pass the hours of darkness in this small cave excavated by some previous crew in the side of the hill at a particularly steep part, not far from Battalion Headquarters. It is so snug and safe that each afternoon you normally have difficulty waiting until the light fades before trekking down the quarter of a mile or so through the snowy woods to the hot meal you know will be waiting for you.

The one and only serious drawback to life in this cave, whose structural stability is dependent on frost, is its proclivity to rain down drops of dirty water over everybody and everything whenever the combined heat of bodies, the Primus stove, and the gasoline lantern warms the air sufficiently to melt the frozen earth overhead. Whenever this occurs, the lantern has to be doused and the canvas door slung open until it cools down enough to solidify the ceiling again.

38

WINTER INTERLUDE

———————————— ✳ ————————————

WHILE NO FORWARD OBSERVATION POST COULD EVER qualify as entirely pleasant or comfortable, particularly in the swirling, bitter winds of what is rumoured to be the worst winter Holland has seen in the last fifty years, you are truly thankful when you again occupy the top floor of this tall black windmill in Groesbeek, where you lie on cushions on the floor and observe the zone through the open fan-window in the cupola.

They told you on the way up this time that enemy mortaring and shelling have cooled off considerably on the Groesbeek sector in recent weeks, and hopefully there won't be the same need for flash-spotting as last time. You sincerely hope they're right, for the air feels as though it's from the Arctic today as you climb up the old, steep, wooden stairs from floor to floor, up to the cupola housing the great wooden gears on the end of the windmill shaft.

It is so cold today, January 20, that when you try ranging on a house with a smoking chimney in no-man's-land, your first rounds fall noticeably short, something that has become a factor since the really cold weather arrived, with ranges increasing as the guns warm up. Recently, right after the guns were calibrated, a testing shoot on all guns, carried out by Ted Adams, Easy Troop commander, showed they fired on average fifty yards short when cold. However, that test must have been done on one of the less cold days, for you've witnessed drop-offs much more than that.

A deep silence lies over the whole front, broken only now and then by a creaking in the ancient wooden shaft of the mill as a gust of frigid wind tries to move the giant, skeleton vanes hanging motionless outside. Your signaller tries to write a letter, but he seems to spend more time blowing on his fingers to keep them from freezing.

Below the window on the snow-covered fields, sloping down into the valley and the German border, lie dozens of broken gliders. In front of the gaping mouth of one is an abandoned Jeep, and in another can be seen the bowed, helmeted heads of American soldiers machine-gunned as the glider landed four months ago.

Four out of every five days mist and fog reduce visibility to a couple of hundred yards. Today is a rare day – sunny and bright, and even colder than usual. They report from the guns that the ammunition thermometers register minus 14 degrees Celsius (4 degrees Fahrenheit).

Across the silent white valley, dotted here and there with lifeless farmhouses, the dark evergreen mass of the Reichswald frowns down from its ridge, mysterious and formidable – so dense and easily fortified it forms the lower bastion of the Siegfried Line.

Although battalions of Germans lie in wait out there, and you are certain that every farmhouse cellar shelters some of them, days go by without spotting a sign of life, though you sweep the valley with your field-glasses from dawn to dusk.

In all the weeks you've taken your turn in the observation posts along the Rhine and this ridge, the only movements you've seen have been some wisps of smoke from a couple of chimneys, a German Shepherd dog trotting between a house and a barn, and one distant German soldier running at full tilt a crazy pattern through the snow-covered open fields in the valley, disappearing and reappearing for more than half an hour, never once approaching one of the farm buildings or giving a clue to his mad venture.

Like the Germans, our infantry lie concealed all day in cramped, straw-floored slit trenches or, if they're lucky, in dug-outs or farmhouses, waiting patiently for hot food and drink to be brought up after dark.

But in spite of the discomforts and long periods of boredom, interspersed with brief periods of fear, morale generally remains at a reasonably high level, and there seems to be no limit to the inge-nuity of men trying to make the most of what is available.*

Where conditions allow, such as back at the guns, dug-outs have been made unbelievably comfortable, with improvised stoves, bunks, and, in the case of 2nd Battery (thanks to the experience of pre-war Hydro lineman Signaller Jack Snowell and the advice of ex-Hydro foreman Sgt.-Maj. Ed Blodgett), electric light tied into a local power line.

Soldiers will work on a project for days, even if it's only trying to lure the sole surviving cow from a forward slope into a barn where it can be safely butchered. Others spend hours modifying their dress to conform to current fads.

For instance, it is currently fashionable among the gunners to cut the arms out of greatcoats and sew them into the armholes of leather jerkins, ever since the German camouflaged parkas, picked up back at Antwerp, were taken away from them, along with German vehicles and Schmeissers they'd acquired along the way. (The reason given by the brass was that you couldn't tell a Canadian

---

* Half a century later, Maisonneuve company commander Jacques Ostiguy would still be marvelling at the parachute-silk walls of the dugout his men secretly constructed as a surprise Christmas gift for him at the front near Groesbeek. Led after dark on Christmas Eve to his new two-room HQ (albeit two tiny six-by-six-foot rooms), Ostiguy was "overwhelmed" by the effect of the white silken walls, shimmering in the candle-light. Affection for his generous men – some of whom had been with him throughout Normandy and the Scheldt – shone through even as he tried to strike a critical note: "Those crazy guys! Imagine . . . risking their lives out in no-man's-land to secure parachutes discarded by Amer-ican glider troops . . . for my dugout!"

from a German without a program, particularly at night when they both were using burp guns.)

After dark, the front comes to life. Rum rations and hot meals are brought up to the troops in the trenches in canisters, carried in wheelbarrows, baby carriages, or on children's sleighs – depending on the weather. Jerry, knowing this, starts dropping mortar bombs along the suspected supply routes.

Our guns open up periodically with harassing fire or diversionary fire to cover infantry patrols making their nightly, agonizing forays into the enemy lines to try to bring back prisoners and satisfy the curiosity of intelligence officers as to whether or not new German units are thickening up this sector in anticipation of our big spring offensive.

Patrol work by the infantry – when a few men, led by an NCO or a lieutenant, creep out into no-man's-land after dark seeking information on enemy locations and numbers, taking prisoners where possible, and now and then engaging in a shoot-out with an enemy outpost – is being carried out constantly all along this front.

Division and Corps seem to have an insatiable need to interrogate fresh prisoners. But prisoners are difficult to come by at any time through patrolling; to surprise an armed man in the dark of night and persuade him to surrender so he can be brought back alive will always remain a difficult feat. And along this front the enemy seems to have developed a high degree of alertness, reinforced by trip wires and trained guard dogs, making it next to impossible to surprise an outpost. With the continuing dearth of prisoners the pressure on all battalions to bring some in has grown.

Even when the big guns are silent, and there are no sputtering bursts of small-arms fire at suspected movement, Very lights rise and fall here and there over no-man's-land throughout the night.

Mail from home comes up with the rations to the forward troops at night, and parcels can be opened and contents enjoyed in the dark. But letters must wait for dawn, and sometimes they are never read when they are buttoned into the breast pocket of a battledress that goes out on patrol and doesn't make it back.

39

SOMETHING BIG AFOOT

———————————— ❊ ————————————

SOME TIME AFTER THE FACT YOU WILL LEARN FIELD MARSHAL Montgomery, on January 21, 1945, issued a directive calling for converging attacks to clear the west bank of the Rhine between Nijmegen and Düsseldorf, preparatory to crossing that great water barrier and engaging the enemy in mobile war north of the Ruhr. While no one at your lowly level will be privy to such precise information for some days yet, on the very afternoon of this directive, you learn something very big is afoot from a brief, but extraordinarily intimate, contact with two famous corps commanders.

From early morning, cold drifting mists have blotted out most of the valley. A heavy hoar-frost covers everything along the road coming up the hill to the Groesbeek windmill: the trees, the bushes, the stiff weeds sticking up through the snow at the side of the pockmarked road. Even the broken power lines, drooping down to the roadway from their shattered poles, are coated with a greyish-white fuzz. On this frigid day the Generals choose to call, you are up in the cupola of the mill, lying on mouldering chesterfield cushions rescued from a house in the village that has gradually been chopped to pieces by the shells and mortar bombs dropping sporadically on this desolate place since shortly after the American paratroopers and gliders landed last September.

You recline beside the huge, wooden gears on the end of the windmill shaft, well back from the fan-light window, and the telescopic sights of snipers or the field-glasses of artillery observers. Not that you have to worry about them today, for the whole valley is shrouded in a cold fog, which the pale winter sun has yet to burn away.

With your field-glasses you try to spot the Americans still sitting with heads bowed in one of the gliders, killed by a German machine-gun that raked their glider as they landed four months ago in the field, only a couple of hundred yards from the mill.

You doze off, but are awakened by the sound of boots thumping up the wooden ladders. When you open your eyes, you are staring at a familiar face under a black beret, barely above floor level, but rising as its owner ascends the last rungs.

With a gut-clutching shock you realize that face belongs to one Lt.-Gen. Guy Simonds, Commander of 2nd Canadian Corps. As you scramble up to salute as best you can in the confined circumstances, another head appears wearing a red-banded forage cap bearing the same rank badges as Simonds. For the moment you are unable to place this thin-faced, grey-haired officer who smiles at you so pleasantly as he scrambles up the last rungs of the ladder and immediately goes down on his knees beside Simonds on your cushions.

You hope the stern-looking Simonds didn't see you sleeping, for your excuse for slumbering, the fog, has now lifted. If he did, he gives no sign, as he requests to be "put on the ground," which consists mainly of your pointing out Kranenburg, Cleve, and the "saddle" along the left end of the Reichswald ridge, and relating each of these distinctive features to the map. The saddle area seems to excite the British Corps Commander for some reason, and in his discussions with Simonds refers to a prominent lump to the left of it as the "Nutterden Feature," as though its placement is of some consequence, and its speedy attainment of prime importance in future operations.

Suddenly you realize this pleasant Englishman, with whom you are literally rubbing shoulders as he waves his expressive hands about and gives expression to his thoughts with such erudition as to seem almost voluble beside the taciturn Simonds, has to be Lt.-Gen. Brian Horrocks, Commander of British XXX Corps, which from Normandy onwards seems always to have been on Canadian Army's right flank, when it wasn't driving for Brussels or the bridge that proved to be too far at Arnhem last Fall.

With growing fascination you watch as the two great field commanders, down on their knees on your dank and scruffy chesterfield cushions, sweep the palms of their hands over the maps and mention army corps and divisions – such and such a division here and another there – obviously planning a very big show.

In their desire to get a still wider view of the front they keep edging closer and closer to the fan-window, until finally you are obliged to warn them not to get too close, reminding them that you have to go on living here after they have gone.

Immediately they draw back, and Horrocks apologizes, remarking that it is most curious that the mill has been left alone by Fritz until now – at least it doesn't show any signs of having been hit by enemy fire. Have you any theories why?

You can only offer your old line: that the Germans must believe that no one in his right mind would occupy such an obvious observation post. But the suggestion amuses Horrocks, who with a roar of laughter slaps his leg and says, "You know, you are probably right!" Soon after that, they leave.

In the days that follow, the mill sees a steady stream of British brigadiers, colonels, majors, captains, and subalterns thumping up the stairs and ladders to the cupola to be "put on the ground."

This, of course, nourishes an old and continuing fear you have always harboured about the mill: that the enemy must come to notice any unusual amount of coming and going. This concern is apparently shared by the brass, for much care is taken by the visitors, and rigorous control is imposed on any movement in the area occupied by 2nd Canadian Division.

A Reconnaissance Report Centre is established at Grave, where all wanting to view the battlefield have to report. The number entering any particular area is controlled by a system of passes allowing them access to an OP for a definite period. And because English battledress is a lighter-coloured khaki, all British officers, before going forward where they might be under enemy observation, are outfitted with darker Canadian battledress. Adherence is ensured by sentries posted at intervals on access routes where passes must be shown.

Of course it has been clear to all at the guns for some time that a major push is being planned for this, the extreme northern end of the Western Front. The heavy ammunition-dumping program that began the second week of January – even as the daily allotment of shells for current firing continued to be strictly limited – would alone be enough to convince the gunners that something big is in the wind.

By January 16, 23,000 rounds were on 4th Field gun positions – a very respectable 958 rounds per gun. Now the complement of H.E. per regiment has been raised to 33,600 rounds, a figure unheard of even during the record-breaking firing back in Normandy about the Verrières Ridge – a staggering 1,400 rounds per gun, over and above first-line standing complement of 144 H.E., 16 smoke, and 12 armour-piercing solid-shot per gun.

This you learn from Col. Mac Young when he comes up to your windmill to study the zone in a remarkably detailed way, his curiosity spiked by sitreps (situation reports) from OPs in recent days that have been providing evidence Germans are being spotted more frequently than usual. Either they have become more careless or there are more of them out there to be spotted.

He asks you to point out every last spot you've seen enemy activity or detected signs of his presence, such as smoke rising from a chimney in daylight, which you noted a few days ago; where you've seen tracks through the snow between house and barn; and where you saw Spandau tracers coming out of nowhere one foggy morning, down the slope out in front near one of the derelict gliders.

And you have to establish for him the area where you heard the hollow *thunk* of a mortar firing, somewhere down behind houses along the road passing the distant graveyard, where a woman's coffin still rests above ground beside an open grave, just as it was abandoned by her mourners last September when the American gliders and paratroopers landed out there and the cemetery became part of no-man's-land.

As is his custom, the CO speaks very little, only when he seeks assistance in establishing a map reference of some spot of interest. But the way he stares for long periods through his field-glasses, it is as though he is charging to memory the complete layout of the valley and the ridge beyond for future reference.

If he knows the details of the upcoming operation, he chooses not to reveal them when you ask, but points out it would have to be a remarkable show to make use of the 33,600 shells now accumulating at every field artillery regiment position in the Nijmegen salient – including eighteen additional positions staked out for British regiments, which won't be occupied until a day or two before the big attack. Canadian arty units presently in position in the salient, including 4th Field, are having to unload and stash away the Brits' allotment as well as their own. When 4th Field gunners have finished digging in their 33,600 rounds, they'll be required to manhandle another 33,600 rounds onto a vacant position next to them staked out by an advance party of Brits.*

After the CO leaves, you amuse yourself calculating that each six-man 25-pounder gun crew will have moved more than eighty tons of earth and steel by the time they have completed manhandling 2,800 rounds (their own and the Brits') and dug a hole eighteen feet long, fifteen wide, and three feet deep to get their own 1,400 shells and cartridge cases below grade. Each ammunition pit will require

---

* Gen. Crerar provided the following illustration of the immensity of the stocks of shells of all calibres dumped in the salient: "If the ammunition allotment for the operation, which consists of 350 types, were stacked side by side, five feet high, it would line a road for thirty miles. Total ammunition tonnage provided from D-Day [February 8] to D-plus-three [February 11] would be equivalent in weight to the bomb drop of 25,000 medium bombers."

excavation by pick and shovel of thirty tons – thirty cubic yards at a ton per cubic yard of earth – while manhandling 2,800 shells and 2,800 cartridge cases (their own and their neighbours'), amounting to another 51.1 tons.

At a briefing today (February 6) you learn that the day after tomorrow First Canadian Army, with British xxx Corps under command, will push southeast from the Nijmegen salient, with the Rhine on its left and the Maas on the right, to clear Cleve and the Reichswald, after which there will be thrusts through rolling farming country dotted with villages, towards another forest – the Hochwald – and the town of Xanten some thirty miles distant.

The enemy front is supposed to be lightly held, but they will be fighting on their own soil for their own soil, and the main thrust of the attack must proceed through a confined corridor, no more than 5,000 yards wide between the rising floods of the Rhine polderland on the left and the dominating Reichswald ridge on the right, and in the process must surmount the strong outpost positions of the Siegfried Line, consisting of an anti-tank ditch, minefields, pillboxes, concrete gun emplacements, and barbed-wire entanglements.

Even Rhineland farmhouses are reputed to have been constructed especially for defence, with loop-holed walls and tremendously strong basements, consisting of interlocking, arched tunnels with cryptlike ceilings capable of withstanding the complete collapse of the upper storeys of the house. Towns and villages are reported to have been turned into fortress positions, and as in Normandy, defences have been constructed in depth. Some ten miles beyond the Reichswald, in front of the Hochwald, is another prepared line – the "Schlieffen Position."*

Clearly it will not be any walk-in. Fighting is bound to be more

---

* After Count Alfred von Schlieffen, nineteenth-century Prussian, whose theories of fast encirclement failed the Germans in the first days of World War I, for lack of mobile supply, but succeeded brilliantly in 1940.

severe than they would have you believe. However, victory is certain, for Allied forces are massive. For the operation Gen. Crerar's First Canadian Army will consist of some 450,000 men from thirteen divisions, nine of them British, and a vast array of Army troops – the largest force ever commanded by a Canadian. And two days after this attack goes in, February 8, Operation "Grenade," eighty miles to the south, will see 303,000 men of American Ninth Army start to cross the River Roer above Roermond, with the object of moving north along the Rhine to ultimately meet the Canadian Army driving south.

Montgomery is in overall command of these joint operations, which, as in Normandy, could lead to the destruction, between the closing jaws of two armies, of the last serious enemy resistance in the West. The plan is to catch the enemy on the west bank of the Rhine between the two armies and force him to choose between withdrawing over the river and setting up a defensive line on the east bank, or fighting to the bitter end on the west bank and ultimately losing all capacity to prevent an Allied crossing and headlong rush into the heart of Germany.

It is assumed that Hitler will require his troops to defend every metre of the Reich and that this will result in a final, bloody battle on this side of the Rhine, from which his forces on the Western Front will never recover. Not only national pride will motivate Hitler, and provide the incentive for his troops to fight on to the death to hold the west bank of the river. Strategically it is impossible for Germany to abandon the barge traffic on the river. The Rhine is the principal artery for the lifeblood of the industries of the Ruhr. Once Allied forces are in position to dominate the Rhine and entirely shut down all barge traffic, particularly that flowing to and from the mouth of the Dortmund–Ems canal halfway between Duisburg and Wesel, the German war machine must collapse.

Thus First Canadian Army, for the third time in the Allied campaign in Northwest Europe, is destined to play the crucial role in a pivotal operation having a significant bearing on the final course of the war – Operation Veritable.

The maps you've been issued for the invasion of Germany have been printed on the backs of maps of England, stored in the thousands by the Germans in a warehouse in Antwerp in 1940 for Operation "Sea-lion" (Hitler's code name for the invasion of Britain), across which the British map-makers, with a delicious sense of irony, have overprinted diagonally, again and again in satisfying repetition, "Cancelled." The ink on some of the maps is still damp enough to smudge. Some idea of the size and complications of the upcoming operations can be gained from the fact that half a million air photos and three-quarters of a million maps have been produced.

But to the gunners, the size and importance of an operation is best indicated by the build-up of ammunition, and no one has seen such mountainous deliveries of shells since Normandy. All of it has to be on gun positions before dawn February 3 so that the roads will be free for guns, tanks, and troops to move up on the last four nights before the attack. And it seems the deadline is met.

In less than two weeks more than three-quarters of a million shells have been accumulated at gun positions – 633,160 of them just to take care of the opening tasks by 1,034 guns and howitzers ranging from 20-pound missiles to 360-pound monsters.

And a further 120 lorry-loads of ammunition have been brought up for 446 more weapons (40-mm Bofors, 75-mm tank guns, 17-pounder anti-tank guns, 4.2-inch mortars, and medium machine-guns) assigned to "Pepperpot" concentrations to beat on enemy infantry and gun positions with such intensity and duration as to convince the enemy that to move above ground would be suicide.

During recent weeks only the normal traffic of 2nd Canadian Corps has been allowed to move on roads in this part of the salient in daytime. All other vehicles require special passes. But when darkness falls, many thousands of vehicles come out of hiding, filling the roads almost nose to tail as they work their loads to designated dumps.

Space has become precious, and so jammed together are the new gun positions, they encroach on each other and on existing gun positions. The Regiment will share its position with a British field regiment – 48 guns in an area no more than 600 yards wide and less than that deep. And directly behind a medium outfit will deploy. This "integration" of positions, you're told, will help to camouflage the fact new regiments are being added.

The Brits were allowed to start bringing in their guns only three nights ago (February 4) so as to reduce to a minimum the time the enemy might have to gain advance notice by air reconnaissance of the buildup. Since then, however, nights have been filled with the muffled sounds of mass movements of lorries and quads dragging guns onto positions.*

To "camouflage" the location of the offensive, 4th Armoured Division (with British commandos under its command) was ordered to wipe out a bridgehead the Germans held over the Maas, forty miles west of Groesbeek. Known as Operation Elephant, it was supported by the field guns of 4th Division, the Polish Division, the 19th Army Field Regiment, the 90th Field Regiment RA, along with mediums and heavies of 4th British AGRA. For the field guns alone, 56,000 rounds of H.E. and 33,500 of smoke were provided. Starting on the bitterly cold morning of January 26, it was to take only a few hours. It took five days and cost 236 casualties (mainly to the Lincoln and Welland Regiment and Argyll and Sutherland Highlanders) while inflicting three or four hundred on the enemy.

------

* 25,000 vehicles and 1,300,000 gallons of petrol were required to bring up the equipment and supplies. To carry this traffic, most of it moving to the extremities of the salient in the area behind Groesbeek, fifty companies of Royal Engineers, twenty-nine companies of Pioneers, and three Road Construction Units built five new bridges over the Maas and improved or replaced one hundred miles of roads. Intricate scheduling was needed to prevent traffic jams, and because all moves were carried out within the hours of darkness, with vehicles required to be off the roads and hidden by dawn, strict traffic control was enforced by 1,600 military police. Among mountains of Compo rations and other essentials accumulated in the salient were 8,000 miles of cable wire, and 10,000 gallons of fog oil for smoke screens. (Statistics from *Corps Commander* by Sir Brian Horrocks and Eversley Belfield, Toronto: Griffin House, p. 178.)

40

PREPARING FOR
OPERATION VERITABLE

※

FOR THE PAST FOUR DAYS SUBALTERNS FROM THE GUN POSI-
tions have been taking turns going up to the OPs to take over the
watch, so that troop commanders and their crews can come back to
the guns and prepare for the days ahead, when they'll be moving
with the infantry in the attack and there will be little or no opportunity for maintenance of their equipment or their persons.

Questionable 12-volt batteries for the big 19-set radio in the
carrier have been replaced, and extra batteries scrounged for the
18-set that a signaller can carry on his back, when you must leave
the carrier and go forward on foot.

Also, a reserve supply of fresh cells have been located for the ver-
satile little walkie-talkie 38-set, which will not only allow you to go
forward a short distance in dicey positions where a second man
might attract too much attention, but, equally important, allow you
to pick up the BBC since it operates on regular broadcast-band frequencies, which means that now and then, during lulls in the
action, you can tune in the news or pick up the familiar strains of
Eric Coates's march "Calling All Workers" – the cheerful signature
tune for "Music While You Work" that the BBC pipes to the men
and women doing their long and often boring shifts on factory
floors throughout Britain – and perhaps catch Vera Lynn earnestly
promising "We'll Meet Again."

New spark plugs are acquired, including one for the often balky, one-lung Chorehorse engine, bolted to the rear of the carrier, powering the generator, absolutely essential to maintaining a round-the-clock supply of charged batteries, without which radio communication with the Regiment and the guns would cease to exist.

Encased in freshly washed long underwear, a clean shirt, and two pairs of new socks (worn in your normal fashion, one over the top of the other) you'll at least start off clean. There's no telling how many days or weeks it will be before you get another chance for clean duds. During long periods of intense action, such as you expect in the Rhineland, equipment maintenance must take precedence over personal maintenance. Cleanliness is bound to take second place to food and sleep; and from experience you know there will never be enough time for sleep.

Still you pack extra socks to allow for a change some night when your boots and socks are sopping. Whatever else you may encounter in the Rhineland, it is certain there'll be plenty of mud and water, and by now you are well aware that dry socks are among the world's greatest luxuries. The profound comfort that comes from the sensation of dry, warm wool pulled over clammy, water-wizened feet just removed from squishy-wet socks, is beyond description.

Just when 4th Brigade, or more precisely the Royals with whom you are to move, will join the attacking forces, is not clear. Initially 2nd Division infantry will have a limited role. Les Fusiliers Mont-Royal will cut the main Nijmegen–Cleve road near Hochstrasze crossroads, four kilometres northeast of Groesbeek, and then the Calgary Highlanders will take the village of Wyler about a mile northwest along that same highway.

Since returning to 2nd Battery as commander of Baker Troop, you have bunked at Regimental Headquarters in the comfort of Rusthuis when not up at an OP, for it made no sense to dig another dug-out in the frozen ground at 2nd Battery for the short time remaining. Early in the evening you visit the guns but you don't

hang around. The command posts are still completing a mountain
of work. The details of the fire-plan for many concentrations and a
barrage, including overprinted maps and traces, accompanied by all
sorts of complicated timing-schedules and scales of fire, were only
received by command post staffs at 7:30 P.M., and the strain of deci-
phering the meaning of it all and working out the fire-plans for the
guns has put everybody in a foul mood. They all pose the obvious
question: If they could build roads and bridges, and move up thousands of tons of ammunition in the sixteen days since Monty gave
the order for the push, why the hell couldn't the arty brass have
completed their plans for the guns sooner?

You return to Rusthuis, and while you wait for the four
hundred heavies of RAF Bomber Command to arrive from
England to flatten Cleve and Goch at 11:30 p.m., and medium
bombers of 2nd Tactical Airforce, following behind, to attack
Weeze, Udem, and Calcar deep in the Rhineland to the southeast,
you pass the time glancing through carbon copies of sitreps based
on the OP logs of today's date, forwarded some hours ago by Don
R to 2nd Division Headquarters and so up the line to Corps and
Army Intelligence.

The log, about which you are most curious, and the one all "I"
officers at all higher levels will be carefully perusing tonight, is that
of Lieut. Bernie Ackerman, Able Troop GPO, who, until the last
hours of daylight this afternoon, was in "OP 45," the windmill in
Groesbeek which you've come to look upon as yours because of
the extent and frequency of your occupancy, and from which, in
fact, you were relieved only a couple of days ago.

Log OP #45 MR 756544

0800 hrs: Occupied OP. Visibility 2,000 yards.
1100 hrs: Nothing to report. Visibility 3,000 yards.
1200 hrs: Suspected enemy strongpoint. Engaged with one
troop. Rounds in target area.

1700 hrs: Registered target with tanks. Visibility 4,000 yards.
1730 hrs: Left OP.

You visualize every "I" officer – from 2nd Division Head-quarters, back through Corps to Army Headquarters – heaving a sigh of relief, as they read this report, and proceeding to reassure their red-tabbed bosses, who, as always, must be counting as much on surprise as on massive fire-power to achieve success.

Obviously, reports from all artillery OPs overlooking the valley in front of the Reichswald will receive careful scrutiny tonight by "I" officers at all levels as they try to perceive any signs of unusual activity in no-man's-land or enemy territory that might suggest the Germans suspect something is about to descend on them.

However, OP 45, the towering Groesbeek windmill, sitting on the startline from which the first 50,000 men will debouch into the valley on their predawn thrust tomorrow, is widely known as an observation post without peer by officers of all formations involved in "Veritable," and most particularly the officers of XXX British Corps leading off the attack.

From personal experience you know that scores of officers, from corps commanders down to platoon commanders in the rifle companies of the spearhead, are aware of this mill and the unrivalled panoramic view it affords an observer. Every day, from the third week of January until a couple of days ago, small groups of officers visited the mill to study the land laid out below them all the way across the broad valley to the forbidding pine-forested ridge, slightly more than three kilometres away.

Having to put each party of officers "on the ground" (mark identifiable landmarks on their maps), and then move out of their way to allow them to get a good view, was at first a bore. But as time went on, it turned into a remarkable learning experience as you watched the visitors reveal wide differences in individual perceptions of war. The direct correlation between the rank of an officer and his general attitude and approach to the coming battle would tickle the humorist as much as it would sadden the grave-digger. In the development of a man's perspective it seems to matter a great deal whether he's been chosen to exercise vast power to plan and direct affairs from command posts and caravans well behind the lines, or go forth with those who will face the enemy in frightful intimacy.

Corps commanders, on their knees in the cupola of the mill, planning the best use of 450,000 men, swept open hands across map-boards as they talked of such and such a division going through here and another over there. Later, division commanders and brigade commanders, reviewing the role of their brigades and battalions, stroked their maps with two fingers held together. Then came battalion commanders using a single finger for similar purposes in meetings with company commanders.

But when company commanders returned with platoon commanders, maps were marked with razor-sharp pencils. Huddling over their maps before the window of your mill with their subalterns, not speaking for minutes on end as they peered out at the ground they knew they'd have to cross – where even a fold in the ground could turn out to be of ultimate consequence to their lives and to the lives of their men – they would sometimes ask, in a quiet voice barely above a whisper, questions like, "Is that a ditch out there, running left at 11 o'clock from that last glider with the broken tail?"

It's these men you remember tonight as you await the heavy bombers from England that are to hit the Rhineland towns.

About 10:30 P.M. the pulsating roar of the first wave is heard passing over on its way to bomb the first major town in the path of the attack – historic Cleve from whence had come Anne, the fourth wife of Henry VIII. You go outside to watch with the new padre, Honorary Capt. Marsh Laverty, who just arrived today to take over from Padre L. D. Begg. It is a mild night for the time of year, but intensely black, with a light drizzle of rain falling now and then.

The southeastern sky is first lit by flares, then sparkling ack-ack, as great flashes begin along the horizon. For a time there is only the sound of the planes growling overhead, but then comes the ground-shuddering string of *crump*s you've learned to associate with aerial bombing. Cleve is at least ten miles away, but the violence of the flashing explosions at times lights up the whole cloudy dome of sky; and soon the reddish glow of fires, mounting higher and higher like an early sunrise along the eastern horizon, makes it appear much closer. Not since Normandy have you seen such heavy bombing, and in your mind's eye you see the awful tumble of rubble in Caen and other Norman towns. Cleve and the Rhineland targets will look like that.*

---

* Cleve was almost wiped out by 1,384 tons of high explosives. Horrocks, Commander of XXX Corps, had decided it must be "taken out" to prevent the Germans from bringing up reserves and reinforcing that "Nutterden Feature" on the northern end of the Reichswald, the dominance of which he considered critical to the success of his advance beyond the Reichswald into the open farmland. In the postwar book *Corps Commander*, Horrocks said the bombing was "the most terrible decision I had ever to make in my life, and I can assure you I felt almost physically sick when . . . I saw the bombers flying overhead on their deadly mission . . . After the war I used to suffer nightmares and literally for years these always concerned Cleve." (Sir Brian Horrocks, Eversley Belfield, and Maj.-Gen Essame, *Corps Commander*, Toronto: Griffin House, p. 184.)

41

THE BIGGEST ARTILLERY
SHOOT OF WORLD WAR II

✳

THE THROBBING ROAR OF PLANES COMING AND GOING AND the rumble of bombs in the distance will go on for much of the night as one after another of the Rhineland towns beyond Cleve and the Reichswald are pounded. So after a few minutes you bid the Padre good night and hit the sack, knowing that at 5:00 A.M. all sleeping will end for everyone in the Nijmegen salient when 1,600 guns, heavy mortars, and medium machine-guns open up on the heaviest fire-plan of the war. But you can't sleep.

Memories of Normandy have been aroused by the scale of the bombing, and all the anxieties and tensions of those days are crawling around within you. The idea of having to leave shelter and go out into the open in an attack with the infantry as soon you must is horribly repugnant. Only now are you aware of the comparatively soft life you've been living and how thoroughly you had built up your hopes that somehow the war might end before you'd have to go back into it again – either by the assassination of Hitler, an uprising in the Reich, or an unstoppable surge by the Russians into Berlin.

Shortly before 5:00 A.M., when the great concentration of guns are to open up, you go out from Rusthuis into the dismal darkness and head across the scrubby bushland for 2nd Battery Command Post, on the rim of the deep railway cutting about a kilometre away.

It's now drizzling rain, cold and miserable – a rotten morning for the gun crews, all of whom have been at their guns for some time now completing the preparation of ammo for the big shoot, taking shells out of their cases, removing safety caps, and stacking them in piles handy to the guns. And as you slosh through mud and stumble up and down over incredibly deep water-filled ruts left by the trucks and quads pulling and winching guns into position around here during the night, you feel for the poor late-arriving British gunners, and most especially for their command post staffs. It must be wicked trying to set up under such wretched conditions for a shoot of such magnitude.

As you pass behind 26th and 14th positions, and in front of other British field and medium regiments that have been slotted into spaces behind and beside them during the night, you can see very little in the windy, wet darkness, but there are faint sounds of voices calling out orders, and brief, glowing flickers of subdued light from hooded lamps-electric hovering over dial-sights of guns getting a final check of their "parallelism" – making sure all are perfectly on line.

Silhouettes of gun muzzles poke up against the night sky where previously there were only scrubby pines. Unseen hordes of gunners, dripping with rain, are now standing to their guns as they carry out last-minute tasks. By the time you make it to 2nd Battery, ghostly faint voices from Tannoy speakers in gun pits are calling "Take Post," an order presently being given on scores of positions. You try to visualize 9,000 gunners arranging themselves in customary gun-drill positions behind their weapons awaiting H-hour, five minutes away.

Until firing gets underway you decide to stay out of the hair of Lieut. Jack Bigg, who is in charge of Baker Troop guns this morning in place of the GPO Doug MacFarlane, who is up in the Groesbeek windmill, one of twenty forward observers who, until H-hour and during a ten-minute pause by the guns scheduled for 7:30 A.M., will report any active enemy guns or mortars to Major J. M. Watson, counter-mortar officer at Division.

You stop at Battery Command Post to visit "Hutch" (Capt. Les

Hutcheon) who, like "Stevie" (Capt. W. D. Stevenson) in 14th Battery, retired from fooing last fall to assume again the duties of CPO when it was decided more experience was needed in battery command posts than could be provided by the current crop of reinforcement officers.

When you fumble your way through the sodden tarpaulin hanging over the entrance to a log and earthen dug-out, you are blinded momentarily by the startling brightness of the electric light dangling over their artillery boards. And even before you can wipe the rain off your face and focus your eyes on anything, Ack CPO Lieut. Bill Craig has placed in your hand a tin cup and "Hutch" is slopping into it a generous dollop of a colourless, oily liquid which he guarantees "will warm the cockles of your liver!"

It's clear that you've walked into a celebration of sorts. With the intense efforts of yesterday and last night behind them, they are relaxing. And while there's still some residual cursing at the "stupid clots" in the higher echelons for not allowing them more time "to work out the most complicated fire-plan for the biggest shoot of the war on any front, from that goddamn pile of rolled-up tables, tracings, and overprinted maps lying over there," most of yesterday's bitterness has dissipated in a golden bliss induced by this firey-sweet liqueur, which, according to an unusually well-informed ack, Gunner H. Buck, resting in the shadows in a cloud of tobacco smoke, is "Danziger Goldwasser." Between puffs on his Stanley Baldwin-style pipe drooping on his chin, he explains that the little dark flecks, floating suspended in what is left of the oily liquid, are actually flakes of gold leaf.

He says that just before you came, he and fellow ack Dick Tanner were speculating on just how badly the Reichswald will be chewed up by the guns, and he calculated the 25-pounders alone will dump more than 5,000 tons of H.E. on the Germans in the forest and round about. At 0459 hours, with only a minute to go, you leave Hutch starting the countdown over his two phones to the troops and go outside to see what you can see. For a few seconds there is deep silence, broken only by the slight rustle of wind and rain lashing the surrounding trees and bushes, covering up the sounds of nearby Tannoy speakers that must now be carrying voices of count- less GPOs counting down the seconds to their gun sergeants.

One faint, distant voice yells, "Fire!" And for a split second, there's a rising chorus of urgent voices on all sides yelling "Fire!" before the night is overwhelmed by furious, flashing, roaring waves of sound and concussion, rending and tearing the darkness with monstrous, theatrical effects such as only 1,500 guns, mortars, and rockets can unleash when deployed in overlapping concentrations on a narrow front – a dreadful stimulant that causes you to shiver as with a chill, even as you begin to perspire.

Most of the 1,034 guns and 12 rocket-projectors firing off the prearranged fire-plan, along with the additional 466 weapons engaged on "Pepperpot" targets, have been crowded into confined clearings in the immediate area – a narrow strip of scrubby pine plantations, about six miles long and two wide, running south from Nijmegen to Mook. The exceptions are the three AGRAs and the 3rd Super-Heavy Regiment now roaring and flashing over on the right from south of the Maas.

No fewer than forty "Heavies," 7.2-inch howitzers on their great rubber tires, are belching 200-pound shells up to 16,000 yards. Two 8-inch guns, with a range of 18,000 yards, are unloading 240- pound shells on the Reich; while the strongest concrete emplace- ments of the Siegfried Line are receiving the attention of four superheavy 240-mm (9.5-inch) howitzers capable of throwing their howling 360-pound missiles up to 25,225 yards (14.3 miles). During the course of the firing this morning each of these great monsters will get off 80 rounds for a total of 320 rounds – adding more than 57 tons of high explosive to the hellish cauldron the guns are creating in enemy-held territory.

What enemy outposts and first-line troops are going through is almost inconceivable. You try to imagine the stunning effects of the airbursts alone, 50,000 from ninety-six 3.7-inch heavy anti-aircraft guns firing on flat trajectories, filling the air with savage showers of shell fragments.

While unable to distinguish in the thunderous cacophony the swooshing rush of sound that marks their passage, you know the first wave of rockets, of the fifteen waves scheduled by 1st Canadian Rocket Battery, must by now be descending on the Reich – about three hundred missiles in each wave, each missile carrying a 29-pound warhead packing the destructive power of a medium shell. Fired electrically from twelve projectors, each with at least twenty-four barrels, or "rails" as they are known (some have thirty-two), in rippling salvoes a quarter of a second apart to avoid collisions in flight, they form a monstrous "flying mattress" of high explosive, which reputedly lands with remarkable accuracy on designated targets.

The 248 mediums are now booming their 100-pound shells onto their prearranged tasks at the awesome scale of 450 rounds per gun, while thirty-two 4.5-inch guns are getting off 15,000 rounds.

Of course the greatest number of shells – 433,000 on the opening concentrations alone – are being fired by the 576 Canadian and British field guns accumulated here.

Adding to the awesome din are the 466 weapons assigned to the Pepperpot concentrations, weapons not required for other tasks: 114 Bofors (40-mm) ack-ack guns, 24 17-pounder anti-tank guns, 60 75-mm Sherman tank guns, 80 4.2-inch mortars, and 188 medium machine-guns. Unequipped for precise and rapid switching on targets not visible to them, and since all the firing is "indirect," Pepperpot weapons have been given the task of beating continuously one or two areas only.

Voice communication is impossible in the Troop Command Post. The Hughes brothers, Morty and Ralph, two of the friendliest, most garrulous acks, just spread their hands as if to say, "Forget it – there's just no way you can converse." Even their booming-voiced GPO Jack Bigg, a man never at a loss for words, can only grin and point down at the troop mascot, the Louvigny hen "Hardtack," carrying on as usual, strutting about, still quite sure of herself and unperturbed by the floor shuddering beneath her feet.

And so you return to Rusthuis where you pass the time working out a breakdown of 13,000 tons of H.E. being fired on prearranged tasks:

Weapon	Rounds	Shell Weight	Tons
25-pounder	433,104	25-pounds	5,413.80
5.5-inch	111,712	100-pounds	5,585.60
3.7-inch	48,420	20-pounds	484.20
17-pounder	5,400	17-pounds	45.90
4.5-inch	14,824	50-pounds	370.60
155-mm	4,688	95-pounds	222.68
7.2-inch	8,640	200-pounds	864.00
8-inch	292	240-pounds	34.80
240-mm	320	360-pounds	57.60
Rockets	5,760	29-pounds	83.52

For the next four hours and forty-five minutes (until 9:45 A.M.), except for one pause, all known enemy localities, headquarters, and communication centres are pounded by weapons of various calibres, so arranged as to ensure at least six tons of H.E. land on each.

Concrete personnel bunkers at Materborn, southwest of Cleve, receive the attention of superheavy 8-inch and 240-mm guns, while mediums concentrate on enemy batteries. The first three "flying mattresses" of the Rocket Battery are aimed at open trenches.

Field guns, in concert with mediums, heavy ack-ack, and rockets, work over a list of ten targets at various times and rates of fire, until 7:30 A.M., when a smokescreen is fired across the whole front and all guns cease firing for ten minutes. As the silence descends it is hoped the Germans will believe the attack has begun behind the smoke, and that all their surviving guns and mortars will come alive, allowing the counter-battery people, with their sound-ranging equipment and "four-pen recorders," to get a fix on them for even more precise concentrations before H-hour at 10:30 A.M.

In the sudden quiet, only one hostile battery opens up, but nineteen mortar positions become active and are identified as gun targets.

At the end of the silent period, the guns start roaring as before and continue until they are turned onto the barrage in support of the attacking infantry and tanks. Many guns, including those of 14th and 26th batteries of 4th Field, continue with what pukka staff officers are inclined to refer to euphemistically as "artillery preparation."

The 2nd Battery guns, placed on the barrage at 9:20 A.M., fire seventy minutes on the opening line alone! At 10:00 A.M. 14th and 26th batteries join in, but without one gun, that of C Sub, Fox Troop (Bombardier Bradley in charge with Sgt. R. B. Brunton on leave). A round, left in the overheated breech when the order "stop" was given for the ten-minute pause, exploded, splitting the barrel and blowing off the dial-sight. The fact the new gun-layer, firing for the first time in action, had just slipped off the layer's seat to stretch his legs, undoubtedly saved his life. Pieces of the counter-poise whistled all over the gun position.

Smoke shells mixed with high explosive provide a frightful screen behind which the assaulting units form up. The barrage starts at a thin rate, gradually thickening until it reaches full power at 10:30, when yellow smoke is fired to indicate the barrage is moving forward. Then tanks and infantry move out, the 44th Brigade of 15th Scottish Division heading for the northern extension of the Siegfried Line, riding in Kangaroos with tanks, Flails, flame-throwing Crocodiles and AVREs.*

The barrage is fired on behalf of the assaulting troops of XXX Corps in the centre only, the 51st Highland Division on the right having chosen to use prearranged concentrations on known target areas.

It is a "block barrage" designed to consume more than 160,000

---

* Armoured Vehicle Royal Engineers: Churchill tank armed with Petard short-range heavy mortar and various devices for bridging and ditching.

shells. The "block" or depth of the concentrated shelling on each lift is 500 yards. This is accomplished by arranging for the field guns to simultaneously shell three lines 100 yards apart, while the super-imposed mediums fire on two lines 100 yards apart – the whole business moving forward in lifts or "blocks" of 300 yards every twelve minutes. The slow forward movement is meant to allow time for the infantry and tanks to make it over the very difficult ground. And to help the attackers in their timing, the guns drop yellow smoke among the high explosive shells one minute before the end of each block.

In a Royals' slit trench on the railway embankment to the left of Groesbeek, Major Jack Stothers has a good view of the opening of the attack. His report will survive as an attachment to his battalion's war diary:

At 10:30 six tanks move out onto the high ground south of the railway. As the Welsh Fusiliers cross the startline, heading over the railway embankment towards the Reichswald, the tanks open up with their machine-guns. All buildings on the immediate front – houses and farms strung out along the roads leading out of Groesbeek all the way to the German border – are aflame or smoking. The infantry keep up a steady advance, and the tanks move up and join them. Masses of armour now move up in a steady stream.

Shortly after this, tanks, Kangaroos, and Flails (tanks with a revolving drum out front, to which pieces of logging chain are welded to beat the ground and explode mines) start to bog down in the soft bottom land in large numbers, but are obscured by smoke from several sources: the barrage, the burning houses, and a smoke-screen laid down on the left flank by 13th and 14th Field guns, adding to a 4,000-yard protective screen streaming out along the Rhine from mobile generators operated by the Pioneer Smoke Companies, which are moving forward as the attack progresses.

Only one Flail makes it through the mud to clear a path through the minefield, and all the Coldstream Guards' tanks following behind bog down.

All but one of the Kangaroos carrying the Argyll and Sutherland Highlanders into the attack on Kranenburg get stuck in a wasteland of mud churned up by tanks and Flails trying to clear a route through a minefield left by the U.S.A. Airborne Division last fall, and only one of the accompanying Scots Guards' tanks makes it to within sight of Kranenburg Railway Station.

Still, steady progress is reported against little resistance. And the long lines of prisoners, escorted back through the gun positions during the afternoon, offer clear evidence of the effectiveness of the stunning preliminary bombardments and the fierce barrage that rolled over them, snuffing out their will to resist. Many of the prisoners are youngsters no more than sixteen years old. Terribly shaken, they report that of thirty-six guns in their locality, thirty-two were knocked out. Their bewildered eyes and strained faces tell the story. Clearly they are still demoralized by the memory of the bombardment. Seemingly they survived because they were able to shelter in well-constructed bunkers. Those in the open were slaughtered. For the first time ever you hear a German soldier say, "*Alles kaput.*" As in Normandy some ask to see the "automatic 25-pounders"!

At the first objective of the Régiment de Maisonneuve, a tiny crossroads hamlet called Den Heuvel two kilometres northeast of Groesbeek, one officer is able to count sixty-four Germans dead from the bombardment "without examining slit-trenches" for bodies.* Survivors, still cringing in cellars from the Niagara of shells that recently descended on them, show clear signs of being in shock when flushed out, according to the commander of a leading platoon of the Maisies, Lieut. Guy deMerlis. The result is the Maisies lose only twenty-four, including two killed, taking their objective.

---

* Reported in Col. G. W. L. Nicholson's *Gunners of Canada, Vol. II*, Toronto: McClelland and Stewart, 1972, p. 407.

And while the Calgary Highlanders, in taking the town of Wyler – 2nd Division's main objective sitting astride the Nijmegen-to-Cleve road – run into more opposition and suffer 67 casualties (twenty-four of them from anti-personnel S-mines when held up in a deep minefield), the will of the defenders is so weakened by the shelling that 322 of them surrender once the Calgarians seal off the town from the rear.

Later at Kranenburg, five miles beyond Wyler and six east of Groesbeek, elements of both the Argyll and Sutherland and the Highland Light Infantry Regiment of the 15th Scottish Division report equally satisfactory results from bombardment by Canadian rockets. With their thirteenth and last salvo, 1st Canadian Rocket Battery wiped out a Moaning Minnie position on the outskirts of Kranenburg – news of the most satisfying kind to all who for the past two months have suffered spasms of agony from countless basins of these awesome missiles descending in all their hellish clamour among the ruins of Groesbeek while you were on your way up or back.

The intensity of the fire from the Pepperpot weapons, including the Bofors of 3rd and 4th Light Ack Ack Regiments, will only be known by those subjected to it, but you get some indication when you learn that eleven barrels of the twenty-four Bofors guns of 38th Battery overheated and bulged from firing their allotment of 800 rounds each, which a Bofors can do at the rate of 110 rounds a minute.

By noon the barrage has been shot, and gun crews go to work on the great mounds of expended brass cartridges – several hundred per gun – boxing and stacking them out of the way, before preparing a fresh supply of cartridges and shells for the next big shoot.

At 5:00 P.M. the guns join in another heavy fire-plan by 2nd Corps' artillery, lasting an hour and a half, on behalf of 3rd Canadian Division attacking across a now deeply-flooded plain dotted with "islands" of farmhouses and hamlets, stretching from the Rhine on the left to the Kranenburg-to-Cleve road now under a foot and a half of water in some places and rising. A sudden surge in the level of the river saw the water rise eighteen inches in only a matter of hours. You don't envy 3rd Division FOOs having to go forward in amphibious "Weasels," and the infantry in "Buffaloes." These ponderous affairs, huge steel boxes shaped like World War I tanks, may not in themselves pose any real threat to the enemy, but they surely must present a terrible façade of menace as they crawl from the water and up a bank, dripping weeds and slime like prowling, primeval monsters.

At about 6:00 P.M. some Jerry 150-mm guns come alive, rocking Able, Baker, and Charley Troop positions with sixteen wicked blasts, some of the 83-pound missiles bursting overhead and some landing with shuddering impact between the guns, sending up towering black spouts of mud and gravel. Miraculously there are no casualties, but most of the windows at RHQ's Rusthuis, which survived the winter intact, are blown out.

By late afternoon the British units have limbered up their guns and left for positions farther forward. By next morning, February 9, only a small stretch of the battlefield in front of 3rd Division on the left and an area south of the Reichswald towards Gennep remain in enemy hands within range of the guns. Nevertheless, this afternoon 4th Field guns are required to join in an Uncle target that calls for thirteen rounds from each of the division's 72 guns; and this evening they contribute to a Victor target requiring six rounds from each of the 216 field guns in 2nd Canadian Corps, drenching some desperate spot in the fluid battle in Germany with 1,296 rounds of high explosive.

Still, none of this appears to impress Regimental Clerk Sgt. A. E. Martin, responsible for the unit's war diary. His ears still humming from yesterday's stupendous shoot, he records: "A very dull day after yesterday's bustle and activity."

Next morning, February 10, the front has moved so far away, 4th Field guns can no longer reach targets even with Supercharge, and so they are taken out of action for maintenance. To be out of action while a big operation is still going on is a new experience, and while everybody is grateful for the chance to catch up on maintenance, including personal maintenance, there is a sense of being left behind.

However, things are clearly going well for the assaulting forces. The fact they have pushed beyond the range of the guns (7.6 miles) means they have not only overrun the enemy outposts and closed with the main Siegfried positions, but have penetrated them. And for the infantry to have moved so far with so many of their supporting tanks and self-propelled guns bogged down in the freshly thawed bottom land on the way to the Reichswald, speaks volumes for the effectiveness of the gun program in subduing German guns and mortars.

You are told that with comparatively low casualties to the attackers, six battalions of the German 84th Division were destroyed, and that of the more than half a million rounds fired by the guns on opening day, not a single one fell short among the attacking troops. This is to the eternal credit of gun-layers and command post staffs who prepared the gun programs, and the last-minute "corrections of the moment" (adjustments of line and range for wind and weather at various levels above the earth through which the shells looped to target) – not forgetting the accuracy of the raw material in the "meteor telegram" produced by the Meteorological Section.

For five days the Regiment does maintenance on guns and vehicles, packs up spent cartridges, and collects unspent ammunition in a central dump in readiness for the Army Service Corps. It's a humdrum time coloured by feelings of anti-climax.

Still, the hiatus provides a fine opportunity for the new Padre to get to know everybody. And very quickly all ranks come to the realization that a cheerful, genuinely supportive personality has been added to the strength of 4th Field.

On February 13 he makes the unit war diary: "Honorary Capt. A. M. Laverty, our new padre, is a going concern and all the men like him."

On the 14th the first edition of his daily regimental newspaper, *Airburst*, makes its appearance, and by the time the order "prepare to move" comes, on the afternoon of February 16, it is as though this charming man, with an amazing ability to remember names, has been around for months, firmly in position to help reduce the growing uneasiness among all ranks at having to leave familiar surroundings and move towards the distant murmuring of guns from that hostile land over there.

All want to see the war brought to an end as soon as possible, and know they can help bring this about, but these dug-outs have been home for most of three months, and memories of life in them are likely to remain vivid for the rest of their lives – particularly the humorous incidents, such as the time Gunner Lorne Galbraith was shocked by a raw 110-volt wire touching his improvised hardtack-tin stove just as he was picking up an aluminum mess-tin full of warmed-up beans. The involuntary spasm of clenched hand and arm flung the whole glutinous wad of beans up and back over his shoulder onto the back of Gunner Bruce Freelove's neck as he sat with his back to him reading a book.

"Don't move!" yelled the quick-witted Galbraith, as he grabbed a spoon, "That's our last can of beans!"

Soldiers remember mostly the humorous and the bizarre, and of all the memories of life here, the one most likely to remain forever fresh for you is the rainy night you were lost in Groesbeek. Just to think of it is to be back in the windy wet darkness, resisting panic as you try to find Riley headquarters.

After descending in the turgid gloom from the windmill to enter the village from the rear and reduce the possibility of stumbling into a Riley outpost with jittery trigger-fingers, you move at a snail's pace along a narrow street stinking with the sour odour of wet charred wood, crunching shards of window-glass underfoot at every step, and now and then startling yourself by inadvertently kicking a skittering piece of broken roofing tile along the pavement, while your hands feel for obstacles along the walls of the ruined buildings. Concerned you may wander out into no-man's-land, you keep bearing right.

Pausing at a corner to decide which way to go, you're surrounded by a teeming cacophony of water sounds, amplified from within the windowless, doorless rooms – dripping, gurgling, and splattering down from thousands of holes in cracked ceilings and shattered roofs. As you listen a pattern emerges, as though the whole thing has been orchestrated: *gurgle-gurgle, tinkle-tinkle, plop-plop, plink-plink*, repeated over and over in a weird, atonal rhythm.

A broken shutter starts clacking violently and rhythmically in the wind nearby, sending a chill up your spine, and bringing you back to reality. Now totally confused as to where the headquarters may be, you still must keep moving. You think you hear faint footsteps ahead, and it occurs to you how easy it would be for an enemy patrol to sneak into the village tonight. And at that instant you almost suffocate with panic when a sodden curtain, wafted by a draught from within a sashless window, sweeps out and envelops your face with ghastly clinging wetness. As you tear at the repulsive icy rag to clear your mouth so you can breath, there's an overpowering stench of mildew.

Now you really push forward, exercising only the over-riding precaution to keep bearing right. After what seems like an age of gloomy blackness, dripping rain, and mounting anxiety, you find yourself at an intersection, listening to a peculiar pattern of *tinkle-tinkle, plop-plop, plink-plink, gurgle-gurgle*, and a broken shutter rattling in a way that's awfully familiar. Suspicious, you hold your arm out in front of your face and move forward – and sure enough, within a few feet, an icy wet curtain curls around your wrist.

Thanking providence there's no witness to your stupidity, you go forward at an even faster pace, and after another age of blackness and rain that soaks your pants to beyond your knees, and raises your anxiety level critically, you again identify the peculiar water symphony at a certain intersection. Now you really have to struggle not to lose your cool. You are not only lost, but somehow trapped in a maze that unfailingly is bringing you back to the same point.

Before starting off a third time, you force yourself to stand still and figure out why you keep circling back here to this wretched spot. Obviously you have become completely disoriented, and while it outrages your sense of direction, you decide to try bearing left instead of right. Of course, it works.

The quads are arriving to limber up the guns when you receive an order to assemble your crew, pack in your carrier, and join the Royals at Mook for a long and roundabout move into Germany. At the same time you receive a roll of large-scale maps, reaching down to Xanten, of such recent vintage the ink is still wet enough to smudge.*

Your crew consists of a driver and two signallers. Your driver, Gunner Steve Reid, is a husky man of energy, quick of wit and quick of movement, perhaps a bit too quick, suggesting an uptight, highstrung nature. One signaller, Gunner Walter Ferry, wears glasses and the greyest complexion ever seen on a man not dying from chronic anaemia. But he is a most likeable lad, always ready with an encouraging smile and an upbeat comment at the appropriate moment. The second signaller, Gunner Mel Squissato, is a highly intelligent, self-contained, polite young man, who, you suspect has hidden reserves of strength that will make him, as time goes on, the leader of the crew. Before being posted to 4th Field, he was on his way to becoming a paratrooper by choice until someone in authority decided that, being of Italian origin, his life might be in double jeopardy if he were required to jump behind the lines in Italy. While all are strangers to you – untried quantities, as of course you are to them – in a couple of days of sharing an existence where survival is most often the prime objective, you'll know them and they'll know you better than brothers from the same womb. But for now there exists an uncomfortable diffidence in their relationship with you, and with each other.

---

* For operations in Northwest Europe forty-nine tons of maps were printed.

PART THREE: FEBRUARY 8 – MARCH 10

The Thirty-Day
Battle for the Rhineland

42

DRIVING INTO HITLER'S THIRD REICH

❊

WHILE ELEMENTS OF 15TH SCOTTISH DIVISION WERE ABLE to surge through the northern end of the Reichswald and reach the outskirts of Cleve on the afternoon of the second day, the smashed and rubble-clogged city is not clear of the enemy until February 11.

And only after nine miserable days of bitter fighting and heavy casualties among the sodden, dripping clutter of shell-ravaged trees, booby traps, and trip wires – along narrow forest-tracks heavily mined and covered by machine-guns every inch of the way – did the 53rd Welsh Division get within sight of the far eastern edge of the Reichswald.

With the battle about to move beyond Cleve and the dismal forest into open, rolling farmland dotted by numerous villages, stretching for miles south to the next fortified line at the Hochwald forest, blocking the way to Xanten some sixteen miles away, Crerar will need all the fresh troops he can muster. By now the American Ninth Army should be threshing north, occupying the attention of many enemy divisions. Instead it is stationary and helpless behind the flooding unleashed by the enemy smashing open the discharge valves on their Roer dam, while nine additional German divisions are allowed to move north to meet the Canadian threat.

Nor have the Germans confined their tactical flooding to the American sector. To inhibit supplies and reinforcements reaching the Allied front at Cleve, they have continued to open holes in dikes on the Rhine, raising the flood waters beyond Groesbeek so that the road through Kranenburg to Cleve is now under several feet of water.

Until another road far over on the right, running from the British sector through the Reichswald to Cleve, came into Allied possession, there existed no road above water serving the Canadian Army front. While the effect of this has been somewhat overcome by all units cut off by the flood waters, taking into use a variety of amphibious vehicles (3rd Canadian Division so extensively they are becoming known as water rats), large-scale movements of fresh formations to the front have been impossible. Even now, with just that one road open, divisional moves are greatly inhibited, and when the order comes for 2nd Canadian Division to move into Germany, all convoys are forced to take a roundabout route via Mook, Gennep, and Hekkins before heading northeast over the hard-surfaced road through the middle of the Reichswald to Materborn and Cleve – a route shared with XXX Corps.

The result is a massive traffic jam in the Reichswald the like of which you have never encountered before. Tanks, covered with infantrymen laden with equipment, as many as a dozen on each tank, are moving up along the right half of the road; while on the left half, also pointed towards Cleve and jammed nose to tail, is an endless line of trucks, Jeeps, and carriers, including those of the 4th Field FOOs.

That this does not end up in impossible entanglement is some sort of miracle for which no staff officer can take credit. Only the extraordinary patience of hundreds of drivers keeps those parallel lines crawling forward all afternoon.

Somewhere in the column stretching back as far as the eye can see, and covered with infantrymen hitching a ride, are the guns that are to deploy beyond Cleve at a town with the improbable name of Bedburg.

The gunners will be grateful for the rest the slow move is providing. As your carrier was pulling out from the old positions to line up with the Royals, gun crews had to use the winches on the quads to haul every gun and limber across the boggy clearings to the nearest forest road. The balmy spring weather during the past week, so welcome while the Regiment sat in limbo, was today cursed heartily by the gunners as they manhandled the heavy winch cables to the hookeyes of guns and trailers. With the frost steaming out of the earth, bushland that had been so firm for moving guns and quads two weeks ago is now a bog. And very little better are the bush tracks that once were gravelled roads but have now deteriorated into channels of deeply rutted, slithering mud.*

There are more than 3,000 vehicles in a division (3,347 in an infantry division including supporting arms, and 3,314 in an armoured division), and all are here, crawling at a snail's pace when not stopped for minutes at a time. How anything is supposed to get back from the front is a mystery that now and then is tested by a vehicle, with ridiculous results. Fortunately casualties are being evacuated by water in various types of amphibious craft.

Once through the Reichswald the pace of movement improves remarkably. At the Siegfried Line, someone has strung some rags on a string between two posts, and placed on it a sign: "The Washing."

---

* When the author visited the area twenty-eight years later, the ruts left by 4th Field quads, leading from indentations that once had been gun pits and dug-outs, including a remarkable officers' mess, though overgrown with weeds and gorse were still deep enough to make a man stumble! Your guide, Jonkheer van Grotenhuis, wartime mayor of Groesbeek (who chose the site for the Canadian Military Cemetery for 2,335 graves overlooking the Reichswald when he discovered a "Canada" button off a greatcoat and an empty package of Sweet Caporal cigarettes in an abandoned trench), recalled that the warm weather of February 1945 aroused such awful odours of decaying flesh, you could smell Groesbeek two kilometres away. And when 2,000 of its citizens who'd taken refuge in Belgium tried to return, he was forced to set up police road-blocks to turn them back until the foul refuse of war, accumulated over the six months Groesbeek lay in the front line, could be cleared.

When finally you arrive in the devastation that once was Cleve, you can understand why traffic was backed up for miles. Cleve is a bottleneck which until a few hours ago was sealed off with a cork of rubble. They still are trying to bulldoze a second track through the mess to allow for a "Maple Leaf Down" route as well as the "Maple Leaf Up" route they have created through the mountains of rubble as bad as or worse than in Caen.

The Royals are ordered to find billets for the night. It seems the leading battalions, who are conducting a very noisy war somewhere up there beyond Cleve, have not proceeded as far as they should have. The flanks have not been been pushed forward to the point where 4th Brigade can gain a startline reasonably free of fire from which they can lead the 2nd Division's push south to the Goch–Calcar road.

The enemy is putting up fierce resistance against 7th Brigade of 3rd Division, who are trying to clear Moyland Wood, a feature on high ground on the left flank of the axis of advance, dominating even the brigade's possible forming-up areas.

However, the guns continue on to deploy at Bedburg in positions reconnoitred and surveyed yesterday by a regimental advance party, at some considerable risk, you will later learn. The guns immediately are drawn into battle in support of other units – their fire rising to the respectable level of 3,200 rounds in the twenty-four hours ending 4:00 P.M. February 18. And Sgt. Hunt's diary entries for the first three days in action in the Rhineland will suggest a return to a high-tension existence reminiscent of the bitter battlefields of Normandy and the Scheldt: "February 16: Battle really raging. Whole Regiment deployed in one field. Fire and counter-fire reverberate up and down the battle line, ebbing and flowing like heavy surf breaking on a rugged beach. Really terrific, with the earth and all therein trembling..."

43

POSTPONEMENTS OF ATTACK
ARE HARD ON THE NERVES

✳

THE BIG PUSH NOW DEVELOPING WILL SEE XXX CORPS attacking Goch, while the Canadians push southeast of Cleve down to Calcar.

Having missed the Royals' predawn "O" group called by Lt.-Col. Lendrum when the messenger failed to find you in the blackout in the dismal tumbledown clutter that is Cleve, you must learn as best you can where you are bound and what is expected of the Royals this day when you catch up with Major Bob Wedd's company leading the brigade line-of-march south through Bedburg on the Cleve–Udem road.

The attack in the centre by 2nd Division, to be led by 4th Brigade, is meant to carry south some five miles beyond Bedburg to the high ground. But before troops can form-up on a startline, Cleve Forest on the right flank and Moyland Woods on the left must be cleared of enemy, for the corridor between those woods is only about a mile in width at its narrowest point. And even as the marching troops and support vehicles, with innumerable unexplained lengthy halts, are slowly picking their way up the shell-pocked and blasted road cluttered with debris, including burned-out vehicles, the Cleve Forest is being rendered untenable by a thundering bombardment by guns of all calibres as a prelude to it being cleared by British XXX Corps. And now and then, over the tremendous racket can be heard the gut-clutching sounds of "flying mattresses" taking off in accelerating *swoosh*es from the uplifted "rails" of 1st Canadian Rocket Battery deployed just to the right of the road.

Long before Cleve Forest is declared cleared it is being treated as though it is by troops moving up, including the Royals. However, the dark woods humped up on the high ground on the left is a different matter, and when the bombardment of Cleve Forest finally ends, the sounds of battle emanating from Moyland Woods make it plain the Germans are determined to remain there. Between the heavy cracks of black airbursts over the trees and the reverberating roars of Moaning Minnies ending their insane yowling flight down among them, there are sustained exchanges of small-arms fire. And before the Royals reach their 11:45 A.M. rendezvous point, they get a message from Brigade that the plan has changed; they are to assist in the attack on Moyland Woods.

But a few minutes later another liaison officer from Brigade catches up with the battalion with orders to proceed on to the original assembly area. There the troops are served a hot meal. As it is being consumed against a background of vicious sounds of battle, you can't resist the thought that for many squatting down on the muddy ground, digging into steaming mess-tins, this could be their last meal on earth. But after the meal you learn the attack has been postponed until tomorrow. The troops are to disperse and bivouac around here for the night.

Your relief on hearing of the postponement is so profound you find it discouraging. The "cellarosis," with which you clearly are infected from those long weeks of relative safety during the winter, is more deeply rooted than you thought. You expected that when you were on the move again with the infantry, the old resilience would come surging back, but this has not happened. And as you accompany the Royals dispersing among the little farms strung out along a side road within sight and sound of Moyland Woods, you find the roar of mortars landing over there very disturbing.

Normally you and your crew would occupy space in the basement of the little house where Wedd establishes his company HQ, but the basement is so small there simply is no room. Deciding it is safer in slit trenches outside than on the ground floor of the house, you dig shallow holes. And since it is threatening rain, you cover them with the green pup tents issued late last fall and never used. This turns out to be a most fortuitous move, for around midnight a cow wanders into the kitchen of Wedd's house and stumbles into the open trapdoor in the floor of the kitchen over the cellar steps — coming to rest with her generous body completely plugging the opening, her legs dangling and threshing helplessly in the dark void below, and bellowing her distress at her predicament.

When Wedd and his men awake in the inkwell darkness, it takes a little while for them to realize what has happened. Then as they try to push the beast up and out of the hole, they find her weight and her kicking a discouraging combination. Still, they can't abide this situation; they must persist and win or eventually they'll suffocate when all the oxygen in the tiny basement is used up. As they redouble their efforts, the excited animal, attacked from below by a monstrous number of hands, becomes incontinent, flooding the basement. That does it! They decide to pull the damned cow down into the cellar, climb out, and leave the problem of how to get her out to the German farmer.

Needless to say Major Wedd is late for the Orders Group called by Col. Lendrum while the cow is still plugging the trapdoor opening, and the briefing for today's push is almost over before the somewhat haggard and agitated Wedd appears in the light of the Colonel's hissing gas lantern in the quiet cellar far removed from his stressful scene.

However, he is readily excused when he provides details of the hilarious circumstances surrounding his tardiness — a welcome bit of relief from the tension that has been building ever since the Battalion entered Germany, and which has not been helped by the numerous changes in orders from on high, including yesterday's postponement of the attack.

Later when everybody is filing up out of the cellar in the predawn light, someone wonders aloud, "How in hell will that poor German farmer ever get his cow out of there?" Major Jack Stothers, never favourably inclined towards anyone wasting sympathy on the Boche, observes that while it may be a helluva problem, it hardly compares with the problems left behind for the French farmers to clean up in the sweltering heat in Normandy, recalling one particular cow, bloated and foul, decaying on the kitchen floor of a shell-ravaged house in Eterville. How would these Rhinelanders like to have that to clean up?*

And you are left thinking it is perhaps good that the war did not end in Normandy – that the Rhineland, where the Germans took their first step towards this war, should experience what war has meant to Belgium and France, something Germany escaped in the First War by requesting an armistice before the Allied armies invaded the "Fatherland."

In Cleve yesterday morning, when your crew made a joke out of "washing up" the breakfast dishes, taking turns tossing them one after another over their shoulders out a shattered window to crash onto the tiled courtyard beyond, you'd felt very uneasy. Vandalism is not your cup of tea. But then you remembered those farmhouses near Falaise in Normandy with all their drawers and cupboards dumped onto tables and beds and floors by the retreating Germans, still looking for loot even as they pulled back into the cauldron of death in the "pocket."

---

* In November 1969, Madame R. Romagne, proprietor of Restaurant des Cultivateurs, in Caen, recalled how she, as a little girl in Eterville in July 1944 (before being evacuated by the Germans), quailed with her family in their shell-wracked farmhouse, enduring the terrible odours of rotting flesh that grew worse each sweltering day from the dead cow lying in their kitchen, where her father had led it, hoping it might survive the shell-fire and provide milk for the children.

44

SPECIAL DELIVERY TO
FRONT–LINE MUDHOLE

✳

ONCE AGAIN TODAY, FEBRUARY 18, THE ATTACK BY 4TH Brigade towards the Goch–Calcar road is postponed.

This time they say it is because not enough artillery to conduct the barrage could be diverted from hammering Moyland Woods and targets called for by units attacking towards the town of Calcar, including 5th Brigade's Black Watch, Le Régiment de Maisonneuve, and Calgary Highlanders, and 7th Brigade's Royal Winnipeg Rifles, Regina Rifles, and Canadian Scottish.

But before the postponement order is received, the Royals assemble in a forward area in muddy slit trenches scattered about a forlorn stretch of soupy landscape drenched with a steady rain. Being uncomfortably close to Moyland Woods and the urgent sounds of battle, you have parked your carrier out of sight behind a barn and gone forward on foot with a signaller to occupy a sodden hole near Bob Wedd and company awaiting orders. As you wait your attention is attracted to the noisy, tortuous progress of a Don R coming up from the rear, "walking" a big, cumbersome Harley-Davidson motorbike through the deep mud. The low-slung heavy bike, designed for high-speed travel on hard-surfaced highways and issued only to despatch riders at Army or Corps Headquarters, is totally out of its element.

Now and then bike and rider pause briefly at a soldier in a slit trench, and from the pantomime of scanning the surrounding landscape and pointing, it is clear the Don R is asking and getting directions.

Spellbound, you watch the roaring, slithering bike turn in your direction, eventually pulling up and stopping with its overheated, steaming engine at eye level beside your hole. In astonishment you hear your name called out in a questioning way. And when you nod your head you hear, even over the sputtering engine, a fervent "Thank God!"

Swivelling around on his seat, he undoes some straps holding a slim, rectangular package about two feet long and some six or eight inches wide and deep, wrapped in a gas cape. As he hands it down to you, he produces a message pad on which is written "Parcel Received," explaining he needs your signature as proof of delivery.

What is it?

He has no idea, but it sure must be important. When they sent him out from Army Headquarters five days ago, his instructions were: "Find this officer and deliver this, and don't come back until you do."

Naturally he is very curious, and so are you, but there is no way you can open a parcel in the rain and mud here. So, with a resigned grimace and a shrug of his shoulders, he turns his unwieldy machine around and starts skidding and lurching back through the mud, still wondering what the hell was worth all this trouble to Canadian Army Headquarters, and to him in particular. And only after word comes up that the attack is again postponed, do you get to return to a dry farmhouse. On removal of the waterproof oilskin cover, you find the brown-paper wrapping enclosing the parcel covered with addresses overwritten with the word "Unknown." Though your last name and rank are clearly printed in capitals, the only address provided is "Canadian Army."

Totally baffled, you pry open the beautifully constructed box and find, taped securely down within it, a gorgeous doll dressed as a Dutch woman in traditional clothes and fancy headdress of the type you'd frequently seen in South Beveland Peninsula last

October – complete with brass "blinkers" and tiny wooden shoes. This could only be the doll the Mother Superior Sister Ignace didn't think could be made by her nuns and the girls at her convent school in the little village about sixteen kilometres west of Nijmegen on the Waal (the southern branch of the Rhine). For several days early last January, you had waited in vain at the convent for Operation "Heaps" to get underway to rescue the Arnhem walking-wounded British paratroopers still lurking beyond the Rhine.

Sister Ignace had assured you they could readily make a doll and costume it, but she despaired locating a china doll's head – fragile things like dolls' heads having little chance of surviving the shelling and destruction the day that the Polish tanks arrived to liberate the town, and their regular convent burned down.

The good Sister had learned of your little daughter (born Christmas Day 1942, six months after you left Canada) when you showed a wad of snapshots to her and another nun – the school's singing teacher and former opera singer – when they joined you early one evening in the music room, where you were amusing yourself at the piano before joining in the nightly vigil on the Rhine waiting for the Very light signal that never came.

You had expressed regret you had been unable to find a doll to send her for Christmas, and this had inspired the singing nun to ask if you could write down the words and music for at least one English song, explaining her girls were sick and tired of singing "It's a Long Way to Tipperary," the only song she was able to sing in English. And so a deal was struck: she and her girls would make you a doll, and you would set down the words and piano accompaniment for the George M. Cohan song that goes "For it was Mary, Mary, plain as any name can be ..."

You had fulfilled your part of the bargain, but the doll had still not made an appearance, when suddenly, in the middle of the night, the order came to pull your guns out of action and rejoin the Regiment at Groesbeek. Now, seeing this masterpiece, you can understand why it took so long. And you visualize poor Sister Ignace walking out to the main Nijmegen road, stopping the first army truck to come along and handing up the parcel addressed simply: "Canadian Army" to a bewildered driver for delivery to you.

Obviously she believed the Canadian Army would show as much compassion for the needs of a child as the people of Nijmegen did before the war began, when they earned the profound gratitude of countless Jewish families in Germany by trying to save their children from what was coming. Nijmegen became the terminal for an "underground railroad" for Jewish children buying one-way tickets in Cleve for the regular train into Holland, which ran along those tracks through Groesbeek and on through the bush where your guns would one day be deployed.

But even she scarcely could have visualized her parcel attaining the status of special delivery by an Army Headquarters despatch rider. You can only speculate that someone with a big heart and considerable authority eventually opened it to see if it justified the trouble it was causing, and discovered the note inside from Sister Ignace, making it clear the doll was a group effort by some nuns and a lot of little girls for a child in Canada who had never seen her soldier-father.

Nailing the lid back in place and turning the brown paper inside out, you seal it up. Then, with indescribable pleasure, you address it to a little lady at "Sleepypeopledom," the name her mother had given to your little apartment in Ottawa during one of those last, incredibly beautiful weekends in another age, in another world, so perfectly described in the lyric of Hoagy Carmichael's song "Two Sleepy People . . . by dawn's early light, and too much in love to say goodnight."

When Signal Sgt. Jim Ryder comes up with the rations, it starts on its way. Before leaving, Ryder tells you that when the guns arrived at a position near Bedburg the day before yesterday, they found they were digging-in out in front of some British infantrymen hunkered down in slit trenches. Even the wagon lines, well behind the guns in the badly smashed village, were harassed by snipers, and Gunner Edgar Brown, driver of an ammunition truck, shot one out of a tree. His pal, Gunner G. Bombardier, got his wristwatch.

There may also have been a "stay-behind" artillery observer, for during the night the village and wagon lines were hammered with some really big stuff. Three were wounded – Sgt. Lawrence Cairns, Gunner David MacDonald, and Gunner John Winn. And Gunner Peter Goodz, the quiet, pipe-smoking equipment-repair man, was killed. Ryder points out it could just as well have been your batman Whitehawk. Goodz and Whitehawk were sharing the same trench. Very tired after helping to carry tons of ammunition in from the road to the guns, they slept through the subsequent German bombardment, oblivious to the shells bursting around the muddy hole they had made more comfortable with armfuls of hay. So when Goodz was awakened by a passing guard to take his turn on duty, he sat up unaware of the danger of flying shell splinters. He made no sound as he was hit and fell back. Whitehawk found him in the morning lying dead beside him as though sleeping.

Yesterday there were two more casualties: Gunner Thomas Price was wounded, and a shell fragment killed Gunner "Jimmy" Lowe, a very popular member of Fox Troop.

Already disturbed by the extent of your relief at each postponement of the attack, and struggling with even more complicated emotions since wrapping up that precious doll for your little girl, Ryder's news is extremely depressing.

It continues to rain steadily, and having discovered last night the tents are far from waterproof – distributing a spray so fine it is felt rather than seen, but wetting nevertheless – you decide to take over the living room of a nearby house. Unlike Wedd's house, this is still intact, but it is very small, so small there is not enough floor space for four bodies without moving some furniture outside. This your men are proceeding to do when the man and woman of the house appear outside the open window. The woman beseeches you not to place her red velvet settee, a stiff-backed Victorian monstrosity, out in the rain. "Nein, nein – gut für schlafen," she keeps repeating, with her hands clasped beside her head, tilted over as though resting on them.

Anger boils up in you at being placed in the position of being embarrassed at tossing this old woman's prized settee out in the rain. And you holler at your hesitating crew holding the settee on the window sill: Dammit to hell, all you are trying to do is get enough floor space so that all of you can sleep in a dry place out of the rain! You'd love not to have to clear a place on their damned floor for sleeping. You'd love to be back home in Canada sleeping in your own bed – and would be too if it weren't for these God-damned Germans!

Stunned by your fury, the couple disappears, and your men slide the settee out onto the ground. But during the night, as you hear the rain pattering down, you suffer pangs of conscience; and are greatly relieved to note, on your way to a pre-dawn "O" Group, that the settee is missing, the owners obviously having found another place to store it.

At the "O" Group, Col. Lendrum assures his company commanders that the attack is definitely on for today, February 19. There will be no postponement this time. Canadian 2nd Division must gain a deep penetration to protect the left flank of 51st Highland and 15th Scottish divisions who'll be simultaneously attacking the town of Goch. The 4th Brigade attack will, it is hoped, also reduce pressure on units of 7th Brigade of 3rd Canadian Division, held up from assaulting Calcar by the stubborn resistance encountered in dense Moyland Woods stretching along the road that leads from Cleve to Calcar.

With the Royal Hamilton Light Infantry and the Essex Scottish leading, and the Royal Regiment in close support, 4th Brigade must gain possession of a lateral road, some four kilometres distant, that runs from Goch on the right to Calcar on the left.

A massive artillery fire-plan has been arranged on behalf of the

Canadian and British attacking forces involving fifteen field regiments (of 2nd and 3rd Canadian divisions, and the British 15th, 43rd, and 53rd divisions), seven medium regiments of 5th British AGRA, and the 1st Canadian Rocket Battery.

A rolling barrage will lead the 4th Brigade battalions.

45

RHINELAND FURIES UNLEASHED

---　＊　---

IT'S 11:30 A.M. – THIRTY MINUTES TO GO. YOU ARE SITTING
with your crew in your carrier among the battalions of 4th Brigade
in an assembly area south of Bedburg, just off a main road marking
the axis of advance southeast through Louisendorf village, which,
according to the map, is laid out in a unique diamond configuration
with roads running out from each corner of the diamond, including one leading on to the brigade objective – the Goch–Calcar
highway running laterally across the front on high ground about
3,000 metres from the startline.

Over on the left mortars crash now and then in Moyland Woods
where 7th and 5th brigades are meeting fanatical resistance, and far
over on the right heavy guns rumble. But here the RHLI, the Essex
Scottish, and the Royal Regiment, with their carriers, anti-tank
guns, and vehicles, lie unnaturally quiet and motionless on the treeless slopes of this natural amphitheatre – waiting. Motors have been
turned off and although the valley is crowded with clusters of hundreds of men, there is no sound of a human voice. It is a time for
thinking, not talking.

For many, perhaps a majority, this will be their first experience in
a massive assault against a seasoned and desperate enemy, and they
are fearful and wondering how they'll do.

And for those who remember the fury of Normandy and the
horrors of the Scheldt and know only too well the meaning of that

strange charge of intensity hanging in the Rhineland air and growing stronger with each passing day, it too is a time for wondering. Those many weeks of relative safety in static positions have had their effect, and you dread, more than ever before, facing that awful feeling of nakedness when H-hour comes and you must move forward across open country among the brutal sights and sounds of battle.

Back at the beginning it looked like an easy go. The crushing bombing of all the towns in the corridor, and the overwhelming fire-plan by more than a thousand guns, most certainly did the job of cutting a swath through the Siegfried Line, and for a while it seemed that the operation would be a piece of cake.

But that was before they opened their dams on the Roer River and immobilized the American army in the south, allowing them to bring nine more divisions into action up here, supported by a great number of guns and mortars, if you can judge by the amount of stuff he's been throwing around Moyland Woods and on the British on the right.

It all sounds, looks, and feels like Normandy all over again: the bomb-smashed towns; the mass movements of tanks, recce cars, trucks, and guns; the rolling countryside, dotted with smashed farms and villages; and the strafing, rocket-firing planes and the artificial moonlight. The chief differences are that here it is cool and wet, where Normandy was usually hot and dusty; and the hard core of the enemy here is formed by paratroop divisions instead of SS divisions.

You find yourself sighing too much, and while your mouth is cracking dry, your palms are damp. You try to concentrate on the Calcar sheet of the maps they've given you to invade Germany, which have been printed on the backs of maps the Germans had printed to invade England. You turn over the map and study the "Grantham sheet of Lincolnshire" – now overprinted with the word "cancelled" – and wonder what the village of Barnaby-in-the-Willows is like, and whether you ever passed through it during schemes like "Spartan" or "Welch."

Suddenly the air is pierced with shrill screams, and you look up towards two soldiers on the opposite slope of the valley dashing hither and thither between vehicles and men after a half-grown pig. Finally they catch it, slit its throat, and butcher it on the spot. As you marvel at such an activity at a time like this, one of the soldiers starts walking across the valley towards you. How at this moment anyone could consider food, let alone raw pork, is beyond you. The soldier draws near, and you see he's carrying a bloody hunk of pig, complete with skin and bristles.

Just then the signal comes to move up and your driver starts the carrier engine. You wait for the soldier to move out of the way, but to your amazement he walks right up to the carrier and plops the pork on the fender, and looking you in the eye yells over the fanning engine, "There's the pork you wanted."

Dumbfounded and speechless you can only nod. But as he turns and starts loping back across the valley, you catch sight of his shoulder flash, "RHLI," and suddenly you remember: Major Joe Pigott's company command post in the tiny house on the forward slope to the right of Groesbeek, and a soldier (Danny Butler) who'd been a butcher in peacetime. For a week he'd provided you and the command post crowd with choice steaks from a "liberated" cow. But after the fourth steak in one day, you'd confessed to having a great desire for pork. But my lord, now? You desperately want to fire the bloody mess into the field, but your hands are helpless. Had it not been butchered, carried, and presented to you before the eyes of the entire 4th Brigade? A *beau geste* if there ever was one!

You move off with the Royals to their startline. Time only for a last cigarette and then the guns start thumping behind. In seconds shells whine overhead and flash orange and black immediately in front of the sunken road. The infantry clamber up the bank to disappear over the crest. For a moment you see Bob Suckling, with whom you've shared so much, silhouetted against the black puffs of the thunderous barrage, pistol in hand, waving his company forward, and then they are gone.

The soggy, ploughed fields will not support a carrier, so you must wheel out on the road and try to stay parallel to their advance. You hope that damned pork will fall off the fender, but a carrier is a remarkably smooth-riding vehicle and the hairy, bloody flesh sticks like glue. German airbursts are now cracking above the stunning din of the barrage, and a couple of hundred yards down the road you pass two freshly killed Canadians lying on the road. You stop the carrier, pluck the revolting obscenity from the fender, fling it into the ditch, and wipe every last drop of blood off the fender before you move on towards Louisendorf and the burning houses beyond. But the damage is done. Your legs are rubbery as you climb back into the carrier, and you find it hard to focus your eyes and find your spot on the map. You earnestly hope it doesn't show, for it will infect the crew. Already driver Reid, with his jerky starts, is showing signs of getting the wind up, stalling the carrier twice before he gets it moving.

The rest of the afternoon is a blur of dashes from farm to farm, black airbursts overhead and fountains of mud spouting in smoky fields: of cracking small-arms fire; of infantrymen peering from behind hedges and burning farmhouses; of wounded and dying men being given treatment in open ground by stretcher-bearers bent over them; and one particularly dicey moment when it appears disaster has struck the carrier.

It happens just after you spot friend Ken Mickleborough, M.D., peering cautiously out of a doorway in shell-wracked Louisendorf, and stop to ask him what the hell the MO of the Royals is doing out ahead of the battalion? He tells you he and his crew were tagging on behind the support company of the Rileys moving up on the left, until they ran into some heavy fire from the next crossroads south of the village. On hearing this you decide to shift your axis of advance over to the next parallel road leading south, even though it means moving broadside to every 88-mm they may have covering that kilometre-long stretch of road, which is without trees or cover of any kind. Leaving the earnest Doctor staring up the road after you, watching for Royals crossing in the fields, you tell Reid to "Push it to the floor and leave it there."

Quickly the carrier picks up speed and is roaring up the perfectly straight, flat, open road, when suddenly there is no road! At least that is how it appears to you, hunched over in the steel bucket, peering out through a narrow port, when a monster crater yawns across the whole road.

Later you will realize that it is fortunate Reid has no chance to apply the brakes, and so, instead of nosing over as it might have done, the carrier sails across the deepest part of the crater, slams into the far side of the great hole, and teeters up onto the road again before conking out. Then, for what seems an eternity, it has to sit there unmoving, a sitting duck, while you and Reid struggle to clear the front compartment of bedrolls, Compo rations, the 18-set and two spare 12-volt batteries, and other lesser items that cascaded forward, inundating you both in truly bruising fashion when the four-ton vehicle came to its abrupt halt.

And all the while you are clawing at the mess, recklessly tossing stuff back to the signallers in the rear, you despair the engine will ever start – and if it does, that the transmission will still be intact; surely it must have been ripped apart by that crashing, jolting stop. That the engine roars into life the moment Reid pushes the starter button, and the clinking tracks roll her along up the road with as much pep as before, seem to you an absolute miracle, equalled only by the total absence of armour-piercing shots slicing through her body during that unscheduled stop at the crater, and during the remainder of its run across that open plain.

At the T in the road where you turn left towards the front (along a road marking the boundary between British XXX Corps and 2nd Canadian Corps) a long line of slit trenches extends out across the field as far as the eye can see, filled with British troops, hunched down "standing-to" with weapons at the ready, peering ahead as though expecting a counter-attack. The sight leaves you wondering what lies ahead.

However, three hundred yards up the road at a farm on the left, you find C Company of the Royals, with Major Jack Stothers peering around the corner of the farmhouse, watching one of his platoons move with due caution among the fiercely burning out-buildings, while small arms snap and crackle in the drifting smoke that obscures the scene.

Over on the left, barely visible through the smoke, is the farm where you must join Suckling's company, but the turn-off into the track leading over there is fifty yards farther up the road, and less than three hundred yards beyond that point, German helmets can be seen bobbing in trenches dug along the verges of the road.

Not knowing how close the Essex are in the field to the left of those Germans (by now the Essex might even be behind them on their objective at the junction of this road with the Goch–Calcar highway) you cannot safely engage those trenches with the guns. But your luck holds. An Ordnance bloke drives in the farmyard with a recce car he is trying to deliver to some outfit. Surprised to learn he is in the midst of a front-line battle and that there are Germans in holes along the road just up ahead, he asks if it would be all right if he took them on with the heavy machine-gun in the car? Assured no one will object in the slightest, he climbs back up, moves the car out into a better position, and again and again sends long bursts of bullets along the ditch where the German heads had been seen. When finally the recce car turns to go back, a little reluctantly you think, and he appears to wave goodbye, he is grinning broadly, obviously quite exhilarated by his experience.

Thankful for his assistance, you lose no time getting underway for Suckling's position while the Jerries still have their heads down. But as you move up the road to where you turn left into the track across the field, you find yourself looking into the faces of Germans not fifty yards away in trenches along the ditch where you had not noticed them before. There is nothing you can do but keep on going, and though they keep their weapons pointing at you and stare intently at your carrier as it comes up and turns left within thirty or forty yards of them, they don't fire a shot. You can only reason they are getting ready to give up.

Halfway across the field, you spot Canadians lying on their stomachs, pointed in the direction of the Goch–Calcar highway about three hundred yards further on. Changing direction slightly you run over there. You discover they are Essex Scottish. Their officer was wounded or killed somewhere back there, and they don't know what to do. A corporal asks if their objective is that road up ahead. You assure him it is, and urge him and all within the sound of your voice to get moving up there to those houses as quickly as possible – that lying out here in the open is courting death. A mixture of fear, bewilderment, and distrust shows in their eyes, and you feel truly sorry for them as you leave them to continue on to where you are supposed to be, and where you can hear the snap of rifle fire and the measured staccato of a Bren.

Cutting in behind the house and stopping at the mouth of the cow stable that is just an extension of the house from the wall containing the kitchen door, you find Suckling's company preoccupied with clearing a sniper from the house across the road, who has already killed one man and wounded several others.

Unfortunately the house is less than thirty yards away, too close for shelling, and when they try to get 3-inch mortar bombs through a window, a mortar-man is shot. It is decided to whistle up a Wasp, a Bren carrier equipped with a large flame-throwing device and a huge tank of fuel. And very shortly, with a terrible roar, a huge ball of flame rolls across the road, instantly setting the house on fire. In a matter of seconds a white sheet appears at a side door, and a German soldier comes out with his hands on top of his head – then another – and another and another – until there are twenty-six strapping paratroopers, including an officer, lined up in the barn-yard, grinning as though it's funny that a monstrous flame-thrower should have been used to burn them out. But the sight of their sneering faces is good for you: it arouses hate and anger – those foul twins that can sustain a man in battle when all else fails, and which, you now realize, have been missing all day. You feel the thickness disappear from your head and the jerky wobble leave your knees.

A young soldier, whose closest buddy was killed by a shot from the paratroopers' house a few minutes before the flame was used, watches soberly as others relieve the prisoners of Lugers, watches, and money. He had been promised his buddy's death would be avenged as soon as they flushed "the sniper" out, and he appeals to Major Suckling:

"Aren't we going to shoot them?"

The Major turns away. But a veteran sergeant puts his arm around the boy's shoulders and says quietly:

"We don't do that sort of thing, kid."

When the seriously wounded are taken away on a stretcher-bearing Jeep, the Royals' walking-wounded start marching the prisoners back over the muddy ploughed fields – the last two paratroopers helping to steady an elderly woman who was just brought up from the cellar of the house. Having just watched as she was tugged, groaning and gasping, up the stone steps by a younger woman (her daughter you think) and the Company Sergeant-Major, so she might be evacuated to a safer place, you marvel she is managing to move at all along those muddy furrows on her swollen, rheumatic legs and feet. Imagining your mother in such circumstances, compassion threatens to overwhelm, until you force yourself to ask aloud of no one in particular: Was she among those who cheered and applauded that day nine years ago when Hitler's legions reoccupied this Rhineland in defiance of the Versailles and Locarno treaties that had declared the left bank of the river a "demilitarized zone"?

As your mind settles down and you are able to reflect on today's events, you can only conclude that luck was with you all the way.

The Essex Scottish are still not firmly on their objectives – three farmhouses along the Goch–Calcar highway, named, according to the map, "Wilmshof, Kranenburgshof, and Schroarnenhof," the latter dominating the junction of the highway with another main road leading back to Cleve. In an on-the-air exchange between Major J. F. Brown and Regiment, you learn Ted Adams, Fox Troop Commander, assumed command of an Essex company and led them onto their objective when the company commander was hit.

The RHLI are on their objectives, but have taken heavy casualties. Among the wounded, you'll learn later, are Major Joe Pigott and his Sgt-Maj. Stewart "Pinky" Moffatt, well-remembered for the filet mignon steak (the fourth that day) he served you one night at Pigott's company HQ near Groesbeek. Today he was knocked down by a bullet smashing through his jaw, and Joe was carrying him into a house where he might shelter until he could be evacuated, when he came face to face with a paratrooper holding a grenade. The German tossed it. Joe dropped Moffatt and took the explosion on his chest. A fragment punctured his windpipe, but the worst of the blast was absorbed by body armour he'd been issued in Normandy – of which he'll say one day: "Most of the boys had discarded theirs because it was heavy. Fortunately I kept mine."*

Even the Royals, the reserve battalion, getting here and clearing this road, suffered forty-three killed and wounded, including four subalterns – Suckling's company losing twenty, seven dead and thirteen wounded.† And you surely would have added to that count had you not run into Mickleborough and been dissuaded from carrying on forward from Louisendorf and turning right into this road to pass within thirty feet of those twenty-six cold-eyed bastards in that house over there.

Now, relishing the prospect of being able to hole up for the night in relative security with a reserve company, you decide to stake out an early claim on some cellar space. As you're passing through the

---

* As quoted on p. 160, *Rhineland*, by ex-Riley Commanding Officer Lt.-Col. Denis Whitaker and his wife Shelagh. Toronto: Stoddart, 1989.
† Three officers of B Company of the Royals – Major Robert Suckling, Lieut. H. J. Harkness, and Lieut. J. H. Poole (who also was wounded) – earned Military Crosses for their "coolness and courage in the attack."

cow stable on your way to the kitchen door, you spot the upturned toes of hobnailed boots poking out of the gloom of the corner on the right. When you stop to examine their owner, a boy in muddy battledress, sitting on the cold, wet concrete floor, his back against the wall, you assume he is dead, for his eyes have the fixed stare of a dead man. But then his toes quiver.

46

BATTLE EXHAUSTION

———————————— ✳ ————————————

FOR MORE THAN TWO HOURS THIS AFTERNOON HE'D RUN, crouched, and crawled behind the furious, flashing geysers and drifting smoke of the roaring 25-pounder barrage, across muddy fields ploughed by enemy mortars and shells, while overhead the grey sky was torn by cracking, black puffs of airbursting 88s. Although he'd been among hundreds moving forward – vaguely conscious of long, irregular lines of men extended to his right and left – he, like every man in the attack, had felt alone. And somewhere back there among those brain-numbing, raging explosions and sights of buddies falling, something inside him snapped.

And when his company reached the farm buildings that were the day's objective, he crawled into a dark corner of the cow stable and sat down on the concrete floor in a puddle of icy water. Now he stares at you with sightless eyes, completely still and unmoving except for the occasional quiver of one hobnailed, muddy boot. When you ask Bob Suckling why something isn't being done for him, he tells you the drill is to leave cases like this alone for a few hours. If it's not really authentic battle exhaustion he'll eventually get up and move around.

It's growing dark when you learn that Ted Adams, who assumed command of a company this afternoon, when the company commander was wounded, is himself wounded and missing.

Soon everybody is preoccupied with a strong German counter-attack supported by several tanks that is threatening to overrun the RHLI positions just to the left of the Essex dug-in along the near side of the Goch—Calcar highway. The guns seem to be in constant demand, and the front begins to reverberate with the roar of the shells, and the airwaves are dominated by the high-pitched Foster-Hewitt-type voice of 14th Battery signaller "Coop" (Bombardier Ralph Cooper), penetrating through the electronic babble of overlapping frequencies to relay urgent calls for fire from FOOs as well as from his own Major Jack Drewry.

Suddenly, however, FOOs are competing for the guns, as the Essex situation deteriorates. Two and three Mike targets are called for at the same time. While the calm drawl of Col. Mac Young, now constantly on the air sorting out priorities, is reassuring, it is clear things are critical when Major Brown, of 26th Battery, who is with Lt.-Col. John Pangman of the Essex, calls for a Mike target on their tac headquarters, and when queried by the CO, replies: "It's our last resort . . . position overrun by tanks and infantry."

It is now 1:40 A.M.

Later you'll learn that, holed up with Brown in the cellar of the farmhouse shown on the map as "Kranenburgshof," are two FOOs, Capt. Jack Cooper and Lieut. Ernie Richardson, along with their crews, and, for a while, Sgt.-Maj. Ken Scott, who drove Richardson up to replace his Troop Commander Adams. When one day Scott gets the chance to recall for you his first and last night with the infantry in the front line, he will have no difficulty remembering the date, for this is his forty-fourth birthday, and he was just in the process of celebrating it, sharing a roast of fresh pork with some pals "sitting at a real table" in a house back at A Echelon, when about 9:30 P.M. he got a call from Lieut. Richardson to drive him up to the Essex Scottish:

We take the road up on the right flank, and when we get to within a quarter of a mile of the Goch—Calcar highway, we are stopped by some guards who won't let us go any farther. They say the Jerries are shelling the crossroads. So we park the Jeep in a farmer's lane and walk through the fields till we come to Essex Tac Headquarters, which we identify by the three carriers and trucks parked at the back of the house.

When we go in the back door we run into a lot of guys milling around, some armed with spoons and partially consumed sealers of fruit, and others with handfuls of eggs waiting for a turn to cook them. It is something of a rat race.

We find our officers down in the cellar with their crews. When I am introduced to Col. Pangman, he asks me to stay all night and be his guest. When I say I can't for no one knows where I am, he gets on the blower and calls our CO at Brigade. And so I'm stuck there for the night. Soon, about five German tanks come up the right flank. Some of the men go and get Piat launchers, but then they find they just have three bombs. They ask for volunteers to go back out there among the tanks to look for Piat bombs. That gets rid of half of the gang. Next they are to get reinforcements from the Royals, who promise to send up sixty-three men. They ask for volunteers to go back and guide them up. That's the end of the gang in the kitchen.

Left alone I start to go downstairs, but at the bottom of the stairs Col. Pangman puts his arm across in front of me and says I have to go out and help defend the building. Having no weapon, I borrow a Sten from one of the signallers and go outside.

There's a lot of tracers flying around, so I make myself scarce, landing up in the pigpen. There are four others in there already: a Lieut. Waltham, a Cpl. Hunington, and a couple of others. When it starts to get light I ask the Lieutenant if he thinks we should get out of here, as I figure the Jerries will come in and get us when it is daylight.

He says he cannot leave if anyone is alive in the cellar. So he goes out to check. When he comes back in about five minutes, he says he thinks all are done for. So that leaves it clear for him to leave. We start out the back door of the pigpen and walk right into a Jerry standing there with a submachine-gun.

When at 3:00 A.M. all communication with Major Brown goes out, you join Suckling outside, peering into the darkness ahead. At first you can make out little beyond some skittering tracers and the growling of heavy tank engines rising and falling as they move from one spot to another. But suddenly this changes when two farmhouses ("Kranenburgshof" on the right and "Wilmshof" on the left) about three hundred yards apart are set on fire by the Germans, using missiles that explode against the walls with spectacular splashes of white sparks in the manner of "hollow charge" bombs fired by Piats and Panzerfausts. As the houses blaze up, lighting the scene, things look bad. Silhouetted against the fires are tanks – three, maybe four – it's hard to tell, for they move about in the drifting smoke, glowing red and wavering from the flames. Now and then German soldiers pass in front of the fires. At first they scurry, bent over, but soon they are walking bolt upright, suggesting they have gained complete control of the position.

Very soon small groups of highly agitated Essex Scottish begin to materialize in the murk only a few yards in front of where you and Suckling are standing. Confronting the retreating men with the stern, confident voice of authority, Suckling inquires if there is an officer with them? They say their officer was hit going in this afternoon.

Recalling the frightened, bewildered guys you came across lying in the open field on the way over here this afternoon, you feel only deep sympathy. That they now should be ordered to return up there would never occur to you. But then you're not an infantryman. The Major, on questioning them as to what has been going on up there (Did any of them actually see anybody shot? Did any of them get a shot at a German?), clearly believes it is not as bad as they think, and he instructs their only NCO, a corporal, to collect them and lead them back up there.

Whatever he may think, the corporal makes no protest, but turning to the men, says quietly, "Sorry, fellows, but we have to go back up."

That they too respond in positive fashion, albeit slowly, turning round one after another and moving off in single file following the corporal back up towards that flaming ridge, says much for the courage and discipline of these men. But before they get halfway there, they meet an even larger group, something in the order of a platoon, coming back, and their newly found resolve dissolves.

When the combined group arrives back, Suckling gives up and orders them to dig-in to the right of his house.

Soon it is clear from the numbers arriving that the battalion has been routed. As each new group arrives they are directed to dig-in over on the right.

No one from 4th Field shows up. But as time goes on you learn that some get back to the guns. Sheltering in the cellar with their officers at Essex Tac HQ, until they are sent outside by Col. Pangman to help defend the position, are Bombardier Ray Bugden and Gunners J. J. Garrigan and Brown. Also hiding in the pigpen building until the captured Essex Scottish and Sgt.-Maj. Scott are marched away, when they get the chance to make their way back to the guns, are Gunners J. Dobson and L. Hager.

Gunners Lowe and Erickson, sheltering in slit trenches near the house all night, until they get the chance to come out under cover of one of your Mike target concentrations laid on an adjoining farm at dawn, hold out no hope for the survival of anyone up there. They say a tank circled the house and shelled it at point-blank range. (In fact, the tank crushed through the walls and ground across the main floor.) They think the foundations of the building collapsed, entombing our men.

When the last stragglers tell you there will be no more, that they saw the rest being taken prisoner and marched off, you are free at last to bring down fire on those rampaging tanks and their escorting troops. You proceed with a vengeance.

To your satisfaction the German foot-soldiers continue crossing and recrossing in front of the fires in almost leisurely fashion, right up to the instant your shells whistle overhead and flash among them. Again and again you drench the burning farms – first Kranen-burgshof, then Wilmshof on its left (east), and then Schroarnenhof on its right – with high explosive shells, each one capable of smashing a tank track or a bogie wheel, or jamming a tank turret. Your main purpose, though, is not to disable the tanks, but to destroy or drive away the screens of foot-soldiers without which tanks can't move and fight at night.

You feel remarkably secure that those flashing hurricanes of 25-pounder shells lashing the Mike targets around the burning houses up there will succeed in driving off the panzer forces that moved in with such speed and ease. It is a confidence born of having been witness to the effectiveness of similar concentrations maintained by the guns for lengthy periods along Verrières Ridge in Normandy when the Fusiliers Mont-Royal, South Saskatchewans, and these same Essex Scottish were overrun by tanks and infantry, and the guns filled the gap with curtains of shell-fire until a counter-attack could be mounted to regain the position.

When the German tanks withdraw, snarling, into the surrounding darkness, you move the shelling around, plastering every area where they might try to regroup for another attack down this way. And throughout the night, whenever the guns are not engaged in desperate support of the Rileys beating off counter-attacks, you shell the area of those smouldering farms along the road up there.*

---

*   The effectiveness of the guns of 4th Field, as they consumed 8,472 rounds (established by the number of flashless NCT propellant charges used only after dark) in smashing the German attack, is confirmed by a chapter in the *History of Panzer Lehr Division* describing their involvement along the Goch–Calcar highway that night: "At 2000 hours Kampfgruppe von Hauser [special counter-attack battle group assembled under one Colonel Baron Von Hauser, commander of 901st Panzer Grenadier Regiment] launched its frontal assault on both sides supported on the right by elements of 6th Parachute Division and on the left [against Essex Scottish] by 116 Panzer Division. *As soon as the tanks rolled across the forward edge of the Canadians' position* [on the Essex front] *their artillery fired barrages which made movement difficult and separated the German infantry from their tanks. Nevertheless by midnight in the struggle for Schwanerhof* [RHLI farm] *it*

The blackness along the front is continually ruptured by roaring, flashing tornadoes of high explosive. At 0200 Major Jack Drewry lays on heavy fire in support of a counter-attack by the Rileys to retake a company position overrun by the Germans. After about an hour and a half the Rileys report that company position restored, but now another company is fighting for its life. Only gradually does the fighting in the Riley area peter out, and you keep expecting the attack by the panzers to be revived over this way. But nothing happens.

By the time the situation stabilizes and you are able to join Suckling in the cellar of your farmhouse in gulping down a scalding cup of tea and a whole sealer of preserved cherries from a well-stocked shelf under the stairs, the first sustenance you've had since breakfast almost twenty-four hours ago, it's getting on towards dawn.

Only then does someone remember the boy sitting in the puddle out in the cold, dark cow stable. They carry him down the cellar steps, still rigid in a sitting position, and put him down on a pile of potatoes. They talk to him encouragingly and try to feed him hot tea, but he doesn't respond in any way. They light a cigarette and shove it into his mouth, but they have to remove it for he makes no effort to puff it. Finally they decide to let him rest until he can be evacuated in the morning. When they try to lay him down, they have to force his torso backwards while holding his legs down. They cover him up with a blanket, but his sad eyes remain wide open, staring up at the ceiling the rest of the night, locked on some secret horror.

------

changed hands several times. But the attack was halted at the Goch–Calcar road. Access to the area beyond it was denied by concentrated fire."

47

SHELTER FROM
THE STORMY BLAST

❋

AT FIRST LIGHT (FEBRUARY 20) YOU ARE OUTSIDE WITH
Suckling peering at the two farms some six hundred yards away, still
smouldering from the fire that consumed them last night, when a
soldier in Canadian helmet and battledress appears in your glasses
near the derelict farmhouse on the left front and casually starts
walking this way.

While waiting for him to arrive, there is much speculation as to
why the Jerries are letting him walk back here unmolested. He
must be some kind of emissary. But for what purpose?

When finally he arrives no one is prepared for his question, presented in a slow Western drawl: "Where's the Essex Scottish?"

He is told that what is left of them are dug-in just over there in
the field on the right. But where on earth has he been, not to know?

"Sleepin' in a trench up there," he replies.

That he slept through the whole night oblivious to roaring Jerry
tank engines charging about the place, the crash of their guns firing
into the houses, not to mention the deluge of 25-pounder shells
you'd poured up there when you believed no more Essex Scottish
were left on the position, is incredible. Nevertheless, he maintains
he didn't hear a thing: "Couldn't believe it when I woke up and
found I was alone!"

But how did he escape being captured by the Germans this
morning? And why did they let him walk back here just now?

"Cause there aren't any Germans up there."

Is he sure?

"Positive – not a living soul up there. Plenty of dead though."

Then sensing the scepticism in his listeners' questions he says, "If anybody wants to see for themselves, come on up there with me. I gotta go back to get my 'loogur' pistol I left in my trench." And with that he turns and starts walking briskly back up.

When this astonishing bit of intelligence is transmitted through Battalion to Brigade, the Royals are ordered to reoccupy the abandoned positions as quickly as possible, and by 1030 hours your old carrier is trying vainly to follow Bob Wedd's company and a troop of tanks across the sticky, clinging mud and turned-over mats of turf of a ploughed and furrowed field, making for the skeleton ruins of the farm on the high ground on the right front that had been Essex Battalion Headquarters.

Soon you are following the example of the tanks, which give up trying to make it up that considerable slope through the gumbo to Wedd's objective, and veer off to the left to harbour on a stretch of unploughed turf lying well down behind the crest and another burned-out shell of a farmhouse. But even on the level your carrier can barely move through the mud, and it takes hours (how many will always be in dispute) to get across four or five hundred yards of ploughed field: now grinding forward a few feet – now backing up to unfold the rugs of mud rolled up in the front bogie wheels – now charging ahead again on a different tack until the engine threatens to stall or does stall – now backing up again to unsnarl the mud – and so on. And all the while shells from a German battery, deployed beyond the crest, scream in and churn the field round and about, blindly ranging on the straining sound of your carrier motor. Or so it seems, for your carrier is the only target being engaged. Those Shermans, with pennants flying arrogantly, sit unmolested up ahead.

It is shelling the like of which you've never experienced before. Always it has been one, two, or three guns firing a round at a time, but now it's a dozen or more firing together, if not salvoes, the next thing to them. Only poor ranging is saving you, and every soul in the carrier knows it. Soon the strain begins to tell on driver Reid. More and more frequently he is stalling the engine when forced to reverse direction to free the mud from the bogies, and you despair he will be able to get this gaping box to firm earth, where he can shut off its tell-tale engine, before one of those random shells drops in it and it's all over. However, their ranging-to-sound remains exceedingly inaccurate, and though, from late morning to mid afternoon, you are surrounded by violent explosions sending up black fountains of mud – now and then close enough to rock the carrier and ensure this day will register in memory as the most terrifying of your life – no damage is sustained by the sluggish vehicle or the white-faced men hunched down within it.

The sense of relief is indescribable when finally the carrier struggles out of the mud onto the firm pastureland where the tanks are huddled. However, it doesn't shake the shelling; if anything it grows worse. Leaving Squissato in the carrier manning the radio, you, Reid, and Ferry get down in a couple of abandoned German trenches next to the tanks. When the shelling continues, with only brief respites, you decide all would be better off in some trenches you spot along the base of the gable wall of the burned-out house up on the Goch–Calcar highway, the only remaining whole wall of what was a two-storey stone house.

During a lull in the shelling you call out to the other two trench-dwellers, that come the next lull you should all make a dash up the slope to the trenches along the base of the derelict house about two hundred yards away. But they either misunderstand or consider the idea mad, for when you call out "let's go" and gallop up the grassy slope to a trench tight against the gable wall, you find you are alone.

For a while you feel sorry for them and for Squissato, huddled down in the carrier, as you relish the sense of security provided by the towering wall, so high it seems almost to scrape the clouds passing above it. No enemy shell or mortar can reach you here. Then, incredibly, the Germans begin to cut the wall down. You know it is madness to think they are doing it to get at you, and later in a saner mood you will consider the possibility they wanted to open up a clear field of fire in case those Shermans moved up the slope. But now, as each solid-shot rips through the wall with a horrible shriek right over your head, showering you with stone chips, you cannot suppress the idea they are determined to get you regardless of what it takes. Rapidly the towering structure weakens until it quivers and sways over your head in a terribly menacing way. If it falls this way, you'll be buried alive – if you aren't squashed to pulp by chunks filling the trench. In your rising panic you abandon logic that dictates the wall must fall away from you in the direction it is being struck with such force at its base.

Often during the Caen to Falaise battles you saw men pray. Though you respected their views you didn't think it logical that a man should ask his God to redirect a shell that could kill another nearby innocent man. Now you are all alone and you wish you weren't, for the long winter lull of relative safety around Groesbeek has done something to you.

When finally you hear the wall crack, and the great mass of stone and mortar comes crashing down, your nerve cracks as well. And when the German field guns immediately start shelling with sadistic fury the newly exposed ground containing your trench, all your resilience collapses. You can take no more.

Later you'll be grateful that no one sees you like this, pushing your face deep into the mud and trying to hold onto earth that won't stand still. But now, you have nothing left to hold on to, and you have the vision of a panic-stricken kitten in the bottom of a pail while tin lids are crashed over its terrified head – on and on and on – Will they never stop? You find yourself listening to a voice mumbling, "Oh God our help in ages past, our hope for years to come, our shelter from the stormy blast . . ." And then you realize it's your own.

Somehow, in the long lull that follows, you manage to rally your composure sufficiently to run down the slope to your crew. There, you order an immediate move up and across the slope to the farm on the right where you know Bob Wedd will be waiting, and where you must be when the inevitable enemy counter-attack comes in. Convinced you can make it faster on foot, and at the same time lighten the load in the carrier, you decide Squissato will accompany you carrying the 18-set on his back, so you'll have communication with the guns through Ferry now manning the 19-set in the carrier if it fails to claw its way up there.

Since all will be taking advantage of this strip of solid turf to get well up the slope before turning right across the ploughed field, where you'll be under observation for the rest of the way, no one must dilly-dally. And before taking off, you lay on, through Ferry, some harassing fire on buildings you assume are infested with snipers, about four hundred yards (according to the map) beyond the highway and that forlorn cluster of burned and broken buildings that is your objective. You order "troop fire" (four guns firing in rotation), "at three-second intervals . . . for ten minutes . . . starting now."

To further reduce the carrier's weight, on Squissato's suggestion, you and he carry the 60-pound roll of remote microphone cable suspended between you on a steel bar inserted through the centre of the spool. How you manage, you will never know. To run unencumbered a three-hundred-yard dash in mud, across an uneven ripple of furrows, would be an ordeal. Encumbered it is pure hell. And Squissato has that damned 18-set on his back. Only the realization you are running for your life keeps you going – gasping for air and churning your legs that burn as though on fire from lifting boots doubling in size to monstrous globs of clay.

Just when your chest is about to burst and your legs seize up in paralyzing spasms, you reach the firm ground of the farmyard and make for the only intact building, a long, low, brick structure extending all along the left side of the laneway to the gateway at the highway.

Plunging in the first open doorway, you and Squissato stumble into a room half-filled with coal. Gasping and heaving, you flop face-down on the slithery, rasping pile, and long after you regain your breath, you lie there clutching handfuls of shiny black anthracite, relishing the strange sense of security it provides. There is about the smell and feel of the stuff an aura of normalcy that has been totally missing all of yesterday and today. And you are still there, beginning to lose a battle with sleep, when Wedd bounces in the door, calling excitedly:

"Foo! Foo! Quick – they're putting a gun in action just out front."

When you scramble to your feet, you find him backed into your doorway, cautiously peering left around the doorjamb in the direction of the gate. Urgently waving you up beside him, he points across the road:

"Look – over there in the field – see it?"

You do, not more than three hundred yards away, a 75-mm you think, when you get your glasses on it. And clearly it is being prepared for action by a crew of four or five men.

Yanking your folded map out of the front of your battledress blouse you hurriedly establish a map reference. But before you can give it to Squissato standing by with his remote mike – which he assures you is now hooked up to the radio in the carrier parked out behind – Wedd restrains you: "Look – we may not need your guns!"

Looking the way he is nodding, back in the laneway to the right, you see the crew of a Royals' 6-pounder anti-tank gun that has just been manhandled into position, frantically readying it for action. And for a few seconds you and Wedd hold your breath as your heads swing back and forth from the gun in the laneway to the gun in the field, trying to judge which gun will get off that first crucial round that will decide the outcome of this deadly duel, for neither gun could possibly miss at that range.

It happens you are bent forward looking around Wedd towards the Jerry gun when the hot smash of muzzle-blast from the snout of the 6-pounder almost bowls you both over backwards, and you barely manage to follow the tracer of the shot as it goes through the shield of the German gun. As expected there is no reply to that shot, or to two more the Royals' gun puts through the shield of the enemy weapon. Nor is there any further sign of the crew, though you search the ground around the gun in all directions with your glasses for several minutes.

Just as you are about to give up, a Bren carrier rolls into view, from the direction of the enemy, making for the disabled gun. At first you think somebody has made an error, driven into no-man's-land, and is racing to get back to the Canadian lines, but when it arrives at the disabled gun, it stops, and men in potty helmets and field-grey uniforms pile out.

With Squissato at your elbow, his remote mike at the ready and the approximate position of that gun marked on the map, in no time at all you have the guns of 2nd Battery pumping up five rounds' gun fire (40 rounds). The Jerries are still in the process of wheeling the carrier around to present its rear hook to the trail eye of the gun, when the shells start arriving. Unfortunately they fall far beyond carrier and gun.

However, when you order "North 100 – Repeat," forty rounds catch the persistent Germans still frantically throwing things into the carrier for a quick take-off, and when the shelling ends there is no sign of life in the field. Still, the Royals' 6-pounder crew, attracted back to their gun by the fuss your rounds are making, ensure that carrier is permanently disabled with a couple of well-placed solid-shot.

In the lull that follows, Wedd tells you that in the cellar of the derelict house they found three 4th Field officers and the Colonel of the Essex Scottish, badly shaken, but otherwise unharmed.[*] However, among the missing and presumed captured are a FOO, Ted

---

[*] Just how shaken is indicated by Company Sgt.-Maj. Charles Martin of the Queen's Own Rifles of Canada in his book *Battle Diary*, describing a brief encounter shortly after with Pangman, who at one time had been Martin's company commander and was chiefly remembered for being "disciplined, a good planner, but stand-offish." The Queen's Own were passing through the Essex on their way up to the Goch–Calcar startline,

Adams, and his Sergeant-Major, Scott. They say the FOO was blind from his wounds when captured.

As daylight fades on February 20, you get an urgent message from friend Suckling, inviting you to join him. His company has moved into position among the houses at the crossroads on the right, filling in the gap the Germans found last night between 2nd Canadian Corps and British XXX Corps.

(And it was some gap! The whole right flank stood empty last night when the British brigade that was supposed to have attacked simultaneously to gain that section of the Goch–Calcar highway to the immediate right of Canadian 4th Brigade inexplicably didn't budge from their trenches way back in that field, where you'd spotted them yesterday when you were making that detour on your way over from Louisendorf.)

Suckling, obviously conscious of his exposed flank and remembering the speed with which Jerry overran these positions last night, is most desirous of your company, and you are outside in the dark, considering the merits of such a move – peering in his direction, measuring the risk of driving up the road instead of using the muddy field behind the house – when you hear the sharp *bur-rup bur-rup* of Schmeissers and see streams of tracers streaking towards the crossroads.

Thus you are in position to instantly get the guns working over the darkness across the road with flashing, roaring Mike targets, Scale 10 (240 shells per target), first in front of Suckling's position, then before Wedd's, and then over on the left in front of Stothers's, before swinging the guns back to the right to plaster the road leading up from the south to the crossroads, which you believe was

---

when he saw Pangman: "He was dirty and gaunt, tears running down his cheeks. It was hard to compare this man with the major I had once known when he said, 'God bless you in this. We took terrible losses and still didn't get the objective.' He'd come to realize how war makes us all equal." See Charles Martin, *Battle Diary*, Toronto: Dundurn Press, 1994, p. 116.

the route used by the tanks last night. The ugly image of a Tiger tank crushing through the smouldering ruins of the house here last night is still vivid, and you pound that road for several minutes. When at last you let the guns rest, no more tracers are coming from anywhere out there.

Whether the guns cooled off a diversionary attack on the right wing of 4th Brigade, or snuffed out a serious attempt to retake these positions they gained so handily last night, is impossible to tell. Whatever they were trying, the guns surely soured their taste for it, for, though the Royals stand-to the rest of the night, expecting the worst as the sounds of bitter action rise about the Rileys on the left, and 4th Field shells frequently roar with grim intensity over there, the Germans leave the Royals strictly alone.

For the Rileys it is a bad night. Two companies are seriously infiltrated. This you learn from monitoring radio messages from the FOOs to the guns. At 0100 hours February 21, you identify the voice of Lieut. Gerry Corbeil, a 14th Battery GPO brought up to relieve a FOO, calling for a Mike target on his own position to flush out the Germans. There follows a terse exchange with his Battery Commander, Drewry, in that peculiar abbreviated way radio messages are passed in the heat of battle – only the barest facts, unadorned by emotion, occasionally camouflaged by facetious expressions such as "big brothers" for medium guns, and frequently punctuated by long, agonizing blanks in transmissions, during which, for minutes on end, you try in vain to distinguish something intelligible amidst the gibberish spilling from earphones.

After hearing Corbeil report "uninvited guests" are about to visit his house, you hear no more for an interminable period, though you strain your ears to identify his familiar accent in the gushing roar of static and overlapping gabble. Just as you are starting to think he must have bought it, he comes on to explain to "Sunray" he had to remain quiet while he waited with drawn pistol to get a bead on a Jerry coming in the door, so he wouldn't miss in the gloom.

Of this very grim night Riley's Col. Whitaker will recall:

Back in the milk factory [Tac Headquarters] we were swamped by reports by the FOOs and my company commanders about this extremely dangerous counter-attack. Panzer Lehr attacked Kennedy's B Company at Schwanenhof [farm] from the south and the decimated C Company from the east.

Jack Drewry and his gunner crew of two – the latter operating the 19-set from a half-track behind my HQ – swung into non-stop action that was to continue throughout the night. Jack was a big, bluff, good-looking, hard-drinking officer who never lost his cool. His gunners were an unlikely crew, both characters: Steve Pinchuk, the driver . . . and "Coop" Cooper, an excellent signaller, who was an accomplished jazz pianist. His favourite tune was "Pistol Packin' Momma, lay that pistol down . . ." Through numerous battles, those three men were responsible for saving many, many RHLI lives; the enemy laid many pistols down.

Drewry had direct call on twenty-four guns of 4th Field (for Mike targets) and on all seventy-two guns in the three field regiments of 2nd Division (for Uncle targets). He called down many Mikes and Uncles that night. It was a "Mike target Scale Five" [five rounds from each of twenty-four guns] that dispersed the enemy from C Company HQ.*

It is nearly dawn when the Germans pull back leaving scores of their dead strewn about (200 would later be counted in the vicinity of the Rileys and the Royals), and 46 prisoners from the Panzer Lehr Division in Riley hands, bringing the total POWs taken by 4th Brigade to 275. Across the front six more enemy tanks are burning, and at dawn an Air OP pilot is able to count eleven derelicts around and about the highway.†

---

* From *Rhineland*, by Col. W. Denis and Shelagh Whitaker, Toronto: Stoddart, 1989, pp. 165-6.

† *Gunners of Canada* gives 4th Field much of the credit for 4th Brigade

In an unusual document prepared for filing with the regimental war diary, the taciturn Col. MacGregor Young will write of this epic two-day struggle to gain and hold the Goch–Calcar highway:

> This operation produced the most violent German counter-attacks the Regiment has seen. On one occasion two officers with separate battalions called down fire on their own OPs at the same time. Three officers spent a whole night in a cellar with the enemy over them. Three other OP parties had the enemy throwing hand-grenades into their OPs, and got into hand-to-hand fighting on two separate occasions . . . Prisoners of war later stated at least three tanks were disabled by artillery fire, and the heaps of dead Germans in front of the various company positions were adequately satisfying.

Clearly life back at the guns remains exceedingly strenuous. Just servicing the round-the-clock demands from the FOOs for tons of shells would be enough to exhaust the gunners. But they must also contend with quagmire fields where every gun has to be winched and manhandled in and out of position, and every ton of ammunition – of the mountains consumed daily – must be

---

holding the Goch–Calcar highway, singling out for special mention Major John L. Drewry, who was awarded the DSO, and his signaller, Ralph Cooper, who received a Commander-in-Chief Certificate. However, credit for nine out of eleven kills of Panzer Lehr tanks was given to 18th Battery, 2nd Anti-tank Regiment – seven by C Troop under Lieut. David Heaps, and two by A Troop under Lieut. F. R. Ray. Both officers were awarded the Military Cross. Major Louis Froggett, who guided a 17-pounder crew from 2nd Anti-Tank into position, would never forget the satisfaction of seeing them knock out four tanks. As reported in *Rhineland* by Col. Denis and Shelagh Whitaker (Toronto: Stoddart, 1989, p. 168), those charging tanks were stopped less than one hundred yards from Battalion Headquarters. Had they made it all the way, Froggett believes they could have "rolled up the battalion."

carried in from the nearest stable road, over cavernous, water-filled ruts, especially treacherous on dark rainy nights to bone-weary gunners staggering under the weight of 110-pound shell boxes. And though the nerve-wracking tension of the front line, which can exhaust a man even when he is doing no more than crouching in a hole in the ground for survival, is less persistent back at the guns and wagon lines, life for the gunner is frequently just as fearful and dangerous. Impressive numbers of German guns and mortars maintain harassment day and night – moving their fire about from gun positions to wagon lines, to road junctions, and back again – while their new jet-propelled assault planes *swoosh* in without warning, streaking through a blur of black ack-ack puffing skyward from dozens of Bofors, to bomb and strafe whatever presents itself as a target.

All of which you must visualize by applying past experience to the bits of information garnered from Signal-Sgt. Ryder when he brings up the rations every two or three days, since you never get a chance to visit the guns. To gain the full flavour of life at the guns, you must wait the chance to peruse Bombardier Hossack's log and his revealing montage of impressions:

The front is aroar with all the guns seemingly firing in unison.

The area is literally packed with all kinds of Allied equipment, and three units divide one small smashed house. Enemy shells fall at the busy crossroads and a Don R is blown to eternity. All German houses have been well "conquered" and all civilians are evacuated to the rear, for our protection not theirs. We find sleeping space on ground floors and cellars of the broken homes, and everything from bedpans to pianos are thrown outside to give us more room. The battle is now an even-stephen affair and civilian rights are not even considered as we vie for supremacy.

Our ack-ack guns can't hit the jet-propelled planes that visit us daily. These [twin-jet M-262s] have a remarkable change of pace. We wear tin hats when ack-ack shell splinters bounce off the tile roof of our small command post. Bombs screech down and we take cover. There's a direct hit on a 14th Battery gun pit killing three and wounding four.*

The shells and mortars that come in day and night bring memories of Carpiquet, Normandy. German larders are full of choice preserves. Pork and beef roam around, and all this finds its way into our cookhouse. Pork chops used to be a memory; now they are a daily occurrence.

An enemy counter-attack gains headway overrunning Battalion HQ . . . Frantic calls come in for Mike targets, and everybody goes to work with a vengeance: gunners doing their work "at the double," signallers perspiring, the officer talking himself hoarse on the Tannoy PA system, as the surveyor (GPO Ack) provides him with the data. Hours later the attack is halted, but not before sizeable losses are suffered by the infantry. In the morning (February 21) congratulations are received from the infantry commander on our efforts: the shooting was "right on the button" and the shells were "on the floor" faster than ever before recorded – just seventy seconds after the radio signal specified a map reference . . .

You hear that Carrier Driver "Palm" Knight and OP Ack Eugene Bowers, who both served on your OP crew last winter, were wounded during the counter-attacks on the Rileys. The Rileys suffered 125 killed and wounded, and the Royals 64. The Essex Scottish lost 205 men and officers when they were overrun: 51 killed, 99 wounded, and 54 taken prisoner.

---

* Killed were Gunner Robert Bilodeau, Lance-Bombardier Ralph Bartlett, and Bombardier Burgess A. Porter. Wounded were Sgt. George Oleniuk, Bombardier Murray Harding, Bombardier John Homan, and Gunner James Garrigan.

48

OBSERVATIONS FROM A PIGPEN

---- ✳ ----

AT FIRST LIGHT FEBRUARY 21, YOU AND SQUISSATO REPAIR to the only place you can get an overview of enemy territory without exposing yourselves to snipers: a pigpen in the far end of this low-slung brick structure abutting the highway. Long shallow shutters, hinged along the top and raised slightly for ventilation, provide a broad view of the zone. And even though you must remain well back in the shadows, when you climb over the wooden barrier and join the grunting, half-grown pigs in the sty itself, you find you can gain a truly panoramic view when you move right and left. And so from dawn to dusk you remain among the agitated pigs while Squissato sits with his remote control outside the pen on a barrel, when he isn't rustling up tea or grub, or spewing handfuls of pig feed from the barrel to a squealing mob of porkers scrambling for position at their trough.

Though the Germans continue sporadic shelling and mortaring across the front, occasionally with awesome intensity, they launch no more counter-attacks this day against the weary battalions along Goch–Calcar highway – no more, that is, if you don't count a crazy attempt by a company of Germans to reoccupy this position late this afternoon, marching this way boldly upright, two abreast, as though on a route march, up a road that joins the highway just left of your pigpen. Obviously new troops, fresh from the south, but inexplicably ill-informed not to be aware that only some thirty-six hours ago German infantry and tanks (116 Panzer Windhund Division), after retaking this very position and inflicting heavy casualties on the Essex, were driven out by your horrendous concentrations of shell-fire; and that only last night when Panzer Lehr units hinted they wanted to return here, they too were dissuaded by another torrent of shells from 4th Field guns.

You have to be alerted to the imminent arrival of these uninvited guests by a Royals' mortar sergeant, so engrossed are you in engaging a distant target barely visible in the haze that your 10-power glasses tend to magnify excessively: a long line of tiny figures, strung out for at least two miles, interspersed with horse-drawn wagons, crawling at a snail's pace across the front from right to left along a road lined with Lombardy poplars. To reach them you are using super-charge (good for 13,400 yards), shelling first the leading end of the column and then moving back along the line of march to troops still upright, plodding along. Then back to the reformed front section and so on.

Quickly you peel off Baker Troop guns from the others working over that distant road and order "ten rounds gunfire" (ten rounds per gun fired as fast as they can) on a point just in advance of the marching column – a point easily established, for it happens to be the centre of the designated DF SOS Target area. And the Germans are still swinging jauntily up the road no more than two hundred yards away when your shells sizzle overhead, and you see them break ranks and start diving for the ditches, before the target area is obscured by a turmoil of violent orange and black puffs erupting on the road, in the ditches, and among the trees lining the road. From that moment you see no further movement out there. But assuming that most of them will have survived that initial blasting and will be crawling away along the ditches making for the farm buildings up that road, you shift the fire of the four guns in stages back along the road to where it runs past farm buildings. And while B Troop engages your latest correction, you go back to tormenting that distant column, again reformed and crawling along to a point where it will disappear from your view.

In the middle of this extraordinary business, you are suddenly conscious that another spectator has joined Squissato and the Mortar Sergeant standing on the trough and leaning on the top rail of the pen behind you. And when you get a chance to turn around to see who it is, you are astounded to find yourself looking into the smiling blue eyes and broadly grinning face of George Browne, who was your troop commander briefly after his escape from France after the Dieppe Raid in 1942, first from the Germans and then Vichy. And he is just as you remember him then, his highly polished appearance enhanced by a gleaming white set of perfect teeth and unusually high colouring, well burnished today by a frigid wind. On the epaulettes of his belted Burberry, so totally unsoiled it could have just come from the dry cleaners, are the crown and pips of a lieutenant-colonel!

Laughing at your speechless disbelief, he advises you to "Carry on – we'll talk when you finish."

But as you return to adjusting the fire on your targets, you feel increasingly uneasy about your appearance and that of Squissato, who is standing beside the impeccably turned-out Colonel. Though your nose has long since lost all sensitivity for any offensive odour a careless pig might release, you must be redolent; and while you've had no access to a mirror for days, you are fully aware that flopping down in a coal bin at night when you get the chance, and observing the zone from a pigpen inhabited by live pigs by day, is hardly conducive to good grooming.

And so you are relieved he is unable to hang around more than a minute or two when you finish – just long enough to explain he is now the CO of 14th Field (since moving over from 1st Field in Italy) and is up here with the Brigadier of 9th Brigade (John Rocking-ham) and the battalion commanders to recce the positions they'll be taking over tonight. Oh, hadn't you heard? 2nd Division is exchanging positions with 3rd Division on the left flank.

You tell him it has been rather a "sticky go" up here.

And he tells you it hasn't been any "piece of cake" on the road to Moyland either, but better than those first few days of "Veritable" when they were earning the title of "water rats." Maintaining arty support for units sailing forward in Buffaloes or walking through water three feet deep to clear "islands" was a trying business. But now he must rejoin the others . . . He saw Mac Young for a moment at 4th Brigade on the way up . . . Must get together for a drink someday. Smiling down at the pigs jostling about your legs, he expresses the hope you will find a less crowded OP where you are going – perhaps draw a luxurious upper room in Moyland Castle from whence he just came. He suggests you look out for Frederick the Great's bedroom with its canopied bed on raised platform, surrounded by curved walls covered with paintings of well-endowed nudes.

You reckon that would be rather splendid.

He wishes you good hunting, and he's gone.

So, there's to be a move tonight over on the left somewhere south of Calcar. You don't relish the idea. It means another sleepless night, and with all those hundreds of men and vehicles moving in opposite directions, the confusion could be horrendous, could draw fire, or even a counter-attack. The pigs are now snuffling around your legs, crowding for position at the trough next to your feet, thinking you are going to feed them. At least you won't be spending tomorrow in a pigpen! For this you'll not be sorry. You are heartily sick of the sight, sound, and smell of pigs, and this you remark to Squissato as you climb out of the pen to rest for a while on his pig-feed barrel.

With this sentiment Squissato heartily concurs and says he doesn't think he will ever be able to eat pork again. This morning, when he went to get something out of the carrier, parked out of sight in a notch behind the pigpen, he found a pig eating the guts out of the dead German lying there.

With that, he goes out to the carrier to rustle up some Compo tea, leaving you to revel in the prospect of a new OP – possibly in that castle that impressed Browne so much.

One day you will read a wonderful description by war correspondent R. W. Thompson of the occupation by the Maisonneuves of the great brick Schloss of Moyland, once the summer residence of Frederick the Great, pitted and scarred by shells and Typhoon rockets:

> ... a dirty white flag was hoisted above the main turret ... sunshine shone upon the dusky red bricks of its mellowed walls and revealed the desolation of surrounding lawns and parklands, laid waste by the violence of the fighting. Two antlered deer, cast in bronze and mounted on stone plinths, flanked the bridge over the outer moat. The swollen body of a dead horse lay in the drive ... Inside a vast confusion of wreckage ... In the great, principal bed chamber ... cooking stoves of a French-Canadian company roared under pans of frying fat . . . In the magnificently appointed bathrooms of the state apartments groups of soldiers washed and shaved for the first time in a week. The place had been a vast treasure house and in scores of rooms all the bric-a-brac of an exquisite home of princely wealth lay jumbled in confusion. In the cellars of the castle Ilse Marie, Baroness Steengracht von Moyland, sat upright in the midst of her white-faced servants, seeming the sole survivor of a world long since dead. It was impossible to believe that a way of life such as hers had persisted until a week ago: impossible to imagine that such a life would ever again be possible.*

But for now your thoughts are of a coarser nature, restricted, by the paucity of detail in Browne's description of the castle made of bricks, to imagining those nude-covered curved walls of the master bedroom.

---

* R. W. Thompson, *Battle for the Rhine*, New York: Ballantine Books, 1959, pp. 174–75.

German artillery bombardment of what is left of the outskirts of Cleve takes its toll of 3rd Division vehicles, February 23, 1945. (National Archives of Canada, PA-46875)

Moyland Schloss, scarred but still impressive, with Frederick the Great's curve-walled bedroom surviving intact. (National Archives of Canada, PA-196815)

Operation Blockbuster (February 26, 1945) begins with Algonquins riding into action through the Rhineland mud on the backs of South Alberta Shermans. (National Archives of Canada, PA-113672)

Don R (despatch rider) in a tank suit, riding a Norton. (Harold G. Aikman, National Archives of Canada, PA-192880)

Six of these 240-mm howitzers, with twenty-two-foot barrels, firing 360-pound shells up to twenty-five thousand yards, were used by the 3rd Super Heavy Regiment Royal Artillery against the Siegfried Line emplacements at the opening of Operation Veritable and in support of the Rhineland crossing. (G. Kenneth Bell, National Archives of Canada, PA-161301)

The thirty-mile-long smokescreen laid along the Rhine for two weeks before the assault crossings on March 23-24 was produced by machines like this, from AO3 Smoke Company British Pioneer Corps, seen here "smoking" the bridge at Nijmegen to obscure it from German bombers. (Donald I. Grant, National Archives of Canada, PA-145657)

Gunner Hardtack with adoring friends. (Collection of the author)

The china hen resting on Gunner Hardtack's grave was scrounged from the rubble of Cleve. Twenty-four years after the war, the author's wife wondered aloud, as she was leaving Groesbeek Military Cemetery, whether Hardtack had possibly been re-buried there as an unknown soldier. Although that wasn't possible, her question was sincere, for she had often heard of the revered hen and her burial as a gunner under a wooden cross. (Collection of the author)

The road bulldozed through Emmerich after intense bombardment and a two-day battle that ended with the 7th Brigade (Winnipeg Rifles, Regina Rifles, and the Canadian Scottish) clearing the city. (National Archives of Canada, PA-151530)

The bailey bridge over the Twente Canal, seven kilometres east of Zutphen, near Almen, erected by the Royal Canadian Engineers under heavy enemy shellfire on April 3-4, 1945 — while the Royal Regiment held off fifteen counter-attacks by the enemy — was still in use at least thirty years later. (Author's photo)

A machine gun tower against the sky was the first indication a 4th Field FOO and his crew had that they were approaching Westerbork Concentration Camp, where more than one hundred thousand Jews were collected from all parts of Holland and sent on to the death camps. (Certified photo from the Rijksinstituut voor Oorlogsdocumentaire [Netherlands War Research Institute])

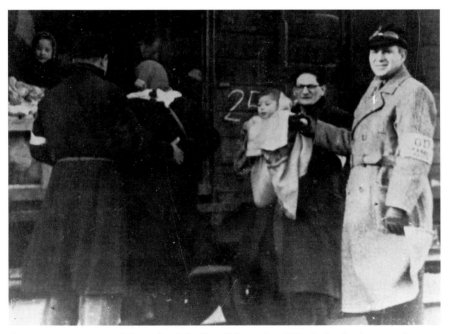

A scene common at Westerbork before Liberation. The baby is about to be handed up by its father to its mother, who is boarding a boxcar filled with women and children unknowingly bound for Auschwitz extermination camp. (Certified photo from the Rijksinstituut voor Oorlogsdocumentaire [Netherlands War Research Institute])

The German staff car that burned on the morning of April 14, 1945, after receiving a direct hit from a 4th Field gun participating in a Mike target called for by a FOO peering out from the great railway station across the canal. (Photo courtesy of Groningen historian Menno Huizinga)

The north side of Groningen's Grote Markt at first light on the morning after its capture. On the right is the Martinitoren (built 1469–82), saved by the Groningen fire brigade after its wooden scaffolding was set alight by the retreating Germans. (Photo courtesy of Menno Huizinga)

Shined up and polished, the faithful old 25-pounders of 4th, 5th, and 6th field regiments (led by Lt.-Col. McGregor Young, DSO and bar, Lt.-Col. E. D. Nighswander, and Lt.-Col. Dale Harris respectively); the 17-pounders of 2nd Anti-Tank Regiment (led by Lt.-Col. J. D. Southam); and the 40-mm Bofors of 3rd Light Ack-Ack Regiment (led by Lt.-Col. G. G. K. Peake), parade past Corps Commander Lt.-General Guy Simonds, Divisional Commander Maj.-General Bruce Matthews, and the CRA Brigadier Frank Lace, May 15, 1945. (Canadian Army photo)

49

A MOONLIGHT DRIVE

IN NO-MAN'S-LAND

❄

AS BROWNE PREDICTED, THE CHANGE-OVER WITH 3RD Division takes place after dark. There is a moon, however, and when not hidden by clouds it is very helpful to the long, snaking columns of shuffling foot-sloggers feeling their way along the rutted and shell-pitted roads, as always heavily laden with weapons, ammunition, packs, and shovels.

During the move you lose contact with the Royals and have to make it to their new location on your own, when you get a signal to report to Battalion Tac Headquarters to pick up a map of the new zone and be briefed by Battery Commander Don Cornett. Because of the confusion of troops and support columns moving up or back in the vicinity, it takes much longer than it should to locate Cornett's barn.

Moyland Woods, after six days of bitter fighting, has finally been cleared, but Calcar, two miles farther southeast, is still in enemy hands. Thus the principal role of 4th Brigade will be to protect the left flank of 2nd Division from attacks out of Calcar, and the Royals, on the left flank of the brigade, will be preoccupied with the east as much as the south.

You are to hole up in a farmhouse that will be Tim Beatty's D Company headquarters on the brow of a hill looking southeast over the rugged country about a mile west of Calcar. By the map there are two routes there: a long, roundabout one which would bring you to the rear of the house; and a more direct route which could present problems of cover as you near the farm. Not knowing which route Beatty and company are taking, you choose the shorter one. However, you have not gone far past dark and silent houses along this totally deserted road before you feel the tension rising as you spot familiar signs that no vehicles or men have passed this way recently. In the moonlight, which comes and goes with the vagaries of the drifting clouds, you see gravelly dirt, twigs, and other bits of vegetation garnishing downed power lines and other miscellaneous debris, blown across the road by past bombardments, totally undisturbed by tracks, tires, or boots.

Suppressing your anxiety that the road may be mined, you let the carrier roll on slowly until you are about three hundred yards from the house, where you should be turning left across a field sloping up to the rear of the house. This, you discover, is impossible, for the road is now passing along a deep notch cut into the hillside. You halt the carrier in the shadows of the cut, and getting down under a piece of tarpaulin, examine the map with a torch. Either you go back and circle around a couple of miles to approach the house from another direction, or you drive one hundred yards or so out into no-man's-land to the mouth of the farm lane leading up to the front of the house. You decide to chance the latter, and speaking softly to Reid, you tell him to be as quiet as he can. Within seconds of the carrier moving out into the moonlight you spot the mouth of the lane. But as you signal Reid to turn left into it, you have to jump up and direct him with hand signals so as to thread the tracks through a dozen or more German bodies sprawled face-down across the lane – the largest number of bodies you've ever seen in such a small area. Only by ingenious swivelling does Reid miss running over hands and feet.

On the way up the muddy track towards the burned-out shell of what had been a tall, white house, still largely white and glistening in the moonlight, you realize a tracked vehicle coming in from no-man's-land could arouse unpleasant action from the occupants of the ruins. So while you are still some distance away you stop the carrier and get out to walk up alone to a sashless window opening, calling out loudly as you go a stream of questions you hope will give the occupants reason to pause before letting fly at you:

"Where the hell is everybody? Are you all asleep? Why am I not being challenged? What's going on? Wake up, you lead-swinging employees of Mackenzie King, and earn your dollar-thirty a day!"

But the white skeleton remains spookily silent until you get right up to a window opening and start to lean in to examine the charred clutter. Then the ugly muzzle of a heavy machine-gun rises up level with your eyes, and a gruff voice demands: "Who the hell are you?"

You tell him you're a 4th Field FOO, and explain why you are coming in from the front. Still, he remains suspicious; nobody told *him* they were going to be relieved tonight. But when, in your best authoritarian voice (not easy with a machine-gun almost touching your nose), you suggest it might be sensible for everybody's sake to get your carrier parked in behind the house as soon as possible, he reluctantly agrees.

Profoundly relieved, you march down the hill and lead the carrier up to a spot behind a low barn untouched by shells and the fire that consumed the house a day or two ago, judging from the coldness of the debris cluttering the ground floor, and the residual heat left in the stone-and-concrete ceiling of the arched alcove that you and your crew take over in the basement, after the remote control from the 19-set in the carrier is spooled out across the barnyard and down the stone cellar steps. At first the mild heat, radiating from the floor above which had withstood the glowing embers of the whole fiery interior of the two-storey house, feels wonderfully comforting after the frigid midnight air outside. But soon you and your men are perspiring, peeling off layers of clothing, and wishing you had access to that marvellous ice-cream parlour in Antwerp.

Suddenly you remember a can of peaches and a can of creamy rice pudding out in the carrier, squirrelled away for a special occasion, on your suggestion, since carrier crews never get to see such exotic items except when errors occur in the letter of the alphabet stencilled on a Compo box to signify its contents.

Miraculously, in recent days two such incorrectly labelled boxes made it past the eagle eyes of ration despatchers at all levels of Army Service Corps and the Regiment. Could there be a better time to sample the contents of those precious cans? When the question is put to the crew, they vote unanimously for immediate consumption.

When you go out to the carrier to rummage for the cans, the mud has stiffened in the barnyard and ice has formed on the puddles. The rich, creamy rice pudding is as cold and thick as vanilla ice cream when it is spooned into mess tins. And garnished with cold sweet slices of peaches, it is the greatest dessert in the history of the world – though perhaps only mouths parched and ravenous for something cold and sweet could be expected to realize this.

When the Royals arrive space is suddenly at a premium, for though the basement is honeycombed with several arched tunnel-like rooms, all are small and some are cluttered, as yours is with a mound of potatoes. Among the stream of people who come to look in on you, checking to see if there is any extra floor space, is the friendly Mortar Sergeant who was with you and Squissato in that pigpen on the Goch–Calcar highway yesterday afternoon. Seeing two of your crew already bedded down and asleep, and another brewing up a cuppa, he wonders aloud how you made it up here so much in advance of everybody else.

You explain about the shortcut, and during the course of your explanation describe the horrific sight of all those German bodies lying in the moonlight down there where your carrier turned off the main road into the farmer's lane leading up to the house.

He is much impressed, but being pragmatic by nature, he decides that when the moon sets about 3:00 A.M. he'll go down and loot them, explaining he soon will have need of extra cash because he is getting married on his next leave.

Sometime before dawn he wakes you up and inquires rather boldly how many bodies you think you saw down there at the road. Sensing your veracity is being questioned, you turn to Squissato, now manning the radio, and ask him the same question.

"About a dozen," says he without the slightest hesitation.

"Well, there aren't any down there now!" declares the Sergeant. Oh, but he must be mistaken. Did he go right down to the road?

"Couldn't make a mistake . . . followed the ruts left by your carrier right down to where they turned in from the road. There are no bodies down there."

The only possible explanation is that all those bodies were alive.

"And one of them at least is still down there somewhere," says the Sergeant, taking off his beret and poking a finger through a bullet hole.

The squeaking tracks of your carrier, resembling a tank, suddenly coming out of nowhere, must have surprised an enemy patrol, and they flopped face-down in the farm lane, feigning death. But then your carrier swung into the lane and they were obliged to maintain a steely coolness almost beyond belief – not moving a muscle as tracks passed within inches of their heads.

50

"NIPPING OFF" SOME
ENEMY TERRITORY

※

AT FIRST LIGHT, THOUGH IT IS FROSTY OUTSIDE, YOU ARE glad to leave that cloying, radiant heat of the cellar and pick your way through the charred trash on the roofless, ground-floor shell of what had been a very substantial house, to a position at the gaping, sashless window you'd approached with such trepidation from no-man's-land last night.

Here you look over a valley of farmland and woods, a striking field of fire for the Bren gunner with whom you share the opening. When you remark on this, he draws your attention to the para-trooper bodies dotted here and there down the slope – all face down, their weapons beside them pointing this way, just as they had fallen to a hail of bullets from this and other openings in the derelict house and barn. He tells you, "Three times, according to the 9th Brigade guys we relieved here last night, the paratroopers charged up the slope yelling obscenities in English."

Those forlorn, crumpled bodies in the dead grass out there provide melancholy testimony to a generation of young men who continue to fight and die for a lost cause. Surely the alert men of the Paratroop and Panzer Lehr Divisions have realized since late December, when their Ardennes' offensive against the Americans ground to a halt after gaining a fifty-mile breakthrough, that all hope of preventing the Allies from overrunning their homeland had disappeared. But still they fight on with an aggressiveness sometimes bordering on insanity.

But not this morning. Stand-to passes quietly.

After registering a couple of farmhouses down in the valley, dropping a ranging round through the roof of each, you retire to the cellar for breakfast. There you find the Royals engaged in an effort to gain more floor space for sleeping, cleaning out everything the farm family had stored in the interlocking, tunnel-like rooms. In the room that until now has been largely the domain of your crew, they are attacking a great mound of potatoes piled up along one wall of the room, shovelling them into burlap sacks and carrying them outside.

A soldier who has just come off duty is asleep on his back on the crest of the pile, snoring away oblivious to the fact his bed is being seriously undermined. Soon there is nothing supporting his head, but mysteriously it manages to maintain a horizontal position as though his neck is locked rigid. By the time the shoveller has undermined his shoulders without any change in his position, the phenomenon has begun to attract a crowd.

Slowly, relentlessly, the potatoes disappear from beneath the upper half of the sleeping man. Still he remains aloft as by levitation. Not until he is undermined almost to his hips does he collapse on his head in a bewildered heap in the corner.

The fact there is no accompanying roar of laughter from onlookers who crowded around to await the inevitable outcome, and are now dispersing without comment, speaks volumes for the depth of the fatigue afflicting all. Even as they marvelled at their comrade's body defying gravity, they had complete empathy with the exhausted man, understanding the capacity of a sleep-starved body to come to terms with the weirdest conditions – maintaining sweet oblivion to every filthy discomfort until the last possible moment before carrying out its next set of obligations, imposed as frequently by visits from uninvited guests from out front as by red-tabbed gentlemen studying well-lighted map-boards in the rear.

However, for the next twenty-four hours all moves, and the sleep-denying conflict they incite, are imposed from the rear, by men using sharp Chinagraph pencils to select limited company objectives designed either to straighten out the line or ensure a more secure startline for the next push: "nipping off" a dominant feature with some farm buildings over there in the valley in front of Major Suckling's B Company; "occupying" a wooded area with farmhouse south of Major Louis Froggett's Rileys company; and "clearing" Ebben, a collection of buildings at a road junction, some four hundred yards in front of A Company of the Highland Light Infantry of 9th Brigade, currently occupying your old pigpen on the Goch–Calcar highway.

But if the objectives are limited, German resistance is not, and in every case their counter-attacks equal in ferocity anything exhibited during their vain struggle to regain dominance of the Goch–Calcar highway. And sometimes you can feel, as acutely at a distance as when directly involved, the tension that exists in the frenzy of a front-line struggle, when the outcome is never certain until you suddenly become aware he is no longer coming at you. A case in point is the furious counter-attack incited by Bob Suckling's company attempting to occupy the farm buildings in front of their position, the course of which you follow squatted down on a milking stool beside Battery Commander Don Cornett, who is poring over a map-board on his lap, in the clammy, draughty cow stable that is Royals' Battalion Tac Headquarters.

Only an hour ago (6:00 P.M., February 23) Cornett, apparently becoming aware that Suckling's position, without the support of a FOO all day, was becoming increasingly vulnerable, ordered you to move over there. However, while you were still packing up, he ordered you to join him at Battalion HQ. Now, with Suckling acting as his eyes, describing as best he can where 4th Field's shells are falling, Cornett is "shooting from the map," sending appropriate corrections back to the guns.

The initial move by Suckling's company to occupy the area of some farm buildings a couple of hundred yards in front of their position began at 2:30 A.M., as a forty-man fighting patrol led by a platoon commander, Lieut. G. H. Matheson. When the rest of the company followed about 5:00 A.M., the farm buildings were still in enemy hands, and were cleared only after some tanks and flame-throwers were brought up to support a second attack about 4:30 in the afternoon. One officer and nineteen paratroopers came out with their hands high over their heads, bringing the total bag of prisoners for the day to forty.

Now with darkness covering their movement, the enemy has mounted a very strong counter-attack behind an unusually heavy and sustained box barrage. Three self-propelled guns have moved up and are smashing shells into the house and barn, and in the glaring light of flares sent skyward by the company's 2-inch mortars, some one hundred paratroopers are seen coming across the field in extended line, providing a target for the Royals' 6-pounder crew until all their H.E. shells are expended.

At this crucial point, you notice Col. Lendrum, the Royals' CO, has been drawn from behind his table and is squatting down beside you in front of Cornett, clearly recognizing that the fate of his D Company is now in the hands of this cool little man, hunched over and all but disappearing within the folds of his great sheepskin coat, in which he has virtually lived since plucking it from that great pile of discarded German winter clothing on the Merxem dock in Antwerp last September.

From the infantry 18-set earphones hanging around Cornett's neck, Suckling's voice is asking: "Can you bring your shells a bit closer?"

Cornett, still studying his map, picks up the microphone of the remote control running out to the 19-set in his half-track in the barnyard that will send his order back to the guns: "Northwest 100 – Scale 5 – Repeat!" And when again the guns can be heard thumping shells into that distant valley, he inquires, "How's that, Bob?"

In a moment Suckling is calling enthusiastically, "You're right on! They're landing right where they should! Keep them coming!"

Again and again Cornett orders "Scale 5 – Repeat," each time releasing another 120 rounds of high explosive on the target area, all the while staring intently at the map-board on his knees, as though willing the shells to land where they should: close to, but not on, that tiny dot representing Suckling's house. Only when he finally allows the shelling to subside, and the expected report from Suckling does not materialize, does he look up with worried eyes. Grasping the 18-set mike he goes on the air to request a sitrep, but when he releases the transmission switch and the gush of static returns to the earphones, no familiar voice disturbs the persistent gabble.

After the running exchange they'd been conducting, the silence is ominous, and the minutes pass slowly as further calls by Cornett fail to draw any response. Then suddenly, to the vast relief of three men huddled around Cornett's map-board, a familiar drawl comes on the air to report: "The Heinies seem to have pulled back."

Later you'll learn his long silence was due to his being fully occupied stalking a paratrooper poking around outside his back door. An amused witness will tell of his Company Commander muttering in disgust – when the grenade he bowled into the court-yard went clattering along the tiles alerting the German to take cover before it went off – "Oh hell, I should have used my pistol!" But then he got another chance when the curious German returned and poked his head in the doorway.

Understrength before the attack, D Company is now down to 20 per cent of its strength, having suffered forty-four casualties, four of them fatal. And by the time Wedd's company arrives to reinforce them, the survivors have been without food and sleep for more than twenty-four hours.

Over on the right, Major Froggett's company of Rileys runs into an equally "sticky go" in moving forward five hundred yards to some farm buildings. During a particularly tense period, their second FOO of the day, Lieut. Jim Nesbitt, GPO of Dog Troop, 14th Battery, sent up to take over from "a wounded and exhausted Troop Commander," Captain Ken Smale, calls down a Mike target on his own position when things become so bad he simply "doesn't know what the hell else to do."

Of this bitter struggle that continues off and on for seventy-two hours, one of Froggett's platoon commanders, Lieut. Ken Dugall, will one day say: "As they tried to jump through the hedge we were shooting them. There were fellows lying there with arms twisted, some shot through the knee and screaming blue murder . . . Oh Jesus, it was terrible."*

Nesbitt will remember the next night as being "a very sticky time at the farm" for him and his crew, including Gunner Al "Dutch" Plomp, his OP Ack. "Before Bren gun fire and grenades send them packing, Germans are running around the place, setting the building on fire with their mortars, and chopping the top almost completely off the 19-set in the carrier with machine-gun fire, rendering it useless."

Next morning, February 25, Capt. Don Edwards, Dog Troop Commander, is sent over to relieve Nesbitt. Thus Edwards is standing shoulder to shoulder with Major Froggett when his company is again involved in fending off a counter-attack of such fanatical intensity that many years after this intrepid company commander will still refer to it as "the grisliest day of the war for me."

Similarly, moves on the same day by battalions of 3rd Division, to improve their startline for Operation "Blockbuster," stir up a hornet's nest. Doug MacFarlane, until recently GPO of your Baker Troop, is in the thick of it, having been promoted Captain and posted to 14th Field Regiment. In fact – though it will be many moons before you learn of it – your good friend is in the process of earning a Military Cross for gallantry in his first tour of duty as a FOO, having gone forward with a leading company of the Highland Light Infantry in a predawn attack designed to clear the crossroads hamlet of Ebben, lying only about four hundred yards south of your old pigsty OP on the Goch–Calcar highway.

By first light MacFarlane has an OP in a building just cleared by

---

* From *Rhineland* by Col. Denis and Shelagh Whitaker, Toronto: Stoddart, 1989, p. 171.

the HLI. Almost immediately it is engaged by an enemy self-propelled gun from about six hundred yards away. Its first shot kills his signaller, wounds him around the face and eyes, and puts his radio out of action. Then the shelling and mortaring about the position knocks out a signal line that has just been laid to his OP, leaving him with no means of calling down fire from the guns. In spite of his wounds and the enemy fire, he traces the line back and fixes the break, returns to his OP, still under mortar fire, and shells the German SP until it goes silent. All day, he shells and disperses Germans jockeying for position to attack.

Meanwhile, the men at the guns continue their exhausting routine. From the day they took up their first position in the Rhineland near Bedburg, the gunners have had little rest. When not being called upon to produce intense fire to beat back counterattacks, which can continue for hours and sometimes overlap, they must conduct long, drawn-out programs of harassing fire to keep the enemy on edge, especially throughout the night. Shell consumption is therefore heavy, and weary gunners have to carry most of it hundreds of yards from heavily laden trucks that can't make it to the guns through the mud. When 4th Field moves February 23 to deploy a mile northwest of Moyland, in fields from which the flood waters have just receded, the quads, wallowing through the mud, manage somehow to drop their guns off fairly near the gun markers, but then they have to winch themselves back out to the road using "ground anchors."

Bombardier Hossack's terse diary notes capture the grimness:

The Padre buries the Jerry dead near us. A bulldozer, digging gun pits, gets stuck in the heavy going. Ammo vehicles cannot get through the field . . . enemy again counter-attacks in strength . . . the guns are literally panting. Quite a few enemy shells, but none among us. . . . Army rations are practically unused as we dine regularly on [the Rhinelanders'] beef, pork, and chicken. Preserves and sugar-cured hams are also in good quantity. We now know that while the rest of Europe was nearly starved,

Germany's Rhineland, at least, fattened on the very best . . .* By treacherous roads to beyond Louisendorf, scene of heavy German counter-attack. Dead Germans are lying around – 25-pounder shells have made an awful mess of many caught out of their slit trenches . . .

Sergeant Hunt's diary for this same day will record similar reflections on the affluence of Rhineland farmers and the awful harvest their country's war of aggression is reaping:

On arrival civilians still in occupation. A white flag droops from shell-torn roof. This overly prosperous farm, which, despite its present condition, suffers a damning comparison when considered with its equivalent in France, Belgium, and Holland, has felt something of the war – something of the fire and tempest that Germany has always kept for export. In the rooms are pictures of a Nazi son in army uniform. Old-fashioned black-edged envelopes indicate a connection more impressive as from the front window may be seen the same uniform on a body sprawled and bloody. *Sieg heil!*

---

* The plight of the Dutch north of the Rhine had by then become known through Underground sources: how the Germans in late February cut off the western, highly populated regions and prevented them from scrounging life-saving food from the eastern hinterlands as a punishment for the continuing support of the population for the general railway strike that began the previous September, and how this already had caused terrible hardship in the regions of Rotterdam, The Hague, and Amsterdam. The result was widespread malnutrition and death by starvation. At one time even cardboard coffins were unavailable, and 235 bodies awaited burial in just one church in The Hague. (Facts derived from Major Norman Phillips, Canadian Army Public Relations, and J. Nikerk, Secretary, Canadian Netherlands Commission, *Holland and the Canadians* [Amsterdam: Contact Publishing, 1945])

51

FOOTNOTE TO

OPERATION "BLOCKBUSTER"

❋

ON THE MORNING OF FEBRUARY 26, SOME 225,000 MUD-caked officers and men of the badly worn, casualty-riddled eight infantry divisions, along with four armoured divisions and four armoured brigades – constituting First Canadian Army – will be required to ignore their battle weariness, accumulated over days and nights of attacks and counter-attacks without number amidst demoralizing sights and smells of death and destruction, arouse their spirits, and push on with all the vigour that commanders expect of fresh troops. Though simply an extension of what has been going on for the past eighteen days, it has been given a fresh name, Operation "Blockbuster," in deference, you suspect, to the tremendous artillery "preparations" designed to get things moving.

Gen. Crerar will again be in charge, though – as in the case of Operation "Veritable" – two-thirds of the units will be British (six of the eight infantry divisions, two of the four armoured divisions, and three of the four armoured brigades), clearly indicating the extent of Field Marshal Montgomery's faith in the Canadian Army Commander.

The intention is to break through between Udem and Calcar, put two brigades on Hochwald Ridge, and exploit through to Xanten. British XXX Corps will attack on the right from about Goch, which was captured by 51st Highland and 52nd Lowland divisions, who cleared the bomb-smashed town street by street, its

fanatical defenders firing from piles of rubble and loop-holed, reinforced cellars of buildings still standing.

The 52nd Division will secure the right flank of xxx Corps, and
the second day (February 27) 3rd British Division will relieve 15th
Scottish Division. 53rd Division, stopped two days ago short of
Weeze, will resume its attack.

British 43rd Wessex Division, which took Cleve and drove south
to capture the escarpment overlooking Goch during the
Goch–Calcar highway struggle, will secure the left flank of 2nd
Canadian Corps along the Rhine – its own flank hidden from the
enemy by a smokescreen produced by mobile generators operated
by the Smoke Companies of Pioneers.

In Phase One, 2nd Canadian Division, supported by 2nd
Canadian Armoured Brigade, will take the high ground south of
Calcar, while 3rd and 4th Canadian divisions combine to clear
Udem and points south.*

As in the last days of Normandy, Canadian units are destined to
play a role out of all proportion to their numbers. Attacking across
open, rising ground on a narrow front from the Goch–Calcar

---

* Crerar's First Canadian Army for "Blockbuster" was grouped as
follows:

Canadian 2nd Corps

Canadian 4th Armoured Division	Canadian 2nd Infantry Division
Polish Armoured Division	Canadian 3rd Infantry Division
British 11th Armoured Division	British 43rd Infantry Division
Canadian 2nd Armoured Brigade	

British XXX Corps

Guards Armoured Division	15th (Scottish) Infantry Division
6th Guards Armoured Brigade	51st (Highland) Infantry Division
8th Armoured Brigade	52nd (Lowland) Infantry Division
34th Armoured Brigade	53rd (Welsh) Infantry Division
3rd British Infantry Division	

highway, they will meet the strongest resistance from prepared positions of the reserve Siegfried Line. For this reason the assaulting units of 6th Brigade (Les Fusiliers Mont-Royal, Queen's Own Cameron Highlanders of Canada, and South Saskatchewan Regiment), leading off the 2nd Corps attack under cover of darkness, will be taken forward as far as practical in Kangaroos and armoured vehicles. Accompanied by tanks and Flails and aided by artificial moonlight, with bursts of red tracers from Bofors ack-ack guns pointing the way with graceful arcs across the night sky, it all will be very reminiscent of the tactics originated by Simonds and his staff for the great breakthrough from Verrières Ridge in Normandy.

And for good reason, for there are remarkable similarities in conditions here to those faced by Canadian Army in its drive for Falaise: a narrow front defended in depth by the finest troops they can muster, presenting fanatical resistance decreed by the Führer who, as in Normandy, has forbidden commanders to contemplate strategic withdrawal beyond a nearby, great river barrier.

Again, as in Normandy, the Americans form the southern jaw and the Canadians the northern jaw, threatening to masticate the Germans west of the Rhine. And precisely as in Normandy (when the Americans were held back by orders from their General Bradley from attacking north until the last moment of the closing of the Falaise gap by the Canadians) the U.S.A. Ninth Army has been held immobile by widespread flooding caused by the Germans opening the flood valves of the Roer dam, allowing them to give their undivided attention to Canadian Army – transferring north, from the American front, nine divisions (between 135,000 and 180,000 men), equipped with the greatest concentration of mortars and guns ever assembled by the Germans anywhere on the whole Western Front – 1,054 guns and 717 mortars.[*]

---

[*] Army Intelligence reported the Germans assembled 451 field guns, 179 mediums, 195 anti-tank guns, 229 dual-purpose 88-mm guns, 581 heavy mortars (80-mm and 120-mm), and 136 superheavy mortars (150-

On top of this, an important change in the tactical approach to operations in the Rhineland has been imposed by the unstable ground conditions resulting from the unusually early spring weather: the use of heavy bombers in support of ground attacks has had to be abandoned. Saturation bombing, as was carried out in Normandy, could turn the low-lying, soggy fields, already treacherous to gun tractors and impossible for ammunition trucks, into a Passchendaele quagmire preventing all vehicular movement including tanks. Thus, apart from stiletto strikes by rocket-firing Typhoons and bomb-carrying Spitfires, the responsibility for destroying enemy strongpoints and neutralizing enemy guns and mortars has devolved on the guns to an even greater degree than usual.

The artillery program, as prescribed by CCRA Brig. Stan Todd (once the CO of 4th Field) will be enormous, involving about the same number of guns as were employed in support of Operation "Totalize" in Normandy. Six divisional artilleries and three AGRAs (Army Group Royal Artilleries) have been allotted to counter-battery and counter-mortar programs.

This massive counter-battery program, in which the Regiment will take part, is to open with a roar at 0345 hours and continue until H-hour at 0430.

Adding to the rolling thunder of 456 25-pounders (nineteen regiments) and 128 mediums (eight medium regiments) will be the deep bellowing of 40 heavies and the hideous swooshing of five successive "flying mattresses," looping skyward from the "rails" of 1st Canadian Rocket Battery to land with awesome violence and their distinctive long. drawn-out roars on the divisional objective before the Hochwald.

Precisely forty-five minutes later, when the counter-battery

---

mm, 210-mm, and 300-mm). Gen. Crerar, himself a former gunner officer, reporting to the Minister of National Defence declared German fire-power in the Rhineland was more heavily and effectively applied than at any other time in the Army's fighting during the present campaign.

program has been shot, 408 field and medium guns will open up on two separate barrages.

In Phase One, on behalf of 6th Brigade going forward in Kangaroos on the right, a fast-moving barrage will be fired to a depth of 4,300 yards; while on the left, in support of the walking troops of 5th Brigade,* a slower barrage will continue to a depth of 1,600 yards.

A program of "timed concentrations" on strongpoints in support of 8th Brigade,† attacking without a barrage on the right flank of 2nd Division, will be fired by 144 additional 25-pounders of 3rd Canadian and 15th British divisions, as well as by 32 mediums.

In Phase Two, on behalf of 3rd Division's attack on Keppeln and the clearing of Udem Ridge by the 4th Canadian Armoured Division, the same targets shelled in the earlier counter-battery program leading up to Phase One will be plastered for another thirty minutes. Then the guns will be switched to supporting the tanks, the M-10s, and infantry riding into action on the backs of the armoured vehicles.

Another thirty-minute artillery bombardment will open Phase Three when 9th Brigade‡ will attack south to take Udem.

Because the planners see all three phases as a continuous operation, it means exceptionally heavy going back at the guns for a day or two. Even before the guns open up, the gunners are involved in exhausting moves to positions well forward, some under enemy observation just behind the FDLs, to ensure assaulting infantry and tanks don't outrun the guns during the early hours of the attack. So limited are suitable areas for gun positions, Brig. Frank Lace, CRA of 2nd Division, does a recce by air in a little Air OP plane.

---

* The Black Watch, Le Régiment de Maisonneuve, and the Calgary Highlanders.
† The Queen's Own Rifles of Canada, Le Régiment de la Chaudière, and the North Shore Regiment.
‡ The Highland Light Infantry of Canada, the Stormont, Dundas and Glengarry Highlanders, and the North Nova Scotia Highlanders.

Slow moves over traffic-jammed roads to quagmire fields where the guns have to be winched and manhandled through the mud into place, and tons of ammo carried for hundreds of yards from trucks confined to the roads, guarantee all ranks are awake and labouring for most of the twenty-four hours before the attack.

Among the clutter of guns, tanks, and vehicles is a radar vehicle designed to pinpoint enemy mortars.* When its crew sets up shop just to the rear of your OP with Jack Strothers on the startline for Blockbuster, you mentally cringe. While you bow to their courage in situating in full view of the enemy (by necessity, if they are to pick up and trace the flight-path of the mortar bombs from source), you are sure their tall, oddly shaped radar aerial will be a beacon for enemy shells or mortars. This you know from witnessing the destruction of another radar crew yesterday morning back there in the barnyard of the Royals' tac headquarters.

It happened just at dawn, when Cornett wakened you to send you over to Strothers. As you were leaving the stable, you had to duck back inside to escape several screaming shells crashing in the barnyard among the vehicles parked there. When you went out, expecting the worst, you found your crew and Cornett's crew unharmed, but the radar crew (of 1st Canadian Radar Battery) in awful shape. The salvo caught them cooking breakfast beside their truck. Two were dead and two wounded. One had his back torn out, and the other, with his right hand dangling on its tendons, remarked with unsettling candour to Turner, the Major's Don R, who'd gone to help him:

"By Christ, I don't think I'll shoot no more crap!"

---

* 1st Canadian Radar Battery came into being near Dunkirk, September 22, 1944, under command of Capt. J. G. Telfer, 2nd Heavy Ack Ack. They taught themselves to pick up the looping bombs on their screens and do the required calculations by firing German mortars west of Dunkirk, and later at St. Leonards, near Antwerp.

52

IN A DISORIENTED
BLUR OF DREAD

*

FOR SEVERAL DAYS NOW, THROUGHOUT THIS WHOLE UGLY business in the Rhineland, you've been living every minute with the dreadful feeling that you are only a few feet away from disaster. It's not something specific you can visualize and prepare for, but the feeling is of such substance that for long periods it tends to dislocate all your other emotional responses.

At times the dread is so all-embracing, it almost disconnects your rational-thinking apparatus, turning the immediate past into a blur, and leaving you with the overpowering sense of participating in an ongoing nightmare: awakening with tremendous relief from one terrible dream, only to descend into another, worse than the one before – on and on in weird, relentless progression.

One of the most terrifying occurs in a little farmhouse on the road marking the front line and the startline for the attack by 5th and 6th brigades, during the first minutes of the barrage opening Operation "Blockbuster" and the heavy enemy counter-fire it incites.

To get a couple of hours' sleep before the guns are to open up on their preparatory tasks at 0345 leading up to H-hour at 0430, you hit the sack shortly after midnight – right after Major Jack Stothers's briefing of his platoon commanders is brought to an abrupt end by the crack of a bullet coming in through a panel of the front door of the little blacked-out living room. He'd barely had time to explain that, though 4th Brigade battalions will be in reserve for the first few hours, all ranks must be standing-to and alert (so as to ensure the startline is secure for 5th and 6th brigades), when there is the vicious slap of a bullet embedding itself in the oak drawer of the sewing machine on which you are leaning your left elbow.

Instantly the lamp is doused, and platoon commanders, fearing still another German counter-attack, rush outside to rejoin their men. But when nothing further happens, and cursory inquiries among the men in slit trenches in the front garden fail to offer any enlightenment as to the origin of the shot, suspicions develop it was only a wayward bullet from a weapon accidentally discharged – a very common occurrence these days. Satisfied this is the case, Stothers gives the order to stand-down. And after producing a generous dollop of rum, he suggests you both catch a couple hours' sleep, for "dear knows when you'll get the chance again."

Gratefully you accept his invitation to share a tiny room off the living room, for you have not staked out any territorial rights in this house or barn since moving back here late today, from a house across the road in no-man's-land where you first had established your OP.

The house over there was your first choice because of its superior view, and you and your crew spent last night over there blissfully unaware there were Germans in the cellar. Squissato had awakened you on hearing German voices coming from the kitchen across the hall. Holding up a finger to his lips for silence, he secured the Bren gun while you, with pistol drawn, joined him at the door. Flinging it open you had confronted not paratroopers, but a middle-aged farm couple, staring at your gun muzzles with anxious eyes. Embarrassed, you had gestured expansively that they should carry on preparing their breakfast. But their sudden, mysterious appearance had unnerved you. Were they really what they seemed, a farmer and wife? Somehow they hadn't shown the proper degree of fear. So when you were called back to an "O" Group at Battalion, you used the excuse to move back within the company area.

While settling down here in your bedroll (fully clothed, including your boots, of course) on the floor beside the cot on which

Stothers is rolled in a blanket, you ask him to wake you when he is getting up at 3:45 A.M. for stand-to.

At this he roars with laughter, pointing out that no one will need a wakeup call when those Tor Scots' 4.2-inch mortars behind the barn start banging away, not to mention the 7.2-inch heavies that will be blasting away somewhere back behind, adding to the din all those 25-pounders and 5.5-inch mediums will be making.

Mildly perturbed by his guffawing, you remind him that gunners are accustomed to sleeping in the midst of guns firing, and that you, having been badly shortchanged in the matter of sleep for some ten days now, will, in all likelihood, sleep through the whole damned show if he chooses not to wake you.

Waiting for sleep, you contemplate the ground-floor window just beyond his cot with suspicion. Recent mortar or shell blasts have blown out all the glass from the window sash, and the wooden shutters, drawn closed over the window from the outside, are so slashed by shell fragments you can see the night sky and feel inter-mittent draughts of icy air pouring down on your head. Is the German who fired that shot still out there? How easy it would be for him to sneak along the side of the house, pull open the shutters, and drop in a grenade. With such forbidding thoughts you roll over on your stomach and fall asleep.

Thus your heart-spasming horror on awakening to find the shut-ters wide open to the furious flashing, blasting night, and a beast, with the weight of a giant, kneeling on your back squeezing the breath out of you, as his hands seek your throat, fulfilling the fearful fantasy you imagined just as you were falling asleep.

In the split second it takes to recognize your predicament, you realize your only chance is to fake unconsciousness, while your right hand – already resting under your pillow – secures the pistol you always deposit there when you bed down.

The beast is uttering guttural mutterings as his big fingers close around your neck and begin to shake it insanely, but it's impossible to make out the words over the hellish racket of the incoming shells. Resisting total panic, you grasp the pistol butt, slip your finger over the trigger, and begin sliding it under your chin with the object of worming it up past your ear and aiming it back over your shoulder at that Germanic muttering . . . which at that moment, sounds curiously like, "Forjeesussake . . . wakeupfoo!"

Instantly the panic level drops, as you recognize the voice of Stothers's huge righthand bower – Sgt.-Maj. Hamm. Rolling him off your back, you sit up gasping for air.

"You okay, Foo? You okay? Can you walk, Foo?" Over and over he inquires of your state of health as he grabs hold of you and hoists you to your feet as he would a child. Then putting his arm around your shoulders as though to steady you, he starts guiding you towards the cellarway through the dark house fitfully lit by the flashing shells landing with horrendous crashes outside. You assure him you are just fine except where his knees landed on your back.

Apologetic, he explains that when Major Stothers sent him up to see what had happened to you, he wasn't expecting to find you still sleeping on the floor. So when he tripped over your feet in the dark and fell on you, and you didn't move, he thought you must be dead. He was feeling for a pulse in your neck, when you woke up . . .

Of course – it all makes sense. But you shudder to think how close you came to getting your pistol in place to pull the trigger.

Down in the brightly lit cellar, assembled around Stothers are all members of your crew, along with his company headquarters group, who react with cheers and applause as the towering Sergeant-Major, holding your arm solicitously as though he still believes there must be something the matter with you, triumphantly delivers you to his Major.

Stothers, while obviously pleased to see you alive and unharmed, wags his head in disbelief that Hamm could find you still asleep with the house literally rocking on its foundations from the bombardment.

He tells you that right after the guns began firing their heavy concentrations, and the Tor Scots' 4.2-inch mortars opened up behind the house, Jerry began to return the fire. And even before he could get out of his bedroll and start for the cellar steps, one round landed just outside, blowing the shutters off the window.

Naturally he took it for granted you would be following him – if you hadn't already preceded him down the stairs. But on checking heads, he found you were missing. Assuming you must have been hit, he sent the Sergeant-Major up to bring you down if you were still alive.

It's clear that henceforth he'll look upon you as a bit of a freak, but a worthy brother-in-arms. Ranking high in his estimation of the quality of a soldier, is coolness under fire – a quality in which he himself excels, sometimes to the point of foolhardiness. (Stothers was the only member of the Royals to sleep above ground at Eterville, near Caen – enduring round-the-clock bombardment by mortars and shells in a brick, two-holer backhouse that miraculously survived without a scar.)

While you know you are living under false colours, there is a certain pleasure in being thought of as "cool," so you don't revive the theme that gunners are accustomed to sleeping next to crashing guns; and though your ribs are sore enough to be cracked in spots, you are so touched by their caring actions, you decide not to share with them the churlish thought that, ordinarily, a person is awakened out of a nightmare, not awakened into one. Nor does it seem the right moment to tell Sgt.-Major Hamm that while he was in the process of scaring you half to death, he came within a hair's breadth of getting his head blown off.

As time goes on, the bombardment eases up in both directions, and you are on your way up to the attic of the little one-storey house to watch 4th Division tanks move off towards Udem Ridge in the second phase of the attack when Col. MacGregor Young arrives with the same thought in mind. Just what you expect to see, you aren't sure, but a vision of hundreds of tanks charging forward with guns blazing was implied, if not actually suggested, by the plan of attack outlined yesterday at Lendrum's "O" Group.

However, though you have a grandstand view by virtue of several holes in the roof, opened among the tiles by airbursts or mortar bombs this morning, there is nothing very dramatic about the attack. The numbers of Shermans and self-propelled anti-tank guns moving forward in ragged extended lines are impressive enough, but nothing in their stop-and-go movements would ever suggest the word "charge."

The soggy Rhineland guarantees a sluggish advance. All the tanks leave deep ruts that immediately fill with water. Miraculously few appear irretrievably bogged down as they snarl and growl across the sodden fields, meeting no opposition of any consequence. Apart from pauses to shoot up buildings in their path, and the odd steamy black fountain of mud from a Jerry shell erupting among them, they crawl forward without incident and disappear over the crest, each with a final, defiant, growling spurt. However, they don't get far before Jerry appears to bring his lethal 88s to bear. Soon, intermingled with the *crump* of shells and mortars and the whine of straining tank engines fading in the distance, are sharp *crack*s of high-velocity tank guns.

Later you will learn that while the armoured assault is effective, 4th Division units lose 100 tanks.

Also on their right flank, opposition is equally severe to the tanks of 2nd Canadian Armoured Brigade supporting an attack on Udem by 3rd Division, and as in all bitter fighting here in the Rhineland, individual courage matters greatly. Though it will be some time before you hear the story, at this very hour, just over on the right at a crossroads clump of buildings called Mooshof, a mile south of the Goch–Calcar highway, a sergeant of the Queen's Own Rifles of Canada is taking command of the survivors of his platoon, "only four in number," and, under heavy fire from a house, is climbing onto the back of a 1st Hussars' tank to direct it to punch a hole in the side of the house, where he jumps down and person-ally kills "at least twenty of the enemy" and captures "as many more" before being killed by a sniper's bullet. With the core of enemy resistance in the village broken, and his objectives secure, the twenty-three-year-old hero was on his way to report to his company commander when the sniper got him.*

As the CO is leaving your OP, he remarks that 2nd Division Headquarters (meaning Maj.-Gen. Bruce Matthews and the CRA Brig. Frank Lace), already conscious of the super way the guns have been responding to the German attacks in recent days, were very impressed by the way they routed the attack by two companies of paratroopers and tanks that hit the Rileys just before H-hour this morning – an attack which, had it been successful, would have destroyed the security of the divisional startline.

When you reveal your total ignorance of the matter, he tells you young Don Edwards, the FOO with the company attacked, put on a super show. It was another strong attack by two companies of para-troopers and some tanks. Not only did Edwards pull down shell-fire with devastating effect, but, when Company Headquarters was directly assaulted by paratroopers, seized a rifle and accounted for several of them himself.

As the minutes to H-hour ticked away and the Germans were still engaging the Rileys, everyone up to Corps Headquarters (and perhaps beyond) who remembered Normandy and the problems unsecured startlines had caused around St. Martin-de-Fontenay and Troteval Farm, began to worry. It was, according to Col. Young, "a very close thing." The startline was secure only five or ten minutes before the gunners had to lay their guns on the opening line of the barrage launching the attack. Years later, Major Froggett will recall with earnest gratitude the contribution made by the guns of 4th Field in quelling the attack:

We were almost completely overrun. There were tanks all around us, and my men were fighting hand-to-hand with the paratroops. It was the grisliest day of the war for me. Men were

---

* Sgt. Aubrey Cosens was awarded the Victoria Cross posthumously.

shouting, punching, heaving grenades, firing pistols, and swinging everything they could put their hands to. Lieut. D. D. Edwards, my FOO, was with me in the little frame cottage when all of a sudden a tank started pushing the wall down. There were forty or so German civilians in our cellar, all screaming. Edwards called down everything the artillery could send directly on our position. The Germans were above ground and they got it. We were pretty well dug-in.*

Of this morning Bombardier Hossack's diary will record: "More enemy counter-attacks precede another 'Montgomery barrage' [of long duration involving many guns]. Breeches jam on overworked guns. Number Four develops a burr in the barrel and is relegated to Ordnance for repairs."

Sgt. Hunt's diary, commenting on the guns managing to repulse this threatening counter-attack, just before having to lay on the opening fire-plan with nineteen other field regiments and eight medium regiments, will express the intriguing thought: "Jerry may not have been overly impressed by our defensive Mike targets [involving twenty-four guns], which he doubtless expected, but at 0400 hours when our Corps barrage [involving hundreds of guns] came down on the very area he'd chosen to play about in, his consternation must have been more than somewhat!"†

---

* Quoted in Col. Denis and Shelagh Whitaker's book *Rhineland*, (Toronto: Stoddart, 1989, pp. 172-3). Lieut. (A/Capt.) Donald D. Edwards was subsequently awarded the Military Cross. The citation read in part: "With complete disregard for his own safety Capt. Edwards remained at his post throughout this period of intense and concentrated fire, and coolly directed artillery fire on the advancing enemy with devastating effect."

† Sgt. Bruce Hunt's unfailingly good humour and leadership – which shone through his diary notes even during the worst days of Normandy, the Scheldt, and the Rhineland – earned him the Belgian Croix de Guerre, 1940, avec Palme.

53

A LIVING NIGHTMARE

---　✳　---

WHEN DARKNESS FALLS YOU GET A SIGNAL TO JOIN MAJOR Bob Wedd's A Company of the Royals as it moves up to thicken up the Rileys who suffered heavy casualties early this morning driving off that fierce German counter-attack and restoring the startline.

Immediately you find yourself plunged into a living nightmare among a massive movement of men and armoured vehicles. As in Normandy the battlefield is lit mistily by artificial moonlight created by playing searchlights on low clouds, though this is hardly necessary, for the whole front seems to be in flames – vehicles, houses, and barns are burning everywhere. Penetrating through the roar of motors and a monstrous barrage they are laying down up ahead, is the terrified squealing of pigs trapped in the flames some-where nearby, and now and then you distinguish the *crack* of an unseen 88 bursting overhead.

A confusion of tanks, Kangaroos, Bren carriers drawing anti-tank guns, and marching troops slogging along the verges in single file are on the move to God knows where, following tracks that may have been roads once but are now churned-up watery bogs. So deep are the ruts, vehicles of all sorts are getting stuck, forcing the columns to keep shifting off to the left or right onto even softer ground, and on such a detour around the rear of some buildings, with the belly of the old carrier bottoming among cavernous, watery ruts left by the heavier tracked vehicles, the transmission packs it in.

While this is hardly a surprise, after the beating it has taken since sustaining such shocking torque, crashing in and out of that great crater in the road back near Louisendorf several days ago, it does create a very awkward situation. By the time you recognize the seriousness of the breakdown, and realize that if you are to keep contact with the infantry you'll have to keep going on foot, a great many vehicles and marching troops have passed by. After getting off a radio signal to the Battery to send up another carrier, you leave your crew to transfer the equipment and gear into it when it arrives, and start off on foot to try and catch up with Wedd and company.

This won't be easy, for you weren't given a specific map reference for their new position. You were merely told to hook up with Wedd's company on its way up to reinforce the Rileys. Even Wedd won't know where his company is to go until he's liaised with the Rileys on the ground and been assigned a role.

All you can do is keep on tramping through the mud, stumbling over the deep ruts, and now and then leaping out of the way of a grinding line of Kangaroos or carriers dragging anti-tank guns behind them, until you catch up with Wedd or find the Rileys.

As you get out into the darkness of open country, away from the flaming farm buildings, and the traffic grows noticeably thinner, you feel the need to orient yourself before you become hopelessly lost. However, to illuminate your map you have to have some cover, for you have only a little bullet cigarette lighter and some matches. It is then you spot, just over in the field on the left a few steps from the road, what looks like the mouth of one of those one-man dug-outs the Jerries dig now and then.

Down inside, sitting on a well-sprung iron cot complete with mattress that almost fills the little dug-out, you exhaust the last of the fuel in your lighter identifying where you are. Still, satisfying as this is, you realize as you make your way back to the road that you have only a general idea where the Rileys might be and where Wedd and company are headed.

But then, just as you start up the soupy road, with your head down taking care not to stumble into a water-filled rut, you almost bump into a figure looming up in the gloom. To your relief it turns out to be Tom Wilcox, captain of the Support Company of the Royals, who is lost and doing a recce on foot to try to establish where he is.

Yes, he knows where Wedd is heading, and could show you on your map if it were possible to find some place to safely show a light.

You suggest the dug-out you've just been in and lead him back to it. Sitting side by side on the cot, lighting matches and scorching fingers, you point out his present position. He in turn points out where you can expect to locate the Rileys and Wedd. He finds it curious that you are separated from them and are walking.

You start to explain . . . and the next thing you know you awake to find yourself alone, lying on your back on the cot with your feet dangling on the floor, which is now lit by the pale light of dawn streaming in from outside.

Scrambling out of the dug-out, you start walking quickly back down the road to where you left your crew. There now is no traffic in men or vehicles in either direction, and only the odd derelict truck and the skeletons of still-smouldering farmhouses, filling the cold, misty morning air with acrid odours of smoke and charred wood, provide evidence of the juggernaut that rolled through here last night.

Apart from the faint sound of grinding trucks in the rear areas, it is now quiet, as though both sides have had their fill of attack and counter-attack, and are now willing just to stand-to this morning, listening and staring out through the mists hanging over no-man's-land.

The sound and the fury of last night now seem like a bad dream. Were you really talking to Wilcox in that little dug-out? You begin to wonder if you didn't dream the whole thing, but then the break-down of your Bren carrier is real enough. When you get back to where you left it, the weary men are just completing the transfer of all the equipment and personal gear to the replacement carrier, which only made it up a half an hour ago, they tell you.

At a late morning Royals' "O" Group, Wilcox confirms he had a map-reading conference with you in a little German dug-out just before dawn this morning – laughing at the way you stopped talking in the middle of a sentence and fell over backward as though hit in the head by a stray bullet or a piece of shell from an 88 just then airbursting above that dug-out. "In fact," says he, "I was so sure you'd bought it, I used up the rest of my matches examining your head. But you were breathing peacefully, and I couldn't find a mark on you. I was going to shake you awake before I left, but then I thought, what the hell . . . any man that exhausted should be allowed to sleep!"

And here the reality is as strange as any dream. That Wilcox – a highly disciplined veteran infantry officer with an advanced sense of duty – should leave you to sleep, simply because you appeared to need sleep, is so inconsistent as to be inexplicable.

Just back from a Brigade briefing, Col. Lendrum is able to report the attacks by the leading battalions of 3rd Division and of 5th and 6th brigades of 2nd Division were entirely successful, with all the initial objectives secure by dawn today. However, it was a rough go. In spite of our guns' extraordinary bombardment of Jerry positions before and during the attacks, seemingly very effective judging from the high number of prisoners surrendering to the assaulting platoons, attackers were still met with severe fire from surviving German strongpoints, especially camouflaged tanks and 88s around the villages and towns.

One day you will learn the details. Keppeln was only secured by the North Shore Regiment after two strenuous attacks, the last one involving a platoon riding on the backs of 1st Hussars' tanks roaring to the objective. In the attacks the North Shore suffered 28 killed and 61 wounded, and eight of the tanks involved in the charge were knocked out.

At the village of Hollen the Chaudières, after being driven back twice and suffering 17 dead and 51 wounded, finally overcame resistance and secured their objective ten hours after they began their attack.

To secure the town of Udem, surrounded by an anti-tank ditch and heavily mined, required an all-night effort by all three battalions of 9th Brigade: the Stormont, Dundas and Glengarry Highlanders, the Highland Light Infantry of Canada, and the North Nova Scotia Highlanders. Only by dawn today was the last enemy counter-attack driven off.

In comparison, the mobile attack by 5th and 6th brigades, with the support of the tanks of the Sherbrooke Fusiliers, the 1st Hussars, and Fort Garry Horse, which took the Calcar Heights, had an easier go – with units of 6th Brigade (the Queen's Own Cameron Highlanders of Canada, the Fusiliers Mont-Royal, and the South Saskatchewan Regiment) reaching their objectives with admirable despatch, even though the Queen's Own Camerons had to manage without their commanding officer. Lt.-Col. E. P. Thompson, at twenty-three the youngest battalion commander in Canadian Army, was among the first killed in the attack.

However, where tank support was not forthcoming due to squadrons getting bogged down in the mud, battalions had a stickier time.

Pinned down by heavy fire in close contact with the enemy holding firm on their objective, Le Régiment de Maisonneuve, of 5th Brigade, suffered a severe bloody nose (93 casualties including 14 dead) before their CO, Lt.-Col. Julien Bibeau, brought up flame-throwers and directed them on targets pointed out by a platoon commander (Lieut. Guy deMerlis).

54

A GUNNER'S MOST

DREADED NIGHTMARE

*

IT IS LATE AFTERNOON ON FEBRUARY 27. THE DANK CELLAR IS lit by a gasoline lantern on a table behind which sits the Royals' Colonel, who is as always looking so extraordinarily neat. Clean shaven, hair brushed smooth, his tie perfectly knotted, he is a picture of orderliness and self-assurance as he outlines the situation in a well-modulated voice. You marvel at his calmness and confidence. In the distance the guns are rumbling heavily, and you know he is perfectly aware of what it is like out there: that this, like every damned attack, will be a messy, confused, bloody terrifying affair, only partially successful on the first try, and that the plan he is outlining will be modified beyond recognition to meet the fluid fortunes of the night ahead. But right now you feel only warm gratitude that he makes the plan sound so simple and straightforward.

At the end of the "O" Group, as he passes on the official word from Corps, spelling out what is expected of the troops, he stares down at the table as though afraid it may sound like a pep talk: "We are to keep on hitting the enemy until he cracks."

But then, looking up at his rumpled, sagging, red-eyed company commanders barely able to hold open their eyelids, and who can stand upright only by leaning against the cellar walls, he adds: "But as we know, gentlemen, a well-known law of physics ensures the hammer takes as much punishment as the anvil."

No one says anything, but there is a general shifting of positions, and tiny smiles appear on drained and haggard faces in appreciation of the sardonic humour of this understanding man. And, as they file out into the night to make their way back to their companies, they go with a lighter and more confident step in the realization their CO knows the score and appreciates what he is asking of them and their men.

Battalion objectives for the attack, that will go in after dark, assigned to each of the four rifle companies of the Royals attacking in the fairly rough terrain just before the Hochwald, are: an area of gullies and scrubby bush on the left front (Bob Suckling's B Company); high ground in the centre (Jack Stothers's C Company); a crossroads on a ridge ascending on Stothers's right (Bob Wedd's A Company); and finally, on the extreme right end, on a promontory curved like a fist aimed at the Hochwald, a lone house, the objective of Tim Beatty's D Company, the company to which you are attached as it moves up to await H-hour at the startline held by the Rileys.

Just before dark, your shells start falling short.

The difference between the sound of 25-pounder shells as they sail overhead, whispering and crackling on their way to targets out beyond your OP, and the deadly sound they create when they are pouring down directly on you, is so remarkable that even when you are braced for it, it's a horrifying experience. Thus when, for absolutely no reason other than gross error at one troop gun position, shells come screaming in behind the house where you know the men of D Company are lounging above ground waiting for the signal to go forward, you are close to sobbing in your panic as you dash out to the kitchen, grab the mike from Squissato, and yell yourself hoarse, getting through to the Regiment:

"Stop! Stop! Stop! Rounds are falling short! Stop! Stop! Stop!"

When at last the shells stop coming, you have a desperate need to know the full extent of the damage they have caused. But almost paralyzed with dread, you can't bring yourself to rise from the kitchen floor and follow Tim outside. You remain kneeling on the linoleum in the gathering dusk, rocking back and forth in a state of utter despair. And this is how Beatty finds you when he comes back in to slump down on a chair at the kitchen table, reporting sadly and quietly:

"Sorry, old boy, but you just killed seven of my men."

Oh God, it could hardly have been otherwise. Without holes to get into, it's a wonder any of them survived. But hearing those dreadful words, *You just killed seven*, is almost too much to bear. You rush to absolve yourself of blame.

Tim listens patiently and sympathetically as you explain how you decided that before all the light was gone you would register the guns on that treeless hump of land about seven hundred yards out in front of here, beyond which you and the Royals will be passing tonight, so that if they come under fire from there, all you would have to do is give the target number and the scale of fire to the guns to get instant neutralizing fire. You intended just to range on it with the first troop to report ready, and let all the other troops, following the corrections on their individual artillery boards in the normal way, record their individual lines and ranges. But when your first round, landing on that barren hump, caused several Jerries to rise up and scurry back up the slope and out of sight, you went into fire for effect with all the troops of the Regiment. The first shells to come up fell precisely where they should have on the crest of that distant hill, just as the ranging round had done. But then rounds began to fall behind the house for reasons you can only guess.

Perhaps an error in passing early survey coordinates to a pivot gun . . . the Regiment had just moved. Things like that have been known to happen, but not with 4th Field – not even during training days.

One of Tim's sergeants comes in the kitchen from out back, and seeing you slumped on the floor in the darkening gloom, rocking in anguish, he inquires: "What's the matter, Foo?"

"Need you ask, Sergeant? I just killed seven of your buddies."

"No, you didn't," says he. "You wounded several, and shattered the nerves of a couple of battle-exhaustion cases who just returned from hospital, dammit. But you didn't kill anybody."

"Oh, but you're wrong, Sergeant," says Tim, "I counted seven bodies out there."

"You mean those bodies alongside the wall at the back of the house?" asks the Sergeant.

"Yes," says Tim.

"Those aren't Royals – those are Rileys killed coming in here."

The relief is like nothing you have ever experienced. It is as though a crushing physical weight has been lifted off you. With an enormous sigh you start breathing again; the nightmare is over.

However, you must make sure it won't happen again. It is now too dark to range each troop on a distant point to discover which guns are in error. So you get on the radio and tell the Regiment some guns are firing short, and until all can be checked in daylight by firing on a distant point, only the ranging troop is to be used.

Reflecting on the matter as you await H-hour, you realize a troop of four guns won't provide much support in turning back a serious counter-attack. But then you remember you can always pull down fire from the other two regiments in the Division, if it is warranted, by simply designating the task an Uncle target.

H-hour is postponed an hour to allow the moon to rise and make it easier for the companies to find their way. Of course, this also helps the enemy spot the approaching Royals. As anticipated this afternoon, the leading companies attract bursts of tracers from that bald hill. But, having registered it with the ranging troop this afternoon, you are able to squelch this fire, and the first three companies gain their objectives without serious opposition, suggesting the Germans have only outposts through here and are holding their main forces just beyond this rugged area of woods, hills, and gullies, in their "Schlieffen Position," a second Siegfried Line, reputedly stretching some twenty miles across the front before the Hochwald and adjacent Balbergerwald.

Still Beatty's company runs into strong opposition only two hundred yards from their objective, when they try to move laterally across the front through a ravine in no-man's-land and attack from the rear the farmhouse which is their objective at the extreme right end of the crescent ridge overlooking the Hochwald. This route is chosen when Beatty and company arrive at the foot of the slope leading up to Bob Wedd's position on the crest of the ridge, and find their line of advance through Wedd's position and beyond startlingly exposed to enemy view by the obscenely bright light of a great moon that has just risen to full brilliance.

This means you must part company from Tim, for your carrier cannot make it up the ravine cluttered with heavy vegetation, let alone follow men on foot when they scramble up the very high and very steep side of the ravine to assault their objective. All you can do is establish an OP along the almost clifflike edge of the ravine in the vicinity of Wedd's company and try to follow their progress in the gully below, judging as best you can when to join them on the objective, and if they run into trouble, bring fire to bear on its source.

Parking the carrier behind the farmhouse on which Wedd's company is centred, you and Squissato go forward on foot a couple of hundred yards to the cliff edge where you find a beautiful, deep slit trench, obviously of German origin, for no Canadian ever dug a trench of such proportions with such sharp sides. Thus you are sitting with Squissato on the edge of this well-constructed trench, with your feet dangling down, looking across the ravine at a house bathed in moonlight well up the slope opposite, when suddenly its interior bursts into flames. In seconds flames are licking out of every window and door, lighting up the barren slope as bright as day, and throwing into sharp relief dark figures in Canadian helmets, momentarily frozen in the glare.

Then tracers start skittering across the slope from three or four directions, and the dark figures start scattering in panic. Some go down and start crawling. Others lie in crumpled positions just as they fell. Others make it down the slope and disappear in the shadows.

When no more figures can be seen running or crawling out there, the tracers cease. And you are down in the bottom of the trench with a lamp-electric establishing a map reference for the fields on each side of the burning house where you think the tracers originated, when you hear men thumping up the slope. They turn out to be three Royals who tell you they were actually with the platoon that was sent to check out the house on the slope when it suddenly burst into flames.

They are convinced it was a well-planned ambush, that the Jerries were waiting for them, for as the Royals went in the front door, the Germans went out the back tossing a match into oil-saturated straw as they were leaving.

Did they actually see them toss the match?

No, but it had to be that way for no house could burst into flames so completely, so quickly, without being prepared with oil and straw. And there were no burp guns until the flames lit up the yard and every Royal was silhouetted against the flaming house.

Just as you begin questioning them as to whether they think you might safely shell the vicinity of the house where you saw Schmeisser fire originating (looking for reassurance that none of the wounded Royals crawled off into the darkness in that direction) there is the unmistakable hollow *plunk* of a mortar firing from over there, and immediately the whisper of its bomb descending.

Being already half in the trench with your legs dangling down, you are first to arrive on the bottom, and are instantly squashed flat under a mass of humanity scrambling to get below grade.

Though scarcely able to take even the shallowest breath with all that weight on you, for the first couple of minutes you are grateful for the extraordinary protection afforded by the mass of bodies stacked four-deep above you, as a wicked stream of mortar bombs crash and flash close to the mouth of the trench. Even a direct hit could not reach you. But when you reflect on this, the prospect of being held captive by several hundred pounds of dead flesh is not something you relish, and you are exceedingly relieved when the mortars cease, and the bodies above you unpile, allowing you to sit up.

Concerned the mortaring will start again when Jerry sees this clump of men reappear, and reasoning that Beatty and survivors of his company should by now be on their way back from the ravine, you decide to get everybody in the carrier and go back down there again to wait for them. And by the time you arrive at the bottom of the hill, they appear in the gloom, pitifully few in number, and most of them walking-wounded.

One of those being carried on stretchers is the company commander. And Tim is not at all in good shape, judging from the weakness of his voice as you bend over him to get what advice he can give you. He figures there are many more of his company back there hiding in the ravine, but he is taking what he has assembled back to Battalion where the company can be remustered under a new commander.

As the men bearing Tim's stretcher start off and you say goodbye to him, he seems so weak you despair of seeing him again. However, a veteran stretcher-bearer, bringing up the rear of the walking-wounded following in behind the stretchers, assures you the Major's wounds are more painful than life-threatening, and that it's the shot of morphine he's been given that's making him so woozy, which is good to hear. This is the third time Tim has been wounded since arriving in Normandy last July, and the second time he has been evacuated to hospital.

Watching the last of them disappear in the thick, cold mists that have begun to block out the moon, you suddenly are conscious of how vulnerable your little group has become. For half an hour or so, a strange quiet has existed along the front here that cannot last. Jerry knows he's shattered a company, and he'll be tempted to probe through the gap that may exist here. You are glad the three lads you collected up on the brow of the hill chose to stay with you instead of following the wounded to the rear as they could have. You wish it were safe to lay a heavy stonk on that ravine, but you don't dare risk it, for many Royals may still be in there crawling back.*

---

* The final casualty count was 26 – 5 killed and 21 wounded – bad enough, but not the disaster it first appeared.

Your immediate need is to make contact with another company, not only to gain local protection, but get back in the battalion picture so as to be of use to them. You recall Wedd's company was to take the crossroads a bit beyond the house where you parked your carrier while on the brow of the ravine watching D Company get shot-up. Being on the right flank, closest to the objective still remaining to be taken, makes it your logical choice: either his company will be ordered to go for it, or you can hook up with whoever it is that passes through him.

But before you move off, heavy small-arms fire, punctuated by the reverberating *wham* of a high-velocity gun, starts up in the wooded area on the left. Taking over the signaller's radio headset, you listen to an exchange between Cornett at Royals' Tac Headquarters and Col. Young at Brigade, which make it clear Royals' Headquarters is seriously threatened by a fighting patrol; and just over on the left among folds in land congested by brush and trees, B Company (Suckling's) is being shelled at close range by a German SP (self-propelled gun). When Cornett reports that B Company is under heavy machine-gun fire and the Germans appear to be getting into position to close in, the Colonel decides to take a hand in proceedings.

Coming on the air, he asks you: "Are you in a position to see where the SP fire is coming from?"

You report you can't see its muzzle-flash, but it certainly is close by.

"Do you have a map reference?"

Anticipating the question, you already have your head under the tarp in the front compartment of the carrier and the dismal glow of a lamp-electric shining on the area of the map just to the left of where the Royals' ravine bends this way, broadening out and flattening as it passes almost on a level with where you are now sitting. You give him the map reference of a point about four hundred yards away.

Nothing happens for a few seconds, then you hear, "Shot SOS." The map reference you gave appears to have coincided with the

designated, precalculated DF SOS target, always placed on the most
vulnerable route. Immediately you hear the guns thumping behind
– all of them, you fear. And seconds later shells are screaming and
bursting all around your carrier in a repeat of their ghastly afternoon performance. With your radio mike readily at hand, hanging
from your earphones, you are yelling, even as the first shells are
landing: "Stop! Stop! Stop!"

When they do, you blow your stack. You address your remarks to
your Commanding Officer in such a way as to give him the benefit
of the doubt, referring to unnamed "boneheads" and levelling
charges of "criminal stupidity" at whoever is responsible for shooting all those guns after you had made it crystal clear at last light that
only the original troop of ranging guns (14th Battery) should fire
until daylight when a proving-shoot can be made on a distant point
to discover which troop or troops are in error. You finish off your
tirade by stating, in the most deliberate and forceful voice you can
muster, that you "will not be held responsible for what may happen
if those guns are fired again before daylight." Precisely what you
mean by this, you are not sure, but your intention is to imply dire
consequences to anyone disregarding your solemn warning.

For a while there is no comment from Sunray. Minutes go by,
and as your overwrought nerves relax and reality returns in the
form of a cold fog seeping through your garments so that you
shiver violently, you start to worry. Perhaps you went too far with
your intemperate comments; after all, no one was wounded.
Eventually, to your great relief, he comes on the air, and in his
calm, slow drawl assures you arrangements have been made for
another regiment to provide "supplementary fire" as may be necessary for the rest of the night.

As you prepare to move off up the hill to Wedd's company, you
are suddenly aware that the *bur-rup bur-rup* of Schmeissers and the
crack of the SP, which brought all this on, are no longer with you.
Short rounds notwithstanding (and perhaps even because of them),
the Colonel's shoot produced a most beneficial effect.

It's after midnight when you and your little raggle-taggle group, now grown to nine including your own crew, check in at A Company HQ in a shallow cellar underneath Wedd's farmhouse where you earlier had parked the carrier.

With the very low ceiling and the vague light from one candle resting on an upturned wooden box, the cellar seems vast, and although there must be a dozen men lying here or there on the hard-packed, wavy, earthen floor, or propped against the walls, there's still lots of room for your group. However, crowding such a large number into a company headquarters doesn't seem quite the thing to do, and you feel obliged to provide the sergeant, squatting beside the box with the candle on it, with an explanation.

Of course he's already guessed, and speaking softly for your ears only, he says: "Most of these other guys in here are from D Company. They've had a bit of a rough go, sir. We'll let them rest for a while, and then get them digging-in outside."

55

THE NIGHT A STEN
GUN DOESN'T JAM!

❋

THE SERGEANT EXPLAINS MAJOR WEDD HAS BEEN CALLED
back to Tac Headquarters. He expects he'll arrive back soon with
orders for A Company to renew the attack on the objective D
Company failed to take. This being the way things tend to develop
for the P.B.I. (poor bloody infantry) he's probably right. It looks
like it's going to be a long night.

As you wait, sprawled against some sacks of potatoes, you pass
the time listening to a couple of the still-agitated survivors of D
Company compare notes on how they escaped the wicked crossfire
of tracers sweeping that bald slope across the ravine when they were
caught in the glare of the burning house.

One soldier confirms the earlier report: "They were waiting for
us – had to be – for when our guys were goin' in the front door,
they were goin' out the back throwin' lighted matches over their
shoulders into the straw and petrol they'd scattered around."

While you had been too far away to see anybody going or
coming from the house before the flames lit up the landscape, the
startling suddenness of the fire – from total darkness one moment
to flaring flames enveloping every room behind every window the
next – would seem to bear out the young soldier's contention.

His buddy, however, couldn't care less how the fire started; he is
interested only in describing what happened when the Jerry

machine-guns opened up, and he was caught like everybody else right out in the open kneeling down on one knee:

"Everybody starts scattering in all directions looking for cover, and I am pounding down the slope, when I spot this partially covered trench. I make a running dive head-first into the nearest open end. Then followin' good old infantry drill of never reappearing where you're last seen disappearing, I roll over a couple of times along the bottom before coming up at the other open end, face to face with a Heinie! I don't know who is more surprised – him or me. But my Sten is almost poking him in the belly, so I squeeze the trigger and hope to God something'll happen. And guess what?"

"She jams," volunteers his friend in ho-hum fashion.

"No, by damn," says he with a real sense of awe in his voice, "she fires!" And he starts to laugh as though he suddenly sees this as being very funny.

Immediately his buddy joins him in hearty laughter, and suddenly the cellar is full of laughter from others who have been listening and who obviously also consider it hilarious when a Sten gun actually fires when the trigger is pulled.

You can't believe your ears. Is it possible you were not listening properly? You question the narrator. Surely he meant he was afraid his Sten might jam from dirt in the mechanism, picked up when he rolled along the bottom of the trench?

"Dirt, hell! There doesn't have to be any dirt, for right after you've cleaned and oiled it, the bastard takes the notion. You never know..."

As if to underline the truth of this, the Sergeant says, "Reminds me of something that happened back at Louvigny in Normandy. Just after we'd jumped into the orchard through a hole in the stone wall blown by the tanks, my pal surprises a German in a trench. And when his Sten doesn't fire, he clubs the guy across the face with it, jumps on him, and strangles him with his bare hands."

Again, everybody roars with laughter.

This is beyond belief. While the meaning is clear, common sense argues they are exaggerating the Sten's unreliability. But when you suggest that surely Stens can be made reliable by proper maintenance, snorts and guffaws on all sides provide you with your answer. Still you persist: Do they mean to say that men will go into the attack carrying a weapon they can't be certain will fire when they pull the trigger?

"Of course, what else," calls out a bitter voice from the far end of the cellar, "the bastards made us turn in all the Schmeissers and Berettas we'd captured and were using last fall back at Groesbeek."

At this there are growls of agreement from many quarters, and the Sergeant quickly jumps in, "It's true, sir, they don't always work the way they should." Then lowering his voice he says, "I think it's time we changed the subject." And in the cunning way all effective sergeants are able to manipulate men under their command, he quickly changes the subject to sex, recounting a crazy story, with suitable embellishments, about a guy on leave in Brussels who was stranded in a hotel room for several days without money or uniform, when the "biddy he shacked up with made off with both his pants and his wallet while he was asleep."

But the subject of the Sten gun doesn't readily leave your head. You recall the first time you ever saw one in the spring of 1943 when they issued them to replace the tommy-guns taken away to give to 1st Division, rumoured to be going into action in the Mediterranean. You and your Troop Commander, Capt. Bill Graham, had been given the job of trying out a couple of them in a chalk pit on the northern outskirts of Worthing, Sussex, where the Regiment had been temporarily posted to relieve a 1st Division unit (3rd Field) leaving for Scotland for special training for landing on a hostile shore.

You remember your initial reaction was shock at its primitive appearance, looking for all the world as though the plumber down the street had improvised it from what he could find in his bin of cast-off pipe; a perfect monstrosity when compared to the sleek gun it was meant to replace, especially the part that rested against your shoulder – a skinny piece of piping with a flattened shoe welded on the end of it, in place of the highly polished wooden stock of a tommy-gun.

There was a stubby barrel crudely welded to a bulgy piece of pipe with slots cut in it. One accepted a long, slender magazine of bullets, sticking out at right angles; another roughly cut opening allowed for the ejection of spent cartridges, if and when the gun felt so inclined; and still another notch was meant to provide a safety catch, accepting the knob attached to the bolt mechanism, when it was pulled back to cock the gun. Turned upwards and hooked in the shallow notch in the casing, accidental discharge was prevented as long as the gun wasn't dropped or otherwise jarred.

While the magazine fitted well enough, neither of you could get your gun to fire a burst of more than three rounds without jamming. Whether the problem was in the magazine or in the ejection mechanism, it had been impossible to discover, since unexpended rounds as well as expended cartridges combined to jam the ejection system. When you'd reported this mulish behaviour to the battery commander, he'd assured you all new weapons had to be worked on by the artificers, and as soon as the sharp edges were filed off, the thing would work perfectly.

While very suspicious of the effectiveness of the so-called safety-catch arrangement, you didn't mention it, for you hadn't yet seen a Sten, on being accidently dropped on its butt end, fire off its entire magazine of bullets, pinwheel fashion – while revolving slowly on its side on the floor – causing everyone in the room to leap into the air as the barrel swivelled in their direction.

At any rate you had accepted the battery commander's assurances, and not having had occasion to fire a Sten from that time on to prove him wrong, you never, at any time during the past eight months, felt any special concern for the hundreds of young infantrymen you'd seen slogging along with Stens slung over their shoulders.

But now – my God – this is really unbelievable. How on earth could a condition like this be allowed to exist? You try to recall all you know of the origins of the Sten gun. You remember being told that the manufacture of these primitive gadgets had been undertaken primarily to satisfy the need for cheap, easy-to-produce weapons that could be dropped to the underground Resistance fighters, that the Sten was chosen because it was of German design and could use 9-mm rimless ammunition which the Resistance fighters could steal from enemy dumps.

In the desperate days of 1941 and 1942, the Sten may have been a justifiable compromise for securing arms for the Resistance, who otherwise would have been weaponless during their brief, infrequent hit-and-run encounters with the Germans. But to supply these totally unreliable weapons to regular troops, who must face the enemy in mortal combat for days, weeks, and months on end, must surely rank among the foremost criminal acts perpetrated on Allied troops in World War II.

The more you think about it, the worse it seems. How many hundreds or even thousands of Canadian and British soldiers have died because Stens failed to fire when they were face to face with the enemy? The numbers will never be known, for dead men cannot recount the circumstances of their death. But these soldiers here tonight, and countless others like them who have managed to survive after being let down in a crisis by its fickle mechanism, would surely agree that the Sten is among the most successful booby traps planted in the way of Canadian and British troops.*

---

* When the British War Office ordered the Sten into production in 1941 they were aware that the design from which it was derived had already been rejected in scorn by the German Wehrmacht. In a rare defence of the freakish Sten, and not one to give the user any real confidence, Lieut. F. Matthews of the South Saskatchewan Regiment reported that in the muddy conditions brought on by torrential rain during the attack on Verrières Ridge, July 20, 1944, they were more reliable than the normally highly dependable Bren. Their Stens worked okay if they were fired "holding the mags vertical and the ejection slot to the bottom, so that if the force of the ejection was insufficient, gravity would push the spent casings out."

56

THE CONDUCT OF
SUPERIOR MEN IN A CRUCIBLE

❋

YOU WILL NEVER GET USED TO THE ASTOUNDING CAPACITY of infantry officers to resist despair, and in the confused, clamorous conditions of battle, to think clearly and coolly – assessing situations which appear to you absolutely hopeless, formulating plans even as the roaring battle ebbs and flows about them, and issuing clear, precise orders in such a calm, quiet style, and in such confident tones, that they breed confidence in all who must carry them out and who, in turn, must persuade others to follow their leadership. Surely this capacity to maintain a constant, positive posture, regardless of how bad things get, must be the ultimate expression of true and enduring courage.

And even as you know you will carry forever the image of the eternally calm and resolute battalion commander, so dramatically displayed by Col. Lendrum at his "O" Group yesterday, the wise and understanding leadership shown by Company Commander Bob Wedd when he returns to this dank and smoky basement at around 3:30 A.M. with orders to attack at 4:00 A.M. is, in a way, more impressive.

Spirits and energy are ebbing to their lowest point as he calls his "O" Group to lay on the attack which must go out through that same defile in which Tim Beatty's company was lacerated. His company has been so reduced by casualties he has only one subaltern, veteran Lieut. "Mo" Berry, and two sergeants to lead his other two platoons.

Thus he must have been grateful to have appear at his "O" Group a subaltern from Beatty's devastated company, who'd come back with the survivors gathered here in the basement. As always, he speaks quietly and confidently in his deep, musical voice as he explains that one platoon (Berry's) will move in against the front of the house while another goes up through the ravine and hits it from the rear, emphasizing that the platoon moving up the ravine will concentrate on the final objective, staying clear of any involvement with the Germans in the area of the smouldering house. The young subaltern from Beatty's company, still shaking from the awful ambush, and assuming he is to go back down there and lead a platoon up through that dark valley of shadows, starts to weep – not sobbing, but sighing deeply and brushing tears from his eyes and cheeks.

Wedd gives no indication he is aware of this as he continues in his calm way. But as he finishes, seemingly without having to pause to consider possibilities, he assigns the leading role for the ravine sortie to one of the sergeants. And the sergeant, to his eternal credit, accepts the assignment without hesitation, as though an obvious decision, and proceeds to get himself organized with such noisy gusto he covers up everybody's embarrassment and diverts attention from the agitated young subaltern who turns away, blowing his nose and sighing with relief.

He'll be LOB on this attack, and by tomorrow night he'll have regained his resilience and be "right as rain," as Harvey would say. You liked Bob Wedd from the first hour you were with him, admiring his cool decisiveness under fire. But now, warmed with admiration for his kind and generous heart, you feel real affection for him as you and Signaller Ferry, with the 18-set on his back, move out on foot with him and the remainder of his company around the rim of the ravine towards the objective, now hidden in fog just over the brow of the easterly end of the promontory, to be in position to rush the burned-out house from the front as soon as the sergeant's platoon hits it from the rear.

And his plan works wonderfully well. With your guns methodically dropping shells on the slope beyond the ravine for fifteen minutes by way of "troop fire – three seconds" (guns of one troop firing in rotation at three-second intervals) to cover sounds of stumbling boots and rattling equipment, the sergeant is able to lead his platoon up the ravine without attracting attention, climb the steep incline, and attack with such surprise that the defenders offer little resistance. The objective is secure before you and Wedd know it is happening, diverted as you are by the startling effect of the muzzle-blast of a Royals' anti-tank gun getting off a couple of rounds at the house. "Mo" Berry will never forget his chagrin at having his "whole platoon bolt for the rear when the gun opened up, just as we were passing it in the dark."

Expecting to be ordered to push on at dawn, it is a relief to be left in place, even though you are forced to remain reasonably alert throughout most of the day, which begins in vastly irritating fashion shortly after dawn. The CO, in an obvious attempt to put you in your place after your undiplomatic outburst on air last night following his bombardment of your carrier with short rounds, sends up "Mac" McDonald (Regimental Quartermaster since last November) to conduct the "proving shoot" to uncover which guns are firing short. And your mood is not improved when the well-rested, "bright-eyed, bushy-tailed" McDonald digs you out of your warm cellar to guide him to a place where he can safely observe the fall of shot on a distant map reference – or "datum point," as he would have it.

It is not a simple matter of leading him upstairs to a spot among the ruins and "putting him on the ground." You don't know how far over this way the heavy enemy fire you've been hearing may have diverted the 4th Division infantry (Argyll and Sutherland Highlanders) attacking the gap in the "Staats Forst Xanten" – between the Hochwald (high woods) on the north and the Tuschen Wald (black woods) on the south – through which a railway line runs east to Xanten. Before dawn there was much high-pitched whining of straining tank motors over there, rising and falling again and again, suggestive of mud-wallowing tanks vainly struggling to extricate deeply embedded tracks.

Then at first light a series of vicious, cracking booms, peculiar to high-velocity tank or anti-tank guns, attracted your attention to some Shermans (South Alberta Regiment) sitting helter-skelter about the soggy landscape down below you to the right, immobilized by mud or enemy fire. There is no infantry in sight.

To be safe, you lead McDonald and Signaller Ferry, again carrying the 18-set, back around the hill to the deep slit trench you occupied briefly last night on the lip of the ravine.

Convinced that whatever was wrong at the guns will have been corrected by now, and anxious to get back to your warm cellar for a bit of shut-eye, you suggest that only the pivot gun of each troop be fired. However, with his sense of mission as inflated as your ego is deflated by the CO selecting him to carry out the shoot, he insists on every one of the guns of 2nd and 26th batteries being fired individually, and that each round be observed and its accuracy noted on the neatly ruled paper clipped to his map-board, before the next round is fired.

Thus the business takes more than an hour, and by the time it is done, you are slumped down in the bottom of the trench sound asleep, totally oblivious to a light dusting of snow then falling, and he has to shake you awake (rather more vigorously than necessary you think) to tell you he found no guns firing short, and to complain of your inconsiderate cluttering of the floor of the trench during the shoot.

You will never know who or what caused those short rounds, but of one thing you are certain: the guns of at least one troop were in error, suggesting an error in communicating survey coordinates or an error in plotting an artillery board. Clearly it was not a gun-laying error, though you can only imagine the fatigue bordering on exhaustion the gunners are enduring at this time: moving in the mud, digging gun pits in the mud, carrying tons of ammunition from the road to the guns through the mud, living day after day in the mud.

Hossack will write in his log: "More rain has made the roads all but impassable, but the vehicles bump and slither their way forward to deploy at Todtenhügel. The command post is dug in deeply and our stoves make it quite comfortable. The Rhine River is far over to our left, and the CO calls for a special target to be fired across the headline waterway. The range required is 11,525 yards. Fierce fighting is taking place at the Hochwald and we fire regularly. Enemy shells land regularly on the road before 26th Battery guns, but the road is used sparingly and there are no casualties."

The succinct Sgt. Hunt records: "Quiet. The slaughter continues."

The diarist at regimental headquarters, equally blasé about the contribution of guns to the progress of the war, will report of this day: "Shot in 2nd and 26th batteries on datum point. Eleven Mike targets engaged. Otherwise NTR (nothing to report)."

Next day, however, the war diary will recognize, "The guns are fairly busy most of the day . . . on Mike targets for our own FOOs and small fire-plans in support of 5th and 6th brigades as they move in to attack the Hochwald."

As 4th Brigade (Essex Scottish leading) joins in the attacks March 3 on the northern half of the forest, 4th Field is again busy firing: two defensive fire targets, twenty harassing-fire targets, a quick barrage, and eighteen Mike targets called for by the FOOs, one of them killing many of the enemy. According to Major Brown, 26th Battery Commander, the deluge of 4th Field shells "caught a German company at change-over. The three prisoners of war taken claimed to be the sole survivors."*

---

* Major J. F. Brown was subsequently honoured by being officially Mentioned-in-Despatches. Other members of 4th Field who were cited for outstanding and/or gallant efforts beyond the call of duty, on one or more occasions, were: Major Wm. P. Carr, Major Don Wilson, BSM E. Blodgett, BSM P. Oleniuk, Gnr. R. Cardinal, Gnr. J. Grenier, Bdr. C. S. May, and Sgt. D. R. Pratt.

57

MURDEROUS FIRE IN
THE HOCHWALD GAP

❋

AT A ROYALS' "O" GROUP, CALLED TO LAY ON AN ATTACK
through the Rileys to clear the extreme northern end of the
Hochwald at 6:30 tomorrow morning, March 3, Col. Lendrum,
just back from a briefing at Brigade, is able to put his company
commanders in the picture as to what has been happening in the
confused and ugly fighting around and about the mouth of that
two-mile-long corridor between the forests.

On the map the gap is about a mile wide at its far eastern end, but
only 250 yards wide at its western mouth near here. Through it runs
a railway right-of-way, but no road. Simonds wants to secure the
railway so the tracks can be ripped up and the firm roadbed used as
a direct supply route for the upcoming battle for Xanten.

It seems that two days ago, when 2nd and 3rd divisions and supporting armour punctured the outer defences of the Schlieffen
Position (the reserve position of the Siegfried Line) with a break-in
near the clearing just in front of here at the mouth of this corridor,
Simonds ordered them to push on and clear the forest flanks of
Germans: 2nd Division, the Hochwald, lying north of the gap; and
3rd Division, the smaller forest, south of the gap. However, before
either division got started, 4th Armoured Division was ordered to
push along the railway line.*

---

* First the Algonquins with South Alberta tanks in support tried it. They
barely got started when they were forced back. Of nine Shermans and

With the woods on both sides of the gap still full of well-camouflaged anti-tank guns and machine-guns, every courageous attempt by 4th Division tanks and infantry to run this horrific gauntlet has been stymied.

When the high-profile Shermans, to avoid getting stuck in the soggy fields, attempted to use the railway, crawling out along the embanked portions of the track, they were potted like ducks in a shooting-gallery. And when they tried the fields, they bogged down and are left at the mercy of whatever Jerry chooses to throw at them and their accompanying infantry.

Clearly no combination of forces can secure the Hochwald gap until the flanking woods are cleared of the enemy. Thus the importance of the attacks that got underway in earnest yesterday, March 1, starting with 6th Brigade (FMRs, Queen's Own Cameron Highlanders of Canada, and SSRs) relieving 10th Brigade and carrying the battle into the Hochwald at the northern shoulder of the gap, while the Essex Scottish led off 4th Brigade's attempt to penetrate the forest on their left flank.

----

twelve carriers trying to do a hook through a railway underpass, only one carrier made it back. Then the Canadian Argyll and Sutherland Highlanders, with another squadron of South Alberta tanks, tried it under cover of darkness. Some elements made it to the eastern end of the gap, but with the dawn they were attacked with murderous fire from all sides and though severely weakened by casualties, they could not be reinforced. Still the Lincoln and Welland Regiment was ordered to pass through them. The attack quickly petered out when all the tanks bogged down, and foot-soldiers came under drenching artillery and mortar fire in fields swept by streams of tracer bullets from both flanks. Similarly an attempt by the Lake Superior Regiment, supported by the tanks of the Grenadier Guards, ended in disarray with the armour bogged down, and the infantry forced to withdraw. On February 28, two squadrons of the Grenadier Guards had only three tanks not disabled 600 yards from their startline. And 4th Canadian Armoured Division (British Columbia Regt., Governor General Foot Guards, Canadian Grenadier Guards, South Alberta Regt.) on February 27 and 28 lost more than 100 tanks.

German resistance aroused by the Essex Scottish was particularly severe. But clearly the recently reconstructed battalion did a super job – driving the Germans from an exceptionally strong log-revetted trench system, and then holding off a succession of fierce counter-attacks by paratroopers determined to regain the security of their deep trenches and spacious, wood-lined dug-outs – some even outfitted with table and chairs.

At the outset the Essex, leading off from the Royals' positions in the rain and sleet and even the odd flutter of snow, were accompanied by a squadron of tanks of the Sherbrooke Fusiliers that took turns pumping H.E. shells at suspicious points up ahead – their high-velocity *whams* penetrating over the roaring furore of the 25-pounder barrage designed to carry the Essex up to the rim of the Hochwald.

But when the tanks bogged down, and the poor foot-sloggers had to carry on alone, you wondered how those poor lads, going into battle for the first time, would make out. Would they again be driven back into the Royals' position as they were the last time you saw them in the attack on the Goch–Calcar highway?

Though Lendrum doesn't refer directly to the fact that the Essex had only a week to rebuild their fighting strength with large numbers of raw reinforcements fresh from Canada (including some of the first conscripts to be sent up to the line), it clearly is on his mind as he recalls in great detail what Brig. Cabeldu reported earlier today about the inspiring leadership of one company commander (until recently the battalion adjutant) who was handling his first attack ever with a rifle company.

He knocked out a machine-gun post with grenades, and though wounded twice, refused to be evacuated when his company was immediately subjected to a succession of counter-attacks. Several times he left cover to cross and recross open spaces to carry ammunition to his hard-pressed platoons, boosting their confidence that the company could hold on, even as it was reduced to fewer than thirty desperate men gathering what ammunition they could from the bodies of dead comrades.

Hit a third time, and lying in the mud and water of a shell crater, barely conscious, one leg blown off and the other so badly mangled it will have to be removed, he refused to be evacuated until he issued firm orders for defending the position to his one surviving officer.*

---

* The summation sentence of the citation for the Victoria Cross awarded Major Frederick Albert Tilston read "By his calm courage, gallant conduct, and total disregard for his own safety, he fired his men with grim determination and their firm stand enabled the Regiment to accomplish its object."

58

FAREWELL TO ARMS
FOR NINE DAYS

※

STAFF OFFICERS BACK AT CORPS OR ARMY MAY SEE THE clearing of the Rhineland as a series of well-defined operations to which they attach stirring names. But for those directly participating, it surely will be remembered as one long, continuous messy business of attacks and counter-attacks without respite, with never a sense of having arrived anywhere in particular or having decided anything of consequence, as another road, another bit of high ground, another burned-out farm or derelict village is taken.

It's enough you've survived the night, or the last hour, or even the last five minutes. And all the while, you lust for sleep. Denied sleep for outrageous periods, it has become the most desirable objective of life. Every chance you get, regardless of where you are, you sleep, if only for a few minutes: usually sitting up and leaning against something, seldom stretching out flat, and, of course, always fully clothed with your boots on. Your body aches arthritically for sleep, your joints are stiff and painful for sleep, your voice is hoarse for sleep, and your brain dull and insensitive to all needs except the oblivion of sleep.

As an officer you have learned to expect a special kind of torture each night, particularly in the wee hours of the morning. Whenever the Battalion is not engaged in an attack, beating off counter-attacks, or exchanging sectors with other units, they allow you to get to sleep and then send up a signal to report back to Battalion Headquarters for an Orders Group briefing on the next attack.

While chronic fatigue has the virtue of dampening down fear and anxiety, it cannot eliminate the conviction, which you must continually suppress, that the only way out of this is on a stretcher or under a mound of earth at the roadside. So when newly promoted Capt. Don Patrick suddenly appears this afternoon and tells you he is taking over your crew so that you can go back and get ready for seven days' leave in England, it sounds like a joke, and not a very good one at that.

You and your crew are just finishing off cleaning out your arched cellar room – not in the interests of good housekeeping, but to rid the windowless cell of a mild but persistent odour of a repulsive nature that all fear will ultimately "do in" the thin, grey-faced Signaller Walter Ferry who is cursed with an overly sensitive stomach. Assuming the vegetables and hams stored in what normally would be a cool cellar were deteriorating from the radiant heat still beaming down from the thick, concrete ceiling, which, the night you arrived, still carried a load of glowing embers from the collapsed and burned-out upper storeys, it was decided everything should be thrown outside. But with every last potato bagged and removed, every last cabbage leaf swept up, and every ham removed from its ceiling hook and deposited outside, that insidious, nauseating odour still persists.

This is maddening because only in the last twenty-four hours, with much encouragement from the rest of the crew, Ferry had begun to keep a little food down long enough to gain a modicum of nourishment. Now everyone is on edge he will start upchucking again if the nauseating odour persists. Only one thing remains on the floor over in a dark corner – a German jackboot – ignored until now as not being a possible source of the odour. But when Squissato picks it up to fling it out, he finds it grossly heavy, and looking inside discovers the stump of a man's foot and leg. Ferry, gagging, barely makes it outside.*

---

* Gunner Ferry was wounded two days later, and Capt. Patrick March 8.

Somehow this repelling incident strikes an appropriate note for your exit from these wretched Rhineland battlefields, or so it seems to you riding back in the Jeep that brought up Patrick, as you try in vain to account for fifteen days and nights since you last saw the guns. You don't remember shaving, and seldom washing, for sleep took priority over everything else. You must have managed to get a hot meal sometime, but you remember only an endless diet of glutinous M & V Stew and Steak-and-Kidney Pudding spooned icy-cold from the can; chips of Compo cheese on slices of sultana pudding; and oily sardines speared from the tin with concrete-brittle hardtack crackers.

Back at Baker Troop gun position the churned-up mud and ruts are so deep you dispense with Jeep and driver at the road and make your way on foot to the Troop Command Post, visiting each gun pit on the way to tell the gun crews how much the infantry appreciate the speed and accuracy of their shells in breaking up counter-attacks. Knowing how the gunners take pride in such messages from the foot-sloggers they admire so much, you find the total lack of reaction on haggard faces and in red-rimmed weary eyes disconcerting until, arriving at the Troop Command Post, you are reminded by your GPO Lieut. Jack Bigg and his acks (the brothers Hughes, Bombardier Morty, and Lance-Bombardier Ralph) of the heavy-going they've been enduring twenty-four hours a day for days on end.

Your barrel-chested GPO, of rich baritone voice, describes how the guns on occasion have glowed red from intense fire on overlapping targets called for by you and other FOOs. His acks tell how Jerry has maintained a nerve-wracking schedule of random shelling, along with aerial bombing and strafing attacks by jet-propelled planes, including the one that killed the 14th Battery gunners. While they are giving you a lively description of an attack the day before on the woods behind the guns by bomb-carrying Spitfires – which were supposed to knock out a Jerry self-propelled gun that had been harassing the guns all day from somewhere in the rear, but mistakenly knocked out six of our tanks instead – you find yourself going to sleep standing up.

Rousing yourself, you ask Bigg if by any chance there is anything left of the monthly ration of officers' booze – officially a bottle and a half per officer per month, normally shared unofficially with the NCOs when there is no officer's mess in action. To your astonishment, he produces a bottle of champagne he had set aside. Thus equipped you ask where you might bed down for the night.

He suggests the battery cookhouse, a reasonably intact house a couple of hundred yards on the road behind the guns, and offers to guide you. While this hardly seems necessary, he insists, taking hold of your arm to steady you when he notices you stagger a little as you turn to make your way across the muddy field deeply rutted by the quads that hauled the guns in here yesterday.

Aware for some time that you are inclined to stagger a bit now and then, you had no idea it was so obvious to others until now. And while it is disturbing to be treated like a doddering old man, you are very touched by the obvious concern of this big, powerful man, and grateful for the support of his firm grip on your elbow, which he does not release until he has deposited you at the door of the cookhouse.

Inside some gunners sit at the kitchen table lit by an oil lamp, playing cards. You open the champagne and offer to share it with them, but they decline. And when it is gone you ask if any of them has anything to drink, assuring them that you will replace whatever they can turn up the first chance you get. One of the gunners pulls out of his pocket a little medicine bottle in which he has been saving his daily rum ration. As he hands it to you, he says you need not replace it for he doesn't touch the stuff.

Gratefully you consume the strong liquor, a sip at a time, sitting on a wooden chair drawn up close to the stove glowing and clicking with delicious heat.

It's only 6:00 P.M., but you know you should hit the sack. Still you go on sitting there, luxuriating in the smell and taste and feel of the heat, as you carry on a desultory conversation with the card players at the table. It is the first hot stove you have been near for more than two weeks, and you fairly drink in the delicious heat.

You could not have dozed off more than a few seconds, leaning against the hot stove, before the smell of burning flight-jacket alerts your companions at the card table and you wake up as they drag you away and beat out the smouldering sleeve of your jacket. But the experience is sufficiently shocking you decide to relax on the floor on your back, with your hands locked under your head.

And this is how you remain, without turning over or changing the position of your hands for twelve hours, until you awake with a line of men stepping over you on their way to pick up their breakfast. Some kind soul has thrown a greatcoat over you, and a good thing too, for the fire is out and the stove is stone-cold.

Relocating yourself out of the way over in a corner, you again go to sleep until suppertime when good old Whitehawk arrives with clean shirts, clean underwear, and clean socks, and your bedroll, which he located still in the back of a Jeep at RHQ. Gratefully you crawl into it and sleep until awakened next morning to get ready for the leave truck that will carry you and several others, including friend Bob Grout, now with 26th Battery, to the Channel ferry dock at Ostend.

59

FOOTNOTE TO

RHINELAND FINALE

❋

WHEN THE NORTHERN PART OF THE HOCHWALD IS CLEARED by the Royals and the Rileys on March 4, and the guns are ordered to move up through the mud, the landscape is so churned up by tanks and shell-fire that Bombardier Hossack will write in his diary:

Roads are just guesswork as we go forward to Neu Louisendorf at the edge of the Hochwald. The woods are strewn with German dead, presenting a grotesque sight. The area is well mined, and we avoid all white-taped places. At midnight the barn containing Regimental Headquarters burns, illuminating the whole area nicely.

Engineers employ bulldozers to knock down damaged houses, producing rubble to maintain roads. An afternoon move (March 6) through mined areas of the Hochwald sees us passing more dead and torn Jerries alongside burned-out tanks and vehicles. We dig-in in a pasture near the badly damaged village of Labbeck [beyond the eastern end of the Hochwald Gap, five kilometres from Xanten]. The new 32-barrel mortars [rocket projectors] are deployed beside us. When they fire, a terrific explosion rends the air and a swish says they are on their way. Toronto Scottish machine-guns, in line behind us, fire frequently. . . . The wagon-lines area is being shelled repeatedly, and our vehicles move to a quieter area.

We are afforded an excellent view of the enemy battling strongly for . . . a ridge on our right front. Shells from our lines can be seen to land among them and beat them back.

Hossack is describing a counter-attack on the British struggling to maintain a foothold on Boenninghardt Ridge on the right flank that overlooks the whole German bridgehead – taken by a small band of 3rd Battalion Irish Guards, and reinforced during two days of bitter fighting by the 4th Grenadier Guards and the 5th Coldstream Guards.

On the left flank of the Canadian drive now threatening Xanten, the leading battalions of the British 43rd Wessex Division, fighting southeast this way along the Rhine, are now within six miles of this fortified town, which provides the anchor for the German rear-guard action to maintain intact the bridge at Wesel, their only escape route. Their encirclement on this side of the Rhine is now complete, for three days ago, March 3, a powerful American spear-head (the other half of the pincer movement planned by Montgomery back in February and long delayed by flooding) driving northwest along the Rhine sealed off the right end of the Wesel pocket, when they made contact near Geldern with XXX Corps then doing a right hook beyond the Hochwald battle.

The American Ninth Army – 375,000 strong – immobilized for fifteen days while waiting for the flooding to subside from the open valves on the Roer dam, on February 23 had begun crossing the still swollen Roer river, the infantry in assault boats, and the tanks on rapidly built bridges. Safely across they swung northwest, well behind the German defences that were designed to protect the Rhine from attacks from the southwest, and drove (if they were tankmen) and walked (if infantrymen) some fifty miles in eight days, now and then confronting and overcoming pockets of resistance, accepting casualties in hastily prepared attacks that were sometimes inadequately supported, so as to carry on "relentless pursuit" of territory thinly held by badly confused and disorganized enemy troops.

Pushing on, along hard, dry roads with remarkable boldness, on occasion with what staff officers like to call "dash and verve," six infantry and three armoured divisions with almost 1,400 tanks had, by March 1, gained half the distance to the Rhine from the Roer. In one week the 13th Corps (made up of 84th, 102nd, and 5th armoured divisions) had taken more than six thousand prisoners. And the 29th Division had "swept a path 20 miles wide and 25 long, containing some 40 towns, the largest being the textile centre of Muenchen-Gladbach with a population of over 300,000," providing "34 accredited newsmen" with great stories of triumphant American troops winning the Rhineland.

However, when they hit the outer perimeter of the German bridgehead near Wesel, soon after making contact with the British right wing of First Canadian Army, they got some inkling of the quality of the enemy troops confronting the Canadian and British troops these past three weeks. Schlemm's forces severely punished the American tank units pushing forward in reckless fashion. Spoiled by the ease with which they had pushed along against weak or non-existent opposition, they were clobbered on March 5 by Panzerfausts and 88-mm guns, as they approached the southern bastion of the bridgehead bunched up (according to 1st Parachute Army General Alfred Schlemm's postwar testimony) in a "wedge-shaped formation of several hundred tanks with little dispersion."

The 8th Armoured Recce Battalion had 50 tanks knocked out in five minutes. Their 36th Battalion lost 41 of their 54 tanks. And their supporting infantry battalion (49th Armoured Infantry) had 343 casualties. According to Lt.-Col. M. G. Roseborough, commander of the 49th, they had no idea what they were getting into:

We were barrelling along against minimum resistance when we ran out of maps and intelligence . . . Our armour [going on alone] just ploughed headlong into a prepared defence the Germans had put in to protect the Wesel bridge. They had a number of their dual-purpose 88-mm . . . ringing the town, and they had a field day . . ."*

Now with their shrinking bridgehead under fire from Allied guns on three sides, Germany's battered First Parachute Army is headed for total disaster if it continues to try to hold territory on this side of the Rhine, particularly if the weather clears enough to allow Allied bombers to locate targets, including the bridges at Wesel, something they've been unable to do.

Nevertheless, with their only escape route at stake, they will make the Allies pay dearly before they withdraw or surrender. They have managed to remove most of their guns and mortars to the far bank of the Rhine and can still reach any point on the perimeter of their holding on this side. And they constantly underline this fact with impressive counter-fire whenever Allied guns pour shells into Wesel, Xanten, and nearby fortified villages Veen and Alpon.

Observing this finale to the awesome struggle for the Rhineland, British war correspondent R. W. Thompson will capture indelible images observed from an artillery OP on the ridge east of the Hochwald Gap:

> . . . in a magnificent and terrible panorama . . . the battle raged with frightful intensity on a front no more than eight miles wide . . . the pounding by artillery and bombing within the confines of that narrow triangle [of villages Xanten, Veen, and Alpon] was awe-inspiring . . .
>
> Thursday, March 8th, had the feel of a day of reckoning . . . the 43rd, 52nd [British] and 2nd, 3rd and 4th Canadian divisions . . . gathered themselves for major attacks . . . supported by an immense weight of artillery . . .

---

* This and the preceding quotes are from pages 251, 252, 255, and 272 of *Rhineland*, Toronto: Stoddart, 1989, by Col. Denis and Shelagh Whitaker.

A white smokescreen streamed across the northern flank . . . shells from batteries of 5.5s crashed into the town of Xanten so that the dark shroud in which the town was hidden flickered incessantly . . . The lovely church and spire . . . seemed to be riding the heavy cloud banks as the battle swathed its base . . .

Crocodiles, Flails, tanks, and men moved in eccentric fashion . . . in the midst of a great turbulence of smoke and flame, Veen lay hidden at the very vortex of the tremendous struggle . . . The whole middle distance was lit hour after hour with the constant flicker and flare of running fires and explosions and the flash of guns.

At intervals farmsteads and ammunition dumps blew up in billows of heavy smoke shot through with flames, and men like ants ran and fell . . .

But even as he recorded this picture of the fighting for Xanten, "the undoubted key" to the wiping out of the German bridgehead, he recognized that "it was easy to see everything and yet see nothing," and there was "no way of knowing reality . . . without going down on that terrible stage."*

---

* From R.W. Thompson, *Battle for the Rhine* (New York: Ballantine Books, 1958), pp. 200-201.

60

SHADES OF SIEGFRIED
AT XANTEN

※

ON MARCH 7, 1945, GERMAN TROOPS ARE SAID TO HAVE begun pulling back over the Rhine at Wesel, nine years to the day in 1936 Hitler, in pointed defiance of France and her allies, sent two battalions of his élite personal guard, SS Leibstandarte Adolf Hitler, marching through cheering crowds over the Hohenzollern Bridge at Cologne, symbolically reoccupying the Rhineland's left bank that had been demilitarized by the Locarno Treaty of 1925.

However, few of the soldiers engaged in attempting to take Xanten and nearby villages – squeezing the last fight out of paratrooper rearguards holed up in previously prepared positions behind mine fields and anti-tank ditches – will have the time or inclination to dwell on such matters, even if by chance they hear the historically conscious BBC remarking on this remarkable coincidence. German resistance, born of desperation, is just too severe. Their searing machine-gun fire from slits in fortified barns and thick bunkers and emplacements rakes the attackers, while hundreds of German guns and mortars of all calibres pound them with unabated fury from across the Rhine.

Xanten, the legendary birthplace of dragon-slayer Siegfried, is the linchpin of the German bridgehead centred on Wesel. Obviously it must be held at all costs if the remnants of their badly mauled paratroop formations (some reduced to half-strength and others to quarter their original number) are to make it back across the river.

For those who remember the wicked confrontations day and night from Caen to Falaise in Normandy last July and August, the Rhineland fighting seems on occasion to reach comparable levels of intensity. Certainly this was so during the struggle for the Goch–Calcar highway when massive concentrations of shells, resembling those dropped by the 25-pounders and mediums on Verrières Ridge, were needed again and again to stabilize the front. And no resistance anywhere along the Rhine is more severe than that encountered during the first days of March, when the words "Hochwald" and "Xanten" become synonymous with flaming battle and remorseless killing by men nearing exhaustion from three weeks of almost continuous attacks and counter-attacks.

A battalion attack by 6th Brigade having failed to take Xanten on March 6, a set-piece attack, involving three brigades (4th and 5th Canadian and 129th British of 43rd Wessex Division), is mounted March 8, to take the town, while 4th Armoured Division captures nearby Veen.

The Wessex units are to capture the main part of Xanten and a hamlet named Beek east of there, while 5th Canadian Brigade secures the high ground south of the town between the railway and the Alter Rhein, and 4th Canadian Brigade clears the western edge of the town. Assaulting units of 4th Brigade are the Essex Scottish on the left and Royal Hamilton Light Infantry on the right, supported by tanks of Fort Garry Horse.

The attack opens at 5:30 A.M. with a sudden rising whine of many tank engines and great splashes of light across the dark skies, as seven regiments of field guns and four regiments of mediums open up with mighty roar from all sides on the shrunken German bridgehead. OP Signaller John Cooper, who, with his Troop Commander, Capt. Gordon Lucas of Fox Troop, is going into the attack for the first time in the turret of a tank supplied by the squadron of Fort Garry Horse supporting the Essex, and will remember every minute of that grim morning:

The enemy position consists of farmhouses and barns built as bunkers with thick, steel-reinforced concrete walls and cellars built in the shape of air-raid shelters – very formidable. The ground leading up to the bunkers, that form part of the northern end of the Siegfried Line, is devoid of all trees and brush – a bare, upward grade without cover. A barrage by our guns is to precede the attackers, but it will be of short duration. The tanks will then take over close support.

We are awakened while it is still dark. Climbing up into the Sherman tank that has been allotted to us as a mobile observation post during the attack, I "net in" the 19-set radio transmitter and receiver to our Regiment. Down in the hull of the tank, there is a driver and a co-driver. Capt. Lucas and I take over the turret. Just after first light, we move off over a ditch onto a road, and carry on for a mile or two, until we turn right into a field that is to be our startline for the attack.

Grave misgivings arise when our wireless goes dead as we are running up to the startline. However, to our relief it turns out we are merely passing through a wireless "dead zone," and soon we regain radio contact with our troop and Regiment.

I feel immensely safe in the tank in comparison with the Bren Gun Carrier we usually use, until the thought of 88-mm anti-tank guns passes through my mind. Still, I think, if a person has to go into battle, there's no better way than sitting down in comparative floating comfort surrounded by thick steel.

All of a sudden our guns open up and the Essex Scottish start forward. Almost immediately a German counter-barrage comes down right on our position. The crashing concussion of each shell is so great, I can only guess they're firing something quite heavy at us – 105-mm or heavier – and I am truly thankful for the protection of the tank, as I look out the periscope and catch sight of some stretcher-bearers attending the wounded among some obviously dead men. It is truly shocking. It all happened so quickly.

The tanks now move up into the clearing close to the enemy

positions and begin firing their 75-mm guns into the bunkers, but without much effect. It is then I notice two or three extended lines of Essex Scottish charging up the incline past our tanks. I'd seen our infantry attack before, but in this case they are attacking across open ground against a very strong position held by German paratroopers armed with many automatic weapons and heavily backed by mortars and artillery. The attacking lines of men are being hit and knocked down by machine-gun fire and well-aimed mortar bombs. I see an infantryman hurled at least ten feet in the air. And the same explosion takes out three or four other men. After taking many casualties, the first line of infantry goes to ground, while the second line charges up the hill with the same result. By this time our barrage has stopped.

Our shells – like those from the 75-mm tank guns – aren't all that effective against these deep bunkers, and for a time the attack is stalled. With our infantry digging in, covered by the tanks continuing to fire on the German positions, the German artillery attempts to knock out individual tanks by firing heavy concentrations on them, and though none are set on fire that I see, they may disable some. The tank in front of us was violently rocked by a heavy shell exploding under the front of its hull.

Now the Essex try to outflank the German positions, and are, to a point, successful. But the main bunkers are still being defended very aggressively, when more German troops are seen coming forward from their rear areas, to dig-in behind the bunkers. Capt. Lucas immediately gives me fire orders to transmit to the guns laying down a Mike target on them. After this they disappear and we never see or hear from them again.

But the stalemate is not broken until about 1500 hours when Crocodiles [flame-throwing Churchill tanks towing trailers of fuel] appear and begin to burn the paratroopers out of their bunkers. The position is finally taken after about an hour of shooting flames and taking prisoners from one bunker after another. As batches of prisoners are being escorted to the rear, some are laughing and some are crying ...*

The Crocodiles also deal effectively with a small, ancient stone fort that "looks as though it could have been built in the Middle Ages."

The Royals' leading companies (Stothers's C and Wilcox's D) are under shell- and mortar fire from the moment they leave their forming-up place, and the closer they get to Xanten, the worse it gets. When they come under machine-gun fire from the old fort on the right and a windmill on the left, they have to resort to crawling up a ditch until they get close enough to rush their objectives in the town.

By now the Rileys are in serious trouble on the right flank of the brigade: two company commanders are dead, and another, the indomitable Major Froggett, in command of a company cut off by counter-attacking Germans, has been taken prisoner.

At noon Brig. Cabeldu, 4th Brigade commander, orders the Royals to renew their attack to help the British 129th Brigade on the left, and take some pressure off the desperate Rileys. They attack with two companies up (Wedd's A and Stothers's C).

Aided by Wasp flame-throwers, Stothers's men quickly gain their objective, but Wedd's company is soon in a very bad way, with his forward platoon pinned down in a group of buildings by such severe fire it is impossible for his other two platoons to move up.

After both of his remaining lieutenants (R. S. Beckley and veteran "Mo" Berry) are wounded and evacuated, Wedd himself is wounded in one leg. Being the only surviving officer in the company, he rejects evacuation and carries on. As he limps towards the factory that is his company's objective in Xanten, he is hit in the

---

* This description of the fighting at Xanten was prepared by John Cooper at the author's request.

other leg, and this time so seriously he can no longer walk. However, until he can get another officer forward to take over the company, he refuses to be evacuated, even though he can't gain shelter in a trench, but must lie on a stretcher above ground in a shallow declivity.

Only when he is hit a third time, the mortar splinters inflicting mortal wounds to his head, neck, and chest, making it impossible for him to protest, are his stretcher-bearers allowed to evacuate him. The delay in evacuation will prove fatal, and he will die in a hospital in England a couple of days later, clearly the victim of devotion to duty.*

By nightfall victory is assured. With 129th Brigade dominating at least half of Xanten, and the rest of the terribly smashed town, where less than 10 per cent of the buildings still stand, dominated by 4th Brigade, the enemy withdraws – even as they keep two companies of RHLI pinned down and inflict 134 casualties on them. The Essex suffer 108, and the Royals 46 while taking 110 prisoners. During the night 5th Brigade passes through to take the high ground south of Xanten, and by early March 10 the last enemy resistance is liquidated.

In clearing the Rhineland a significant Allied victory has been achieved, and there is an appealing ring of honest understanding about the signal from the Supreme Commander Eisenhower to General Crerar to be passed on to the Canadian and British troops under his command: "Probably no assault in this war has been conducted under more appalling conditions of terrain than was that one. It speaks volumes for your skill and determination and the

---

* At a dinner with the author in London after the war, Col. Lendrum of the Royals expressed his earnest regret he had not recommended Major Bob Wedd for the Victoria Cross instead of a medal that could not be awarded posthumously. He certainly would have, he said, had he known the seriousness of Bob's wounds, which at the time, though serious, were not considered life-threatening.

valour of your soldiers, that you carried it through to a successful conclusion."

And xxx Corps Commander Horrocks, a veteran of the mud of Ypres and Passchendaele of the First World War, and who, but for fourteen months recovering from life-threatening wounds suffered in 1943 in North Africa, served continuously in battle zones in this war since before Dunkirk – will one day feel obliged to declare in his book *Corps Commander:* "This [the Rhineland] was the grimmest battle in which I took part during the war. No one in his right senses would choose to fight a winter campaign in the flooded plains and dense pinewoods of Northern Europe, but there was no alternative. We had to clear the western bank of the Rhine if we were to enter Germany in strength and finish the war."*

As in Normandy and along the Scheldt, the vastly superior fire-power of Canadian and British field guns had guaranteed success. The unique fire-control system embracing all field regiments in all the divisions in the corps, developed in late 1942 by a British officer, Brig. H. J. Parham, to allow FOOs of lowly rank to concentrate the fire of many widely dispersed regiments on a "target of opportunity" – twenty-four guns on a Mike target, seventy-two on an Uncle target, and two hundred and sixteen on a Victor target – had, throughout the Rhineland, delivered massive concentrations with a speed and accuracy beyond the wildest dreams of even field marshals and five-star generals of other nations.

"A very impressive technical achievement," will be the grudging tribute paid by German General Schlemm to the weight and accuracy of the concentrations regularly laid down by the guns of First Canadian Army on his First Parachute Army units, as they were decimated and driven back over the Rhine. While remaining scornful of Allied tactics, which he will claim during postwar interrogation "never surprised" him – that he could always "determine from the kind and location of artillery fire, and from the assembly

---

* Sir Brian Horrocks, *Corps Commander*, Toronto: Griffin House, p. 204.

positions of the tanks, where and when the attack would take place" – he will admit Canadian Army gun fire was so intense at times, he marvelled any German soldier managed to survive.

He concluded: "Two qualities are necessary if troops are to stand this *Hell Fire* – energy and resistance. Deep and narrow foxholes for one or two men have to be dug. The men have to have nerves of steel."*

Though the Germans had managed to assemble almost 1,800 guns and mortars to drench the muddy fields with storms of flashing geysers, and fill with shattering airbursts the woods through which white-faced, wincing men had to pass, they never came close to matching the hurricanes of high explosive which Canadian and British FOOs regularly called down on them from 25-pounders and their slower, but heavier cousins, the 5.5-inch mediums.

For the month ending March 7, shell consumption by just the field guns and the mediums – the work-horses of every battle – tell the story: almost 2,000,000 rounds by the 25-pounders and almost 360,000 by the mediums.

During twenty-one days, from February 17 to March 9, 4th Field alone fired 84,072 rounds, averaging 4,000 rounds per gun per day.

In just the last two days (March 8 and 9) 4th Field consumed 15,288 rounds (637 per gun), representing almost eight tons of shells per gun crew, participating in 22 Mike (regimental) targets, one Uncle (divisional), and two Victor (Corps) targets, a small barrage, two counter-battery shoots, and a harassing fire-plan, all one night.

---

* 1st Fallschirmtruppen (paratrooper army) report of commander, prepared by General Alfred Schlemm at #11 POW Camp Wales. (MS #B-084, National Archives, Washington, U.S.A.)

61

THE BILL

--- ✳ ---

GERMAN LOSSES IN THE THIRTY-DAY BATTLE FEBRUARY 8 to March 10 were estimated at more than 89,000: 38,000 killed and wounded and more than 51,000 taken prisoner. Their 116th Panzer Division that had confronted 2nd Canadian Division on the Goch–Calcar highway alone lost almost 3,000 men.*

But the "butcher's bill" was also very high for the Allied armies: 22,934 – the American Ninth Army suffering 7,300 casualties during its seventeen-day campaign, and First Canadian Army accounting for double that, with 15,634 killed, wounded, or missing, 5,414 of them Canadians.

Almost half the Canadian casualties were suffered in only twenty-one days by just one division – 2nd Canadian Infantry Division. As in Normandy the previous July and August, the men wearing the dark blue shoulder patch had the highest rate of casualties of all Allied divisions engaged in the clearing of the Rhineland: 2,307 killed and wounded, surpassing the 2,243 suffered by the 53rd Welsh Division with thirty days' strenuous service that began in the Reichswald on February 8.

---

* German casualty figures from Col. G. W. L. Nicholson, *Gunners of Canada, Vol. II*, Toronto: McClelland and Stewart, 1972, pp. 420-1.

Casualties by Divisions Under Command Canadian Army
February 8 to March 11, 1945

Canadian		British	
2nd Cdn Inf Div	2,307	53 Welsh Inf Div	2,243
3rd Cdn Inf Div	1,530	51st Highland Inf Div	1,583
4th Cdn Armd Div	1,117	15th Scottish Inf Div	1,495
2nd Cdn Armd Bde	88	43rd Wessex Inf Div	1,244
2nd Cdn Corps Tps	177	3rd Brit Inf Div	945
1st Cdn Army Tps	84	52nd Lowland Inf Div	681
	5,303	11th Armd Div	679
		Guards Armd Div	587
		30th Brit Corps Tps	254
		6th Guards Armd Bde	197
		8th Armd Bde	194
		49th West Riding Div	172
		34th Armd Bde	46
		1st Brit Corps Tps	18
			10,348

(National Archives Records RG 24 Vol 18502 File 133.009 D-6)

PART FOUR: MARCH 11 – MAY 15

Crossing the Rhine to
Sever Holland from Germany

62

A THIRTY-MILE-LONG SMOKESCREEN

OPERATION "PLUNDER," AS THE RHINE CROSSINGS ARE TO be known collectively, requires the assembly and camouflage of stupendous quantities of supplies – particularly bridging stores amounting to some 22,000 tons for the use of 8,000 Royal Engineers, including Royal Canadian Engineers who will build near Emmerich the last of the five bridges to be thrown across the swift-flowing river.[*]

No fewer than 260 miles of steel-wire rope and 80 miles of cable (originally designed for tethering barrage balloons) will be needed: first, by RAF volunteers of 159 Wing to winch ferries and rafts back and forth; and second, by the engineers stringing together and holding in place some 25,000 wooden pontoons under the bridges, and sustaining an anti-mine boom strung across the river upstream by the Royal Navy in case the Germans try floating down explosive charges to blow up the bridges. Then there are 2,000 assault boats, 650 storm boats, and 120 river tugboats, as well as mountains of ammunition to be brought up.

And with the far bank of the Rhine somewhat higher than this side, exposing most of the rolling open country to enemy observation, it is necessary to lay down, right up until D-Day on March 24,

---

[*] 155 Engineers were killed or wounded while bridging the Rhine.

a dawn-to-dusk smokescreen along a thirty-mile stretch of river. To maintain the white blanket, billowing from hundreds of smoke generators using 200 tons of zinc chloride and fog oil a day, without leaving any gaps to expose Allied activity, is a tremendous engineering feat requiring constant adjustments for wind and atmospheric conditions.

Canadian Army's Meteorological Group's special "Met Officer," Capt. M. E. Comfort, the only one of his kind in the British–Canadian forces, provides Smoke Control with reliable forecasts of atmospheric and wind conditions, advising on the best beaming points for fog-oil generators to meet changing conditions, and moving them as necessary.*

For twelve days, until March 23, when artillery units are allowed to move up into positions prepared in advance by discreet work parties, the Regiment, along with the rest of the Division, bivouacs in the southeast corner of the Reichswald, which escaped the worst of the "Veritable" bombardments that smashed or denuded 70 per cent of the trees in the great forest.

It is here, far from the sounds of battle, with a degree of relief you find embarrassing, you catch up with them when you return from seven days' leave in England. All the way back you had been plagued with dread at the thought of having to return to action. In vain you had tried to suppress the sickening feeling you were returning to your doom, a feeling that deepened with each passing mile as the racing train from London closed on Dover and the ship that would carry you back across the Channel.

---

* In the planning and distribution of smokescreens that moved up the Rhine as the front moved from near Nijmegen to Wesel, blocking the enemy view of the left flank during the thirty-day campaign, and for two more weeks before the Rhine Crossings, other key officers were: Lt.-Col. W. R. Sawyer, GSO 1 Chemical Warfare; Major J. T. Hugill, RCA; and Capt. J. C. Bond, Chemical Warfare, awarded a Military Cross for his gallant and dangerous work of reconnaissance for deployment of generators often in front of the FDLs, and sometimes in mined areas.

From the outset of your leave, you were totally ill at ease. Finding yourself in London, only hours after being pulled back from an OP at the Hochwald, was a shock. The contrast between survival in the muddy, shell-swept Rhineland and life "laughing onward" in the West End – callously indifferent if not totally oblivious to what was going on over in the Rhineland – was almost too much to bear as you studied every edition of the papers trying to picture what was happening to comrades left behind.

While fully appreciating the British must be sick to death of war news – and that Londoners, of all people on earth, surely had earned the right to ignore the war for a while now the rocket blitz had ended – you still were unable to restrain your temper when a churlish hotel clerk or snotty headwaiter treated with cold disdain your request for a modicum of service. And this was particularly so the day you learned, through a chance meeting with Royals' Major Tom Whitley on Piccadilly, that Bob Wedd had died of wounds in a Limey hospital and been buried that day in Tom's presence in Brookwood Cemetery south of London.

Time and again good old Bob Grout (invited to accompany you on a visit to your wife's relatives in Birmingham) dragged you away from situations in the West End before they developed into something really serious, but in the process further enraged you by begging the offended parties to make allowances for his slightly unbalanced companion. Of course, on cooling down each time, you knew it to be true; you had never really recovered from the unwitnessed but very real breakdown in that isolated Jerry slit-trench on the Goch–Calcar highway. And as your leave was drawing to an end, you took to worrying that under similar conditions another breakdown was not only possible, but entirely likely, placing at risk the infantry depending on you to deliver the support of your guns at a time of desperate need.

And when two attractive, young ladies, volunteer hostesses at the regular Saturday night dance for officers at the Overseas League, where you and Bob had spent the previous evening, arrived uninvited at Victoria Station to see you off, it seemed clearly an ill omen.

After years of coming and going from British station platforms without greeting or farewell from a living soul, this gesture by these two young women from two of the best families in London, with bags of other things to occupy their Sunday afternoon, was just too remarkable.

Then, just as the train was about to pull out, and all the doors along the platform were *thunking* closed, one of the girls reached up and kissed you. You knew it meant no more than "Cheerio – take care – sorry you have to go back there – best wishes for a safe return, for you seem a decent enough chap." But deep feelings you had almost forgotten existed stirred within you. And as the train tore for Dover, you felt your mind, body, and soul surrendering to a rebellion you had suppressed all the time you had been in the U.K., and you unloaded your worries on Bob.

You told him about breaking up in that hole, and of your continuing fear that when you'd be most needed by the infantry, you'd cower in a hole. You swore that if there was an honourable way to get out of it all, you'd take it in a minute – that you'd do almost anything, short of a self-inflicted wound, to get out of going back.

An officer sitting opposite you in the compartment, a total stranger, incensed by your desperate talk, which he clearly felt was unbecoming to one holding a King's Commission, undertook to give you a pep talk, pointing out the obvious disadvantage of allowing the mind to dwell on something that might never happen, while advising against any course of action for which your conscience would never forgive you.

While not helping in the slightest to solve your dilemma, he at least shut you up, as you realized that only someone who'd been driven to the brink could really understand what you were talking about.

Over many months, observing those around you, you have to believe that though men have an extraordinary capacity to absorb and manage fear in all its shades, from breathtaking anxiety to shivering terror, every man has his limits. By suppression or repression, or whatever, a man can appear to carry on indefinitely, holding fear at bay if conditions are not too severe. But even as he blotters it up and puts on a brave front, fear is relentlessly taking its toll. And one day he finds he's had his fill: he can take no more.

It's clear you've lost your resiliency through cumulative effects of having lived too long with fear, cowering too often under shell and mortar blasts, and, on too many occasions, steeling yourself to go forward when every part of your being ached to remain hidden in a hole.

So when you read in a letter from your wife (the first of several awaiting you) that Gen. McNaughton, Minister of National Defence, has approved of an application, made by her father (senior naval member of the Dependants Allowance Board) that you are to be flown home on compassionate grounds to aid in the convalescence of your mother recovering from a serious illness (until now hidden from you), it seems heaven sent.

But the next letter (in chronological order) tells how your dear mother, persuaded she shouldn't let her needs interfere with the war effort, assured a bewildered nurse from Defence Headquarters, filling out a routine form at her bedside, that your return was not necessary.

At first you feel only crushing disappointment. But then you are overwhelmed by the realization you now have an obligation to stay alive even greater than before: if you buy it now, your mother will surely die of anguish, believing she condemned you to death. You've no choice but to go begging. At RHQ you find the CO is up at Division acting as CRA, and the second-in-command has left on long service leave to Canada.* So it's to Adjutant Sammy Grange you confess your plight, holding back nothing.

To your amazement, he reveals your removal from front-line duty is already in the works! He wasn't supposed to tell you in case

---

* Major Gordon Savage, who by then had earned a DSO for his aggressive reconnaissance and forward planning of regimental moves to ensure continuous support of the infantry.

it didn't work out, but the Colonel has recommended you for a job back at the reinforcement depot in Ghent in Belgium. Why? Well, it seems he discovered, through an investigation he undertook from his elevated position at Division, of the longevity records of current FOOs (no doubt inspired by an inquiry from McNaughton's office) that you've survived as a FOO longer than anyone else in the Canadian Army. And to make sure you get the job, he saw to it that only your name went forward. Still, knowing the ways of the military, the appointment could be weeks coming through. Meanwhile, do you think you can hang in there?

In your happiness you assure him that knowing relief is nigh you will have no difficulty. However, later, when the euphoria wears off, you decide you are not going to die twice – that when the time comes to move out with the infantry again, you'll have one of those rum-filled water-bottles, now cluttering the floor of the carrier, always buttoned into the front of your battledress blouse where it'll be handy whenever you feel you are getting the wind up.

With remarkable satisfaction all ranks welcome the news that when 1st Canadian Army goes back into action across the Rhine, it truly will be an army of Canadians – 1st Canadian Corps (including 1st Infantry Division, 5th Armoured Division, 1st Armoured Brigade, and all their Corps and Army Troops) having been brought up from the Italian front, where they'd been fighting since the summer of 1943. This is first learned from Gnr. "Babe" Hughes (kid brother of Bdr. Morty and L/Bdr. Ralph, of Baker Troop, 2nd Battery), who, about a year ago, was posted from 4th Field to Italy. He says all 1st Division arty regiments are now bivouacked in the Reichswald.*

---

* Entering battle in Holland for the first time over the Rhine, 1st, 2nd, and 3rd Field Regiments answered calls for fire from 7th Brigade, of 3rd Division, moving against Deventer.

63

MORE FIRE SUPPORT
THAN FOR D–DAY

✳

WITH THE REGIMENT OUT OF ACTION AND AT EASE FOR THE
first time since those four days last November at Rumst after the
Scheldt, and blessed with sunny days and balmy spring nights, the
gunners enjoy a lazy period of maintenance and recreation. Daily a
certain number are trucked into Nijmegen where wet canteens and
a "hamburger joint" have been set up, and some forty-eight-hour
passes to Brussels are issued.

With the war seemingly far away from the peaceful security of
this bushland, the tragic death of Gunner T. E. Brydges, of 26th
Battery, by a mine on the second day the Regiment is here, seems
monstrously unfair.

A few days later, Gunner E. F. Fyles, an RHQ Don R, narrowly
escapes death when he's swept from his motorbike by the concussion wave of an awesome explosion that rocks the Reichswald and
blows to eternity several Engineers attempting to disarm two huge
piles of mines that had been lifted from the forest floor and stacked
beside the main road.

All ranks are warned against wandering off routes established by
white tape, and you find yourself examining every inch of ground
you are going to pass over, as you recall the advice of an infantry
pioneer officer: If you hear a pop underfoot, leave your foot there,
pressing down, for it could be an "S" mine designed to pop up in
the air about three feet before exploding. Held down, it will

explode underground – blowing off your foot perhaps, but saving your life.

"Long Service Leave" comes through for nine Other Ranks and your GPO, Lieut. Jack Bigg, who leave immediately for England en route to Canada. How wonderful for Jack, and for his wife and seven-year-old daughter who was only a babe of seventeen months when, just before Christmas 1939, he left Winnipeg as a newly enlisted gunner with C Battery RCHA for Halifax and England.*

Again assigned to Baker Troop – Don Patrick having been wounded by a sniper near Xanten – you are ordered to go up beyond the smokescreen and establish an OP overlooking the Rhine and the sizeable town of Emmerich across the river. Collecting your old crew, which now includes Gunner L. R. Cunningham, replacing Ferry who was wounded in the Hochwald, you go forward after dark to an infantry outpost in a lonely farmhouse, sitting out in the open fields about four hundred yards from the river and a couple of hundred yards in from the main road leading to a ferry dock. There you park the carrier out of sight in the barn which, like so many in Holland and Germany, faces the road as an extension of the house.

Of course no one must be seen outside the house in daylight. Thus, next afternoon, when two Provost Corps types in a Jeep, followed by a water truck, casually start down the road past the

---

* Even after fifty years, Gladys Bigg would recall with painful clarity "the empty, lonely feeling of every single minute of those five and a half years Jack was away" that began with the agony of parting in the Winnipeg Railway Station on December 4, 1939: "There was such a crowd, you couldn't move. I was trying to hold baby Phyllis up so she wouldn't be hurt. People were like maniacs. I lost my hat. And there was such weeping and wailing! I look back on it as a scene from hell. When Jack left, I had fifteen dollars to look after myself and Phyl, and his assigned pay [$30 of the $39 a month earned by a gunner] and dependants' allowance [$35 for wife and $12 for the child a month] did not come through for another six weeks. Christmas, shared with the wife of another C Battery gunner, was unforgettable – broke and desolate."

farm, stopping now and then to nail up on a telephone pole another directional sign to the "Water Point," you are restricted to shouting yourself hoarse while they ignore your frantic arm-waving from your obscure position in the shadows of the open barn doors screening you from the windows of Emmerich. Helplessly you watch them drive right down to the dock, get out, and stand talking and pointing at Emmerich in total unconcern, until shells begin to flash and crack around them, and they disappear in the smoke and dust. In a couple of minutes they reappear, running bent-over back down the ditch along the road. More shells burst on the road and they drop out of sight again. From there on they must crawl, and you see them no more, but their vehicles remain at the dock – monuments to poor intelligence, and not just in the military sense.

Still they proved there is at least one artillery OP in Emmerich. Until now your dreary vigil in the smoky mists – nauseatingly oily when the wind shifts this way – studying the dead city had produced nothing. During March 19 and 20, behind the smoke, 4th Field work parties prepare gun and ammo pits near Cleve, while regimental "ammunition numbers" dump 700 rounds per gun.

On March 22, you are pulled back for an officers' briefing by the CO on the Rhine crossings – Operation "Plunder" – scheduled for 9:00 P.M. next day. Units of Ninth U.S.A. Army will cross on the right flank of British 21st Army Group, whose units will cross between Wesel and Rees. Curiously, Wesel and Rees were the first towns in Germany hit by Allied bombs in World War II, when in May 1940 the RAF tried to prevent the Germans reinforcing their *blitzkrieg* in the Low Countries. And Wesel will be flattened by bomber Command dropping 1,100 tons of bombs on it tomorrow night.*

---

* During the last three days leading up to Plunder, Bomber Command dropped 10,000 tons of bombs on enemy airfields, bridges, along supply routes, and on gun positions. And 2,500 heavy bombers of the U.S.A. 9th and 15th Airforces have daily added to the distant, heavy rumbling beyond the Rhine.

Tomorrow's assault, over a twenty-mile stretch of river, is being made with heavier artillery fire support than was provided for the D-Day Landings in Normandy (*see* Appendix A).*

The only Canadian infantry taking part in the initial crossing will be 9th Brigade attached to the 51st Highland Division, the assault division of XXX Corps. Once on the far bank, the rest of 3rd Canadian Division will cross to extend the bridgehead westward through Emmerich. However, though few Canadians will be involved in the crossings, all the Canadian guns including 4th Field's will add their voices to the roar that will rise from more than 3,400 barrels and rocket projectors – 766 more than used in support of Operation "Veritable."

Of this total, 1,780 are field guns, mediums, heavies, heavy ack-ack (in a ground role), and rocket projectors. Together they will engage in a complicated plan of diversionary fire, counter-battery fire, and incredibly heavy neutralizing bombardments – one of which will be maintained continuously for three days!

---

*   Operation Plunder, planned and controlled by Field Marshal Montgomery, was really five major operations: "Turnscrew," at 9:00 P.M., March 23, led by 51st Highland Division crossing at Rees, followed by the 43rd Wessex Division, the 3rd British Infantry Division, and the Guards Armoured Division; "Widgeon," at 10:00 P.M., involving five Commando brigades (1st Army Commando Brigade leading, and 3rd and 6th Army Commandos following, along with 43rd and 46th Royal Marine Commandos) landing near Wesel to surprise the Germans from the rear; "Torchlight," at 2:00 A.M. next morning, led by the 15th Scottish Division, crossing from Xanten; "Flashpoint," at about the same hour, by American 9th Army, led by 79th and 30th Divisions, crossing at two points near Rhineburg, south of Wesel; and finally "Varsity," at 10:00 A.M., involving landings among the German gunlines by 14,000 British and American airborne soldiers from U.S.A. 17th Airborne and British 6th Airborne Divisions, dropping by parachute or sailing down in gliders after being unhooked from tug planes. Of 6th Airborne's nine battalions, six parachute in and three arrive in gliders.

The remaining guns – anti-tank guns, tank guns, and light ack-ack guns, along with medium machine-guns and heavy mortars (not included in the totals) – will fire on selected targets across the Rhine a series of "Pepperpot" concentrations of awesome intensity.

At 11:00 A.M., March 23, the Regiment begins its move into the prepared positions near Cleve, and by 1:00 P.M. all three batteries have reported ready. Command posts receive traces and task tables for the operation, but the Regiment's involvement is not great.

During the afternoon an Air OP observer registers five targets over the Rhine utilizing one 4th Field gun – swooping his little Auster back and forth over the batteries, gunning his motor to climb up to observe the fall of each shot, and quickly dropping down again to pass over the guns with motor shut down in a long, whistling glide almost at ground level. All of which is part of a deception plan, you are told.

Precisely at 5:00 P.M. the guns of 3rd Division, over on the left, open up on their counter-battery work that will last sixty-five minutes.

At 6:00 P.M. on the right of XXX Corps, where XII Corps is to move early tomorrow, another bombardment by 700 more guns begins.

And during the evening, with horrific swooshes, salvoes from 1st Canadian Rocket Battery loop overhead towards targets north of Rees.

At 8:30 P.M. the Canadian guns switch from counter-battery work to direct support of the assault.

Pepperpots are now being fired across the Rhine at rates of fire that cannot be sustained by the 40-mm Bofors ack-ack guns. Designed for very rapid fire, but in short bursts, their barrels soften and bulge from the white heat accumulated from sustained fire, and only by stripping parts from other guns do some remain in action to complete the required expenditure of 750 rounds per gun.

At H-hour and again at H plus-45, 2nd Corps guns fire a counterbattery program designed to neutralize all enemy batteries.

Then they engage on call all batteries that can be identified as still active.

Early next morning, March 24, after firing the prescribed bombards, 4th Field, along with the other field regiments of 2nd Division and 4th Division, joins 2nd AGRA in firing a diversionary plan on Emmerich.

At 10:00 A.M. all the guns go silent as the great air armadas of planes and towed gliders of 6th British Airborne Division (including 1st Canadian Paratroop Battalion) and 17th U.S. Airborne Division stream over ahead. The first waves are the 1,795 transport planes carrying 8,000 paratroopers, and soon, far beyond the Rhine, myriads of white parachutes blossom in the clear blue sky. And as they drift down and disappear, amidst heavy flak, hundreds more planes come over from the direction of Belgium, towing over a thousand gliders (1,305) filled with troops and fighting equipment (109 tons of ammo, 695 vehicles, 113 light artillery pieces).

While the smoky mists lying across the landscape beyond the Rhine swallow up parachutists and gliders as they descend in the distance, the great amount of cracking and booming, though distant and faint, suggests they have aroused a storm of fire from 88s on the ground. You shudder for those poor guys descending through tornadoes of flak, hanging on parachutes or buckled in flimsy wooden gliders, as you remember the broken gliders lying askew in front of your windmill at Groesbeek, including one laden with dead paratroopers still sitting in the open-mouthed glider with a Jeep half in and half out.

Very high casualties would seem to be guaranteed among the 8,000 British, Canadians, and Americans who dropped over there today.*

That they accomplished their tasks is a miracle. But by noon there are reports of success by all assaulting formations, although

---

* 1,100 parachutists, glider men, and aircrew died, and 1,800 were wounded.

fighting continues, and Canadian 3rd Division units are meeting resistance in Emmerich.

By the time darkness falls, there are reports that the airborne troops have linked up with the assaulting ground forces expanding the bridgehead inland from the river, and that in the process have taken 3,500 enemy prisoners.

For the next three days the guns of 2nd Canadian Corps fire Victor targets every ten minutes, and the three batteries of the 2nd Heavy Ack Ack Regiment each contribute 5,000 rounds of 3.7-inch airbursting shells, as an uninterrupted program of harassing fire is conducted on behalf of XXX Corps expanding the bridgehead north and west.

Counter actions by German guns and planes is not great, but for four nights (March 24—27) there is some shelling, and nightly a few planes arrive on schedule, growling in the darkness overhead in a menacing way before dropping their bombs and strafing the area.

Fortunately, though this action is nerve-wracking, no 4th Field personnel are injured by the bombs or strafing – at least, no *human* personnel.

However, Baker Troop's beloved mascot, "Hardtack," the long-legged hen that has travelled with them since Louvigny eight months ago, is found dead under a truck on the morning of March 25.

64

GUNNER HARDTACK

———————————— ✳ ————————————

"HARDTACK" MAY HAVE BEEN ONLY A HEN, BUT ON A GREY March morning just south of Cleve, she is tendered a soldier's burial by the men of Baker Troop, 2nd Battery, 4th Field Regiment. In the midst of heavy gun fire rolling over the Rhineland, a sound to which she'd long become accustomed, appropriate words are murmured over her grave marked by a wooden cross, inscribed: "Hardtack B Troop 42 [4th Field unit sign] – Died March 25, 1945." And on the mounded sod they leave a china nesting-hen.

What exactly caused her death is not known, though it's assumed to have been enemy action. German bombers were over last night dropping flares and anti-personnel bombs close by, and though it was thought they missed the guns, one of those lightly fuzed missiles that leave no crater could have been the cause. At dawn she was found dead without a mark on her under a vehicle where she'd taken shelter. Nearby was a broken jam jar that some gunners suspect played a role in her death.

She will be sorely missed. During the past nine months, she not only won the complete affection of everyone who knew her, but there was a widespread belief throughout the Troop and Battery that Hardtack possessed an uncanny ability to foretell the arrival of enemy shells. And now their little sentinel is no more.

While you followed the Hardtack saga from way back at Fleury-sur-Orne in Normandy, first as a neighbour and nodding acquain-

tance while still with Able Troop, and then as her troop commander after your posting to Baker Troop before the Rhineland attack,
you never were back at her gun position long enough to witness a
demonstration of her clairvoyance. But there is no shortage of witnesses, and Gunner "Buck" Saunders will testify in no uncertain
terms to her eerie capability:

> That bird was the greatest living air-raid warden . . . She could
> sense something was pointed in her direction long before
> anybody else heard anything coming, and just take off and run
> for cover, like down in the command post if it was dug, or back
> under a truck still on the position. On the outside of TL vehicle
> the boys had built a box for her and whenever they were going to
> move, they'd open the door of the box, slap their hands a couple
> of times and say "let's go," and that bird would head over and hop
> up into her box. Then, when they got to the next position,
> they'd open the door and let her jump down and wander.
>
> But if you watched that damned bird, you could get a warning
> something was coming. You wouldn't hear a sound . . . absolutely
> quiet . . . then all of a sudden she'd look up and start to wander
> around looking . . . you know . . . poking around looking for
> cover, like under GA or in a hole. And if you were on your toes
> and didn't want to run any risk, you'd follow that bloody bird
> and take cover yourself! That bird would go and take cover
> twenty seconds before anything came in. I am sure she could
> hear the breeches closing on the German guns! And when she
> took off to one side there . . . oh-oh . . . you knew something was
> coming!

Among the chief witnesses to her extraordinary conduct were
the bird's principal guardians: Gunner W. J. Brewster, who drove the
TL vehicle, and Lance-Bombardier Ralph Hughes, a Baker Troop
Command Post ack.

According to Hughes they'd found a scrawny, woebegone half-
starved pullet, wandering aimlessly in the rain among the dripping

ruins of Louvigny, her bedraggled feathers filthy with rubble dust. By some miracle she had survived a succession of hellish days of torment, beginning with the stupendous concussions from Allied bombs tumbling down on the village and cratering the surrounding fields from early morning of July 18, followed by horrendous concentrations of shells later in the afternoon from 4th Field guns, only to be subjected all next day to periodic bombardments by Moaning Minnies, whose arrival in the village was heralded by blood-chilling wailing and screeching so loud it penetrated even over the continuous roar of your 25-pounders in the field across the road. Finally on the afternoon of the 20th, the sky really fell on her when torrential rain began pelting down, continuing all night and well into the next day, making life entirely miserable for all living creatures forced to survive without shelter.

And she had looked even worse after her first night at the gun position, tethered by a string on one leg to a stick stuck in the floor of Sgt. Morley Jeffries' gun pit, only slightly less close to the crashing gun than the gunners attending their weapon and serving up an endless stream of shells on targets called for by the FOOs.* At dawn she was a pitiful sight, having dropped all her feathers in a premature moult. (While Gunner Hank Prentice, who grew up on a farm, would not rule out the possibility the shedding of her feathers was caused by her terrifying introduction to the unholy racket of a 25-pounder gun position, he thought it more likely it resulted from having her feathers saturated by the torrential rain that fell that night, for hens are known to moult after a thorough soaking.)

At first it was thought the long-legged skinny bird was a rooster, and the only reason to rescue it was to fatten it up for a future feast somewhere down the road. But by the time she'd earned her name "Hardtack" from her principal diet of those brittle biscuits (if not her favourite food, certainly the most consistently available), and

---

* The heaviest twenty-four-hour consumption of shells by 4th Field ever – 1,000 rounds per gun.

had learned to live without fear down among a world of restless boots and dusty gaiters in the Command Post dug-out, which shuddered day and night with the concussion of the guns firing away just outside, no one would have dared suggest a chicken dinner.

A coop was built on the tool box on the side of the TL vehicle (the vanlike HUP), and each time orders came to move, it became part of the command post drill to scoop up Hardtack and button her into her coop, to bump along through dust or rain or darkness until released at the new position.

One dark and stormy night a fast move was called for, and they neglected to pick up Hardtack, each member of the command post thinking the other had put her into her travelling cage. However, it didn't worry them too much. They knew she would not wander far, and they would go back for her in the morning. But when they arrived at the new position, to their astonishment Hardtack jumped down from her coop, having hopped up into it herself when the truck was pulling out, and ridden all night with the unbuttoned door flapping open – determined to stay close to these men of gentle hands.

As days turned into weeks, and weeks into months, and the troop moved through dozens of new positions, farther and farther north, deeper into Europe, Hardtack became "one of the boys" while still retaining a distinctly individual personality.

First, she went through the whole Caen-to-Falaise maelstrom, and crossed the Seine to drive in triumph through Rouen up to Dieppe – saw a couple of Channel ports – lived a placid life on the docks of Antwerp before suffering the mud and water along the whole length of South Beveland peninsula. All winter in the Nijmegen salient she'd put up with the rain, the sleet and snow, including a brief move south over icy roads to hole up in reserve at Boxtel for a few days during the Battle of the Bulge – all the while laying soft-shelled eggs, demanding her share of tidbits from the parcels the boys got from home, and fuzzing up her wings and cackling like a fighting-cock when a brash newcomer to Baker

Troop, Lieut. Jack Bigg, tried to shoo her out of the way in the crowded Troop Command Post.

To the sad gunners who leave their little pal under a mound of fresh earth this day, it is only right that she lived long enough to pass through the Siegfried Line into Germany for the last big battle on the Western Front that crushed all resistance west of the Rhine.

For the next three days, as xxx Corps expands the bridgehead west and north, the guns of 2nd Canadian Corps fire Victor targets every ten minutes, and three batteries of British 2nd Heavy Ack Ack Regiment each contribute 5,000 rounds of 3.7-inch airbursting shells to an incredible uninterrupted program of harassing fire.

By March 28 all three brigades of 3rd Canadian Division are across the Rhine, and after a two-day battle, rubble-clogged Emmerich is cleared of the enemy.

At noon, wicked Pepperpot concentrations blanket the eight-kilometre stretch from Emmerich west to the village of Elten. Again the intense firing is hard on the thirty-six Bofors of 8th Light Ack Ack, wearing out a total of forty-three barrels in expending 2,400 rounds per gun.

At the same time the guns on the tanks of four regiments, firing intermittent salvoes that use up two and a half rounds per gun per minute, expend 1,600 rounds per gun, the heaviest concentration ever fired by any army's tanks anywhere.

And rattling away periodically, at the rate of thirty rounds per gun per minute, thirty-six medium machine-guns of the Toronto Scottish Regiment beat their assigned target areas across the river.

But the target singled out for heaviest treatment by the massed 2nd Corps artillery – a Victor target involving every gun in the Corps every ten minutes – is Hoch Elten, a heavily forested hill shaped like an overturned soup bowl, rising dramatically out of the otherwise flat terrain north of the Rhine halfway between Emmerich and Elten village. Only 1,500 metres from 4th Field gun positions just north of Cleve, it clearly would dominate both banks of the Rhine for miles, providing superb observation for enemy guns and mortars, if left unmolested.

When the three-day continuous bombardment of the hill begins, it is thickly covered by forest. Gradually barren spots begin to appear. By the time the last instalments of some four million shells are exploding on it, Hoch Elten resembles the badly shaved head of a female collaborator. At the beginning of the bombardment, each of the field guns is required to fire only eight rounds an hour, but with each gun crew in the Corps firing at their own discretion during each hour, some shells are always landing on that tortured hill.

Then, after twelve hours of this, the procedure is changed to massive time-on-target salvoes. This means the firing of each troop of guns is so timed that, regardless how far away or how near they are to the target, their shells will land at the same time as the shells from all the other guns in 2nd Corps.

And when finally it comes time for the Regiment to pull out to go over the Rhine, to be replaced by a British regiment, only two guns at a time are allowed to go out of action during the change-over. Thus the relentless pounding of the dismal hill with time-on-target Corps salvoes is allowed to continue without interruption.

At 1030 hours on March 31 the change-over is complete, and 4th Field guns cross the Rhine near Wesel at 1530 hours via the rumbling, spongy planks of a floating bridge called Blackfriars. Rolling east through the smashed and smouldering ruins of Emmerich, the guns pass just below the giant shaven mound that was Hoch Elten.

Seen close-up, the ravaged hill reveals a few shattered buildings jutting bleakly up from a barren expanse of stumps and blasted tree trunks. It's hard to believe there could be any resistance left in those still alive on that hill when 3rd Division units moved in, but it will not be reported clear of the enemy until later today.

Poor roads, heavy traffic, and blown bridges combine to make it one of the slowest moves ever, and it's midnight before the guns get into position near Ulft in Holland.

65

A DASH FOR THE TWENTE CANAL

---　✳　---

FOR A COUPLE OF DAYS AFTER CROSSING THE RHINE, 4TH Brigade units and their supporting arms muck about in aimless fashion, moving hither and yon around a rural landscape from farm to farm, until you move back across the border into Holland and arrive at a town called Doetinchem, the occupation of which (by 5th Brigade) is still being disputed.

There, in a quiet part of town on the night of April 1, you learn the Royals have been assigned the task of securing an objective sixteen miles farther north, a bridgehead over the Twente Canal said to be vital to the future progress of the whole Canadian Army and the ultimate success of its attempt to cut off all lines of retreat for the German occupying forces in Holland.

A significant assignment indeed, but Doetinchem to you will always be the place where the mundane demands of the military combine to deny you the chance to sleep the night through in an exotically perfumed bed billowing with pastel eiderdowns in the front bedroom of a beautifully furnished but mysteriously unattended modern home.

At the outset the night seems blessed. Even as you and your crew explore this delightful billet (using a candle, for there is a power blackout in the town) and you sit down to try out the shiny, black grand piano bathed in bright moonlight spilling in through the filmy curtains on the living room window, Bob Suckling's driver

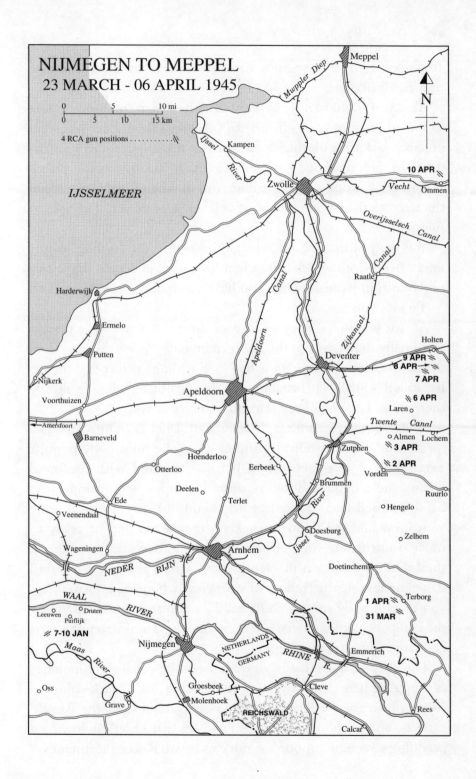

NIJMEGEN TO MEPPEL
23 MARCH - 06 APRIL 1945

```
0        5       10 mi
0    5    10    15 km
```

4 RCA gun positions . . . . ⫻

N

IJSSELMEER

Meppel

Muppler Diep

Ijssel

Kampen

10 APR

Vecht   Ommen

Zwolle

Overijsselsch Canal

Canal

Raatle

Harderwijk

Ermelo

Putten

Apeldoorn Canal

Zijkanaal

Deventer

9 APR
8 APR
7 APR

Holten

Nijkerk

Voorthuizen

Apeldoorn

6 APR

Laren

Amersfoort

Barneveld

Hoenderloo

Twente   Canal

Almen   Lochem

Otterloo

Eerbeek

Zutphen

3 APR

Deelen

Terlet

Brummen

River

Vorden

2 APR

Ruurlo

Ede

Hengelo

Veenendaal

Doesburg

Zelhem

Wageningen

Arnhem

Ijssel

NEDER   RIJN

Doetinchem

WAAL

RIVER

Terborg

Leeuwen   Druten

Puiflijk

1 APR

7-10 JAN

31 MAR

Maas   River

Nijmegen

NETHERLANDS

GERMANY

RHINE   R.

Emmerich

Oss

Groesbeek

Molenhoek

Cleve

Grave

REICHSWALD

Rees

Calcar

comes over from next door to tell you the battalion won't be moving until dawn.

Alas, you should know by now that the order "no move before dawn" never applies to officers, and that you should not squander precious sack time playing the piano. But that extraordinary instrument, in such fine tune – something totally lacking in most pianos in Western Europe – is irresistible. And so when finally you ascend the stairs to the sweet softness of your elegant bower, it is close to midnight.

You are just drifting off, snuggled down in the rustling, white, linen sheets from which arise the most exotic of scents, suggestive of a beautiful woman, when you hear a distant voice, calling, "Foo ... Foo ... Foo ..."

At first you think it is part of your dream. But the voice persists and finally draws you to the open casement window, where, from the street below, you are informed by Suckling's driver that the CO has called a "balls" at battalion ... that Major Suckling is already there ... and that he's been sent back to collect you.

"Balls" being the unique, if irreverent, label currently in vogue for Royals' orders groups (springing from the universally popular expression of exasperation "Oh balls!" uttered with profound feeling most frequently by exhausted company commanders on being aroused from deep sleep to attend "O" groups), you wake your crew and tell them to pack up the carrier and be ready to move immediately you get back. But then a few minutes later, at the briefing, you learn the actual move won't get underway until dawn. Imagining the feelings of your crew when you inform them, you involuntarily mutter, "Oh balls!" – arousing chuckles among the company commanders, and even drawing a smile from the concentrated and earnest Colonel.

The Royals' objective is a bridge over the canal six kilometres east of Zutphen. The Royals are to form part of a "jock column" riding on the backs of tanks of the Fort Garry Horse, the Royals' carriers, and in the quads of 4th Field (in that order), following a prodding screen of armoured scout cars of 8th Recce Regiment's A

Squadron. You and Able Troop Capt. Bob Haig, a newcomer, will attach yourselves to the spearhead of five scout cars commanded by a Lieut. Lorne Mackenzie.

Lendrum, with long experience with middle-of-the-night "O" groups, wastes no time in laying on the operation, and you are looking forward to still getting a goodly stretch of shut-eye, when on the way out of the meeting, Major Jack Cooper (now battery commander, replacing Don Cornett who is now counter-mortar officer at Division) tells you to pick up from the CO at 4th Brigade, somewhere on the south side of town, a roll of maps covering the move, withdraw what you and Haig require, and deliver the rest to him. Cursing your luck, but still optimistic you can get a couple of hours' sleep if you hurry, you start out on foot.

However, as you discovered long ago in Antwerp, nothing is harder to find than a military headquarters in a built-up area in a blackout. By the time you make it back to your demoralized crew slouched around the kitchen table, staring at you with reproachful eyes from under drooping eyelids, the dawn is arriving overcast and dismal. Then as you pile in the carrier to join other vehicles grinding out of town to the forming-up point on a road leading north to Vorden, Hengelow, and a hamlet called Almen, rain begins to fall and bone-chilling gusts of wind swirl across the open carriers and the Royals shivering on the backs of tanks and vehicles. From this point on it's to be a "dash" to the bridge, or bridges to be exact, for there is another small bridge over a narrow stream at Almen a kilometre before the canal. Clearly whatever chance there is of "bouncing a bridgehead over the canal" (Corps Headquarters' dainty way of putting it) will depend entirely on the degree of surprise achieved during the final run for the canal, for certainly all bridges over the canal will be blown the instant they spot the first armoured car rushing up the road.

As your carrier takes its place in the column behind the last armoured car, just before H-hour (6:00 A.M.), you begin to experience the familiar symptoms of rising anxiety – the shallow breathing, the frequent deep sighs, and the desire to urinate – which occupants of armoured cars must experience every time they set forth along uncleared roads to feel out the opposition, presenting themselves as bait for enemy outposts, inviting them to fire and expose their presence and position.

Just before the column moves off, you and Haig get an unusual signal from Sunray. Because your carriers may not be able to keep up with armoured cars (capable of 50 mph), you are to hitch rides with them, taking along your 38-sets for communicating with your carriers when they fall behind. As Haig passes your carrier on the way to climbing up on a recce car, he stops a moment to grin broadly and stare quizzically at you as though asking, "Is this really happening?"

Suppressing your misgivings as you leave your own familiar, steel cocoon – telling yourself that at least you'll be warmer and drier inside the turret of an armoured car – you scramble up onto the rear deck of one of the rumbling monsters, a map stuffed in the front of your jacket and your 38-set hanging from your neck, competing in a clashing-duel on your chest with your dangling field-glasses. Though the deck is only about five feet above the ground, it seems much higher, and you are looking forward to getting inside, when to your dismay you discover a hitchhiker on a Daimler armoured car rides *on* the car, not *in* the car, there being no room for an extra body within.

It takes more than four hours to traverse the sixteen miles to the canal – sometimes rumbling along at a steady pace, sometimes halted while field-glasses scan farms far across the fields ahead in an attempt to identify distant figures as welcoming Dutchmen or Germans, and sometimes spurting ahead with what seems total abandon. But mostly the lead vehicle moves with timid caution, particularly along confined roads through bushland of sinister aspect. And never once do you cease wondering what kind of fire you may attract. Will it be the *bur-rup, bur-rup* of an MG 42, the *pom-puh, pom-puh, pom-puh* of a hopper-fed ack-ack gun, or the ungodly *whack* and *ee-ow* of an 88?

However, apart from a gun nest at a crossroads barn early in the drive, from which one survivor, devastated by the death of a close comrade, is flushed by an awesome burst of fire from the leading car's coaxially-mounted Besa machine-gun and 2-pounder gun, there is no opposition along the road. Emboldened, the Daimlers increase their speed to a level that might properly be called "a dash" as they draw near the bridge over the narrow little Berkel Beek at Almen.

Then, just as the road breaks out of a large forest into a recently cut-over area full of stumps and piles of brush, and Almen can be seen some seven hundred yards away, the recce cars pause to lace with machine-gun fire two figures standing suspiciously close to the far end of the bridge as though preparing to blow it up. As tracers streak at them, one disappears and the other goes down and does not move again.

Your carrier having just caught up, and the Twente Canal less than two kilometres away, you decide to drop off your precarious perch on the recce car and proceed the rest of the way in your own steel bucket. At this moment two of the recce cars, including the one to which Bob Haig is still clinging, roar forward to the bridge where they pause to check if it has been mined or booby-trapped.

Days later Haig will still be marvelling at the courage of the 8th Recce man he watches jump down in the water and swim across the little stream to dismantle explosive charges wired to the bridge abutment, never knowing whether or not a hidden German sentry is about to push down a plunger detonating them.

At the bridge, they discover to their profound regret the corpse on the roadway, killed by their bullets, is of a Dutch civilian, while the German sentry, with whom he'd been conversing, is able to arise unharmed, hands over his head, from a roadside round "pothole" trench. However, many of his comrades in the vicinity are not so lucky. By now the guns are deployed back at Vorden, and you are able to bring down fire on points where you think the enemy may be concentrating.

Haig will later report coming across Germans killed by fire from 4th Field shells, or by bursts of MG fire sprayed in likely places by

8th Recce while they lift some twenty mines from the roadway and dump them in the river, along with the explosive charges from the bridge, a brand new MG 42, and five Panzerfausts, one of them dropped by a German cut down by a burst from the Besas of a recce car as he approached with the thing resting on his shoulder ready to fire.

Then revving their engines the cars roar over the bridge and disappear up a road that wiggles left between trees and houses in the direction of the canal bridge, with the rest of MacKenzie's troop and your carrier following. As the first car approaches the canal there is a monstrous explosion, and a black cloud billows up full of debris from the bridge, which spatters down, pelting the ground in all directions.

Obviously they were prepared and waiting. And now surely they'll be waiting for anyone foolish enough to try a water crossing within sight of that destroyed bridge, and this thought haunts you late into the afternoon as you join Suckling's company, designated the first to cross. And as you wait with him for canvas assault boats to be brought up to an isolated, dockside warehouse on the canal bank about a kilometre east of the blown bridge, the knowledge that, on orders from Lt.-Gen. Simonds, the Royals will not be reinforced until a bridge is built, is equally disquieting. As Lendrum explained at a Royals' "O" Group, the Corps Commander is prepared to sacrifice one of his battalions securing the bridgehead, but no more until a bridge is in place.

Late in the day the skies clear and the winds drop, and as the sun is going down and the crossing gets underway, there is not a breath of air rippling the water in the canal.

Though clearly every man in the boat you are in is white with apprehension, having waited so long for the boats to be brought up, no shots ring out, no mortars flutter down to crash about the boats, and no airbursting 88s crack overhead. It is uncannily quiet since the 72 guns of 2nd Division finished firing the smokescreen and the diversionary shelling on the left near where the bridge used to be.

Paddling over the still water, glowing blood-red from the stunning sunset now in progress, with only the gentle sound of dipping paddles and gurgling water breaking the silence of the balmy spring evening, it is as though there are no Germans anywhere within miles. And when you walk half a mile with Suckling and company, directly into the blinding rays of the setting sun, across quiet green meadows and pastures lined with trees and hedges, without arousing any enemy fire, everybody relaxes. It would seem the Corps Commander was unduly concerned.

Even after dark as you and Suckling stand outside the little farmhouse that is to be his company headquarters, listening to nearby sounds of horses and wagons and guttural voices, which, to your untutored ear could be German or Dutch, you don't worry. That you drew no enemy fire getting here encourages you to conclude the sounds are of a Dutch family removing themselves and their belongings to a less dangerous place. And as darkness deepens, it all seems so peaceful, friend Suckling decides to treat himself to a real night's sleep in a real bed in the house, even donning a new pair of silk broadcloth pyjamas he recently received in a parcel from home.

That the sounds of horses and wagons might be associated with guns and mortars being deployed does not occur to you until dawn when Jerry begins counter-attacking with such force, and shelling and mortaring with such intensity, it becomes clear he means to wipe out the bridgehead. His bombardment is particularly heavy back at the crossing point on the canal where overnight the Engineers put into service a heavy rafting operation using a section of Bailey bridge on pontoons, which brings over your carrier, Bob Haig's, the Royals' Carrier Platoon, and some tanks of the 10th Armoured Regiment. But it's a hazardous crossing, and Gunner W. H. K. Locke, of Able Troop's carrier crew, is killed on the way.

Becoming aware of the mounting aggressiveness of the enemy, but unable, because of clumps of trees and dense woods on the right, to observe anything of the early attacks on the centre of the bridgehead – against the companies manning the east–west railway embankment and a group of houses (Boschhouk) on the extreme right flank – you take advantage of the arrival of your carrier to wheel over that way.

On the way, wearing your signaller's helmet, passed up to you from the rear compartment, you listen to the boyish, high-pitched voice of the sixteen-year-old signaller Bill Knox, passing orders back to the guns from Bob Haig, with Wilcox's D Company. They are obviously under heavy shelling, and Haig calls down a roaring Mike target on the German infantry and tanks attacking them.

Just before the road you are following east bends left towards a railway crossing, you are attracted to a tall, nobly proportioned house that turns out to be Major J. K. Shortreed's B Company headquarters. You barely have time to establish yourself at the third-storey landing of a tower with a circular staircase before rifle shots snap from a couple of Royals snipers stationed at the lower tower windows and you are calling for fire on the field north of the railway embankment behind the house, helping to beat off a counter-attack by infantry that manages to get within fifty yards of the rail line. Accompanying tanks are growling about, menacing Haig's position on the left, but you can't see them because of the bush, which is a worry until you are told a couple of self-propelled anti-tank guns of 2nd Anti-Tank are now positioned over that way.

66

THE WAR CORRESPONDENTS' VIEW OF BRIDGEHEAD

✳

ONE DAY YOU'LL BE SHOWN CLIPPINGS OF STORIES FILED BY war correspondents about the crossing of the Twente Canal, including the front page of the Toronto *Telegram* of April 5, 1945, carrying an eight-column banner line: TORONTO'S ROYAL REGIMENT WINS GATEWAY TO NORTH HOLLAND.

In the story, filed by Allen Kent, there'll be a picture of a smiling Major Bob Suckling, who led the first company across the canal in "canvas assault boats." While Kent's story will be as confusing as the actual events, subheadings manage to summarize with reasonable accuracy what went on from the evening of April 2 to dawn April 4: "Vital Holland Bridgehead Won by Toronto Royals . . . Held Under Heavy Attack . . . First Real Fight Since the Rhine was Crossed Carries Unit Across the Twente . . . What First Appeared a Push-Over Turned Into Grim Struggle to Remain."

And John Clare in the Toronto *Star* will tell how the Royals held the bridgehead "through 15 counter-attacks," quoting company commanders:

"They seemed to be using about a battalion of infantry, although they never did use them all at one time," said Major Stothers. "One counter-attack would have 80 Germans in it, and another of our platoons would report 10 or 12 taking a poke at them, and that is how it was." The major looked fresh and full of bounce after a night spent fighting off the Germans.

The Canadians killed many of the attackers. Bodies of the enemy lie thick on the ground before Major Stothers's company. Among them is the body of a German officer, who led his men right up to the Canadian foxholes. Lieut. George Ackhurst dropped him with one shot (through his eye) ...

The whole bridgehead area was lashed with artillery fire. The Colonel [Lendrum] of the Toronto regiment described it as "intense and accurate." It was so heavy and intense that Canadian Engineers bridging the canal were forced to take cover, and field engineers, ferrying the vehicles and tanks across the narrow strip of water on rafts, were subjected to a hail of metal.

The Germans also threw tanks at Major Stothers' company, and when two of them bore in on the Canadian infantrymen, tanks from a western regiment [10th Armoured] scored a hit on one of them ... All Tuesday night (April 3–4) the Canadians could hear the screams of the wounded and dying Germans lying where they fell in their desperate rushes at the Canadians.

They threw tanks at Major Shortreed's men too. His Piats went into action and when one of the two tanks moving in was hit in the turret they both fled ... The second attack on Major Shortreed's positions was the biggest one of the day, as a company of Germans, walking beside two tanks, moved in on the Canadians. What Major Shortreed called "a beautiful piece of shooting" ... A succession of barrages [concentrations] were laid down virtually on the infantry's (Royals) own position by the forward observation officer ...*

------

* The war diary of 4RCA for April 4 will refer to the extraordinary overnight demands on the guns: "Altogether we fired 11 Mike targets, two Victor, and two Uncle targets in addition to a harassing fire program."

Targets from FOOs may have been upgraded by the 4RCA Colonel, but more likely the Victor targets, at least, were fired by the CRA to cool down enemy shelling holding up the bridging operation.

67

OVERRUN

———————— ✳ ————————

JUST AS THE SUN IS GOING DOWN, THEY COME – IN EXTENDED
line across the grassy meadow towards the railway embankment
along which two platoons of Shortreed's B Company are dug in,
about three hundred yards behind the house. From your third-
storey window, in the tower on the east wall of the house, you
could count them if you had time, for the setting sun, casting dark
shadows, makes each of them stand out sharply. Having helped
abort a morning attack from this direction, you're able to bring
down fire quickly. Instantly they disappear in the tall grass, and all
you can do is work over the field for a while to persuade them to
crawl back rather than forward.

Just as you are becoming smugly satisfied that once again the
guns have snuffed out an attack, staccato bursts of machine-gun
fire draw your attention sharply right to a small copse five
hundred yards away on this side of the railway, just after the road
comes over the crossing and turns this way for a short distance,
before turning to its left and swinging in behind trees and houses
on your right in a long curve that will bring it this way again past
the front of the house.

Tracers lace the trees and undergrowth only a few yards from the
snout of a beige-coloured German tank, the first of two sitting on
the road with their guns pointing to their right at the copse. Soon
all firing ceases, and for the first time ever you watch, with a sick

heart, men in Canadian battledress, their hands held high over their heads, surrender to German soldiers now appearing in numbers around the tanks. Then, as though taunting you – knowing you can't fire on them – the Heinies take their time searching their prisoners, and dusk descends before they march them away. You are still studying the darkening scene with your glasses, held helpless by concern that more Royals may be lying doggo in the bushes up there, when the muzzle of the gun on the first tank swings around to point directly at you. Instantly there's a flash and a horrible rip as a solid-shot passes through the tower just beneath where you and Squissato are standing, and two more tear through the tower as you and he scramble to a lower level.

With darkness closing in, and guided only by muzzle flashes and the sound of straining tank motors suddenly rising and abruptly falling off as though proceeding in stop-and-go fashion up the road this way, all you can do is estimate how far they and their accompanying infantry may have come, and call down Mike targets.

Your shells set fire to a barn four hundred yards east of your house. By the light of the flames, you can see cows standing facing into the open barn doors, close enough to be singed by the heat, but drawn to seek sanctuary in their familiar barn. Two actually stand inside the barn amidst flames and smoke. Confused and paralyzed, the poor beasts bellow in terror, but remain, swaying slightly, right next the fire. It's only a passing image, as you vainly try to see beyond the drifting smoke that is now providing cover for the advancing German tanks and their infantry screen, but you know it will remain forever vivid.

When a few survivors from the overrun platoon manage to crawl back, Shortreed is reminded his anti-tank gun at the railway crossing is out of action, and sends his 2 IC, Capt. Ross Newman, rushing back up the road in a Jeep to where Sherman tanks are harbouring, to lead a couple up for anti-tank protection. When the frustrated Captain returns to report the tanks refuse to come forward in the dark, Shortreed suddenly shouts: "B Company

Headquarters, follow me!" And out the side door he goes, leading every last man from the house except your crew.

Watching them, hastening back in the dusk towards the woods three hundred yards away, you are tempted to follow. However, you must be able to communicate with the guns if you are to be of any help in restoring the situation, and the only way is through the big radio now removed from the carrier and resting on the tiled floor of the entrance hall before the front door which, like the side door, is wide open to the gathering gloom that suddenly takes on sinister aspects.

Too late you realize you should have sent your crew back with Shortreed. They must be hidden in the crawl-space under the back kitchen. Advising them to grab their greatcoats from the carrier near the side door, for it will be cold lying on the damp earth under there, you lead them behind the house. Removing a section of the latticework skirting, they crawl in. You join them long enough to utilize a lamp-electric under a greatcoat to memorize the map reference of the house so you may use it as a reference point for any target you may have, since from now on it will be suicide to show a light.

Cautioning them to remain hidden until the position is retaken, as it's bound to be in the morning, you replace the lattice skirting and start back through the garden for the side door. Heavy small-arms fire is now snapping along the railway embankment. Clearly the attack from the field beyond the track has been renewed. Gaining the front hall, you follow the hissing gabble from the ear-phones to locate the radio mike. Gratefully you get through to the guns on your first try.

You give them the target you registered during the earlier attack in the field beyond the tracks "south 400" so the shells will drop four hundred yards closer to, and you hope, just beyond the embankment where skittering Schmeisser tracers are originating. Since the shells will land close to the infantry, you start with "Scale 1." But when the flashing storm erupts where it should, you order

"Scale 20 Repeat," and go outside and up the garden to judge its effectiveness. Halfway to the embankment you meet the Platoon Sergeant on his way back to Company Headquarters, which he thinks is still in the house. With remarkable aplomb he receives the news. He assures you, that with the support of your guns, his platoon will hold: "But please move your fire away a bit – no sense wasting rounds on us on the embankment!" It was to deliver this droll message that he was on his way back.

In the silence following your shelling, the absence of Schmeisser fire suggests the attack from this quarter has been extinguished, at least for now. Assured he will continue to have your support "a bit farther out," the Sergeant returns to his platoon and you turn back towards the house. Just short of the side door your heart almost stops when a dark figure materializes in the gloom – another sur- vivor from the overrun platoon. Weaponless, having thrown his Sten away when expecting capture, he'd be of no use to the platoon on the embankment. You lead him into the house to shelter in the cellarway, opposite the side door, which descends into inky black- ness you've not had time to explore.

Leaving him there, you feel your way towards the tower staircase to see what you can by the light of the burning farm, now reduced to the odd flickering flame among glowing ruins. Before you reach the stairs, the hall is lit by a tremendous flash accompanied by a shocking *wham!* And for a split-second through the open front door you see the hulking outline of a German tank opposite the gate firing down the road to the right. That you are being subjected to muzzle-blast only is a relief. But the feeling is shortlived when it occurs to you the tank is leaving the clearing of houses to the infantry.

You can expect visitors at any moment. That tank would not have come this far in the dark without its screen of foot-soldiers you'd seen moving with it at last light. Again it fires into the dark- ness down the road, as you kneel on gritty fragments of plaster and shards of glass, fumbling for the microphone – guided by the hissing storm of static and garbled voices from the earphones. Locating it you call for acknowledgement, and after several attempts, you hear the high-pitched squeak of "Coop" (L/Bdr. Ralph Cooper) back there somewhere over the canal with Rileys in reserve, but always alert to the needs of the FOOs.

You call for a Mike target "Scale 10" giving the map reference of the house "south 25" yards. As you transmit your fire orders, you are grateful for the racket the tank is making, its engine rumbling when it isn't firing, for you are no more than thirty yards from it as you kneel at the radio, and though you hold the rubber mouthpiece of the mike right up against your lips as you speak, you still must speak sharply to cut through all that electronic interference and be understood.

Since intruders may prevent you from getting back to the radio for a while, you order: "Fire until you're told to stop." Then, dropping the mike, you head for the cellarway, certain that shells will airburst among the trees out front and some may hit the house itself.

On reaching the door to the stairs, you find there is barely enough room to back in with the infantryman occupying the top step. Breathing down the back of your neck, he tells you all available space in the cellarway is filled with Dutch people, and when your howling shells start flashing and crashing among the trees out front you hear children, down in the dark behind you, whimpering in terror and women reassuring them. For a moment you are plagued with the thought you may drive the Germans to take cover in here with awful consequences.

A shell strikes on or near the front of the house, sending a hurricane of dust and debris flying past your doorway, and a child starts screaming inconsolably, setting off the others.

Trapped in your shallow alcove by your own fire, you wonder how you are ever going to get out to the radio to stop the guns pouring shells up here, when suddenly, mysteriously, they stop.*

---

* The CO of 4th Field caused the guns to stop. Though all FOOs were not aware of it, the order "Fire until told to stop" had been outlawed, for

In the silence, the infernal babble of voices and static spewing from the radio earphones out there, amplified by the echoing emptiness of the tiled hall, seem horribly loud – a perfect beacon to draw the Germans into the house to investigate. You easily imagine them creeping stealthily this way, stopping now and then to listen. Still standing in the mouth of the cellarway opposite the side door leading to the garden, you draw your pistol and hold it in readiness, pointing at the darkness beyond the open doorway. A Browning automatic may be no match for a Schmeisser, but you'll get the first one.

As you strain all your senses, trying to pick up anything that could give warning, you resign yourself to the fact that death is both imminent and inevitable, for no quarter can be expected in the dark. This, then, is how it must happen: a shattering burst from a Schmeisser or the blinding flash of a grenade flung in from an open door. And with the sense of resignation comes an extraordinary sense of calm; gone is all the inner turmoil and panic you've been resisting ever since you heard Shortreed call out, "Company headquarters follow me!"

From the earphones on the hall floor comes a high-pitched insistent voice, penetrating through the unintelligible cacophony, but so strained and garbled you can't quite make out what it is saying. Could it be, "Message for Baker One . . . Are you receiving me?" You think you hear, "Describe your situation?" But are they calling "Baker One?"

Oh, God, if only the children would be quiet!

To hell with the radio! You must concentrate on the gloom out there beyond that open doorway to the garden. All you'll get is a fleeting glimpse of a moving silhouette against a patch of night sky that now is only slightly lighter than the surrounding blackness.

---

the sound reason that if a FOO were killed or his radio blown up after giving the order – a distinct possibility in such circumstances – the guns would keep on firing until they ran out of ammunition.

Then suddenly one of those unaccountable surges in the strength of wireless transmission that occur periodically allows you to clearly distinguish your call signal, and the high-pitched, strident voice of "Coop" passing on "a request from Sunray for a sitrep."

Let him call . . . there's no way you can take your eyes off that doorway. They'll get their situation report in due course . . .

But now, with uncanny perception, the soldier standing behind you starts patting you on the back and talking to you in a low-pitched, soothing voice, barely above a whisper: "That's you they're calling, ain't it, Foo? Yuh have to go, Foo. They need to know we're still here. You have to answer them, Foo. We're all depending on you, Foo."

Unquestionably the weaponless man is just trying to help in the only way left to him. But his hand patting your shoulder is enraging, and his preacherlike intonations, obviously meant to be reassuring, going on and on as you try to listen for the faintest stir of stealthy footfall on the gravel outside, are intolerable. You turn on him, hissing fiercely, "Shut up!"

The very instant you turn your attention back to the gloom outside a dark silhouette looms up in the doorway. And as you are raising your pistol to take aim, the hulking form comes directly towards you – making it impossible to miss. Just as your finger starts its fatal pressure on the trigger, you discern the outline of a British-style helmet.

Assuming it's another survivor of the overrun platoon who has managed to make his way back, you whisper hoarsely, "Who goes there?"

"Squissato," comes the reply.

For a moment you are speechless, knowing how close you came to pulling the trigger – a split-second less hesitation and he surely would have died. You are at once thankful and furious: "My God, Squissato, I almost shot you! You were told to stay put with the others out there under the kitchen."

"Yes, sir, I was. But I don't think it's right that you should be up here alone. I can at least help you by handling the radio."

Instantly your anger fades away. He knows perfectly well you can handle the radio by yourself. He has left a perfectly safe hiding place to take his chances out here with you, purely out of compassion. You know you should send him right back into hiding, but you can't. Your need for the company he offers is just too great.

On many occasions throughout the Normandy campaign last summer, along the Scheldt last fall, and recently in the Rhineland, you have been humbled by the courageous conduct of men under fire, but never more so than now when you are the beneficiary of the selfless action of this brave man. Until dawn he will lie on the floor beside the radio, clutching his microphone, stretched out among the scattered shards of glass and chunks of brick and plaster from the front wall of the house, much of it blasted over him by one of the first basin of shells you have him call up after he takes over the set: "Scale 10 – repeat" of that last Mike target on the tank whose idling motor still mutters menacingly at the front gate. The wayward shell, striking just above the front door, not ten feet from where he is lying, sends a shower of jagged fragments and debris whipping past him. Miraculously he suffers only a minor cut on the back of his neck.

In the quiet that follows, you discover the tank is no longer out front. During the shelling you thought you heard its engine rising to a roar, indicating it was removing itself from the hurricane of shells, any one of which could blow off a track, jam its turret, or set it on fire. But in the confusion of screaming shells, blinding flashes, and stunning concussions, you were unable to maintain the wits to tell if it was going forward or back. You assume it was back, for it would be extremely vulnerable going forward in the dark without its infantry screen; and the tank commander would be as convinced as you that no foot-soldier could possibly remain alongside the tank and survive the torrent of high explosive poured down on the road around it out there.

At a window high up in the circular staircase, you listen for receding tank engines, and move your shelling in graduated corrections back up the road as it curves north towards the railway crossing and the copse where you first saw them in the dusk last night.

Then, still nervous there may be survivors lurking near the house, you move your shelling around and about, a few rounds here and a few there, with longer and longer listening periods between your bombards. During this sweeping process, a cumulative error in your calculations results in your shells dropping farther west than you wished. Again some strike the trees and house, showering the front hall and Squissato with bits of brick and mortar, once more leaving him shaken, but otherwise unharmed.

Eventually it becomes obvious that the tanks, abandoned by their infantry, have gone and will not be heard from again.

By first light, the whole bridgehead is completely quiet. The Germans have even ceased shelling their favourite target, the crossing point at the canal where the engineers have been trying to erect a Bailey Bridge to replace a rafting operation blown to bits by hostile shells yesterday afternoon.

You send Squissato out to release Reid and Cunningham from their cramped and clammy crawl-space, while you take up vigil on the third-floor landing in the circular stairway in the tower, sweeping the zone beyond the railway track with your glasses for any movement. But all is still. The blackened skeletons of buildings at the farm across the field on the right, set on fire by your shells at dusk last night, still smoulder, glowing and smoking in the pale, dawn light. Otherwise the landscape is one of peace.

Presently the women and children from the cellar can be heard assembling in the kitchen, where they create the friendly sounds of cutlery and china plates being set out on a table and a steel spatula scraping a frying pan. When the smell of frying potatoes drifts up to you, you realize, that with all the counter-attacks and other concerns, you and your crew have had nothing to eat since early yesterday.

As you descend into the hall, you discover you have a visitor, a tank captain. He tells you he has a squadron of Shermans on the road out front, and wants to know where you think he should place them. You are greatly tempted to tell him precisely where, but restrict yourself to asking how tankers have the gall to show up now that the enemy has withdrawn? Why weren't they up here last night when they were needed – when all the infantry anti-tank guns were overrun?

He makes no attempt to answer your insulting charge, but listens patiently until you tell him it's a good thing you weren't the one that went back to bring him up last night, for you think you might have shot him dead when he refused to bring his tanks up the road in the dark.

This arouses him to protest that he and his tanks were not even on this side of the canal last night. His squadron crossed over only a few minutes ago with orders to join you up here – immediately after the Engineers got the Bailey Bridge in place.

Flustered and sorry for your mistake, but still bitterly critical of his fellow tankers lurking somewhere back in the woods, you are left mumbling incoherently in embarrassment. Fortunately, Shortreed and his company HQ gang are now clumping in through the side door and down the cellar steps to set up shop; and you lead the tank captain down and turn him over to the weary Major, who looks particularly haggard by candlelight as he bends over the tanker's map spread out on a table improvised on a vegetable-storage bin.

Leaving them to sort out where the tanks should be placed, you are amusing yourself looking over rows of dusty bottles of wine lying on shelves beyond a wire grill, when a remarkably cheerful woman, coming down the stairs with a basin to get more potatoes, catches you staring covetously at the bottles. Instantly, in perfect English, she invites you to, "Help yourself if you see anything you fancy."

You pick out a bottle of German brandy and a bottle of Black and White Scotch with the date 1936 pasted on it, and head upstairs to the master bedroom at the front of the house on the second floor. Shaking the bedspread vigorously to rid it of layers of broken window glass, you pile into bed with a bottle cradled in each arm, and sleep until late afternoon. By the time you awake, the whole Canadian Army seems to be on its way up the road past the house, which, you discover on descending to ground level, is now both Battalion and Brigade headquarters. Your crew requests a twenty-four-hour rest back at the guns, and you approve as soon as they can get up a temporary replacement crew.

Finding all four Royals' company commanders assembled in the front yard, fresh from a battalion "O" group at which they were informed they will rest in reserve at least until tomorrow, you make the mistake of offering them a taste of your 1936 Black and White whisky. Instantly you become the object of a fierce competition as each tries to entice you to spend the evening at his headquarters. Stothers wins hands down with the offer of a well-tuned piano. But then the losers, expressing a desperate need to partake in a musical evening, follow along anyway.

You had forgotten the invigorating strength of prewar whisky. One bottle is more than enough to turn the evening into a heady event for four company commanders and one arty captain. And there is still a respectable heel of the bottle left when the three visiting majors – Caldwell, Suckling, and Shortreed – sensibly decide they should return to their own company headquarters while they still can find their way.

Fortunately for all concerned there are no Germans left anywhere within miles of the Royals' positions, a point Stothers proceeds to prove in a most original fashion immediately his guests depart. Irritated by the stream of persistent requests he has been getting all evening from Battalion Headquarters to supply them with "a precise disposition of his troops," he lurches out behind the house to where his Jeep is parked in the misty darkness, closely followed by his Sergeant-Major Hamm who signals you in an urgent way to follow him.

Stothers, brushing aside the protests of his devoted sergeant-major, climbs behind the wheel, starts the engine, and turns on full the high-beam headlights over which no blackout screens have been installed.

Appealing to you to bear witness to the necessity of his action, the giant Hamm leans over Stothers to turn off the ignition. Stothers, recognizing he is about to be physically restrained, pulls out his pistol and threatens to "hold a field court martial on the spot" if either of you lays a finger on him.

With that, Hamm, totally disgusted, waves you back, growling: "To hell with him – let him get himself killed if that's what he wants."

And so, with headlights blazing, Stothers wheels the Jeep around the yard and roars off towards what last night was no-man's-land. And for the first and only time in the war, you see the headlights of a Jeep bouncing about the front like miniature searchlights, as you walk back to a dimly lit slumbering house of big maps, signallers speaking in subdued voices, and sleepy duty officers – the whole building exuding a sense of confidence and security so very different from the way it was here last night for you and Squissato.*

It seems hardly possible it was only last night. Already the whole business is taking on the fuzzy outline of a bad dream, from which you recall only certain moments with gut-clenching clarity.

However, of one thing you are certain: until your last hour on earth, the name Mel Squissato will have a special place in your heart, along with "Coop" – the indefatigable Bombardier Ralph Cooper – without whose timely intercessions, relaying your target information to the guns, you and Squissato might well be lying out there in the garden tonight under two more mounds of freshly turned earth.[†]

---

* The 21st Army Group Commander-in-Chief's Certificate, signed by Field Marshal B. L. Montgomery, awarded Gunner A. Mel Squissato, February 8, 1946, read as follows: "It has been brought to my notice that you have performed outstanding good service, and shown great devotion to duty during the campaign in North West Europe. I award you this certificate as a token of my appreciation, and I have given instructions that this shall be noted in your Record of Service."

† "Coop" survived the war and became widely known as the perennial

————

jazz piano-player and hilarious commentator on life and people at the old Hotel Metropole in Toronto, where, between his musical numbers, he interspersed jokes and original skits commenting on the passing parade. Unfortunately, like many other veterans, he brought home from the war an unusual attachment to an enemy that eventually did him in – booze. One night he fell to his death trying to escape from an upstairs bedroom in which he'd been locked to sober up. New York *Variety* ran the following obituary:

> Damon Runyon would have felt right at home in the "guys and dolls" impromptu wake held last Tuesday at the Metropole Hotel for veteran pianist Ralph Cooper who plunged from a fourth-storey hotel window to his death the night before. Cooper, 44, a Toronto native, had been a regular at the hotel's dining room for 17 years. He had been "performing" after hours for several cabdrivers on the street when he tied two bed sheets together and attempted to swing out of the window down to them. The sheets came apart and he landed headfirst on the pavement. The next night prominent city lawyers, racetrack habitués, cabdrivers, veteran newspaper reporters – all without previous arrangement – congregated in the dining room for the city's first such wake. Hotel owner Sid Straus arrived and the mourners gathered at his table, drinking, smoking and only occasionally passing a remark about Cooper. For most of the evening Cooper's piano stand was empty. But several mourners bought drinks and ordered them to be placed on the piano. One wry incident marked the wake and it was repeated throughout the evening . . . A lawyer asked a waitress to place a drink on the piano. "He's dead, you know," she replied. "Yes, I know. Come to think of it you'd better make that a double – he always drank doubles," the lawyer said. "Well, that will be $1.30 – if you really want a double," she answered without the slightest tinge of sentimentality.

68

YOUR CREW IS OFFERED A
CHANCE ON A UNIQUE POOL

❊

GUNNER ANDY TURNER, WHO SERVED AS THE BATTERY Commander's Don R from when he joined 4th Field last July in Normandy, is now your carrier driver, thanks to several happenings only tenuously related.

First, there was one of Turner's unauthorized junkets on his old Norton motorbike, in which he seems to have an uncontrollable urge to indulge whenever "the war stops for a while" – to use his own words. This he had decided was the case back at Cleve. The guns were back in action firing across the Rhine, but 4th Brigade infantry were still holed up in the Reichswald. He'd headed for Nijmegen to get a haircut (or so he told the Provost), not knowing that town had been declared out of bounds. No longer protected by a tolerant battery commander (Don Cornett having become counter-battery officer at Division), Turner was paraded before the CO, who gave him fourteen days' C.B., "Confined to Barracks," having no meaning in action apart from being confined to 2nd Battery gun position. His only real punishment derived from being divorced from his beloved motorbike, and being denied the life to which he'd become accustomed at Royals' battalion headquarters. But this was enough to make him "chafe at the bit."

Then there was the overrunning of your OP position at the Twente Canal, which, according to witnesses at the guns that night, became of great personal concern to Sgt. Ryder, a concern that deepened as the crisis over the canal deepened, until he was charging about "like a man possessed," from gun to gun, and into command posts, exhorting everybody to respond "faster . . . faster" to your calls for fire – as all off-duty acks and signallers carried hundreds of shells to guns glowing red in the dark.*

The strain of that night caused your crew to ask for a rest back at the guns, which was supposed to be only twenty-four hours but became a great deal more when on arrival back there, they were offered the chance to buy into a pool which, they were told, would be won by the man who most correctly foretold the day and hour Baker Troop FOO "got it."

While agreeing it was certainly a unique contest, they felt obliged to ask why their particular FOO.

Oh, didn't they know? He'd acquired the reputation of having outlasted all other FOOs in the Canadian Army. Now, obviously a FOO with that reputation has long since outlived his luck, and will be buying it any day now. The only question was when. All they had to do was write down on this piece of paper the day and the hour . . .

To your frazzled crew, this was a most disturbing revelation, and an immediate vote was taken, resulting in a majority decision to split from your carrier while the splitting was good.

While disappointing news, you were not greatly concerned until you discovered, just as you were suddenly ordered to move off with the infantry, that no one in your replacement crew knew how to

---

* Ryder's unusual involvement was explained by diary notes of Sergeants Johnston and Foley: "Had helluva time getting guns in. Very deceptive ground which broke as soon as quads drove onto position – a freshly cleared area full of stumps and very boggy. Opposition counter-attacked and gun fire targets came thick and fast. Ammo vehicles got stuck. Help sent for in order to feed the guns. Sigs and Acks appeared . . .")

drive a tracked vehicle. Thus you were forced to take over the job yourself until you could get a driver, and it is at this point that a relationship among the foregoing happenings shows up. Bringing up the rations, Ryder caught up to your carrier grinding along a road behind a column of infantry. On seeing you driving with a map spread out on your lap underneath the steering wheel, his sense of fairness was so outraged, he threatened to go back and "shoot the bastard responsible for sending you up a crew without a driver." But then he remembered Turner eating his heart out back at the guns. Would you take him?

Of course you would. But could he drive a carrier?

"Don't worry," he shouted, over the roar of his motorbike as he took off back down the road, "we'll see he can before he comes up!"

This morning, April 9, he arrives in a Jeep accompanied by Turner, the two of them smiling from ear to ear – Ryder, happy he's able to do something for you, and Turner, pleased as punch to be back up with the infantry, even if he won't be riding his beloved Norton.

With equal pleasure you turn over the steering wheel to Turner, exchanging the righthand bucket seat for the left, where you can ride standing up – a preferred way when studying the road ahead for mines.

Obviously an apt pupil, with an affinity for tracked vehicles, Turner turns out to be surprisingly smooth in nursing the old carrier around sharp corners and through narrow gateways and the like, and by noon you've relaxed and have almost forgotten you have a rookie driver. But then during a pause at a nondescript farmhouse with Jack Stothers's Company awaiting orders, you discover life with Turner will be full of surprises.

Just as you are about to partake of a feast of scrambled eggs the infantry are whipping up in the kitchen from a basket of eggs found under a bed, a Royals' sergeant comes in and asks you a ridiculous question that sounds like, "Are you aware your driver has both tracks off your carrier?"

Preposterous of course – obviously a crude device for getting you to come outside for some sort of surprise. But when you go out in the barnyard, there, before your incredulous eyes, hang the naked bogie wheels of your carrier. Lying flat on the ground beneath them are two pathetic-looking tracks, while Turner whales away with a sledgehammer at a great rivet holding one of the links at one end of a track, aided by your other crew members – Signaller Sam Kotyk and Signaller H. L. Doherty, an American from Dearborn, Michigan.

Spotting you, Turner calls out cheerfully: "Don't worry, Skipper, we'll have her ready to go when you have to move!"

Just how the hell he would know when that will be, when no one else has a clue, is beyond you, and you tell him so, adding some well-chosen comments you think are appropriate to the situation. Unabashed by your obvious displeasure, this overnight-expert on Bren carriers declares the tracks were getting much too loose and needed to have a link or two removed to tighten them up.

To save your sanity you go back in the house to finish your mess of eggs, leaving him under a threat of dire consequences if the carrier isn't ready to move when you are. As it turns out, it isn't ready when the infantry move off up the road, and by the time you finally are moving, they are out of sight. However, the road is hard-surfaced and there is no fear of mines, so Turner is able to press the accelerator to the floor. Soon you are sailing along full-out through a wooded area, where along the left side of the road, every hundred yards or so, sit camouflaged stacks of huge, black aerial bombs. Just as you are approaching one of these dangerous-looking piles, there's a shocking bang under the carrier, announcing the separation of one of Turner's newly formed track links.

Desperately you yell: "Don't touch your brakes or try to steer!"

Instantly grasping your meaning – that applying the brakes to the one surviving track will send the carrier into an uncontrollable spin – he lifts his hands off the steering wheel and lets the carrier roll to a perfectly peaceful stop, riding on bogie wheels on one side and track on the other, still in the middle of the road.

When you look back, stretched out on the road like a flattened boa constrictor, lying right opposite a big pile of those black, bulbous bombs, is the wayward track. Thoughts of what might have happened, and *didn't*, help suppress most of the irritation at this new predicament, as you walk back with Kotyk in the balmy air that has turned almost sultry, to drag the track up the road to the point where Turner can back the carrier's bogie wheels onto it. This is accomplished much more easily than you imagined it could be, and with equally astonishing speed he links up the open ends of the track with a bolt from the toolbox, and you're again on your way.

Fortunately the infantry meets no opposition until late in the afternoon, and then it is very light; and by the time you catch up with them, they've been ordered to consolidate for the night. Stothers has established his headquarters in a barn and house combination, typical of these parts: the "front" of the house facing into the fields, and the barn doors facing the road, obliging you to pass through the cow stable on the way to the kitchen door.

The few Jerries they'd encountered appear to have withdrawn, but they've left behind a very disturbed Royals' company, not knowing whether their revered stretcher-bearer, Pte. Faubert, has been killed or taken prisoner. Faubert's reputation for fearless service to the wounded is special even among his peers, all of whom daily exhibit out-sized courage. When he disappeared, he was conducting an errand of mercy far out in front of the Royals' lines checking on German casualties.

By the time it grows dark it is raining heavily, and you are most grateful for the dry comfort of the farmhouse kitchen. The infantry has just received a large shipment of parcels from home, and Stothers and Company Sgt.-Major Hamm are in the process of opening boxes addressed to boys long dead. To facilitate dividing up the goodies among the living, the contents are sorted into appropriate piles: chocolate bars here, packages of peanuts there, and gumdrops, jelly beans, and candy kisses in still another pile. Brownies, fruit cake, and other crumbly homemade cookies make up a special pile; while canned goods, razor blades, each have their own pile – as do home-knitted socks, scarves, and sweaters.

In each parcel (strictly against regulations of course) is a one-page letter from the sender. Jack, you notice, carefully unfolds each note and reads it, and then spreads it out on the table in front of him – carefully, gently, almost reverently flattening out the wrinkles before placing it on top of the growing pile of letters.

Becoming aware you are watching with interest, he hands one across the table to you without comment. It is a hand-written note of only a few lines: "Dear Son," it begins, and the words blur as you read of a mother's deep concern for her boy – she sounds so much like your own mother. "The papers tell us that it is very wet where the Canadians are fighting now. So please, Dear, always be sure to wear your rubbers and keep your feet dry."

When you look up at Stothers, he tells you that her boy is the one lying dead outside the back door, face-up in the rain.

For a long while you sit with him at the table, consuming a goodly amount of over-proof "issue rum" as you discuss homes and families. This becomes truly absorbing when you discover that he, like you, has never seen his firstborn, and you take turns imagining what it will be like meeting for the first time a child already in her third year: what she will expect of you, and what might you reasonably expect of her? But neither of you, of course, can visualize the mental development of a three-year-old, and you are forced to conclude that what you don't know about the early stages of child development would fill a football stadium, and are left with an uneasy feeling that life has been rushing onward while you have been standing still.

When, well sedated with rum, you finally bed down out in the clammy hay in the draughty loft over the cows, with the cold rain drumming the roof, sleep comes slowly. Try as you will, you can't shake the image of that boy lying outside there in the rain, and a loving mother back in Canada, perhaps at this very moment writing him another letter of concern for his welfare. And fuelling your melancholia is the nagging thought that a lottery is still being run back at the guns on the day and hour you are to "buy it."

69

LIBERATING A
CONCENTRATION CAMP

✳

PUSHING NORTH BEYOND HOLTEN, THE GUNS OCCUPY SIX positions in four days, maintaining support for the swiftly moving infantry and inspiring the regimental war diarist to record: "Sleep is becoming a memory."

This apparent ease of passage by the Brigade could be traceable to confusion sown among the enemy by a drop of French paratroopers across the axis of advance of 2nd Division five nights ago. Though the front line is lit each night by artificial moonlight, and mysterious fires sometimes flare up in no-man's-land, you see or hear nothing of them until today (April 12), when you are told that some turned up at 2nd Battery gun positions claiming the Germans had captured and shot some of their comrades.*

On April 12 the objective is Assen, the last sizeable centre before Groningen, in the upper reaches of the map of Holland, the ultimate objective in the Canadian drive to sever Holland from Germany.

---

* From the 2nd and 3rd Régiment de Chausseurs Parachustistes of the Special Air Service, they were trained to operate in small groups. They were dropped on a wide area between Zwolle and Groningen, to secure bridges. First ground contact was made with them on morning of April 9, by 18th Armoured Car Regiment (12th Manitoba Dragoons) near Meppel.

At about 4:00 P.M. the Essex Scottish encounter the enemy in strength at Hooghalen. To help reduce enemy resistance, the Royals are ordered to utilize the Kangaroo troop carriers for a flanking movement northeast, through the tiny village of Rolde, three kilometres to the right of Assen, on a plunge deep into no-man's-land, that is to curl left, some three or four kilometres behind Assen, through the village of Loon, to cut the Germans' main supply road from Groningen at the tiny crossroads hamlet of Peelo. So it is that you and your crew find yourselves roaring up a sandy track across flat moorlands in your carrier, trying to keep up with a column of Kangaroos carrying Bob Suckling's A Company but falling farther and farther behind with each passing kilometre.

Coming towards you along the right side of the road, silhouetted against the red April sky, are the watch towers of a huge prison camp surrounded by a high, barbed-wire fence and a very deep ditch. As the Kangaroos, far up ahead, roar past the camp and disappear, you see people running out of the huts and massing at the barbed-wire gates halfway along the fence parallel to the road you are following.

And as you pull abreast of the camp, they have the gates open and some of them are running down the road right up to the front of your carrier. In a moment you are surrounded by men and women of all ages yelling and whimpering, their eyes full of pure, raw joy. Skinny arms reach out to touch you. Weak hands clutch at the sleeve of your battledress and stroke the side of the carrier as though reassuring themselves you are real, even as you and your crew throw them chocolate bars, cigarettes, and bread. After handing out all the canned goods you can spare, you realize you must leave immediately if you are to catch up with the others. But how? You are hemmed in by a dense crowd of delirious people that is growing larger with each passing moment. In desperation you pull out your pistol and wave it in their faces.

The men standing immediately in front of you fall back groaning in dismay, wagging their heads and spreading their open hands in supplication, as if to say: "Oh no, not now . . . after all we've been through!"

Suddenly you are aware of the unfeeling harshness of your pistol-waving to people who until only moments ago were surviving in cruel bondage at the whim of brutal SS masters. Still it has the effect of bringing a deep hush to the crowd, and you are able to ask, "Does anyone here speak English?" One man, holding up his hand, says, "A little."

You tell him to explain to the others they must clear a corridor and allow you to move on. The war is not over – you must catch up with your comrades on their way to fight the Germans up ahead.

The Dutchman takes over like a sergeant-major, and in a minute the road ahead is magically clear, though you notice as you race past the gate, men and women, ill or weak from hunger, still shuffling slowly out, obviously intent on greeting a liberator. Turner says one of them told him they are all Jews.*

The Kangaroos are by now completely out of sight, but their tracks are easily followed. Shortly after pulling away from the camp, they took off, bearing right, across country, a boggy moor laced with deep drainage ditches. While these ditches presented no problem to the Kangaroos with their powerful tank engines, it is very tough going for your old carrier, and before long, it bottoms

---

* Westerbork was the most notorious of the concentration camps in Holland, being a collection centre for Jews. From there 100,000 men, women, and children, including Anne Frank, were deported in boxcars for extermination. Today there is a telling memorial at the spot where all left on their final journey to the gas chambers and ovens. Behind the bumpers of the railway siding is a plaque with a quotation from Lamentations: "They hunt our steps, that we cannot go in our streets; our end is near, our days are fulfilled, for our end has come." The rusting steel rails, still bedded on their worn ties and oil-stained gravel, run out in the direction of Germany for about fifty yards, and then are twisted up in grotesque and tortured fashion as from intense heat.

out coming out of a ditch. For a while it looks like you are destined to spend the night on the moor – an uninviting prospect as the gathering dusk deepens across the gloomy, forbidding landscape.

But suddenly you hear tank motors coming up from behind, and soon another troop of Kangaroos come roaring up. One of them wheels around in front of you and stops, and a sergeant piles out and hooks a chain from the Kangaroo into a ring welded on the front of the carrier for this purpose. With remarkable ease the carrier is hauled across the spongy land where all previous Kangaroo tracks now glisten with water. You are not set adrift until you are on an established, gravel road leading to Rolde.

At Rolde you find Suckling and Company have already taken off in their Kangaroos on a four-kilometre sweep through no-man's-land, north and then west towards a bridge over a canal west of the village of Loon, from which Tom Wilcox's company will later attack the Royals' final objective, the crossroads at Peelo north of Assen, thereby cutting the German's main supply route from Groningen.

A few minutes after leaving Rolde, you see, far up ahead, about where the village of Peelo should be, a great many tracers, a sure sign of German machine-guns. While they'll do little harm to the thick-skinned Kangaroos, you fear for you and your crew when you start passing there. Unquestionably they were taken by surprise by the Kangaroos roaring up the road, but they will be alert now, with their Panzerfausts armed and ready when you come along.

Worried, you have Turner halt the carrier while you get down under a piece of tarpaulin and study the map with the aid of a lamp-electric, searching for another route that would bypass that hornet's nest. But there is only one way to get to that bridge, up the road through Peelo. Advising your crew to unlimber the Bren gun, and get their personal arms, you are about to tell Turner to start the engine, when you hear the whine of the now-empty Kangaroos coming back down the road.

Here of course is your answer: get one of them to take you and your signallers up to Suckling's canal house. But when you stop the leading Kangaroo, the lieutenant says he can't, that he has to go right back to collect more troops for transport elsewhere.

They pull away and you and your crew are left alone in the dark and eerie silence. But only momentarily, for suddenly you hear up ahead the sound of boots running this way on the paved road, getting louder and louder as the runner comes closer. Bewildered, you wait for whoever it is to appear out of the gloom. Finally a hatless soldier, dripping wet from head to toe, staggers up and flops exhausted over the front of your carrier, oblivious to the muzzle of the Bren pointed at him by Doherty from a rear compartment.

Gasping for air and shuddering violently from the effects of the icy night air on his wet clothing, he is totally incoherent. And for a while his overwrought condition appears to border on madness as he rocks from one foot to the other, moaning and wringing his hands.

Kotyk produces a blanket and Turner huddles it around his shoulders, as you haul up one of the water-bottles full of rum from the floor and persuade the shaking man to take a couple of really long belts of the fiery liquid.

And shortly you make out the words: *I killed my Sergeant!*

What does he mean – killed his sergeant? A couple more slugs of rum and the story comes gushing out:

He was the driver of the last Kangaroo in the troop, concentrating on the vague outline of the one ahead of him. He got too close to the edge of a culvert over a creek . . . his right track slipped over the edge and the thing toppled upside down in the water. His Sergeant, standing upright and peering ahead when the thing went over, was caught and pinned under the water by the rim of the open body of the Kangaroo. He tried to pull him free but it was impossible. With the water rising around him up to his chin, he grabbed a rifle and was about to shoot himself in preference to drowning, when he noticed the water had stopped rising. Remembering there was an escape hatch in the floor, he felt around on what was now his ceiling until he found it, undid the catches, and climbed out.

You suggest he climb aboard and come with you – eventually there'll be a farmhouse with a nice warm stove where he can dry out. With this he readily agrees, but asks you to stop for a moment at the dark creek culvert. There you accompany him on a silent pilgrimage to where you can look down on the scene of his recent ordeal.

There, just as he described it, is the upside-down Kangaroo with the dark, glistening water swirling gently around it, filling the quiet night with little bubbling and chuckling sounds so cheerful and so out of harmony with the horrible death of the poor man down there somewhere under the water. At last your companion turns away wiping his eyes.

As you are returning to the carrier, you ask him about the prospects for a German ambush in Peelo up ahead. Of this he is entirely unconcerned, believing they have pulled out of Peelo, since they didn't fire at them on their way back. And he may well be right, for not only does your carrier draw no fire on the way through the dark, silent streets of Peelo, but the village remains sound asleep when Tom Wilcox's company tramps through it an hour or so later, in contrast to the fields a couple of hundred yards past the farmhouse at the canal where Bob Suckling has set up his company headquarters. Wilcox's leading platoon suffers some casualties from heavy small-arms fire – sufficiently heavy, you decide, to bring the guns to bear on the source, Kotyk having just gotten through to the guns by adding so many extensions to the short whip aerial of the 19-set that the unwieldy thing towers above the house.

At dawn, April 13, Wilcox, moving up to the crossroads where he can dominate the road and deny its use to all German movement in and out of Assen, ambushes three truckloads of Germans stopped right at the crossroads for a break. Machine-gun fire combined with a blast from a flame-thrower, which sets the trucks on fire, kills almost all of them. The few who are captured are old men called up to fill the ranks of Hitler's "people's army." One white-haired man sitting on a log with his head in his hands, tells Turner, who can manage some German, that he was a bank manager until a few days ago.

Why the death of these old men seems so awful would be difficult to explain. After all, they had a chance to fulfil their lives in many ways, something the youngsters, who make up the bulk of the dead of the war, will never have. But you cannot shake off the sense of tragedy hanging over this smoking crossroads and the burned-out trucks with forty-five charred bodies strewn about. And you are glad when you get busy shelling distant enemy troops retreating north along another parallel road. The target is at 13,800 yards, requiring super charge, the greatest range fired by 4RCA.

While so engaged you spot a German tank crawling forward on that same road towards Assen, and point it out to the crew of a 17-pounder just then putting their gun in action at the crossroads. They knock it out with three shots, easily followed by the streaking bright tracers.

Kangaroos, carrying Rileys, pass up the road, and in some astonishment you look up to see your own guns rolling by.

70

THE FINAL SEVERING OF
HOLLAND FROM GERMANY

❋

"GENTLEMEN, WHEN WE HAVE SECURED GRONINGEN, WE effectively will have severed Holland from Germany."

That impressive opening sentence of Col. Lendrum's briefing of his company commanders on the situation that will be confronting the Royals at dawn when they join in 2nd Division's attack on this, the most northern of Dutch cities, is the last you consciously hear before you fall asleep with your head on your arms, leaning on the rug-covered table behind which he sits in the dining room of a farmhouse on the southern outskirts of the city.

When you awake about 3:45 A.M. (April 14) the room is dark, Lendrum has disappeared, and the company commanders, who were lining the walls of the little room when you fell asleep, are stretched out snoring here and there on the floor. The almost total denial of sleep the last two days and nights, while the unit was either moving or fighting, has clearly overtaken everyone. As you are wondering what the plan is and where you are to fit in, their Adjutant comes in and starts waking everybody up.

From Majors Suckling and Shortreed you learn there is to be a canal crossing in assault boats at 4:15 A.M. in a southern section of the city not far from the principal railway station, which is the ultimate objective of the Battalion. Two companies (Stothers's and Wilcox's) will cross first and secure a base for the assault on the station by Shortreed's company. You will go with Shortreed.

He says they've been warned to be on the alert for suspicious civilians. Lendrum at the "O" Group reported that the RHLI, in the southeast outskirts of the city yesterday afternoon, were sniped at by Dutch SS posing as civilians. Apparently Dutch SS units exist here, and many of them, afraid of what their fellow countrymen will do to them when their German masters are no longer in control, have changed into civilian clothes. But some seemingly can't resist sniping from apartment-building windows.

A walkie-talkie 38-set being totally inadequate for this crossing, you take along "Junior" – as Signaller Kotyk is now affectionately known by his buddies Turner and Doherty – to carry an 18-set. After walking with the infantry for some time, Shortreed's company is broken off in the shadow of a building a block or so short of the canal.

Hunched down beside you as you sit on your heels with your back against a dark building, Shortreed says that if you were asleep throughout the whole "O" Group, you probably didn't hear that President Roosevelt is dead. This is sad news indeed, for FDR was a stalwart friend of Canada and Britain, and the only U.S.A. president during your adult life. But for the moment you are more concerned with the coming canal crossing, which you earnestly hope will be in the dark, for you've come to hate crossing water obstacles in assault boats. As it turns out, the first companies over the canal run into sniper fire from some apartment buildings over there, and are forced to systematically check out every suite, and it is after first light before Shortreed gets the signal to move up to the canal and the boats.

Before rising from the shadows to move with the Royals down the street, now plainly visible in the grey light of the coming dawn, you take a deep pull from the water-bottle of rum you now always carry buttoned into the front of your battledress, hoping to head off the mounting dread. You know from past experience with canal crossings that it will threaten you as you crowd into that bobbing boat cluttered with men humpbacked with small packs dangling cups and trenching-tools, bulging in front with bandoliers of ammunition draped over webbing pouches jammed with extra Bren magazines, but still cossetting their weapons as best they can as they paddle with desperate strokes, knowing they are totally vulnerable to unseen hostile muzzles.

At this crossing snipers could be taking aim from a hundred windows, and choking tension persists until you arrive on the far side, scramble up the high canal bank, and, with Shortreed, cross the street that runs parallel to the canal for a prearranged rendezvous with Stothers in front of a substantial housing block.

He warns that accepting coffee from civilians over here could be hazardous . . . that it could be poisoned . . . a couple of guys in the first company over became deathly ill from coffee given them by civilians who, according to the Dutch Resistance, could have been Dutch SS posing as friendly civilians. Apparently there are Nazi sympathizers in this area, and some of them have been active collaborators. Until they are rounded up by the Resistance, it will pay to be very careful.

While all is peaceful here in the street during the brief meeting, as soon as Shortreed's men start moving left along the canal bank in single file, they attract small-arms fire that seems to originate from a row of shaggy bushes stretching across the far end of the street and marking the boundary of railyards containing several tracks, separated by raised passenger-platforms, which will constitute a formidable obstacle course on the final dash from the hedgerow to the main station platform.

Instantly all the infantrymen drop down below the edge of the roadway, and henceforth move forward with care, keeping their heads down and sidling crablike along the sloping bank – all except your old friend the intrepid Mortar Sergeant, who chooses to join you and Kotyk in going forward in spurts from doorway to doorway up the line of row housing abutting the narrow sidewalk on the right-hand side of the street. Recessed deeply, the doorways provide good shelter from the bullets buzzing down the street, as you pause in your periodic dashes to stay parallel with the bobbing helmets of the infantry appearing and disappearing along the opposite curb.

Suddenly a door opens behind you and a smiling Dutch youth hands you steaming coffee in a delicate china cup, complete with saucer. Only ten minutes ago you were warned against accepting coffee offered by the civilians who could be Dutch SS with poisonous intentions. But the general air of innocence in the joyous eyes of the young man, and the effect of the odour of coffee on taste buds that have had nothing to work on but undiluted slugs of issue rum since yesterday noon, is irresistible. Just as you raise the cup, the leading soldiers of the leading section, of the leading platoon, of the leading company, of the leading battalion of the leading division of the Canadian Army, spot you. A howl of protest goes up that must surely be startling to the Germans up ahead:

"Look at that! Coffee yet! Leave it to the bloody artillery – they always get the best of everything . . ."

The young Dutchman looks worried: "What do they say?"

Raising your cup in a mocking toast to the hooting soldiers, with your little finger extended in the best provincial fashion, you facetiously tell the Dutch lad, "They want one too."

To your astonishment he rushes into the house for two more cups, complete with saucers, and dashes across the roadway, leans down, and serves the two leading soldiers their morning coffee. Then oblivious to the bullets that buzz down the street, he waits to retrieve the cups, kneeling on one knee like a waterboy at a football game.*

You wonder what the generals and their earnest staff officers

----

* After thirty-two years, through the curiosity of Groningen's war historian, Menno Huizinga, author of two books on the liberation of northern Holland and assiduous collector of wartime memorabilia, and the help of a Groningen newspaper, you learn the "Koffiejongen" – J. E. Spakman – dared not return to the flat of his future mother-in-law (Mrs. Narold) without her precious porcelain. While sternly rejecting his suggestion that "ordinary mugs would be easier to carry" – preferring to follow the tradition that one "must always stay polite to foreigners and

back at Army Headquarters, or the newspaper editors back in Canada plotting their black arrows on maps showing the most forward advance of the Allied Armies, would say if they knew why the tip of the arrow of the great war machine had stopped moving this morning.

Further along you are again peering out of another recessed entry, when the door opens behind you and a most pleasant-looking woman, doing her best to smile in a reassuring way, while warning you with her eyes full of distress, points discreetly over her shoulder into the house, and whispers so softly you have difficulty, with her Dutch accent, making out what she is saying. It sounds like "the Boche – the Boche," but it could be "the Deutsch – the Deutsch." At any rate you do make out, "I think they will surrender."

As you follow her inside, you come face to face with two German soldiers, who immediately drop their rifles and raise their hands. This is fortunate, for, when you feel for your pistol, you find you have dropped it – holster, web-belt, and all – somewhere back there during the canal crossing. However, the alert woman, realizing you are unarmed and brazening it out, passes unobtrusively by you into the kitchen and out the back door, as you order the Germans, with suitably aggressive gestures, to undo their black leather tunic belts, on which dangle potato-masher grenades, and let them slide to the floor.

Presently you'll learn that the first Canadian soldiers she meets up with are your signaller Kotyk and the Royals' Mortar Sergeant. She tells them, "Your officer has just been captured by two Germans!"

This brings them crashing through the front door, with their Sten guns ready to spray the room, only to find you intent on

---

give them the best you have" – the good woman's hospitality did not extend to having her best china abandoned on a muddy canal bank, war or no war, liberation or no liberation!

counting thick wads of guilders and marks from two billfolds, while the Germans, with their hands clasped behind their heads, stand quietly watching.

Tipping back their helmets, your "rescuers" dissolve into laughter, and for the moment the nobility of their instant, unhesitating gallant response to the woman's report that you'd been captured, is lost – overwhelmed by the comic opera aspects of the real situation. But as they usher the prisoners out into the street, and you have a chance to reflect on their actions, you are swept with a wave of immeasurable gratitude. When they rushed in here, they didn't know they wouldn't be met by a hail of bullets. That two men were willing to risk their lives on your behalf will remain forever a treasured memory.

The prisoners, sent running on the double down the street towards the rear where someone will eventually take charge of them, need no urging. Obviously fearing they may be shot by their own men, they run as fast as men can with their hands clasped behind their heads. Their passage arouses a storm of contemptuous hooting from a long line of helmeted heads that pop up along the rim of the roadway, as far back as you can see, causing you to wonder how much action these current Royals have seen, that the sight of a couple of Germans would excite them so.

Returning to the business of moving along from doorway to doorway, you find you must hustle, for the leading section of the Royals has reached the end of the street and several men are kneeling down along the bushes from which the German snipers appear to have withdrawn.

By the time you and Kotyk join the Royals clustering at a gap in the bushes, they are taking off, a couple at a time, on a weird obstacle race over that succession of tracks and waist-high platforms raked by machine-gun fire from a signal tower bridging the tracks on the right, but far enough away that none of the galloping Royals are knocked down as far as you can make out.

At last you take off followed by Kotyk. Unencumbered, as he is with an 18-set on his back, you gain the first set of tracks and, prancing over them, clamber up onto the platform where you dash across and jump down on the next set of tracks as fast as you can, only to gallop across the next set of tracks to climb out again on the next platform – and so on for four or five of them (you lose count) – until at last, with lungs threatening to burst, you crawl exhausted up onto the main station platform, and huddle among a long line of infantrymen pressed tight against the station wall.

Everybody around you is gasping for breath. When you are capable you call for Kotyk, but there's no answer. He must have been hit. Weighed down by that damned radio – no wonder. You call again and again, and just as you are becoming certain he bought it, a voice calls out:

"He's here – he's okay – he just hasn't got the breath to answer."

An empty passenger train stands at the platform, with all lights on in the coaches, its air-brake compressor thumping away. Luggage sits on the platform.

As you move through the various empty offices, telephones are ringing incessantly, and in one office a switchboard is lit up with winking white lights. Baggage sits on counters and floors just as it was dropped. Suddenly there is a tremendous explosion. Dust and smoke roil out of one of the doorways. They assure you that it is not enemy action – the Pioneers have blown the safe and are unloading thousands of guilders from it.

Somehow this seems perfectly natural. For the moment the idea that they are safecrackers and thieves doesn't occur to you. Assuming all public services like railroads have been operated for the benefit of the Nazis, you can readily understand why the Pioneers would consider them fair game. However, as you go looking for a spot in the station to establish an OP, you remain mildly astonished at the priorities of some people in the middle of a battle.*

In a baggage room, a Dutchman (the only visible member of the

---

* Shortly after VE-Day, the chief safecracker was easily traced and the

station staff still on the premises) helps you push open the sliding truck-doors a crack, just wide enough to allow you to observe north across the turning basin of another broad canal (Verbindingskannal) running off at right angles west from the north–south one you crossed.

Immediately you spot, in a tree-lined street just beyond the canal, two German camouflaged staff cars sitting in front of a large house. As you give the map reference to Kotyk for transmittal back to Doherty manning the big 19-set in the carrier, who will send it back to the guns as a Troop target, you see a German rush out to the car with a package and rush back in. Obviously this is some sort of headquarters and they are packing up to leave.

After much shouting into his 18-set, twisting of dials, banging on the microphone, and changing positions here and there in the station, Kotyk gets through, and shortly you hear shells whining in from the left. Instantly the tree-lined street is filled with flashes and dust, and when it settles, a whoop of delight goes up from the infantrymen who have collected to watch, for one car is burning fiercely (maybe both), sending up columns of black smoke.

It will be your only effective target in Groningen, for though you try to hit single German vehicles periodically appearing on an overpass that loops north over the tracks a kilometre west of the station, you are unsuccessful, though you have perfect observation from the Station Master's bed-sitting room on the second floor of the station. Even when you lay the guns on the overpass, well in advance of the appearance of each prospect for destruction, your shells always manage to arrive too late.

Around noon your carrier arrives – Turner grinning from ear to ear in that unique way you have come to expect whenever he has

---

money recovered through the fact the naïve fellow inexplicably had deposited it all in a Groningen bank in his name. When the Dutchmen most directly concerned with the matter learned the safecracker had already volunteered to fight in the Pacific, all charges were dropped.

been through a dicey period, and Doherty frowning and wagging
his head in wonderment that they managed to escape being potted
by an ack-ack gun covering the wooden drawbridge (Parkwegbrug)
they used to cross the canal some seven hundred yards south of the
station.

However, though you get the impression the trip up was a bit of
a shocker, with Turner joking about it and the reserved Doherty
exhibiting his usual reticence, you get no real picture of what was
involved until much later when you're given a vivid description by
26th Battery Signaller Gunner John Cooper, who, with Gunner
B. S. Laycox, comes up via the same bridge in Gordon Lucas's
carrier driven by Gunner L. E. Erickson:

Capt. Lucas is the FOO moving up with the Essex Scottish carriers, to pass over the canal and through the Royals to attack west
from the station and secure an important bridge over another
broad east–west canal. Fortunately the Jerry ack-ack gun covering this first little drawbridge is only a 20-mm and not an 88, for
the carriers draw its fire, as well as fire from machine-guns,
resulting in three casualties, including an Essex Scottish
stretcher-bearer riding on our carrier. After crossing the bridge,
the carriers turn off to the right for the protection of some buildings. One carrier, carrying a Toronto Scottish machine-gun
officer, fails to make this turn, and drives right up the street into
the face of all this fire. Somehow, it manages to get turned
around and gets back, intact, but smoking badly from direct hits.

The Germans respect the red cross on the ambulance Jeep
that comes up, and stop firing while the wounded are being
picked up and transported back over the canal. But immediately
after, when the Essex try to deploy a 6-pounder anti-tank gun
in the street to knock out the opposition, the gunners become
casualties.

Now a 17-pounder is brought up and positioned to shoot up
the street. We, on the other side of the canal, almost directly in
front of its muzzle, don't realize that before it can lay on its target,

a nearby five-foot-high stone wall, running along the canal, has to be shot away with H.E. shells.

The double, almost instantaneous, smashes of sound – first the violent muzzle blast of the gun and then the shattering roar of the shell exploding only twenty-five yards in front of its muzzle – make us dive for cover, and cause near panic among the civilians in the houses around there, especially the children, as the tiles from the roofs in the vicinity lift and slide to the ground like snow. Once the German gun is visible, the 17-pounder makes short work of it, and we are able to move up to the railway station.*

Next day, with 5th Brigade moving in from the west and 6th Brigade passing through the bridgehead secured over the canal by the Essex Scottish, 4th Brigade is pulled back for a rest in a rather posh neighbourhood in the southern suburb of Haren. Fighting in the flaming, smoking city goes on street by street, and in some cases building by building, for another three days. The tanks of Fort Garry Horse punch shells into strongpoints, and the infantry moves cautiously forward to escape the snipers' bullets, attempting to get a shot at a sniper at a basement window, or at a window high up – sometimes creeping along the walls and hedges in the street in front, but most often through the shrubbery and fences of back gardens to hit the buildings from the rear.

Late in the afternoon of May 14, the leading company of FMRs, commanded by Major Elmo Thibault, pushing north along the main artery from the Essex bridgehead over the canal – with the SSRs clearing streets on their left flank, and the Queen's Own Cameron Highlanders of Canada winkling out snipers and machine-gunners along the streets on their right – reach their objective, the

---

* Lieut. H. P. Croome, 2nd Anti-tank Regiment, who, when his six-pounder was knocked out, went back over the canal under fire to bring up the 17-pounder, was awarded a Military Cross.

central city square. There the veteran Thibault, who has managed to survive with a rifle company since early last August in Normandy, is peering around the corner of a big building where his street meets the square, when he hears his name called from across the street. Looking over he sees Colonel Jacques Dextraze, now in command of the battalion, waving an envelope at him:

"Major Thibault," he calls, "a telegram from Southampton."

"Please open it," Thibault calls back, "and tell me what it says."

A slight pause, and Dextraze shouts: "Congratulations! You are the father of a nine-pound-eleven-ounce boy!"

And good fortune continues to smile on Thibault next morning, when he goes forward to inspect his platoon positions and spots a number of Germans up ahead with rifles slung on their shoulders, milling about in front of the big University of Groningen building – a number of them rushing in and out of the noble edifice. To Thibault's astonishment, one of the Germans, on spotting him, doesn't unsling his rifle and bring it to a menacing position, but walks over to him. When Thibault asks him what is going on, the German tells him in good English that they are trying to decide whether to give up. Asked about his excellent English, the soldier explains that before the war he worked for Ford in Detroit.

Thibault advises him to tell his comrades they are surrounded and have no future – that they should follow him back to his battalion headquarters. This turns out to be a persuasive argument, for soon after the German carries it back to his comrades they begin to form up three-abreast in a column, which grows until it numbers 375 men, with several officers in the lead, and then they follow Thibault back to where Dextraze takes charge.*

In the meantime the southeastern part of the city is being cleared by the Camerons, and the northern half of the city by the Black Watch, the Maisonneuves, and the Calgary Highlanders.

---

* Dextraze survived the war, fought in Korea, and eventually became Chief of the General Staff of the Canadian Army.

The German garrison commandant surrenders on April 16, but some pockets continue to resist for another day. In all, the four days of fighting cost 2nd Division a mere 209 casualties, while causing the Germans considerably more casualties and capturing 2,400 prisoners. In eighteen days 2nd Division advanced 195 kilometres and captured 165 officers and 6,031 Other Ranks, at a cost of 44 officers and 768 Other Ranks killed, wounded, or missing. More than 15,000 miles of signal wire had been laid, and divisional engineers had constructed eighteen bridges.[*]

And in twenty-six days, 3rd Canadian Division thrust from the Rhine to the North Sea, clearing the northwest of Holland from Deventer to Leeuwarden, building 36 bridges and capturing 4,600 prisoners.[†]

---

[*] Major D. J. Goodspeed, *Battle Royal* (Toronto: Royal Regiment of Canada Association, 1962), p. 558.
[†] Col. C. P. Stacey, *Six Years of War, Part II,* the official history of the Canadian Army in the Second World War (Ottawa: Queen's Printer, 1955), p. 557.

71

IT'S AWFULLY
WINDY IN A TANK

———————— ✳ ————————

EVERY NOW AND THEN A FOO IS INVITED TO USE A TANK IN an attack that is closely supported or led by tanks. Usually you decline the offer, preferring to take your chances in your carrier — even though its roofless box is an open invitation to anything descending from the heavens, and its relatively thin sides (12-mm of armour plate) provide puny protection compared to the thickly armoured tanks. The lower profile of a carrier offers less of a target for an 88, while guaranteeing you an independence of decision and movement not possible in a tank that's part of a group of tanks subject to their own peculiar set of controls, habits, customs, tactics, and disciplines associated with the steel cavalry.

However, this morning (April 23) you set aside these considerations and accept the reassurances of the thick hide of a Sherman at the rear of a troop of Fort Garry Horse, moving with Tom Wilcox's company towards Falkenburg and Kirchkimmen along the road west from Delmenhorst to Oldenburg.

You need all the reassurance you can get these days. In spite of the frequently replenished water-bottles of rum, carried day and night buttoned into the front of your battledress, you are beginning to "get the wind up" more and more frequently. You know the war is going to end soon . . . you've made it this far . . . you've got to make it the rest of the way. Shell fragments and Spandau bullets can't penetrate the turret of a tank, and apart from mines (which you think a tank can more readily absorb) these are the chief hazards these days.

The war has degenerated into crossroads ambushes, with the Germans showing no tendency to form a line along here. They appear interested only in delaying the advance to Oldenburg, and Wilhelmshaven about thirty miles north of there. Rumour has it they'll make a stand at a formidable water barrier, the Ems–Jade Kanal, just south of the big naval base.*

And they have been able to slow the advance to a crawl with very small expenditures of ammunition and manpower simply by mining all the major crossroads, and blocking them by exploding collars of explosive around the huge trunks of living trees (lining many of the roads along here), only partially severing them in such a way as to drop the massive trunks and branches over the roadway, while leaving the splintered butt-ends still firmly attached to stumps standing several feet above the ground. Then when your column comes up to the tangled mess, a hidden ack-ack gun starts punching airbursts overhead, and one or two Spandaus open up from the flanks, making it very uncomfortable for the halted infantry and their arty carrier crews waiting for the pioneers to come up with their saws to sever the tree trunks into manageable pieces that a tank can tow out of the way.

Usually you drop some shells around and about where you think the gun might be, judging from its barking, and now and then they seem to be effective for the firing ceases abruptly. But then you find it along with the Spandaus waiting for you at the next crossroads, and you suspect you merely encouraged them to withdraw a little

---

* That this could be a real bloodbath was indicated by their stand two days before at the Küsten Canal when they absorbed 1,700 casualties in suicidal counter-attacks against the Algonquin Regiment, who were holding the bridgehead while a bridge was built for 4th Division tanks.

sooner. Casualties are not high, but there are enough that one will be able to follow the route of each brigade by the sad mounds of fresh earth with their lonely new wooden crosses, left along the verges near crossroads lined with the splintered and ragged stumps of trees.

And you are far from feeling reassured up in the turret of your tank as it rumbles down a hard-surfaced road through rather close country, your nerves stretched taut as a drum. You had forgotten the awful sense of confinement that exists in a tank, and how windy it is from air sucked into the turret by fierce ventilation fans, which must be welcome in summer, but which today, with its frosty air, is bone-chilling.

Soon your teeth are chattering and you are wishing you had worn your tank suit, a recent issue to all personnel moving in tracked vehicles – a light beige affair with hood, made of dense, denimlike cloth thickly lined with khaki wool, large enough to be worn as a coverall over battledress, but, unlike the sad-sack look of coveralls, presenting a rather dashing front covered, from chest to thighs, with zippered pockets and special crevices to hold Chinagraph pencils and other necessities not easily recovered from interior pockets when the two long, heavy-duty zippers are run up from ankles to collarbones.

You seem to be occupying the position of the gun-layer, and would be delighted to stay down in the turret amusing yourself looking out through the telescopic sight as you revolve turret and gun, but you immediately realize that if you are to continue to keep track of your precise location on the map – absolutely essential for an artillery FOO – you'll have to ride with your head out the top of the turret. And it is then you are struck by the arrogant height of these vehicles – you must be at least ten feet up in the air – a big target for an 88-mm gun, or for a Panzerfaust for that matter. You've seen what the "hollow charge" of a Piat or Panzerfaust bomb can do to a tank and its crew.

Early on in Normandy you'd peered inside burned-out tanks,

and been shocked by the charred remains of the crew still sitting there in position, reduced to skinny black cinders, their white teeth showing in the grin of death, though the only visible damage to the turret of the tank had been a tiny hole on the outside, leading to a funnel-shaped hole on the inside. However, those concave, brassière-like depressions represented, you were told, the amount of steel that had been instantly turned into white-hot, molten pellets and been sent careening around inside the turret killing all the occupants and setting the tank on fire.*

Now you find yourself studying the ditches on either side of the road, particularly where thick bushes are growing, and each time the column stops, you crawl down onto the road. After a while it appears your nervousness is transmitted to your signaller Kotyk, for he also begins to vacate the tank each time it stops, climbing back up again when the column starts to roll.

Thus when a sparkling explosion suddenly puffs up on the roadway, just to the left of the tracks of the leading Sherman, inducing it to reverse direction with a roar, its heavy machine-gun almost cutting in two the young German still standing upright in a slit trench holding the Panzerfaust projector that had missed its target, you drop down on the verge of the road. And there you are standing, right of your tank, next to the ditch, as some very young prisoners come marching back down the road with their hands behind their heads.

Just as they are coming close enough for you to study their faces

---

* The Panzerfaust was a hand-held, one-shot, throw-away German anti-tank weapon, weighing only 11 pounds, capable of piercing 80 mm of armour at up to 80 metres. The British Piat was effective up to 100 yards and could be used as a crude mortar, but weighed twice as much and was awkward to carry, cock, and fire. The American Bazooka fired a projectile too light to penetrate the frontal armour of German tanks.

and discover they are mere boys (cadets from a naval academy you'll later learn), a rapid snapping of rifle-fire starts up from across the field on the left, apparently from a bordering hedge-row that runs diagonally across the field towards the road up ahead, meeting it just about where the Panzerfaust incident had taken place.

As you jump into the ditch to the right of your tank, the Royals already deployed along the ditch start firing across the road at the puffs to be seen in the hedgerow. The prisoners, caught between the two lines of fire, drop their hands and start running towards the Royals. Immediately some Royals' rifles are turned on them, and several are dropped in squirming heaps on the pavement before you, and a bellowing Royals' sergeant further up the ditch, can get them stopped.

Calling on Kotyk to follow, you scramble up into your tank, and get him loading an H.E. shell in the breech of its 75-mm gun as you squat on the gun-layer's seat and start the gears whirring to swing turret and gun in the direction of the hedge. Though you hadn't expected to actually fire the thing, you had, before setting out this morning, sought instruction in loading and aiming. When the middle of the offending hedgerow swings into your eyepiece, you lower the crosshairs onto it and pull the firing lever. As Kotyk will always remember: "It damned near blew my ears off."

The numbing crash of the gun in that confined space, the sting-ing whack of the rubber-cushioned eyepiece on your cheekbone, and the rather unspectacular single puff of black smoke on the hedgerow combine to inspire the question: With two dozen 25-pounders at your disposal, why the hell are you playing around with this one gun?

Giving Kotyk the map reference of a point midway along the hedgerow for transmittal to the guns, you order a Mike target, going into fire for effect without ranging. The rounds arrive promptly, but most plough the field in front of the hedge. However,

"Northwest 100 – Repeat" brings them bang on the hedge, and before you can "repeat" the order again, several snowy-white pillow cases or sheets are thrust forth to festoon the greenery of the hedge in a way you have never seen before. It is as though someone in authority – loyal to the Führer, but not wanting inexperienced boys slaughtered – instructed them to come prepared to surrender rather than face such an eventuality.

The Royals will record they took 180 prisoners today – a most satisfactory bag – but the image of those young boys running to your trench for safety with terror in their eyes, and being shot down and left squirming on the roadway, will haunt you for days, and perhaps never will be blotted from your memory. At least one of them was shot by the young Royal next to you, before you could knock down the barrel of his rifle. And when you yelled at him, "Why are you shooting them – can't you see they're just trying to take cover?" he'd replied remorsefully, "I don't know … everybody else was shooting … I guess I thought they were taking advantage of the situation to make a break for it."

Like the burning of the truckload of white-haired businessmen in ill-fitting uniforms back at the Loon crossroads, this is something else to feed your hatred of Hitler and his Nazi gang – sending kids, untrained and ill-equipped, to be slaughtered for no useful purpose.

But soon your concern for German schoolboy cadets and elderly Volkssturm troopers wanes as you learn, by way of BBC broadcasts, of the death by starvation threatening 40 per cent of the Dutch men, women, and children in the heavily populated western part of the country – shut off with the strong military forces of their German masters in "fortress Holland" (as the Germans call it) by the 1st Canadian Infantry and 5th Canadian Armoured Divisions. The Canadians are halted somewhere west of Appledorn by orders from Einsenhower while negotiations proceed with Seyss-Inquart, the Reichskommissar in the Netherlands, for a truce to allow truckloads of food and fuel to be brought to the desperate people of Amsterdam, Rotterdam, and The Hague. The citys' inhabitants are reduced to eating tulip bulbs, if they are lucky enough to have some, and burning furniture and cupboard doors for fuel to cook them.*

---

* An average working man requires three thousand calories a day. In the last week, before foodstuffs began to drop from the skies from Allied bombers on April 28, the daily ration dropped to 250 calories, and insiders knew there would be no bread at all by May 5. Malnutrition and starvation oedema (dropsy) touched hundreds of thousands, killing tens of thousands. And when the Allied food convoys finally got to roll through the lines on May 4, thousands were too weak even to feed themselves. Facts from Maj. Norman Phillips, Cdn. Army P. R. Services, and J. N. Kerk, Secretary, Canadian-Netherlands Committee, *Holland and the Canadians* (Amsterdam: Contact Publishing, 1945), p. 27.

72

YOUR DRIVER GETS A LETTER
FROM A MAJOR-GENERAL

---------------- ✳ ----------------

THE SULLEN, DOWNCAST, WITHDRAWN GERMAN TOWNS
and countryside are in great contrast to the joyous, festive, flag-
bedecked, liberated Dutch towns you passed through as you
retraced your route south from Groningen, down through Assen,
Beilen, Hoogeveen, and Hardenberg, and then turn east and re-
enter Hitler's Reich towards Lingen, before turning northeast to
Haselunne and Lahden past Meppen and the Krupp's vast testing
range for all the various weapons spawned by those vile merchants
of death for both world wars.

You hear all actions by 1st and 5th (Canadian) divisions, who have
been pushing northwest through Arnhem and Appeldoorn, have
been halted to allow for negotiations to proceed with Nazi
Reichskommissar Seyss-Inquart to allow Canadian–British convoys
of food to move across no-man's-land to the starving people of
Western Holland; that 3rd Division has swept clean Northwest
Holland from Deventer to Leeuwarden; that the Brits are in
Bremen; and that thousands of German troops are being taken prisoner by the Russians in the outskirts of Berlin.

Obviously the war could end any hour now. And each day, as a
few more Canadian helmets are left hanging on wooden crosses
along the verges, it becomes a little harder to suppress the growing
anxiety that you may get it just before it's all over.

By all rights, it should have happened yesterday. For some inexplicable reason you were standing up in your carrier, which had barely begun to move, grinding along with the leading platoon as it led off into the day's action. Maybe the carrier dipped a little, or jerked forward, but that first shot from the hedge didn't miss by much. It passed so close it stung like a hand slapped across your left ear, leaving it deaf and ringing for a good hour.

When the infantry attacked the hedge, running recklessly at the black, raging puffs of your exploding shells, they captured the lot without a casualty. They were a motley gang in ill-fitting uniforms, and you wondered which of them had been assigned to start the firing by picking off that stupid officer standing up in that carrier. The incident so bothered Turner (B Company Sergeant-Major later told you) that when you and Kotyk, carrying an 18-set, went ahead on foot with Shortreed's company through the thick bush, leaving him and Doherty behind in the carrier, he'd stewed and fussed like a "wet hen," particularly when the inevitable light ack-ack gun started pumping airbursts into the trees where he saw you and "Junior" disappear.

That he is a man of large and tender heart, who would like you to think otherwise, was further exposed when he was able to bring the carrier up at dusk to the farm where company headquarters was set up for the night just beyond the bush. Full of remorse, he immediately sought you out to describe how the arrival of his carrier had indirectly resulted in the death of a Royals' lad, who, at the moment of his arrival, was coming from the barn with an armful of straw:

"Jerry has the road covered right where it leaves the woods and I have to make a right turn into the laneway to the farm. So as we come out in the open, we are hit by machine-gun fire. And when I make my turn and start up the driveway, the fire follows me. Just as I am coming up to the barn, this soldier with an armful of straw is walking towards me from the barn on my right. And as he gets close to me, his forehead just opens up from a shot through the back of his head."

Of course you assure him he was in no way to blame, but all last night he was tormented with regret, and repeated again and again:

"All the poor bastard wanted was a bit of straw to make the bottom of his trench a little more comfortable for the night. And if we hadn't pulled in just then and attracted that machine-gun . . ."

Turner is the best thing that could happen to a carrier crew with a FOO who'd begun to lean too heavily on a water-bottle of rum buttoned into the front of his battledress. He's always grinning, even when the going is at its roughest. The briefest pause and he whips up a pot of steaming tea. Chicken stew, fried eggs, and German sausages appear from nowhere. And at the end of a long day he'll pack you and the others off for sack time while he takes an extra long shift on the radio set.

A few nights ago waiting for dawn on the side of a bald hill in a lonely listening post, he told you about himself. Of Hungarian birth, he'd run away from his home in Toronto, changed his name to Turner from Spirnyak, and gone to sea at the age of fifteen. Christmas 1939 he'd piloted a Canadian tugboat bound for Siberia, through the Panama Canal, when all other crew members, with the exception of the captain, were drunk. He'd learned to speak German in a Hamburg jail shortly before the war, when he missed his ship and was held for months before release to the British.

And just before coming to 4th Field in Normandy he rounded out his experience by doing time in the infamous "Glass House" (detention centre) after being picked up in London in civilian garb on his way to shipping out with the merchant marine on the North Atlantic run – where he felt he'd be "doing something useful" instead of endless training in an army that never seemed to be anywhere near the fighting.

While claiming he harbours no resentment for the severity of his sentence, fully realizing how foolish he'd been, he understandably will never forgive the sadistic treatment meted out by the guards on him and his fellow prisoners. According to him, men sent to the Glass House are completely at the mercy of their guards, without resort to any form of appeal, and those attracted to the job of guarding prisoners (some of whom, admittedly, are deemed incorrigible) enjoy bullying them.

For instance, frequently at morning inspections, a burley NCO would grind the sole of his muddy boot on the gleaming toes of the boots of a helpless prisoner standing rigidly at attention, daring him to protest as he snarled, "Do you call them boots polished?" And if a prisoner's endurance broke, and he lashed out at his tormenter, he was thrown in "the hole" – a totally blacked-out, tiny cell – and kept on a diet of bread and water until released some days later, temporarily blind from his eyes having become accustomed to living without light.

And now and then, in the middle of the night, the lights would come on in the barrack room and a roaring voice would demand to know "Who's been smoking in here?" Getting no answer, since smokes were impossible for prisoners to come by, the inquisitor would proceed with a kit inspection. Finding nothing in the kit he'd spewed all over the floor, he would dump the contents of each straw palliasse-mattress out onto the helter-skelter of each man's kit, on the pretext of examining the straw for hidden cigarettes. On finding none, he would then order the prisoners to return every last piece of straw and bit of chaff to their palliasse bags, without the aid of a broom or dustpan. And when, hours later, the last man had picked up the last bit of straw, returned the last bit of kit to his kit bag, and settled down for some sleep, the lights would go on again, and the roaring order for kit inspection would bring Turner and his fellow prisoners standing again at attention at the foot of their bunks to watch, with grinding teeth, their unsated inquisitor proceed with exactly the same routine as before.

Last winter his kid brother, Frank (who'd retained the family name of Spirnyak), died from a sniper's bullet while serving with the Royals at that island position you once occupied by boat in the area of Mook. He'd gone looking for brother Frank as soon as he heard he was wounded, and had caught up with him at a Casualty Clearing Station:

"Too late – he was already wrapped in a blanket. And there was this Sergeant who was just too damned casual – I nearly punched his goddamn head off! I know he had his hands full, but he knew what I was looking for. Throwing a thumb over his shoulder he said, 'There he is – over there.' Over there was a whole line of bodies sewed up in blankets awaiting burial."

In recent days Turner has been carrying clippings from several London papers – photographs taken at the recent liberation of Bergen Belsen and Dachau concentration camps – showing piles of unburied, naked, emaciated bodies, and hordes of hollow-eyed, hollow-cheeked living-skeletons in prison suits. And at the first sign of arrogance or resentment by German civilians, particularly those who are using Polish slave labourers at the time of your arrival, Turner pulls from his breast pocket a double-page spread of horrifying pictures.*

After carefully opening it on a table, he demands in German they look at the naked bodies stacked up in their tangled repulsive piles, and study the faces of the freed prisoners, distinguishable from the dead only by the fact their mouths are not quite as noticeably agape. Invariably the reaction of the Germans is disbelief, charging the newspapers with propaganda. This, of course, always sends Turner into a rage, causing him to smash his fist on the table and shout that Hitler and his Nazi swine are the liars, not the pictures. Whether or not they believe him, at least they are impressed with his fury and never pursue the argument, thereafter speaking very little, and always in low tones.

In one farmhouse yesterday a Pole, wearing a jaundice-coloured P in a circle of faded purple cloth on his shirt, denoting his slavery status, driven slightly mad either by past treatment or by the intoxication of his liberation – or a combination of the two – went completely berserk after telling you in German (with Turner translating)

---

* While front-line soldiers seldom saw newspapers, tons arrived daily in the theatre of operations – 946 tons from 6 June 1944 to 8 May 1945.

how he'd been denied the means of writing home to his family during all his years of slavery. As you followed his rampage through cupboards, desks, and bureau drawers, you thought at first he was after loot. But soon it was clear he had in mind the singular objective of destroying every piece of writing paper he could lay his hands on – shredding it and scattering it like confetti as he laughed and danced in childish glee.

At another farm, Turner saw to it that the woman of the house mopped the kitchen floor under the supervision of her ex-slave, a young Polish woman who, having exchanged her rags for her former mistress's best clothes, sat with her feet up enjoying a cup of coffee she'd been regularly denied.

Yesterday, he shook you awake in a haymow over a cow stable, and spilled on your chest the contents of an envelope he'd just received. A strange multicoloured ribbon fluttered down with a letter from Maj.-Gen. Bruce Matthews, Commander of 2nd Division, informing him that he'd been awarded the Croix de Guerre With Bronze Star for wheeling his old Norton motorbike back and forth over shell-pocked roads keeping communications open in some foul spot on the road to Falaise.

Grinning from ear to ear – ready to deprecate the gallantry that had brought him this high honour, claiming that "Fred Brohman [another member of the Major's crew] should have had it or one just like it" – he still saw some practical advantage arising from it and could hardly wait until you'd finished reading, before proposing:

"Wouldn't a bit of leave to wet my gong be in order, Skipper?"

Totally in agreement, of course, you were able to get approval from RHQ for a forty-eight-hour pass, and helped him sew the colourful ribbon on his chest beside the faded and crushed CVSM ribbon (Canadian Volunteer Service Medal), borrowed from your chest, he having lost his own somewhere along the way (probably during events leading up to his trip to the Glass House).

And after a couple of stirrup cups with Doherty, Kotyk, and Major Suckling, you packed him off to Antwerp where he figured that ribbon would be worth a lot of free booze at his favourite watering-hole. But just in case, he took along an impressive piano accordion he'd picked up along the way, which could readily be converted into several hundred Belgian francs.

73

YOUR LAST DAY IN
A UNIVERSAL CARRIER

——————————— ✳ ———————————

DAWN THE LAST DAY OF APRIL BREAKS MISTY AND COLD, AND all parts of the carrier are clammy and wet as you and your crew climb into it to move out with the infantry.

Everything in an open carrier including its passengers, being completely exposed to the elements at all times when on the move, cannot escape accepting whatever weather the elements choose to deliver – from baking sun and sudden cloudbursts in summer, to the drenching, cold rains of fall, and the black frosts and freezing snows of winter. Moreover, the coarse and unfeeling characteristics of the thick steel box in which you are immersed for hours on end tend to magnify the discomfort of all the extremes of weather – radiating suffocating heat at bake-oven levels in July, and in January doing its best to freeze you stiff by drawing from your shuddering frame, shrinking from its frost-biting touch, the last bits of precious body heat.

Usually when you stop for the night, or are in a static position in foul weather, the rear compartments and the equipment carried on top of the engine amidships are covered by a tarpaulin, and this was in place last night. However, the old tarp has so many slits in it from mortar and shell splinters, including some from your own shells air-bursting in the trees around your house on the Twente Canal, that everything is miserably cold and wet, including the thin slabs of sponge rubber that pass for upholstery on the metal bucket seats.

The Royals, with whom you are to move, are to provide protection to the left flank of 4th Brigade as it moves up to the outskirts of Oldenburg, preparatory to taking this major centre. During the day it is expected you will run into enemy outposts.

Setting off at 0800 hrs, with D Company leading, you roll slowly up a bleak secondary dirt-road, and while there is no sign of the enemy, it takes an hour to cover two kilometres because of the enemy's cratering and the muddy condition of the road.

During the morning there is a steady drizzle of icy rain, and by mid-afternoon this has turned to snow. Though most of it melts as fast as it falls, the thickness of the flurries swirling around the carrier makes it seem even colder than it is.

By late afternoon, as a result of all the rain and snow, the unpaved road you are following with Bob Suckling's A Company, now leading the advance, is very muddy.

From the ruts your carrier is leaving in it, these roads are bound to deteriorate fast with the passage of all the trucks and other wheeled vehicles coming behind, including the quads and their heavy ammunition limbers and guns. You pity the drivers who'll be coming up later along this stretch of road. It is distinguishable from a mere farmer's lane only by the deep ditches running along both sides, which make it imperative your driver steers carefully along its crown so as to not slither off and get bogged down.

Clearly your carrier is the first vehicle to use this road for some time, for there are no tracks in the soft mud before you pass along. Thus you ride standing up to better study the roadway for any sinister signs of mines.

One day you must try to calculate how many thousands of square feet of road surfaces you have peered at in nervous fear, on many occasions walking in front of the carrier to get a closer look at cobblestoned roads and unpaved tracks like this one when it has been obvious your vehicle was the first to pass that way. And though you have never spotted a single mine in all those hundreds of miles of studying every foot of the ground before you, the process has become second nature, as have all survival habits of importance.

Lately you have become exceptionally wary, having seen a number of vehicles blown up by mines, and frequently piles of mines, lifted from roadblocks, stacked up beside the road.

Just this morning you learned that the legendary former sergeant ack of 2nd Battery, Emile Dalgas (an officer in World War I and militia major at the outset of this war, who resigned his commission so he might serve overseas) was killed when his Jeep ran over a mine on his way up to visit 4th Field. Overage for "the field," he'd got his commission back as an instructor at the Canadian School of Artillery

Now as you are coming up to a crossroads – some forty or fifty yards short of it – you spot a very faint, rectangular indentation in the wet, undisturbed soil of the road, lying at right angles to your carrier's left track, no more than twenty feet from it. Thrusting your clenched hand down in front of the driver, you yell, "Stop!"

Immediately he brings it to a rocking halt, and you jump out and go forward to the indentation. It is the exact shape of a box mine, obviously planted when the ground was dry. The rain has settled the thin layer of soil that was smoothed over it – just enough to allow you to see the outline. And no more than fifteen feet further on, in line with the right track, is another indentation of identical size and shape.

When Suckling comes up and examines the indentations, he agrees with you and sends a message back to the Pioneers to come up and lift the mines. He tells you his company will go ahead and consolidate around the farmhouse at the crossroads, and will try to get permission to give his troops a breather while the mines are being lifted. They have been walking since early morning and have had nothing to eat since breakfast. And that is how it works out. By the time the Pioneers come up with their mine detectors, lift and stack almost three dozen of the deadly devices at the crossroads, and it is safe for your carrier to proceed, Suckling and company are back on the road, trudging forward again. Now the countryside changes from bleak, open fields with few trees and even fewer buildings, to a more tree-lined road along which are distributed a succession of respectable-looking farms.

A few hundred yards past the crossroads, the leading platoon comes under small-arms fire from somewhere up ahead – the first contact with enemy rearguards the battalion has had in three days. Fortunately your carrier at that moment is just approaching a farm-house close to the road on the right, and as the infantry jump over the rain-swollen ditch and run, crouched over, to take up defensive positions around the house and barn, you are able to spot a culvert a bit farther along, that allows your driver to swing the carrier into the laneway and get it out of sight behind the house in a matter of a few seconds.

Joining Suckling under a dripping, shaggy hedge on the far side of the house, in the midst of several of his riflemen, you sweep the glistening fields and bushes with your field-glasses, but can spot no movement of any kind. He decides the firing probably came from the vicinity of the next farm, partially hidden by trees, a few hundred yards further along the road up ahead, and leaves you to go to his Company's 18-set, somewhere behind the barn, to exchange views with Battalion Headquarters and receive fresh orders.

As you focus in on the distant house, vaguely outlined in the grey mists now forming over the sodden fields, its yard and gardens appear as innocent as hundreds of others you've passed in the past few days. But as you continue to study them, their very deadness presents a sinister aspect. And as the minutes drag by, and your arms grow tired holding the glasses to your eyes, you ponder how many hundreds of hours you've spent studying dead buildings and dead landscapes in the past ten months since Eterville and St. Martin-de-Fontenay – without losing one iota of your sensitivity to the lurking menace suggested by unnatural stillness and absence of movement.

Before it grows dark, which will be very soon with all this fog, you want to register those buildings as a potential trouble spot, and at the same time intimidate the opposition round and about here, with the tremendous fire-power available to the sparse and weary column they tried to shoot up as it was trudging up the muddy road towards them a few minutes ago. So you call down a stormy

Mike target on them, and while you ask only for "Scale 3" (three rounds for each of the regiments's twenty-four guns) the seventy-two roaring explosions are so concentrated in space and time, they can't help but be impressive, particularly if the enemy troops in the target area are anything like those poorly-equipped inexperienced "Volkssturm" (people's army) you have been running into in recent days.

At any rate there's no more fire from there. Now C Company, which was diverted to the left from the crossroads (where the mines were lifted this afternoon) to move north on a road parallel to this one, has bumped the enemy. Judging by what you can pick up from radio exchanges, their skirmishing is no more serious than what has been going on here. However, upper echelons seem to suspect these are enemy outpost positions in the first line of defence of the city of Oldenburg which, according to intelligence reports, will be defended vigorously as the main anchor in their defensive plan for the region leading up to Wilhelmshaven. With darkness falling and visibility worsening by the hour, the Royals are ordered to consolidate and dig-in here until daylight.

The snow has stopped, but with the darkness a real pea-soup fog descends, cutting visibility to zero. The very clean, cosily furnished farmhouse, immediately taken over for company headquarters, looks exceedingly comfortable after the long, cold, wet day; and you look forward to spending the night here, as do the infantry.

With luck, Jerry will keep his distance, so that all but the sentries will be able to take advantage of the shelter of the house and barn. But before you get settling down in one of those comfortable chairs, Bob gets a signal to be on the lookout for a wayward Panther tank spotted by C Company somewhere over beyond their line of march just before it grew dark.

This is most disturbing news. You recall hearing a distant motor over that way and wondering what it meant. All the fears you've been trying to suppress are aroused. With all that fog out there, it would be so easy for them to overrun this position before you could fire a round.

You go outside and listen for the whine of a motor and squeaking tank tracks, but all you can hear is the rustle of the cold air through the trees and bushes.

When you finally decide that Jerry is probably just as uneasy as you are, and has grounded his tank or tanks for the night, and return inside, there's a signal waiting for you: you and your crew must report back to Battalion Headquarters immediately.

This turns out to be the house you'd noticed this afternoon back on the northeast corner of the mine-cleared crossroads. When you report in, you find Col. Lendrum and Major "Paddy" Ryall, his 2 IC, waiting for you. They tell you that you've been called back to take the place of your battery commander, Jack Cooper, who it seems got stuck in the mud somewhere back there this afternoon and then got lost in the snowstorm. Now with this dense fog, he has sent up a message that he is not going to try to find his way up tonight.

As you listen, you find their manner a little strange – leaning towards a chummy, man-to-man manner – not at all typical of either of these officers who normally are inclined to hold themselves politely aloof except when conducting military business with you. And when well-filled tumblers of good whisky are poured all round, they broach the subject they really want to discuss with you. It seems they are not satisfied with Don Cornett's replacement, and intend to approach Mac Young with a request that you be made battery commander in his place.

You hasten to point out that, while you are flattered, in the artillery promotions are made on the basis of total service seniority, not just within the Regiment, and the new major has bags of seniority built up in coastal defence in Canada from early in the war.

However, Lendrum will not be put off. He says Don Cornett showed just how effective a first-class artillery rep at the battalion level can be, and he is not prepared to accept anything less. He says you must have noticed that for days now at "O" Groups he has been addressing his questions to you on the most effective application of the guns in each move, and to which company you think you should be assigned. And tonight was the last straw. He intends to approach MacGregor Young forthwith, but before doing so, he wanted to get your blessing.

It is such a staggering idea, holding out such possibilities, that for a moment your head swims and you are tempted to say, Yes, why not? But before you can commit yourself, there's a rap on the door, and in comes a remarkably cheerful, young anti-tank officer looking for advice as to a safe route to C Company on a parallel road over on the left.

It seems he is responding to a call for a 17-pounder anti-tank gun to be brought up and positioned with C Company on that parallel road over there where a Panther tank was roaming around before dark. He needs to know if the connecting road, leading from the crossroads outside the house here to that other road, has been cleared of mines?

While no one can answer that for certain, you are able to tell him that the Pioneers cleared a big stack of mines out of the crossroads while you watched this afternoon. You don't know if they cleared the side roads, but surely they would have cleared the connecting road to the left knowing that C Company was going to use it. And the Royals' RSM, who came in with the anti-tank officer, says at least one Royals' carrier must have pulled a 6-pounder up that connecting road late this afternoon.

Finding all of this reassuring he is about to leave when Paddy Ryall suggests a tot of whisky for the road, and the very likeable, outgoing chap seems grateful for the suggestion. After only a brief discussion of the atrocious weather that has now turned to drizzling rain – during which he describes the gargantuan disgust of his gunners at being yanked from a warm farmhouse to come up and stand-to all night in the fog and rain – he tosses off the whisky and goes out into the filthy, black night.

The conversation is slow to pick up again on the subject at hand, and you are still recalling what a pleasant, refreshing chap he was, when there is a heavy, dull boom that rattles the windows.

All look at each other questioningly as the Sergeant-Major goes out to investigate. Shortly he returns to report: the 17-pounder only started up the side road – got no more than twenty-five yards – when the carrier towing the gun hit a mine. The whole crew bought it.*

Oh God . . . he was such a pleasant fellow! And you visualize him riding along in the front of the carrier unable in the dark to see the tell-tale indentation in the soggy roadway that had saved you and your crew from a similar fate this afternoon . . .

For a while no one speaks, and when Lendrum and Ryall resume the discussion of your accelerated promotion, you find your taste for the subject has vanished. When they suggest that if there was any sense or logic to the artillery promotion system, you would have your majority by now through your long experience as a FOO, you find yourself pointing out the guy didn't invent the seniority system – which is the way he put it the day he informed you, almost apologetically, he had become your battery commander.

It wasn't his fault he built up his long service as a captain in Canada where no one is killed, wounded, or promoted, and he clearly had paid his dues as a FOO since joining the Regiment back on South Beveland last November – a good long stretch – a lot longer than most.

You can see your infantry friends, who have never had to contend with such broad seniority rules when making promotions in the field, have mixed feelings when you tell them you could never give your blessing to their plan.

Later in the day you are given cause to wonder if they went ahead anyway, and thus triggered a sequence of events that sees your position suddenly change drastically to one where you have no further regular regimental duties in the front line or at the guns.

––––––

* Lieut. H. P. Croome, who, the week before at the canal bridge in Groningen, won the Military Cross for going back under fire and bringing up a 17-pounder; and his gallant crew that had faced the German ack-ack gun at point-blank range, and subdued it.

Mid-morning Capt. Don Patrick, who only recently came back from hospital after recovering from a wound suffered at Xanten, suddenly appears, just as he had back in the Rhineland in front of the Hochwald, and announces he is to take over your crew again, so you can report back to Regimental Headquarters for a "special assignment."

Your first thought is that the job back at the Reinforcement Depot in Ghent has finally come through. But when you locate RHQ in a working windmill, Adjutant Grange tells you it has nothing to do with the Ghent posting; the 2 IC, Major Wilson, has asked to see you.

And where is he, this morning?

"Standing behind you," says a familiar, well-modulated voice.

When you turn, to face him, expecting to be warmly greeted, you are bewildered by his cool demeanour. Dammit, you haven't seen each other since he was your troop commander in Easy Troop way back at Barnham Junction in the fall of 1942! But he hasn't changed one iota. After a perfunctory greeting he is all business, getting on with what he wants to say in those abrupt, abbreviated sentences you remember so well – expressed in the low, restrained tone he always affected when his great barrel-chest was about to burst with indignation.

At first he gives the impression he is disgusted with you for having survived so many months as a FOO – a matter that has come to his attention only this morning.

But then it becomes clear his complaint is not with you, but with those "strange souls" who left you up there so long. Then, after pointing out "your fooing days are over," he proceeds, in all seriousness, to appoint you "third-in-command" of the Regiment, stating that while it is beyond his capacity to improve your rank, he can, and will, see you benefit from all the privileges and respect due a "3 IC."

When you go along with the joke to the extent of asking him just what a "3 IC" is expected to do, he replies with such sober intensity, he almost has you believing that there is such a job. "The

3 IC will be attached to A Echelon, but will have no duties or responsibilities except one: he will take advantage of every opportunity to live like a king – always comfortably, and in luxury wherever possible. And I warn you, I shall be checking up on you, and if I find you are not carrying out this responsibility to the best of your ability, it will be back up to the front line forthwith."

Tonight, May 1, the BBC reports Hitler is dead. You hear it in a cold, stinking cow stable, as you are stretching out to sleep beside a pigsty adjacent to the kitchen door in a barn chosen by someone as a billet, wondering how you'll ever gain the elevated lifestyle expected of a "3 IC" if this is the way A Echelon lives. In the morning when you decide to treat yourself to some hot water for shaving from the warming reservoir on the kitchen range, and the German farmer and his wife make no effort to hide their resentment, you find yourself wishing you had those London newspaper clippings of Belsen that Turner's been carrying.

For a couple of days you follow Wilson's instructions, taking no responsibility for anything, except responding to a request to all officers to come up with names of persons who may have been overlooked or turned down for medals for outstanding or gallant efforts beyond the call of duty.* But when life continues to revolve around dismal cow stables, you decide you must take a hand in the selection of billets if ever you are to fulfil your obligation in the matter of securing a princely lifestyle. So on the afternoon of May 4, you take over the job of reconnoitring billets for the night.

The move is north of Oldenburg, its surrender having been arranged by telephone calls involving Major Jack Drewry and Col. Whitaker from Riley's Tac HQ on the south side of the canal to the

---

* Members of 4th Field who subsequently were awarded Commander-in-Chief Certificates from Field Marshal Montgomery were: Capt. P. C. Voloshin, M.D., L/Sgt. W. J. Neill, Bdr. Ralph H. Cooper, Gnr. E. L. Bowers, Gnr. J. L. Dobson, Gnr. L. J. O'Connor, and Gnr. J. P. Pelletier.

Bürgermeister on the north side, warning him that his beautiful, old city (until then largely unscarred by war) would be reduced to rubble starting at midnight if he didn't persuade the garrison commander to remove his troops. The phone call was simply following up on propaganda leaflets, printed in nearby Delmenhorst and showered by the thousands across the ancient city by 26th Battery guns airbursting smoke shells from which smoke canisters had been removed to take wads of pamphlets. At first the *Bürgermeister* said he couldn't influence a military decision. And with negotiations at an impasse, the seventy-two guns of 2nd Division were laid on to deliver a city-rocking salvo on the town's central square at thirty minutes after midnight. With only four minutes to go, the *Bürgermeister* phoned to say the military had agreed to withdraw all troops from the city by dawn.

And there is more good news: Captain Ted Adams, blinded and captured on the Goch–Calcar highway when the Essex were overrun, is in a hospital in North Holland, his sight restored by German doctors; and L/Bdr. Ken Munro and Gunner Hans Neilson, captured last July in Normandy, have been released by an American spearhead.

74

JOURNEY'S END

--- ✳ ---

ABOUT 10:30 A.M. (MAY 4) THE REGIMENT IS WARNED OF A move to new positions north of Oldenburg on the road to Wilhelmshaven. This time you move with the advance parties as they make their way through the narrow, winding, medieval streets of a city that apparently held little attraction for RAF bombers on any of their frequent nocturnal visits to the Reich, including nearby Wilhelmshaven and Bremen, though residents had provided for such eventualities by constructing a truly massive concrete bunker several storeys high just outside the city centre.

The sergeant driving your Jeep, who speaks some German and is able to talk to the people he encounters, concludes that the lack of major scars in the city is due to Oldenburg's being utilized as a hospital and convalescent centre for the wounded from larger cities, and, as a consequence, the number of buildings with red crosses painted on their roofs.

On reaching the allotted area, well out in the country, you turn right up a lane to a clutch of buildings, set back some distance from the road, which you selected before setting out simply from their designation on the map as "Distillery." The name suggests affluence of more than one kind, but especially substantial buildings attached to an enterprise that rates identification on a map. And your assumption proves correct: while the distillery itself is a gloomy, dusty, cavern of pipes and vats, there is a row of spacious warehouses, and quite a splendid house providing both office and residence for the manager of "Hullman Korn" distillery.

Though the yard is uncannily reminiscent of a farmyard with its arrangement of out-buildings, no one in A Echelon will sleep with stinking cows or pigs tonight. When you check out the distillery it appears long dead, full of dust and cobwebs. In the basement, in behind a floor-to-ceiling grating formed from heavy industrial-fencing and securely padlocked, is a huge rectangular galvanized tank, which you presume is empty though you can't check it, for the two-inch pipe, protruding from the bottom rim, is fitted only with a plug, not a tap.

You take over the main part of the house for officers and NCOs. And using your sergeant-interpreter to communicate with the mistress of the house, you lay on "a chicken dinner with all the fixings to be presented on her best dinner service at 8:00 P.M.," promising that on the basis of the quality of the dinner, a judgement will be made whether the family will be allowed to occupy the servants' quarters or be forced to find accommodation elsewhere.

It is, of course, your intention to show off your high standard of living while at the same time getting the chance to have a chinwag with Don Wilson over dinner. And as soon as the Regiment comes up and the telephone line is laid to RHQ, you intend to invite him, Adjutant Sammy Grange, and Padre Marsh Laverty to share in the feast.

But within minutes after the arrival of the main body of troops, they've discovered that a dusty 2,400-gallon tank in the basement is full of alcohol, have shot the padlock off the barrier, knocked the pipe off the bottom, and are carrying away pails full of the stuff. Of all this you are blissfully unaware until one Sgt. G. Whitley comes in the house seeking advice on what you think should be done about it. When you go rushing out to see for yourself, and are striding across the yard, you are accosted by a laughing pair who offer to pour you a tin cup full from a teakettle they are carrying. Brushing them aside, you make for the stone stairs leading down into the basement. As you descend in the gloom you note the bottom step has disappeared under a glistening, dark lake of alcohol that is being fed by an unimpeded *glug-glugging* flow out of the ruptured tank. As you stand there wondering how you are going to maintain sober guards at this cistern of alcohol – the fumes of which are enough to make you dizzy – a gunner comes down the stairs with a pail: "Excuse me, sir," says he, as he bends down to dip his vessel in the pungent pool and lift out all it will hold.

Guards are placed, but they have to be changed frequently.

When you phone RHQ to invite Wilson and the other two for dinner, you are told to call a muster parade of your group immediately and call back when it's ready.

Why, for gawd's stake?

You needn't know! Simply report when every last man is on parade.

Just then the mistress of the house passes on a warning from her husband lurking in the background: the alcohol is not meant for human consumption, but was manufactured to pep up the fuel in V-2 rockets! Frantically you call the MO, Dr. Veloshin, and ask him if he can test it to see if it's poisonous? He tells you he can't test for higher forms of alcohol – that "they all may be blind in the morning."

It begins to drizzle rain as the men start mustering in the yard. Most of them can still walk, but some cannot, and those who cannot are dragged out and laid face-down in the line. After every nook and cranny of the premises has been searched, there are still a couple missing. You try to get Grange to release the others, for it's now raining steadily, but he tells you they must remain until you locate every last man.

Surprisingly, the men take it all in good humour as the minutes crawl by and still the remaining two can't be turned up. Finally Adjutant Grange arrives with a military policeman and two women – a young woman and an older woman who appears to be her mother – who go down the line peering at each soldier's face, including the faces of those lying in the mud, whose heads must be raised for examination. "Nein ... nein ... nein ..." is heard over and over as they pass on from one to the other.

When you spot the Padre, you ask if he knows what this is about. He does. Shaking his head and grimacing in disgust, he tells you it is a revolting tale of rape involving men with 4RCA on their shoulders.

Though relieved the culprits are not found among these men, when permitted to break off the parade, you keep them standing a few more minutes to tell them what the parade was about and how damned lucky they are not to have been picked as a rapist. How could they have defended themselves in their condition? You tell them to take their sodden comrades and themselves out of sight, and to remain out of sight until morning. You tell them you are taking the guards off the alcohol, but if you see a drunk out in the yard, you'll beat his brains out with a rifle butt ... might as well, for he'll probably be blind or dead in the morning anyway! The intemperance of your lecture – most of which would have sounded silly under normal conditions – impresses, and where they were giggling and simpering before you spoke, they leave the parade supporting their limp comrades in a very subdued and reflective mood.

What they don't know is your decision to remove the guard from the alcohol in the distillery is no gamble at all, for you learned from Sgt. Whitley, just before you spoke, that soldiers are now coming from far and wide to take away jerrycans full of the stuff from railway tank cars sitting on a siding over in the field.

Inside the library of the house, a little 38-set on the mantel plays "Workers' Playtime" from England. You wait until all the goblets are full of Mosel from the case you'd had brought in from a large cache in one of the warehouses, and then you ask the Padre to propose a toast. But before he can speak, the music ceases abruptly and a woman's voice says: "We interrupt this program to bring you a very important announcement. Field Marshal Montgomery's 21st Army Group Headquarters has just announced the surrender of all German forces in Holland, Northwest Germany including the Frisian Islands, Heligoland, Schleswig-Holstein, and in Denmark.

The cease fire will take place at 0800 hours tomorrow, May 5th. We repeat this very important announcement . . ."

You sit stunned and speechless with relief and thankfulness. The Padre rises as though on cue and gives a beautiful toast to peace, to loved ones at home, and to the memory of comrades who have died helping to bring about this moment. Silently you drink this toast, and for a long time no one speaks. Then Paymaster J. D. Macdonald turns to you and in his kindly fashion says earnestly: "Well, it's all over."

Overwhelmed with relief that you are going to live and will actually be going home, you can find nothing to say. Nor can anyone else. In the silence, there is a knock at the door and you hear a woman's voice: "Dinner is served."

Silently, you all move into the dining room and sit at a table of polished silver and crystal, sparkling in the light of a candelabra. Dishes are passed and plates are filled before Sgt. Whitley breaks the spell – "How in hell did you know the war was going to end tonight, sir?" A roar of laughter, and then as though a dam has broken, everyone starts talking at once.

There's a tapping on the hall door behind you, and when you open it, the woman of the house reports they have just discovered a casket of valuable jewels has been stolen, and can you help them get it back. Ten minutes ago you would have told her "tough luck" and closed the door, but it is no longer "spoils of war," but theft – criminal and punishable. And so you get Whitley to go out and spread the word that if the jewels are returned, no charge will be laid. In a few minutes a gunner delivers a heavy metal casket to you after getting you to come out in the hallway to the foot of the stairs.

Standing alone in the dark hallway after he leaves, staring at the tiaras, bracelets, and necklaces sparkling in the shaft of light coming through the crack of the door, you are greatly tempted to take something for your wife. But the splendid reverent feeling for the gift of life itself, presently flooding your being, forbids it and you deliver the casket intact to the grateful woman in the kitchen.

As you undress for bed in the unnatural silence, you relish the strange, almost-forgotten feeling of safety. There'll be no orders group tonight, or any other night. If only there was some way of notifying your wife that you have made it safely to the end. And you go to sleep imagining how wretched it must have been for her, and all the other wives and families, never knowing . . .

In the morning you are awakened by the unmistakable crashing of 25-pounders firing nearby, and you dress hurriedly, cursing that it has started again.

But when you go over through the bush to RHQ in the great mansion that is the home of the owner of the distillery, they tell you it was just some rounds of red, white, and blue smoke, fired first by the three field regiments of 2nd Division, and then by selected 4th Field "1939 gunners" – a crew from each of the original four batteries – so timed as to land at precisely 8:00 A.M. and stream victory hues across no-man's-land as the last rounds fired on the Western Front in World War II. And you were not the only one disturbed by the sound of the guns. Grange hands you a signal just received from Army Headquarters:

"First Canadian Army will cease fire. Fourth Field Regiment will cease fire!"

There are no boisterous victory celebrations on this north German plain. It is enough to relish the deep relief and gratitude that the fighting is over and that you have survived – that you have been spared a final battle with well-armed enemy forces concentrated north of a formidable canal before Wilhelmshaven. (Just how well-armed will become known when 4th Field helps collect 1,400 artillery pieces from the Germans north of the canal for towing to the Krupp gun park at Meppen.)

On Sunday, May 6, in barns and sheds for miles around, thousands of men in stained battledress kneel on rough concrete floors to utter genuine prayers of thanksgiving as they participate in regimental memorial services. The men of 4th Field assemble in the barn beside the regimental headquarters' mansion, and listen with profound sadness as the Colonel reads the names of their dead.

Word also comes that the officers and men captured at Dieppe in August 1942 have been released.*

On May 8, officially declared VE-Day (Victory Europe Day), the unit assembles in a nearby field to hear a broadcast from the King. Still there is no celebrating. Everyone is tired, emotionally drained, and with unlimited opportunity for sleep many find it difficult to drop off in the disconcerting stillness. While others, who haven't been conscious of having dreamt in months, start having dreams and nightmares.†

There is an unreal, aimless quality to these first few days. Free of censorship and those personal restraints you imposed on your letter-writing when you thought you might not live to get a reply, you can now write long letters home and say exactly what is in your heart. And every time you get a chance to be alone, you study snapshots and try in vain to recall the sound of her voice.

Now and then you experience a wave of exultation combined with profound thankfulness that you survived – death passed so close so many times. Then you hear friend Capt. Jimmy Else, formerly of 4th Field, who landed on D-Day as a 13th Field FOO with the Chaudières (Major Michel Gauvin's company), and was wounded twice – once on the beach and again farther on, and had to be ordered three times to seek medical treatment before he did so – was killed on VE-Day. His Jeep ran over a mine.

---

* See Appendix B.
† Some were unable to grasp the full reality of peace for months. Major Elmo Thibault, who, from when he joined the FMRs in Normandy, projected the image of the cool, confident, self-possessed company commander, was so uptight by the time peace came that, for months after, to go to sleep he had to have his loaded pistol under his pillow – even on leave with his wife in Southampton. And bad dreams pursued many for years – some up to the present. One very common recurring dream is of being back in action, with the sense of having awakened from a sweet dream of peace into the reality of a war still going on.

75

THE RESTING OF THE GUNS

* * * ❋ * * *

THE DREAM OF GOING HOME WILL NOW ACTUALLY COME true. The thought is intoxicating. But try as you will, it is impossible to suppress the feeling that this is only a temporary pause before another push, or at least another training scheme – there has always been another. So it is a striking day of truth when at an isolated spot along a tree-lined, sun-dappled country road near Oldenburg, you take part in a solemn ceremony, "Resting of the Guns," preparatory to handing them over to the Dutch Government.

The reviewing stand, on which the commanding officers of all nine infantry battalions and their brigade commanders assemble with the Corps Commander, the Divisional Commander, and the CRA to salute the guns, is quite a noble affair – or so it seems to you who, with Major Don Wilson, are responsible for its design and manufacture. Erected on the steel girders of a Bailey Bridge, the platform is backed by three great billboards painted by an Oldenburg artist and paid for by that wad of marks you took from those two German prisoners delivered to you by the Dutch woman back in Groningen. The outer two boards resemble 2nd Division shoulder-patches with golden "C-IIs" on royal blue. The middle board is a great stylized maple leaf crowned by a huge artillery crest. Finally, as a reminder of the origins of these regiments, Major Don Wilson and Major Geoff Brookes, of 6th Field – suitably attired in forage

caps, serge jackets, Sam Brownes, riding breeches, and highly polished riding boots – sit stiffly on horses flanking the stand.

Except for the officers, NCOs, and drivers conducting the guns
past Lt.-Gen. Guy Simonds, flanked by Maj.-Gen. Bruce Matthews,
and CRA Brig. Frank Lace, all personnel of the five gunner regiments
(4th, 5th, and 6th Field, 2nd Anti-tank and 3rd Ack Ack) line both
sides of the road leading up to the stand. Then, following the
example of 4th Field's CO, all officers riding in Jeeps at the head of
each battery, after passing the reviewing stand, dismount and join a
growing line of officers at the side of the road saluting the slowly
passing guns.

No drums roll. No voices call out orders. Each gun sergeant,
standing proud and tall, his head and shoulders protruding through
the roof-opening of his quad, automatically does eyes-right as his
gun, glistening with new paint, oil, and polish, approaches the
reviewing stand. Still there is something about the simple, quiet
solemnity of the affair that affects you deeply.

As the first gun rolls slowly by, chuckling and clinking on its
limber hook, there's a growing awareness of just how deeply these
cold, steel machines have endeared themselves to you. It's as though
you're saying goodbye to old friends you shall never see again.

Remembering the revulsion you felt on first being introduced to
the death-dealing capacities of an old 18-pounder by an enthusiastic lieutenant at summer camp, you marvel at your feelings. Has
time, training, and experience perverted you? Can it be right for a
man to look with affection on killing machines?

But as you stare at those passing guns, you decide a man would
truly be perverted if today he was unable to feel gratitude for those
trustworthy old weapons that subdued countless counter-attacks
and unquestionably saved the lives of many, many men, including
your own.

D Sub's gun is going by, and you look for the holes in the shield
through which the bullets came that killed Sgt.-Major "Lefty"
Phillips. Its breech shines like silver in the sunlight. What a mountain

of cotton waste and oily rags must have been consumed over the years in the tender care of each gun – of each tiny part of the breech and firing mechanism. Inexplicably you recall in every detail one particular day in a gun shed in the sheep and cattle market at Barnham Junction, Sussex. It's December and it's raining. A chilly wind blows through the open-sided shed, but gun crews have the breech mechanisms spread out on oily canvas breech-covers on the ground, and are rubbing each little piece with a bit of oily cotton waste . . .

Now you see those breeches, in blasting recoil, splashing in the reddish, muddy water of the gun pits of Louvigny as the gunners, stripped to the waist, respond to calls from desperate FOOs for over-lapping fire: "40 rounds gunfire – enemy tanks . . . 50 rounds gunfire – SS attacking . . . 60 rounds gunfire . . . Fire until you're told to stop!"

Then you hear a voice, as though from a great distance, saying: "Well now . . . let's go and find something to drink." And you realize the ceremony is over.

The last gun muzzle is disappearing around a bend in the road on the right, followed by the two majors on horseback. And when they disappear, the road is deserted except for a solitary German soldier walking barefoot up from the south, making his way home – dusty and unshaven, his unbuttoned, rumpled tunic flapping open, and his jackboots inexplicably slung around his neck on a piece of string.

Col. Lendrum of the Royals comes down from the platform and joins you to walk over to the refreshment marquee in a nearby orchard.

It is obvious he too has been much affected by the ceremony. His voice is husky with emotion as he earnestly expresses his regret that all the infantrymen of 2nd Division were not invited to turn out and line the road to salute the guns.

Then he stops and proceeds to read aloud with great feeling from the printed program entitled "Farewell Review of the Guns" issued to platform guests, Rudyard Kipling's famous words of gratitude from a surviving front-line soldier:

> Ubique means that warnin' grunt
> The perished linesman knows,
> When o'er his strung and sufferin' front
> The shrapnel sprays his foes,
> And when the firin' dies away
> The husky whisper runs
> From lips that haven't drunk all day
> "The guns, thank God, the guns."

APPENDIX A

GUN STATE FOR OPERATION "PLUNDER"

MARCH 23–24, 1945[*]

(A) In support of the 2nd Canadian and the VIII, XII, and XXX British Corps:

3.7"	75-mm	105-mm	25-pr	4.5"	5.5"	155-mm	7.2"	8"	240-mm	Totals
30	–	–	912	48	320	76	40	4	6	1,436

Rockets	3.7"AA	40-mm	37-mm	20-mm	17-pr	6-pr		
24	144	870	–	54	675	–		1,767
						sub total:		3,203

(B) In support of XVIII U.S. Corps:

75-mm	105-mm	25-pr	6-pr	17-pr	37-mm		
60	12	12	80	12	32		208
					Total:		3,411

If each of the 32 firing "rails" on the 24 rocket projectors is counted a "barrel," another 744 barrels (768 minus the 24 already included above) could legitimately be added: 744

                          Grand Total: 4,155

Not included in this total are 2,000 additional guns firing on behalf of Ninth U.S.A. Army crossing southwest of Wesel at 10:00 A.M. that same day.

The monstrous fire-power represented by these totals can best be placed in perspective when compared to other remarkable assemblages of guns:

El Alamein (N. Africa)	980	guns
Hitler Line (Italy)	786	guns
Gustav Line (Italy)	1,060	guns of all types
Operation "Veritable" (NWE)	2,645	guns[†]

APPENDIX B

4TH FIELD POWs TAKEN

AT DIEPPE AND LATER FREED

The *only* field gunners on the Dieppe raid for the purpose of taking over a troop of German guns and turning them on the enemy at Puys, these officers and men of 4th Field were prisoners from August 19, 1942. They were manacled with steel handcuffs, joined by a chain only fifteen inches long, from December 2, 1942 to November 21, 1943. They were released on May 1, 1944 by British tanks:

Capt. Thomas D. Archibald	Gnr. Fulton James Adams
Lieut. Tait M. "Moose" Saunders	Gnr. M. D. C. Eager
Sgt. Leonard Joseph D'Arcy	Gnr. Charles Stanley Gray
L/Sgt. Irving Heller	Gnr. Joseph Krawda
L/Sgt. James George Potter	Gnr. J. Carl Killeen
Bdr. Deans Cummings Lansing	Gnr. David Brown McIntosh
Bdr. George Leslie Gow	Gnr. Archie Mills
Bdr. Harry Hancock	Gnr. Horden J. Phillips
L/Bdr. Morris Allen Demeray	Gnr. Wm. Mortimer Scott
	Gnr. Wm. Egill Sveinson

Also captured (up on the Puys headland with Lt-Col. D. E. Catto of the Royal Regiment of Canada), Capt. George Browne, within hours, managed to escape and make his way, with the help of the French Underground, to "Unoccupied France." When, soon after, it was "occupied" by the Germans, he was jailed by the Vichy people. But again he escaped and got to England via Lisbon with information of crucial importance to the planning of the Normandy invasion, for which he was awarded the DSO (Distinguished Service Order).

Sgt. John W. Dudley, L/Bombardier F. H. Lalonde and Gnr. Donald McLean, along with eight officers and 201 Other Ranks of the Royal Regiment of Canada, with whom they went ashore, died on "Blue Beach" at Puys – a skinny stretch of sea-lapped gravel, which for Gnr. Carl Killeen, a signaller with Browne that morning, will forever be "littered with dead bodies."

INDEX